Understanding
PostScript
Programming

UNDERSTANDING
POSTSCRIPT®
PROGRAMMING

SECOND EDITION

DAVID A. HOLZGANG

SAN FRANCISCO • PARIS • DÜSSELDORF • LONDON

Cover design by Thomas Ingalls + Associates
Cover art courtesy of Adobe Systems Incorporated
Book design by Julie Bilski

ACKNOWLEDGMENTS

Although nothing is more solitary than the practice of writing, turning an idea into a book requires both personal and professional support and assistance, and I have been lucky enough to have both.

On the professional side, I would like to thank Bill Gladstone for encouraging me to turn my ideas into a proposal and for his guidance on the most effective format for doing it. I would also like to thank Chuck Ackerman at SYBEX for believing in the proposal and guiding it into a project. And I would like to thank Yvonne Perry at Adobe Systems for her help and advice.

Once the project was under way, I was particularly helped by the constructive and supportive editorial staff at SYBEX. David Kolodney gave invaluable advice on organization and approach. Jim Compton organized the work, clarified my prose, and generally put up with the first-time author's crises and traumas with good humor and consistently constructive advice. Elizabeth Forsaith scrupulously edited the manuscript, and Jeremy Elliot worked through the examples and critically reviewed the technical information. Ruthanne Lowe prepared the index. All of their contributions have produced a final prodiuct that is more accurate and easier to read than I would have achieved on my own.

The SYBEX production staff also made significant contributions: Olivia Shinomoto and John Kadyk, word processing; Michelle Hoffman, graphics production; Julie Bilski, design; Ingrid Owen, artwork; and Savitha Pichai, proofreading.

On the personal side, I would like to thank Frank for getting me into this and Colman for advice and for not laughing when I told him. And I would like to thank Shirley for setting the alarm every morning and not minding.

For this second edition, I would like to extend additional thanks to those who have helped me review and revise the book. At SYBEX, Marilyn Smith provided the detailed editorial support and Barbara Gordon provided the overall editorial direction, both with their usual combination of patience, precision, persistence, and good humor. I would also like to thank Glenn Reid of Adobe Systems for his continued willingness to answer my questions and share his outstanding technical expertise. Thanks also to those who "put the pieces together," including Bob Myren, word processing; Rinaldo Benet, proofreading; and Helen Bruno, pasteup.

TABLE OF CONTENTS

INTRODUCTION: AN OVERVIEW OF POSTSCRIPT AND THIS BOOK

This book is a guide to understanding and using the PostScript page-description language. PostScript was designed and developed by Adobe Systems Incorporated as a general-purpose programming language that also contains a large number of graphics operations defined within it. The entire concept of programming in PostScript, as you will learn from this book, is to combine the basic PostScript operations into powerful procedures that you can use to create and print complex pages of text and graphics.

WHAT IS POSTSCRIPT?

PostScript is a *page-description* language. It has been designed specifically to communicate a description of a printable document from a computer-based composition system to a raster-output printing system. This description is a *high-level* description, because it describes pages as a series of abstract graphic objects rather than describing them at a detailed, device-limited level.

PostScript is embedded in an interpreter program that generally runs in an independent device, such as a laser printer. The interpreter program (or just the *interpreter*) translates PostScript operations and data into device-specific codes and controls the output device to generate the graphics being described on the page. The interpreter processes each element (a name, string, array, number, or whatever) that is presented to it completely before it proceeds on to the next element. You will learn all about these *syntactic objects* in the following chapters as we discuss PostScript programming and its requirements.

This Introduction will help you understand how to use this book and how the book was set up to help you learn PostScript. The first section introduces you to the PostScript language and discusses how to "think" in PostScript. Because PostScript embodies many new concepts, particularly those oriented toward graphics and page structure, you will want to understand some of the unique characteristics that give PostScript its distinct flavor before you start learning the language itself. Although all of these characteristics are more fully explained in the body of the book, you will find the work easier and more understandable if you have a survey of the language before you get caught up in the specifics.

The second section of this Introduction deals with the purpose of the book and the structure that has been used to support that purpose. PostScript is a rich and complex language, and as with any such language, there is more to be said about it than can be reasonably contained in a single book. This section sets out in detail the objectives that this book is designed to meet and relates them to the reader's expected needs and background.

This book is heavily oriented toward examples and illustrations; it adopts a "learn by doing" approach. Because of this approach, the second section of this Introduction also contains information about the setup of hardware and software that will enable you to run the examples.

THINKING IN POSTSCRIPT

PostScript represents a new and exciting way of creating complex pages of output that include both graphics and text. In many ways, PostScript seems to me to return us to a time of artistry and craftsmanship, when the creation of a page of output was not a mechanical operation performed by high-speed presses, but an interaction between a human hand and mind and the physical output. PostScript has much more in common with lettering and calligraphy than with offset presses and typewriters.

By design, PostScript treats letters as graphic objects, as shapes to be painted onto the output page. Moreover, PostScript provides features and operations that will allow you to control the precise rendering of text and graphics in ways that are not possible with the traditional typesetting and printing technologies. You can stretch, bend, shade, and clip letters, using their shapes as graphic elements to create interesting (sometimes even bizarre) effects. The net result of these possible controls is to create an environment where you can design pages in ways that are more reminiscent of a medieval manuscript than the front page of a newspaper.

One of the driving forces behind the increased use of PostScript is the need to be able to represent the potential range of output on raster devices in a high-level, device-independent way. Graphic artists have come to realize that a new, effective tool is available to them, one that can do the old tasks well, reducing the repetitive portion to a minimum, and also provide scope for new, innovative approaches that were not feasible before. This feeling has been enhanced by the development and acceptance of electronic page-composition systems that use PostScript as their link to the individual devices, thus greatly expanding the potential for high-quality output. To appreciate the potential range of opportunities embodied in these applications, you need to understand PostScript's unusual capabilities as a computer language.

PREVIEW OF THE POSTSCRIPT LANGUAGE

The PostScript language has several distinctive characteristics that are important from the viewpoint of the PostScript user and programmer alike. It is both a programming language and a page-description language, and its special characteristics derive directly from this dual nature. It is

- Interpreted
- Device-independent
- Graphically powerful
- Page-oriented

These characteristics are important qualities for you to understand before you begin working in PostScript.

INTERPRETED

PostScript is an interpreted language, like BASIC or APL. This means that PostScript operators are understood and acted upon by another program, the interpreter, which generally resides in the controller of the output device (laser printer, typesetter, or other device). The use of an interpreter provides both advantages and disadvantages to the programmer. On the plus side, it allows definition of many program requirements as the commands are being executed, which provides both flexibility and sensitivity to the current state of the output and the output device. It also allows for immediate feedback, error recognition, and command execution, which makes interpreted languages easier to debug and correct.

However, there are some negatives to an interpreted language as well. In particular, because the interpreter is itself a program, there is an additional layer of software being executed. This can slow things down.

In PostScript's case, the loss is usually not great, since the interpreter is running by itself in the output device and therefore doesn't take up the resources of your computer.

Interpreted languages do not, in themselves, impose any specific structure on a program. Therefore, PostScript does not place any required structure on a document description, which is the PostScript equivalent of a program. This can be a negative point, if the programmer doesn't impose a clear structure on himself or herself. Generally, attention to such requirements—and the self-discipline to enforce them—comes only with experience in the language. There is both discussion and practice of recommended formats and conventions in the following chapters precisely because this kind of self-discipline is essential in an interpreted environment.

PostScript has already established a recommended structure and approach, which we will discuss more fully in Chapter 3. The use of these conventions is not required for creating successful PostScript page descriptions (programs), but following them makes clear to yourself and others what each part of the program is doing, so that programs can be easily compared and modified.

DYNAMIC

Because PostScript is an interpreted language, it is able to provide feedback to the programmer or the PostScript application. This feedback is particularly valuable in determining the current state of the execution environment; for example, whether a specific font is currently loaded and available. This is one sense in which the PostScript language is dynamic.

Another sense is that PostScript page descriptions can be defined and modified as they are created by defining new operations from the basic set of graphic and procedural operators. This dynamic process, which also is a function of the interpreter, makes PostScript significantly more powerful than traditional page-description mechanisms.

DEVICE INDEPENDENT

One of PostScript's great strengths is that it is independent of any specific output device. The basic set of PostScript operators is designed to be appropriate to the general class of raster-output devices upon which the language can be implemented. Adjusting and converting PostScript commands to the specific device's requirements is the interpreter's problem. However, where there is a need for specific, device-dependent information in order to construct a page or an image, PostScript can do that as well.

This freedom from the constraints of a specific output engine provides two major benefits to the PostScript programmer. First, you can generally remain unaware of the specific requirements of the output device. Second, a page described in PostScript can be proofed on one device and then produced on another with no modification of commands or operators. Pages can be proofed, corrected, and reset quickly by means of a convenient, relatively inexpensive output device, such as a laser printer; but they can also be generated for final printing on a typesetting machine once the proof and correction cycle has been completed. In this way, you gain the benefits of automated processing and quick turnaround, while still having the quality of output only available from the high dot-density devices. This is the benefit that has created much of the excitement about "desktop publishing" in the business community.

GRAPHIC POWER

PostScript is especially designed for the creation and manipulation of graphic objects on a raster-output device. This orientation toward graphics is such a major component of the language that I believe that the best way to think of PostScript is as a method of drawing electronically. In a sense, it is electronic calligraphy. Almost 30 percent of the operators deal with graphics; and many of these operators are intuitively similar to the actions of a skilled calligrapher handling a pen: raising it, positioning it on the paper, inking it, and then stroking each character onto the page. PostScript provides powerful primitive operators, such as **scale** and **rotate**, which can be combined in many ways to produce dramatic and surprising output. A number of examples in later chapters demonstrate this power.

This flexibility makes PostScript the language of choice for serious work, particularly work that combines text and graphics on one page. Where other languages or mechanisms are impediments to combining text and graphics, PostScript makes it easy and natural. This facility in combining the two modes derives in a large measure from PostScript's approach to text. Within PostScript, the individual characters that make up the text are themselves graphic objects that can be positioned, scaled, and rotated as required.

PAGE DESCRIPTION

Finally, PostScript is a page-description language. A raster-output device essentially prepares one page of output at a time, by setting each point on the page to a precise value. For black-and-white output, these points, or pixels, are set to either zero or one, representing either black or white. The page description is therefore a complete map of these values for the entire surface to be output—usually a full page, but sometimes less because of hardware limitations.

There are fundamental drawbacks to the pixel-by-pixel method of page description. Three of these issues stand out as particularly undesirable from the user's viewpoint:

- The description is particular to a specific device. It can only represent one array of values for a given page, even though different devices (of differing resolution or format) may require different values to represent the same page.

- The full description of a page is inevitably large. It requires one value for every addressable point on the page. For example, this comes to more than 72,000 values per page for a typical laser output device.

- The mathematical process of deciding which points get what values for the representation of a given image (called scan conversion) requires a substantial amount of computation and may not be possible to do at an acceptable speed on a small machine like a personal computer.

PostScript provides a mechanism for the description of a page of graphic objects rather than a page of pixels. It does this by using powerful primitive operators, which correspond in a relatively natural way to how you ordinarily handle graphics. These operators can be combined to produce a wide range of complex output.

POSTSCRIPT OPERATORS

One of the strengths of PostScript is its extensive set of basic operators, which cover both ordinary program tasks and graphic operations. The library of PostScript operators can be divided for this work into five major groups, as follows:

- **Stack and mathematical operators**. This group covers the operations of stack handling, array and dictionary processing, and all mathematical operations.

- **Graphics operators**. This group consists of all operators that handle graphics on the user page, except those operators specifically related to font definition and handling. This includes operators that handle path construction and painting as well as those that control PostScript's internal graphics memory.

- **Font operators**. This includes all operators that define and control fonts.

- **Program-control operators**. This set includes operators that handle relation tests of various types and file operations, as well as alter or control the sequence of execution.

- **Device-control and status operators**. Finally, this group contains all the operators that set or report the current state of the output device being used.

Do not confuse this grouping of operators with the standard groups presented in the *PostScript Language Reference Manual*. Even when the names are similar, the above groups are generally more inclusive and are presented and used here for the purposes of conceptual organization and discussion.

These operators represent a rich set of possible operations, and each has a specific, useful place in a programmer's PostScript lexicon. However, as in English itself, you will probably be able to accomplish 90 percent or more of your work with 15 percent or less of the operators. Because this book is directed toward understanding the basics of the language, it will concentrate its examples and discussions on the most useful 15 percent or 20 percent of these operators.

This is a reasonable and effective method for mastering a new programming language. In many ways it is analogous to learning a foreign language. You want to learn the structure and flow of the language—the "grammar," if you will—and then learn a useful "vocabulary" of frequently used operations. Once that is accomplished, you should try to add one or two new operators to your repertoire with every new programming opportunity. This will help you to grow in confidence and competence and to master the full range of PostScript's possibilities.

BOOK PURPOSE AND STRUCTURE

The purpose of this book is to teach you to understand and use PostScript. PostScript is, as has been said repeatedly, a powerful language. Unfortunately, the power of a computer language is generally directly related to its complexity, and PostScript is no exception to this relationship. PostScript is not inherently difficult to use; it is only unfamiliar and complex. This book is structured to minimize the complexity by introducing you to PostScript operations step by step, which helps you become familiar with PostScript through practice and discussion of many examples, and thus opens up to you the range of power in PostScript procedures.

The structure of this book has been developed from long experience in using and teaching interpreted programming languages. PostScript, like most interpreted languages, provides an interactive mode of operation. In this mode, the interpreter holds a dialogue with the user, immediately performing each operation and reporting back any results or errors. This mode of operation is an advantage for learning a language because it allows you to see the effect of each command as it is executed. In this way it pinpoints the place where a program has gone wrong or done something you didn't expect it to do. This mode also allows you to stop at any point, try out alternative commands, and see how the page looks as a result. Thus, you can see the changing page as you reshape its description. The book takes advantage of this immediate response by using exercises that are designed to allow you to develop and test them interactively.

There is one point of caution for readers who are running on an AppleTalk network. You will need some special help to get interactive access (or as close to interactive access as AppleTalk will allow). Please read Appendix D, "Configuration Data and Setup," which contains specific instructions on how you should set up and run the exercises.

The book also includes in its structure three proven techniques that can help you build your understanding of PostScript. First, the book follows a course of study, a plan that is designed to present the various operations in PostScript in a natural way. The book also proceeds in a cumulative manner, with each topic and exercise building on the previous ones. Finally, the book provides ample exercises and examples to help you practice the concepts presented in a concrete setting and allow you sufficient drill to make these concepts and operations really familiar.

OBJECTIVES OF THE BOOK

As stated previously, no single book can adequately explore the complete range of PostScript operations. Therefore, objectives that are discussed here represent the primary criteria that were used to determine what materials were included and in what order and depth those subjects were covered.

At the broadest possible level, the goal of this book has already been stated: to help you understand and use PostScript. This statement, however, is too expansive to provide much guidance for the construction of a satisfactory work. Therefore, three more specific objectives have been defined and arranged in a priority ordering.

The first objective is to teach you to read PostScript code. This means more than just looking up the operators in a manual. Sometimes that kind of reading is necessary, but it is not the kind of fluency that we want to develop here. This objective means that you should be able to understand PostScript concepts and operations with depth and accuracy. You will learn the basic PostScript vocabulary and structure, so that you can follow most PostScript code without recourse to a reference guide (either this book or any other). By the end of the book, you should be able to follow most PostScript programs, especially ones that you have not written yourself, and comprehend at a general level what the program does and how it does it. In other words, you should be able to read PostScript in much the same way you can read English—sometimes referring to a dictionary or grammar, but mostly able to follow ordinary constructions without difficulty.

The second objective is to teach you to work with PostScript. This means that you will be able to set up PostScript in its various modes of operation and, particularly, be able to invoke and use the interactive mode for debugging and testing. From the exercises, you will be familiar with defining PostScript operations and analyzing PostScript problems. Overall, you should have a good grasp of how PostScript works and what facilities it has available.

The last objective, but by no means the least important one, is to teach you to write PostScript programs. You will learn to analyze and set up page output. You will use these setups to generate the necessary procedure definitions, and you will then program those procedures to generate the pages that you have analyzed. This process of structuring pages, designing solutions to create the pages, and then implementing them in PostScript is at least as important a component of learning to write the language as is the use of the various operators.

Obviously, these objectives are intertwined so closely that each supports and makes use of both of the others. Like any good text, the book does not distinguish each objective, but tries to teach all three of them with each exercise or lesson. In this way, you will learn both the individual PostScript operators and the process of combining those operators into PostScript procedures in a unified way.

REQUIREMENTS

What do you need to get the most out of this book? To begin with, you should be willing to work through the examples. PostScript is like any other language in that ease and proficiency come from practice. So you should do the exercises and examples, perhaps even more than once. I would encourage you to try alternative approaches and print out your variations to see how you are progressing. One of the most interesting things about PostScript, in my experience, has been how much fun it is to play with. You can generate an amazing variety of graphics, just by trying options and operators. Please enjoy this experience; it will make the whole process more satisfying for you.

General computer concepts are not covered here. Although I try to define precisely all terms that are intrinsic or even related to PostScript, there are certainly a number of concepts that apply to computer operations and computer languages generally that are undefined. Things like what a file is and what a computer language does are taken more or less for granted. If you find yourself having trouble with these kinds of things, look in Appendix E, "Bibliography," for some recommended books on basic computer concepts.

The general matter of computer operations also is not covered here. I'm not going to tell you how to turn on the computer or the printer, nor tell you how to start up your programs (other than PostScript). The issue of computer operations is particularly sticky with PostScript, since it can be run on any computer onto which you can hook an RS232 port and connect a PostScript-equipped device. In particular, PostScript is widely used on both the Apple Macintosh and IBM PC lines of computers, both of which (to make a vast understatement) are quite different. The general tendency in this book has been to avoid device- or operating-system-dependent text and examples and allow you to work out how to talk to the PostScript device on your own. This presumes, of course, that you are familiar with the computer that you're using. If you have trouble, first look at the operations manual (or manuals) that came with the computer, then try the device manual for your specific output device, and finally try this book and Appendix D of the *PostScript Language Reference Manual*.

You will want to know what resources, besides this book, you might want to have handy. To begin with, you will almost certainly require a PostScript output device. Although it is possible to follow the examples in the book without actually doing them yourself, the learning experience will be immeasurably improved if you can input and execute these examples. The book expects you to do so, and meeting the second objective above can only be accomplished through a "hands on" approach. If you don't have a PostScript device available for your own use, there are a number of places (at least in Northern and Southern California) that rent time on their PostScript-equipped Apple LaserWriters for reasonable fees. It would certainly be valuable for you, under these circumstances, to rent a little time and at least try the larger exercises on a PostScript device.

If you are going to do much PostScript work, you will also want to own the book mentioned earlier, the *PostScript Language Reference Manual*. It is written by Adobe Systems, the creator of PostScript, and is the definitive source for all PostScript operators and operations. You don't need it to use this book; all the required definitions are provided here for your use and reference. Even if you have other references, you don't want to flip back and forth between several books while you are trying to learn the material. But as you grow beyond what you have learned here, you will need precise and complete definitions for every possible PostScript operator. That is what is provided in the *PostScript Language Reference Manual*; it is the ultimate reference and referee for all PostScript operations. There are several places throughout this book where you are referred to the *Language Reference Manual* for further detail or explanations of various operations.

STRUCTURE

The book follows a regular pattern that grows naturally out of the objectives discussed above. It is organized in a sort of spiral, in that certain topics reoccur in regular succession but with increasing depth and complexity. Thus you will first encounter simple text output, using the most basic operations and relying, as much as possible, on default parameters in the language. Then you will explore PostScript procedures and dictionaries, followed by basic graphics. You will return to text processing again, this time using the procedures and graphics techniques already developed to help you build more complex text output. And so on, through advanced fonts and dictionaries, more text, and finally, very advanced graphic concepts.

TASK ORIENTATION

The basic orientation of the book is to do first and talk after. You will have a much better appreciation of the discussion of what the program means after you have executed it, instead of analyzing it to death before running it. This is an excellent basic approach to language instruction generally, whether natural or computer languages—just ask Berlitz.

However, this approach cannot be followed entirely. Page composition is inherently a process that depends on analysis and planning to work correctly. Moreover, some choices have to be dealt with before you start programming; otherwise, the program and the associated procedures will look entirely arbitrary and capricious. To this extent, the exercises include preliminary setup and analysis. Beyond what is required for that reason, no preliminary programming is undertaken. Instead, the exercises and examples all have extensive discussions, usually line by line, after the program is presented and run. The intention is to provide you with the concepts necessary for the program before you write it, to use the actual program as an example, and then to discuss the specific use and results of these concepts as embodied in the program after the exercise is completed.

EXERCISES AND EXAMPLES

The programs included in this text are broken down into two informal groups: examples and exercises. The examples are short, usually simple, and designed to illustrate one or two specific points from the text. The exercises are longer and more complex, and generally combine several previous techniques into one larger program.

Both the exercises and examples are to some extent cumulative. Because of the structure of the PostScript language, it is both appropriate and useful to create procedures that perform specific tasks and reuse these procedures over and over, occasionally reworking them in small ways to fit the current need. That is not to say that you need to work the examples in order; most of them are complete programs in themselves, and can be entered and executed on their own without error. However, the explanations that accompanied them initially are not repeated in the text when the procedure is reused. Therefore, if you are skipping around and find that you need to look up a specific procedure to understand a point, you will have to look back at the first instance of its use in the book to find a complete discussion.

The concepts used in the book are also cumulative. As you might have guessed from the earlier discussion of the spiral nature of the material, much use is made of previous concepts and techniques as you proceed further into the book. Indeed, some of the material in the later chapters will be almost incomprehensible if you are not fully familiar with particular PostScript operations and ideas that have been explained, discussed, and illustrated in earlier portions of the book. This is, to some extent, a process of developing the vocabulary to enable further discussions to proceed quickly and precisely.

If you do want to skip around in the book, I would recommend that you use the "Operator Review" sections at the end of the chapters as a quick guide to the material covered in the chapter. I would also suggest that you at least read through the exercises before you skip the chapter. If the exercise is clear, well and good, then you can proceed with the assurance that you understand the work done so far in the book; if the exercise is not clear, however, you should read the explanations and discussions before proceeding.

DEVICE USE

All of the work in this book, both text and examples, relies on generic PostScript features and is not tied to a specific implementation of PostScript in any specific device. Any exercise or example should execute correctly on any PostScript-equipped device, and the concepts and techniques that you will learn are as applicable to a typesetter as they are to a laser printer.

The work in the book is based solely on PostScript. With the single exception of requiring the use of a separate editor in one exercise (merging application data and a form generated by PostScript), no language or program other than PostScript is used in this book. You can complete all of the examples using only a PostScript-equipped device and a terminal, if necessary. Note that this would be an impossible request if it were not the case that PostScript is a good general-purpose language as well as a specialized one.

Obviously, each reader will have a specific configuration of hardware and software. The book is structured for use by everyone; but what do you do if you have a specific problem? Unfortunately, we are not able to provide detailed information on every possible configuration. However, Appendix D, "Configuration Data and Setup," contains specific information for two common configurations: one for an IBM PC and the other for an Apple Macintosh. Even if your specific setup is not included, you may want to read whichever of these is most similar to your configuration if you have a problem. It may give you some ideas or information that will help you.

CHAPTER SUMMARIES

This book contains seven chapters (besides this Introduction). These chapters illustrate the spiral or recurring nature of the topics that we discussed above. The general contents of the chapters are listed as follows:

Chapter 1: Getting Started

This chapter covers the basic functions of PostScript and starts you working in the interactive mode. It also introduces specific PostScript concepts that are essential to understanding and working with PostScript operators. The chapter includes a number of exercises to illustrate these basic functions. The examples and exercises all produce a variety of text output onto a simple page.

Chapter 2: Dictionaries and Definitions

This chapter covers two important PostScript facilities. The first is the PostScript dictionaries. PostScript uses dictionaries heavily for a variety of processes. Here is your first encounter with these vital objects and with an associated set of examples to help you use their basic operators. The second is the facility within PostScript to define procedures. This is at the heart of PostScript programming, and the exercise here provides a good illustration of how to use procedures in PostScript. The chapter ends with a section on naming and structural conventions, which are extremely important in PostScript.

Chapter 3: Introduction to Fonts and Graphics

With these basic concepts under control, this chapter introduces the first use of graphics in the book and shows the connection between the creation of characters in fonts and general graphics operations. The chapter starts with a number of small examples that illustrate the basic graphics operations: creating a line, creating closed figures, and shading or filling an area on the page. Then the chapter discusses basic font mechanisms: how you establish and use the PostScript fonts. Finally, the chapter returns to the use of graphics and discusses curves and coordinate transformations. Again, there are a number of examples, culminating in an exercise that links many of the preceding functions to create a logo for an imaginary company.

Chapter 4: Basic Documents

This chapter is entirely devoted to a large and complex exercise. The chapter discusses the basic types of documents and then goes on to create a simple invoice form using PostScript exclusively. The form is designed to be filled in with data output from a simple spreadsheet application. The chapter concludes by preparing the data from the spreadsheet and inserting it onto the form, so that the complete document prints out with all the data inserted as required.

Chapter 5: Creating and Modifying Fonts

This chapter returns to our discussion of the PostScript font machinery and how it works in actual use. The chapter covers typical operations of the font mechanism in detail, and then begins to review the possible changes that the programmer can make to a font. These changes are categorized into two simple sets: the modification of all characters in the font simultaneously and the modification of characters individually to achieve certain effects. This also includes a general discussion of adding fonts to PostScript either by creating new ones or downloading them. The chapter contains a variety of examples that illuminate the techniques involved.

Chapter 6: Advanced Text Topics

This chapter builds upon the concepts discussed in the previous chapter to develop advanced techniques for handling and displaying text. The chapter has only a few examples, because of the complexity of the issues, but there is a full discussion of string handling and manipulation along with a discussion of word and character justification. An exercise on text justification is included as an example and an inspiration. Next, the chapter discusses joining application output with PostScript programs. This is an important topic, which includes information on how to read and interpret the PostScript code generated by several typical applications.

Chapter 7: Advanced Graphics Techniques

This last chapter primarily deals with specialized graphics processing. The first section of the chapter discusses the PostScript advanced graphics controls and operations. The first of these concepts is clipping, and some examples of its use in typical situations are provided. This is an important topic for PostScript programmers because it is a powerful tool to aid them in producing some of the most typical PostScript effects. Additional advanced graphics controls cover line handling, arbitrary curves, and various transformations. The second part of the chapter covers image processing, a complex and demanding process. You will read all about the basic concepts and parameters that are necessary for processing both sampled and synthetic images. Finally, the chapter (and the book) closes with a discussion of device-specific information that you can access within PostScript.

Appendix A: Summary of PostScript Operators

This appendix presents all the operators that you have learned throughout the book in one place and in a common format.

Appendix B: Structuring Conventions Version 2.0

This appendix updates the discussion of program structure in the book with the latest revision of the recommended PostScript structuring conventions, published by Adobe Systems, the creator of PostScript, in late January, 1987.

Appendix C: Encapsulated PostScript

This appendix describes the use of Encapsulated PostScript (EPS) files which are primarily used to produce illustrations.

Appendix D: Configuration Data and Setup

This appendix contains two subsections: the first discusses a typical IBM-PC setup (hardware and software) as required to run an Apple LaserWriter; the second section presents a similar configuration for an Apple Macintosh.

Appendix E: Bibliography

This appendix is a short list of books that are related to various topics discussed in the body of the text, including advanced graphics computations, typography and design, page layout, and other areas of interest to different readers.

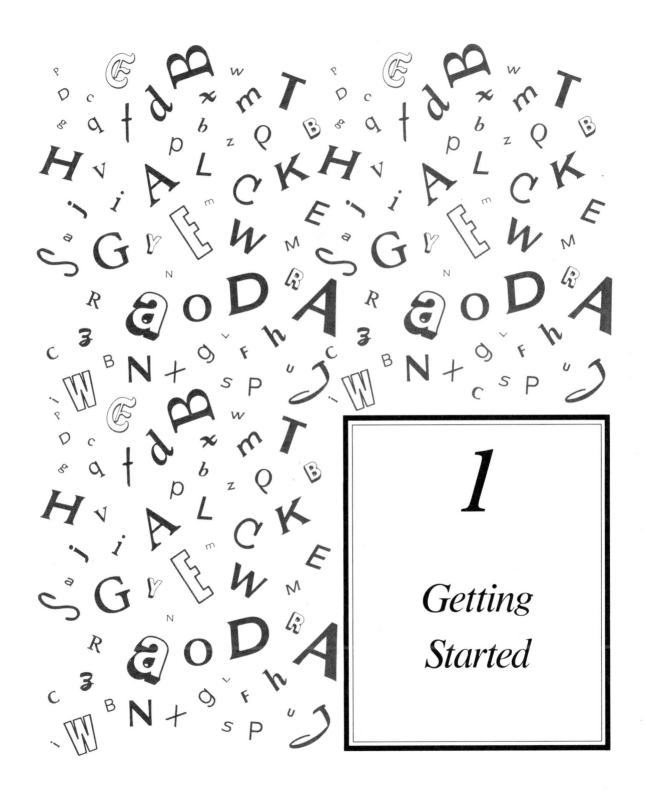

1

Getting Started

IN THIS CHAPTER YOU WILL BEGIN TO EXAMINE POST-SCRIPT OPERATIONS AND OPERATORS IN DEPTH. THIS chapter, together with the next, "Dictionaries and Definitions," is intended to give you a clear understanding of how PostScript operates and of how you read and write PostScript code. You will be introduced to a number of PostScript operators, which command the PostScript interpreter to take various actions. These operators form the basic building blocks of PostScript procedures and programs.

The chapter is centered on two exercises intended to acquaint you with actual PostScript coding without becoming too complex and bewildering. Because PostScript is a relatively complex language, these first exercises will be kept simple, to avoid an excessive—and tedious—amount of explanation before you can see any output.

Before you can start the exercises, however, you must understand how PostScript describes a page of output and how to use these page-description concepts in your work. So the chapter begins with a section on PostScript page structure and concepts.

In addition, you need to understand issues relating to starting and operating your system, such as communicating with the PostScript interpreter, typical screen presentation, and possible error conditions. You also need to understand the basic functions that must be performed within your program in order to print even one line of text. So you will read about the basic start-up issues and about text initialization and positioning.

After these necessary preliminaries, you will execute the two programs that constitute the first exercise, each of which outputs a line or two of text onto the printer. The simplicity of these programs allows you to start working in PostScript and to become familiar with the interactive mode of the interpreter without being too concerned with program errors. Each program is given in detail and includes a complete discussion of what each line is intended to accomplish.

With the successful completion of the first exercise to motivate you, you continue the chapter with a section on PostScript programming in general. After your first excursion into the world of PostScript, you will naturally have questions and will have observed some unusual qualities in the PostScript code. Such points, including PostScript stack operations, notation for PostScript examples, and a short discussion of how PostScript handles strings of characters and comments, are covered in this section.

The next section in the chapter consists of a second exercise, a longer program. This program sets several paragraphs in a text-and-commentary, two-column format. This exercise will show you how you can easily use PostScript to accomplish things that may look difficult. As before, the actual program is preceded by a discussion of page setup issues and requirements and is followed by a line-by-line analysis of the program so you will understand exactly what was done and, more importantly, why it was done.

The chapter ends with a brief review of the basic PostScript operators that you have encountered so far. This final section is intended as a review and a reference, and it provides in one place and in one standard format all the operators that have been previously discussed.

WORKING WITH POSTSCRIPT

The PostScript language contains more than 240 primitive operators for performing various functions. These are the operators that are defined in the *PostScript Language Reference Manual* and are implemented within the PostScript interpreter. They are called "primitive" operators because they define the specific functions that the interpreter knows how to perform. These operators form the basic building blocks that make up the PostScript language.

Before you begin writing or modifying PostScript code, you need to acquaint yourself with a basic subset of those operators and become familiar with the unusual structure of PostScript itself. While PostScript is by no means unique in its format and structure, it is distinctive; and some time spent on understanding and appreciating its characteristics will pay off in quicker comprehension and easier handling of PostScript programs.

The PostScript interpreter processes a series of entities called *objects*. This is a convenient name for describing the different things that the PostScript interpreter can work with and understand. For our purposes objects can be grouped into several intuitive categories: literals, names, and procedures. Literals are what you would expect: numbers, characters, strings, and so forth. Names are basically labels for other objects—literals and procedures—that are entries into the various dictionaries. Procedures are groups of objects, meant to be executed in sequence, that are treated as a unit and stored in PostScript memory. All of this sounds more complex than it is, as you will see when we get to the examples further on.

MODES OF OPERATION

There are two basic modes of operation: batch and interactive. These two modes are much the same in that the interpreter behaves the same way in both of them; they differ in the source of the PostScript objects that are being processed by the interpreter and in how error messages and status information are reported.

In the *batch mode,* the PostScript interpreter is presented with a series of objects, usually from a file that it processes sequentially. Generally, such a file is generated by an application program or by a programmer and is intended to create a description of a page or pages. That description is then used to generate output onto the raster device controlled by the interpreter. Most of the interpreter's work is in the batch mode.

INTERACTIVE MODE

It is also possible to interact directly with the interpreter when it is implemented in a dedicated device (such as the Apple LaserWriter). In this *interactive mode,* each PostScript object is sent by the user directly to the interpreter using a terminal and a communication link, or an equivalent mechanism. The PostScript interpreter acts on each object as it is presented, carries out the requested action, and returns any error or status messages back through the terminal. This mode then creates a kind of "dialogue" with the interpreter, which is particularly useful for learning PostScript and for debugging PostScript programs. For this reason, the interactive mode will be used in our examples almost exclusively.

As we proceed through the examples in this chapter, we will display the entire contents of the screen so you can see what is going on. Since we will be using the interactive mode, you will see both the input and the interpreter response, which will help you see what PostScript is doing.

OPERATION OVERVIEW

There are a few points that you need to know before proceeding. All of these points will be discussed in depth later.

The first key concept is that PostScript works through a *stack* mechanism. This is a place where PostScript operators look for data and return results. For now, you can think of it as a temporary storage area within the interpreter.

As you know, PostScript is a language of operators and each operator performs a single function, although sometimes that function can be complex. Most operators require some type of information to work with; this required data is called *operands*. Our second key point is that in PostScript, unlike most other computer languages, the operands must come before the operator. This makes life easy for the interpreter, but hard for the user. It means, for example, that you must enter the coordinates for where you want to go on a page before you can tell PostScript to move there. This is a little disconcerting at first, but you'll soon get used to it.

PAGE STRUCTURE

A unique and powerful characteristic of PostScript is its design as a page-description language. A page is the natural unit of output on a raster output device, and PostScript operates within that unit in an easily comprehensible way by means of its operators. In this section, you will examine more closely what is meant by a "page" and how PostScript's operators work within it.

CONCEPTS

PostScript maintains a simple conceptual model of a "page" as a two-dimensional space. Images are "built" on the page by placing "paint" in selected areas. The paint may be put on the page in the form of letters, lines, filled shapes, or halftone representations of photographs. The paint may be in color, black, white, or any shade of gray. It is always opaque, so that the last mark on the page completely overlays any previous marks. Any element may be cropped, as it is painted onto the page, to fit within a desired shape or border. Finally, once a page reaches the desired form, it may be rendered onto an output device.

In all these things, PostScript follows the natural model of moving a pen or brush across a page of paper. Even though the "page" may be a metal drum and the "paint," electrons, the concept remains the same.

The major conceptual change follows from PostScript's ability to generate a path and fill it in. This is similar to an artist lightly pencilling in a letter or figure, filling in the outline with ink or paint, and then erasing the original line to render the final object—except that PostScript's "pencil lines" are invisible. Nevertheless, both the power of PostScript page descriptions and the natural way they behave, particularly for the graphic artist, can be readily understood.

CURRENT PAGE

The PostScript artist (or programmer) begins work on an "ideal page," which is independent of any specific output device. PostScript calls this the *current page,* and this is the two-dimensional space where PostScript makes its marks.

When PostScript begins, the current page is blank. Painting operators, which form a subset of the complete set of graphics operators, place marks on the page. The principal painting operators are as follows:

Operator	Function
fill	fills in an area on a page
stroke	marks lines on a page
image	paints an image, such as would come from a scanner or similar device
show	paints character shapes onto a page

Each of these operators (and the other graphics operators) has various operands, both explicit and implicit, but we will fully discuss these in Chapter 3.

CURRENT PATH

Most of the painting operators (**fill, stroke,** and **show**) have one common and important implicit operand, which is called the *current path.* This is the invisible "pencil line" we discussed before, and it marks for PostScript where to apply paint on the current page. The current path is an arbitrary sequence of points, which may be both connected (as in a line or curve) and disconnected (as a separate point). Taken together, this sequence of points describes shapes on the page and further describes the position and orientation of the shapes with respect to the overall page. The last point on the existing current path is the *current point*.

You can construct more than one path on a page. There is no requirement that a page be output before you start a new path. Of course, only one current path can be on a page at one time.

PATH CONSTRUCTION OPERATORS

The current path is built through the use of PostScript path construction operators. Each of these operators alters the current path in some way, generally by adding a new segment to the existing path. Typical path construction operators are the following:

Operator	Function
newpath	starts a new path
moveto	moves from the current point to a defined point
lineto	creates a line from the current point to a defined point
rlineto	creates a line from the current point to a new point defined by its relation to the current point; also known as **relative lineto**

Remember that all these operators only move the current path; they do not mark the page. All marking is done by means of the painting operators.

MEASUREMENT AND COORDINATES

As you might expect, paths and points are specified on a PostScript page in terms of coordinates. Since a PostScript page is two-dimensional, two coordinates are required: x and y. With this method, every point on a PostScript page can be described by a pair of numbers (x, y) that conceptually define its location on the page. You must understand that, at this point, these coordinates have no relationship to the actual output device. They are ideal coordinates that always maintain a fixed relationship to the current page. This coordinate system is called the *user space*.

DEFAULT USER SPACE

In order to understand precisely where a specific pair of x, y coordinates puts us on a page, we must define three things:

1. Location of the origin: point (0, 0). The point (0, 0) or the *origin* on a PostScript page is at the *bottom-left corner* of the page.

2. Direction of the x-axis and the y-axis. The *positive* direction on the x-axis extends *horizontally to the right* across a PostScript page. The *positive* direction on the y-axis extends *vertically upward* on a PostScript page.

3. The scale, or unit of measure, on the x-axis and the y-axis. The length of *one unit* along both the x-axis and the y-axis is *1/72 inch*.

If you are not familiar with printing, the choice of 1/72 inch may seem like a strange value to use; in fact, this is almost precisely a printer's *point* (which is fractionally larger than 1/72 inch). In this way, the default x and y values become the equivalent of point values as you move around the page. You will find this useful as you begin page composition. You should also notice that, by this choice of the origin and orientation, every point on the page is described by a positive value of x and y.

This entire set of conventions now precisely defines every point on an ideal page in units that are easy and natural to use, from a printing and graphics standpoint. This set of conventions defines what is called the *default user space*.

Like many PostScript conventions, this set of coordinates, although perfectly logical, is a bit difficult to get used to. The natural coordinate system probably would start at the top-left corner of the page rather than the bottom, and a positive value of y would move down the page rather than up. The PostScript convention is more traditional in that it conforms to the standard mathematical notation, but it does require a change in thought patterns as you work on a page of output.

FIRST EXERCISE

For the first exercise, there will be several examples displaying a line of text in various positions. Each of the examples has a specific purpose, and each will help you understand how PostScript handles a page of output. Each example displays a slightly different line of text (for identification purposes), and each line is displayed at a different place on the page.

SETUP

In the best epic tradition, we are going to start "in the middle of the action" in order to provide some concrete examples of PostScript output. This has a real benefit in that it helps structure and motivate the learning process; computer languages generally—and PostScript in particular—are sufficiently complex that they can best be assimilated and understood by using practical, explicit examples rather than abstract discussion. However, PostScript has almost no default options or structure, and therefore we need to do some setup work before you can do the exercises.

The requirements for setup and the concepts behind the setup functions that have not already been explained will be covered in detail. However, in these initial exercises, you will have to enter each line of the examples exactly as shown. Because PostScript is an interpreted language and we are working in the interactive mode, you will get appropriate error messages if you make a mistake. Don't worry if that happens; just reenter the statement with any necessary corrections. But do be aware that PostScript, like most computer languages, is particular about format and syntax. Later in the chapter we will cover this subject in detail; for now, you only need to copy the exercises exactly.

In entering each line, there are two points that you should know about PostScript syntax. First, PostScript requires at least one space between words or data, but won't mind if you use more than one. If you have any doubt whether there is a space in a line, put one in; generally, it won't hurt anything. Second, PostScript distinguishes between uppercase and lowercase letters; you must use the same letters as the examples do, both upper- and lowercase. Sometimes this may look strange, but it is important. We will discuss the issue of names and naming conventions (which is what this relates to) in the next chapter.

COMMUNICATIONS SETUP

This section discusses the setup of the examples in general terms. Specific details on how to set up your personal computer and interact with the output device are contained in Appendix D. Since the Apple

LaserWriter is the most common—and most inexpensive—PostScript-equipped output device, we will assume for example purposes that this is the output device. Nevertheless, all the example programs will work on any standard PostScript interpreter. The examples all assume that you are running in the interactive mode, using either an IBM PC (or compatible) or an Apple Macintosh in terminal mode as an input into a LaserWriter. In order to run your personal computer in terminal mode, you will have to run a communications program. There is a discussion of this point, with specific recommendations of programs for this purpose, in Appendix D.

In order to communicate with the LaserWriter, you must set the select switch (at the rear of the printer) to either the 1200-baud or the 9600-baud setting. I recommend the 9600-baud setting unless you are having difficulty in communications or unless the printer is located some distance away—approximately more than 50 feet of cable. After setting the switch, turn on the printer. You should receive the standard start-up sheet, indicating the correct operation of the printer.

Next, start up your communications program, using the following settings:

- baud rate set to 1200 or 9600 (depending on what you set on the printer)
- 8 data bits
- no parity
- 1 stop bit

Open a direct communications link with the printer. This is done by not using any telephone number or modem commands when you establish the connection. Some communications software has a direct-link option that you can use. Set up your communications program *not* to echo your input. Depending on the communications program you are using, set the local echo off, or set duplex to halt to suppress the echoing. The LaserWriter will automatically echo once you have started PostScript in the interactive mode.

If the program supports it, you should set it up to use the XON/XOFF protocol. If your program has this feature, it will be a menu or a command option. Check your software manual for details. If you don't have this protocol or can't find it, don't worry about it. The XON/XOFF protocol is a way for the printer and the computer to exchange information about when the computer can start sending data and when it must halt, usually because the printer cannot handle more data. Since you will be using the interactive mode, you are not likely to cause this condition. The protocol is most necessary when you are sending large amounts of data (or a large and complex program) to the printer, such as you might do with a batch file.

TYPICAL PRESENTATION

Once your communications software tells you that you are connected to the printer, type in the word "executive". At this point you will not see anything on the screen, since you set "echo off" in the communications program and you have not yet started the interactive mode with the PostScript interpreter. The command "executive" is the command that starts the interactive mode.

You should receive the following response after you enter "executive":

PostScript(tm) Version 38.0
Copyright(c) 1985 Adobe Systems Incorporated
PS>

The version number may differ depending on when you got your printer. The PS> prompt means that the interpreter is ready for you to enter a command.

At this point, there are several possible problems you might encounter. These usually arise because of a problem in the communications link between the PC and the printer. Although we can't cover all the possible problems, let's discuss one or two of the more common glitches. Even if something goes wrong that isn't covered, this discussion may help you diagnose what is happening.

In the first typical problem, your screen shows one or two lines that look like comic-book curses. It may look something like Figure 1.1. Actually, this is not as bad as it may seem; at least you're talking to the printer. Generally, this kind of display is caused by incompatible communications parameters between the terminal and the printer. Check the baud-rate settings on the printer and in the communications software. If these are set correctly, check the settings for data bits and stop bits (8 and 1 respectively) and check for correct parity (none).

A second typical problem is more difficult to diagnose. In this case your communications software tells you that you are connected, you type in "executive" (which you can't see), and nothing happens. Basically, you are not communicating with the PostScript interpreter in a way it can understand; unfortunately, there can be many reasons for this.

The first thing to do is to check all physical connections between the devices. Review Appendix D and the hardware manuals for the PC and

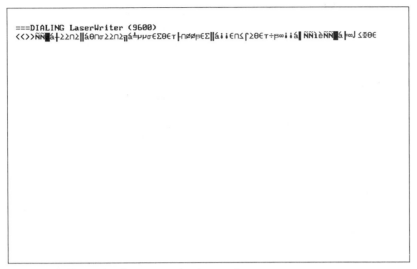

Figure 1.1: Example of a communication settings error

the LaserWriter for specific advice and directions. If the physical connections and switches all appear correct and firmly in place and you still have a problem, turn off the LaserWriter for a minute and then turn it on again. After the test page is produced, reinitialize the communications software on the PC. Make sure all the communications parameters are set correctly, and then type the "executive" command again. This should resolve most of these problems.

Finally, you may get an error response from PostScript when you start up, as in the following:

    = = = DIALING LaserWriter
    %%[Error: undefined: OffendingCommand: ATDT]%%
    %%[Flushing: rest of job (to end-of-file) will be ignored]%%

This is caused by the communications program, which sent something (in this case a modem command to dial—ATDT) to the PostScript interpreter before you entered the "executive" command. This generally occurs because the communications software is programmed to talk over a dial-up telephone line, through a modem, rather than to talk over a direct communications link. Therefore, the program sends modem-control signals such as ATDT to direct the modem. Any such automatic dialing or other modem commands should be deleted from your communications software or be disabled while you are accessing the LaserWriter. If this problem does occur, you will have to send an end-of-file command to the PostScript interpreter before it will recognize your "executive" command. As you can see from the screen, PostScript says it is going to skip all commands until it receives an end-of-file character. To send an end-of-file command, send a Ctrl-D (ASCII 4)—Command-D on the Macintosh—command from the keyboard. Then enter the "executive" command as before. The result looks like this:

    = = = DIALING LaserWriter
    %%[Error: undefined: OffendingCommand: ATDT]%%
    %%[Flushing: rest of job (to end-of-file) will be ignored]%%
    ♦
    PostScript(tm) Version 38.0
    Copyright (c) 1985 Adobe Systems Incorporated.
    PS>

TEXT SETUP

This first exercise will produce text output on your printer. Since almost every page that is created for output on a PostScript system contains text, this seems like an excellent place to start.

Text is presented and manipulated in PostScript as *strings*. A string is a line of characters, enclosed in parentheses, like this:

    (This is sample string number 1).

In fact, this will be the string you will use for display in the first example. Of course, strings may contain other characters, and later in the book we will discuss all the varieties of strings.

PostScript displays strings by means of the **show** operator. This is one of the PostScript painting operators that place marks on the current page. In this case, the marks are in the form of letters, as described by the currently active font. Each font contains a description of letters and symbols that defines for **show** how to mark them on the page.

PostScript contains built-in descriptions of several common fonts. These include two character fonts, Times-Roman and Helvetica, along with a Symbol font that provides mathematical and other special characters and a typewriter-like font, Courier. There are a number of additional fonts available for PostScript, including Palatino, Avant-Garde, Bookman, and others. Any or all of these additional fonts may be loaded into the PostScript interpreter and used in normal PostScript operations. The examples in this book will only use built-in fonts, to ensure that any setup will be able to run the exercises as shown. You can easily substitute other fonts if you have them installed; it won't affect the exercises at all—although, of course, it would change the output to the selected font.

There are three essential font operations that must be done before the **show** operator can do its work. First, you have to tell PostScript what font you want to use, by supplying the name of the font to the **findfont** operator. Second, you must specify what size you want the letters to print. This is done by giving a size number, in user units, to the **scalefont** operator. Since you will be using the default units, this size will be in points—which is a natural and convenient measurement for text. Finally, you must tell PostScript to make your selected, scaled font into the currently active font. This is done by the **setfont** operator. The whole process can be done in one line of PostScript and looks like this:

/Times-Roman **findfont** 12 **scalefont setfont**

This sequence of operators finds the Times-Roman font, sets it to 12-point size, and makes it the current font. Now when you issue a **show**, PostScript knows what font you want and what size you want the letters to be.

POSITIONING

There is one more thing that must be set before you can use **show** to paint a string of text. You must set the current point so that **show** knows where on the page to paint the desired string of text. Anytime you start a new page, the current point is undefined—remember, there are almost no defaults in PostScript. The **show** operator paints a string of text beginning at the current point, and it resets the current point to the end of the string when it's done. In this way, successive **show**s will place strings one after another, as you would expect and want. However, the operators will not sense when the text goes off the side of the page (or top or bottom, for that matter); you will lose the part of the string that exceeds the page margins, and you will get a current point that is off the page. It is up to the programmer, or the application program, to keep track of the current point and break the string when it is too long to fit across the remainder of a line.

Going back to our initial problem of setting the current point, for this example you will display the line of text 5.5 inches from the bottom of the page and 1.5 inches from the left side of the page. Recall that PostScript coordinates are in points (1/72 inch) and that you need a pair of coordinates (x, y) to define the desired point. Therefore, the desired point on the page has the coordinates (108, 396).

The current point is set by the **moveto** operator. This operator takes a pair of numbers—the x,y coordinates—and sets the current point to them. The command looks like this:

108 396 **moveto**

FIRST EXAMPLE

Now you understand what needs to be done before a **show** will execute correctly. You have to take the following actions:

- define the font you intend to use
- set the point size of the font
- set that font and size as the current font
- establish the current point where you want the text to print

This sequence can be done in two lines of PostScript commands: one line to set the font information and a second to set the current point, as shown.

/Times-Roman **findfont** 12 **scalefont setfont**   %1
108 396 **moveto**   %2

TEXT OUTPUT

Now you can issue a set of commands to print a string of text onto a page. This will require two more lines of PostScript commands as follows:

(This is sample string number 1) **show**   %3
copypage   %4

This sequence introduces two new elements. The first is the sequence of numbers %1, %2, and so on to the right of each line. In PostScript, the % indicates the beginning of a comment, and everything beyond the % is treated as a comment by the interpreter. For these exercises, numbers will be used in the comments as line references. So there are four numbered lines in the first exercise. You can include these in your work or not, as you choose; their presence or absence will not affect the output.

The second new element is line %4, which consists of the operator **copypage**. The PostScript interpreter builds pages in memory according to the commands it receives, but it doesn't actually output a page until it gets a specific command to do so. The **copypage** operator is such a command; it causes the interpreter to print the current page and to retain an image of the current page internally so we can continue to work on it. You will discover how important and valuable it is to be able to control precisely when a page gets produced on the output device.

Figure 1.2 shows the four lines of PostScript code as they would look on the screen, and Figure 1.3 shows the page of output that they will produce. That completes our first program example—simple, but effective.

EXAMPLE STRUCTURE

Let's look at this example. Even though it consists of only four lines of PostScript code, it provides some important points for discussion regarding PostScript structure and control.

You have already covered the requirements of the **show** operator. Obviously, from the previous discussion, lines %1 and %2 had to be executed before line %3. In the same way, you had to paint the characters onto the page before you printed it; therefore, line %3 must come before line %4. You can think of this as inking the press before printing: if you set the type but don't ink it, nothing will be printed. Similarly, you need

```
===DIALING LaserWriter

PostScript(tm) Version 38.0
Copyright (c) 1985 Adobe Systems Incorporated.
PS>
PS>/Times-Roman findfont 12 scalefont setfont
PS>108 396 moveto
PS>(This is sample string number 1) show
PS>copypage
PS>_
```

Figure 1.2: First program example

This is sample string number 1

Figure 1.3: First (partial) output from the first exercise

to paint characters, lines, or shapes using the appropriate PostScript operators before you output the page.

This still leaves the issue of sequence for lines %1 and %2. You may think this order was arbitrary; indeed, from the point of view of the interpreter, either line could come first. All that is necessary is for both operations to be completed by the time the interpreter reaches line %3 (the **show**). But to you as a programmer, the order is important. Font changes and scaling take time and consume resources; for efficient

PostScript programs, you want to minimize how often they occur. In addition, all of the text in a given portion of the document is likely to be in the same font and point size. Movement around the page, however, occurs all the time; it's one of the most frequent actions you will take. If you were going to print multiple lines of text, you would probably have to move on every line. For these reasons, you should habitually set the font first, followed by the **moveto**, which is how they were done in the example.

SECOND EXAMPLE

While you are still in PostScript and in the interactive mode, let's do a second page. Here again, the output will be two simple lines of text, with some small variations. This example assumes that you have successfully completed the previous example and are still in the interpreter; that is, you still have the PS> prompt on your screen.

Here is the code for the second example:

```
(! This is sample string #2.) show            %5
108 432 moveto                                 %6
(And this is sample string #3.) show           %7
showpage                                       %8
```

If you have done this example immediately after the first example, your screen will look like Figure 1.4, and you will get output that looks like Figure 1.5.

There are several distinctive points that you have probably already noticed about this example. The first and most obvious one is that the previous text is still on the page where it was in the first example. This happened because you used the **copypage** operator, which saved a copy of the page being printed, to print the first page. In this second example, you have used the **showpage** operator (on line %8) to print the page instead of **copypage**. The **showpage** operator clears the current page after it prints, whereas **copypage** saved the current page. Because you used **showpage**, the page is now blank and all the previous data is gone; if you issued a new string and printed it, only the new string would show on the page.

The **showpage** operator is the usual method for your output. The **copypage** operator is useful for testing or (as in this exercise) as a learning tool to help you see what you've already placed on a page.

```
===DIALING LaserWriter

PostScript(tm) Version 38.0
Copyright (c) 1985 Adobe Systems Incorporated.
PS>
PS>/Times-Roman findfont 12 scalefont setfont
PS>108 396 moveto
PS>(This is sample string number 1) show
PS>copypage
PS>
PS>(!  This is sample string #2.) show
PS>108 432 moveto
PS>(And this is sample string #3.) show
PS>showpage
PS>_
```

Figure 1.4: Second program example

The second point that you probably noticed is that you didn't have to set or scale the font anywhere in this program. Since you performed these operations once before, the interpreter will continue to use the previous settings until you end the program, by using the **quit** operator (which we will discuss shortly) or by turning the printer off, or until you explicitly change one of the settings by issuing new font operators.

EXAMPLE ANALYSIS

Keeping these two observations in mind, let's discuss this second example, line by line. In line %5, you again give the interpreter a **show** command. You remember that there are certain requirements for **show**: a current font must be active, and there must be a current point. The **copypage** operator, as we discussed above, has left both of these unchanged from the first example. This is illustrated graphically by the placement of the ! as the first character in the second string (on line %5), which shows up right behind the first string (see Figure 1.5). This also illustrates the point made earlier, that the **show** operator adjusts the current point to the end of the string when it paints the string; the next **show** will begin where the previous one ended.

In line %6, you deliberately reset the current point by means of **moveto**. The x-coordinate is reset to 108, where it was for the first string. This will line up the beginning of the new string with the beginning of the first

And this is sample string #3.

This is sample string number 1! This is sample string #2.

Figure 1.5: Final output from the first exercise

string. The y-coordinate is reset to 432, which is ½ inch up the page from the first string, which was positioned at 396. Remember that the positive direction for y is up the page; if you wanted to position the third string below the first one, you would have to subtract 36 (½ inch) from 396 instead of adding it.

In line %7, you paint the third string on the page, which appears in the same font as the two previous strings but is positioned at the new current point set in line %6. Line %8 prints the page on the printer and creates a blank page for the next operation.

PROGRAMMING IN POSTSCRIPT

As you continue in this chapter, text examples will be provided so that you may gain a clearer understanding of the concepts. These examples will be given in addition to practical exercises such as the ones you've just completed. To facilitate this process, we will define here a few mathematical operators for use in these examples:

Operator	Function
add	adds two operands together
sub	subtracts two operands
mul	multiplies two operands
div	divides two operands

Each of these operators requires certain items of information in order to execute; you may recall that we named these *operands*. All of the mathematical operators are presented and discussed in a later section of this chapter.

These are probably the most intuitive operators to use; you should not find the examples difficult to follow. Where the operands come from and where the results go are the subject of the next section.

STACK OPERATIONS

One of the important characteristics of PostScript is that it works through a series of stacks. You have already been introduced informally to the work of the stack in the previous examples. Now you need to know more about PostScript stacks.

Physically, a stack is an area of memory that holds items to be referenced by the PostScript interpreter. PostScript uses four distinct stacks, as follows:

- execution stack
- dictionary stack
- graphics state stack
- operand stack

All of these stacks are independent of one another; what happens to one doesn't have any direct effect on the others. Each stack has its own method of access, but all of them are similar in concept and operation. If you understand how one of the stacks works, you will understand how they all work.

The first of these, the *execution stack,* is directly under the control of the interpreter and can be interrogated by the PostScript program but not modified. For our purposes, we can treat it as a black box. The second and third stacks, the *dictionary stack* and the *graphics state stack,* are special stacks controlled by specific operators. We will examine the most useful of these operators later in the book. They have particular importance in program structure and control.

The last stack, the *operand stack,* is the most important stack for our purposes. This stack contains the operands for PostScript and receives the results as operators are executed. The majority of PostScript operators either get their data to operate on from this stack, or return the results of their execution to this stack, or both. This is the stack that we mean when we refer to "the stack," and it is this stack that we will now discuss in detail. Remember that all the other PostScript stacks operate in essentially the same way.

The operand stack (like all PostScript stacks) is a push-down, pop-up stack. It can also be described as a last-in, first-out (LIFO) stack, but the push-down, pop-up terminology is easier to visualize. You may have seen a plate stacker in a restaurant. That's a spring-loaded hole in a counter where a pile of clean plates is loaded. As needed, a plate is taken off the top of the pile, and the plate underneath pops up, ready to be used. As fresh, clean plates come out of the kitchen, they are loaded on top of the stack of plates already there, pushing down the old ones. And that's how you can visualize a push-down, pop-up stack. Not exactly high-tech, but it works.

Let us visualize how this stack might appear in operation. Suppose we present the number 25 to the PostScript interpreter—for the moment, let's not worry about how the number got to the interpreter. The interpreter will take the number (the first "plate") and put it on the operand stack, which then can be visualized like this:

25
‾‾

This would be a cutaway view of the plate stacker from the side of the counter, if you're following the visualization process. Next the interpreter gets the number 60. Now the stack looks like this:

60
‾‾
25
‾‾

Finally, the interpreter gets the number 10. The final state of the stack is shown here:

10
‾‾
60
‾‾
25
‾‾

   Whatever image or analogy you choose to help you understand the stack mechanism, there are three points to keep in mind. First, the next item available is always the one on the top of the stack; nothing beneath it can be reached without moving the top item. Second, the next item down becomes the top item automatically when the top item is used or otherwise removed. Third, as you begin to construct reasonably complex procedures, you must remember to think ahead about the desired sequence of operands and results on the stack. These points will be made clear in the following examples.
   Let us consider the following series of actions an example of stack operations. Consider this series a dialogue between us and the PostScript interpreter; this is an example of the interactive mode of operation, which was described earlier in the chapter.

a.

20	60	**add**	80
	20		

b.

20	60	**sub**	−40
	20		

c.

$$\underline{2} \qquad \begin{array}{c} \underline{6} \\ \underline{2} \end{array} \qquad \textbf{mul} \qquad \underline{12}$$

Note that, in *b*, the number on top of the stack, which is the last number presented to the interpreter, is subtracted from the number below it, which was the first number presented to the interpreter. The sequence of presentation is of major importance.

The issue of sequence can perhaps best be thought of as an extension of the problems of order of operation, which are usually solved in mathematical notation by means of parentheses. For example, let's compute the following equation in PostScript:

$$25 - (3 \times 4)$$

This can be accomplished as illustrated in *a* below. As you see, the presentation is different from our intuitive sequence, which is shown in *b*. Note that, when the sequence of operands is different, we get different results. This illustrates why we must think ahead in planning PostScript programs. This different kind of thought process is inherent in the PostScript language, as you will discover in the next section.

a.

$$\underline{25} \qquad \begin{array}{c} \underline{3} \\ \underline{25} \end{array} \qquad \begin{array}{c} \underline{4} \\ \underline{3} \\ \underline{25} \end{array} \qquad \textbf{mul} \qquad \begin{array}{c} \underline{12} \\ \underline{25} \end{array}$$

$$\begin{array}{c} \underline{12} \\ \underline{25} \end{array} \qquad \textbf{sub} \qquad \underline{13}$$

b.

$$\underline{3} \qquad \begin{array}{c} \underline{4} \\ \underline{3} \end{array} \qquad \textbf{mul} \qquad \underline{12}$$

$$\underline{12} \qquad \begin{array}{c} \underline{25} \\ \underline{12} \end{array} \qquad \textbf{sub} \qquad \underline{-13}$$

NOTATION

Because of PostScript's interpreted nature and stacked operation mechanism, it requires an unusual syntax for execution. Recall that, in the examples above, the interpreter executes an operator when it receives it, taking the necessary operands from the stack. Operands must precede their operators in order to execute properly. This is known as post-fix notation. While this is eminently rational, and both easy and practical for the PostScript interpreter, it is not how we usually write operations. We would normally use either "1 plus 2" or "add 1 to 2" where PostScript uses

1 2 **add**

So you need to begin thinking "backwards," in a way, in order to read PostScript. This becomes especially necessary when you start to read procedures (described below), which may contain several nested levels of operation. This way of thinking was also reflected in the issue of sequence illustrated above, in which the operands had to be presented in "reverse" order to get the desired result. PostScript has operands to help with this sequence issue, as we will see.

EXAMPLE NOTATION

The examples above were presented graphically, showing the stack during execution, to help you follow how PostScript operates. However, we cannot continue presenting it this way for obvious reasons. We need to establish a standard notation for writing PostScript statements.

We will assume that the PostScript interpreter reads statements from left to right, as we do. That means that the sequence of operations presented in our first stack example would be written as follows:

25   60   10

and our second stack operations example would become

20   60   **add**

20   60   **sub**

2   6   **mul**

From now on, the examples will be written across the page as illustrated, and you must envision them going onto the stack and being pushed down, or popped up, as required. This may seem foolish, but as I tried to show you with the examples on sequence, visualization of the current state of the stack is essential to successful PostScript programming.

Also in the examples, we will need to show the result, which generally is returned to the top of the stack. Where an explicit result is returned to the top of the stack, we will illustrate that as follows:

$$20 \quad 60 \quad \textbf{add} \quad \rightarrow \quad 80$$

$$20 \quad 60 \quad \textbf{sub} \quad \rightarrow \quad -40$$

$$2 \quad 6 \quad \textbf{mul} \quad \rightarrow \quad 12$$

OPERATOR NOTATION

We have established how we will write PostScript operands and operators in a program context. Now we must also establish how to write the operators for general reference purposes, since the conventional notation that we established above was specific to a program context. For example,

$$20 \quad 10 \quad \textbf{add}$$

adds two specific numbers and returns the specific result, 30, on the operand stack. Now we need to establish how to write operators so that you will know as you read them how they work, what operands they require, and what results they return.

Let us establish the following conventions for writing operators. On the left of the operator we will show the operands required in the same order as we agreed to write them above; that is, with the last operand (the one on the top of the stack) as the rightmost operand. Where no operands are used, we will use the symbol —. And we will use names that are suggestive of the characteristics of the operands: for example, num (for numbers), int (for integer numbers), proc (for procedures), and so on. Thus we would write

$$num1 \quad num2 \quad \textbf{add}$$

On the right of the operator we will show the results in the same order as the operands: again, with the rightmost result on the top of the stack.

This is similar to the notation we established for writing explicit results above, except that we omit the → before showing the result. Where the operator does not return a result, we will show —. Then our full set of notations will look like this:

Syntax	Function
num1 num2 **add** sum	adds *num1* and *num2*
num1 num2 **sub** result	subtracts *num2* from *num1*

These are the same conventions used in the PostScript manuals.

STRINGS AND COMMENTS

You were introduced to the use of strings and comments in PostScript code in the first exercise. There is additional information regarding these objects that you will want before we begin the next exercise. This information is still not a complete discussion of either object; that discussion will come in the next chapter where you will read about all the types of PostScript objects in one section.

STRINGS

You saw strings used in the first exercise as the operand of the **show** operator. This is probably the most typical use of strings in PostScript, since strings are the natural method for representing and handling textual material.

A string usually consists of a collection of characters bounded by left and right parentheses. The string begins at the initial left parenthesis, (, and is terminated by the matching right parenthesis,). PostScript strings are extremely flexible and have no restrictions on what characters can be placed within the delimiters. Even the characters (and) can be put inside the string, as long as each is part of a matched set. You will see an example of this useful feature in the next exercise.

COMMENTS

Every programming language must provide a method to allow a programmer to annotate the code being generated, for self-preservation, if for no other reason. PostScript is no exception. Such annotations are called *comments,* and they are markers for the interpreter that indicate the end of the PostScript-readable material and the beginning of a line of code "for your eyes only."

A PostScript comment, as you have already learned, begins with the character % and ends at the end of the line. The PostScript interpreter ignores all information after the % and only starts processing again on the next line. This means that once you have begun a comment with the %, you can continue with any characters or words you want, including more %'s, operators, strings, or whatever. The PostScript interpreter will ignore everything until a new line begins. There is no method of continuing a PostScript comment onto a second line; each line of comments must begin with its own %. The only exception to this rule is that the character % can be used within a string without starting a comment; in this case the interpreter will not recognize the % and will continue to process the string (and the rest of the line) normally.

The exercises use comments within the PostScript code itself for two purposes: first, to number the lines for reference, and second, to point out important issues within the code itself. You will find examples of both uses in the second exercise.

SECOND EXERCISE

The second exercise consists of a single program designed to show you how you (or an application program) might set multiline text. To make the full exercise easier and more understandable, however, we need to review the PostScript operators and do some additional work with program fragments before we move on to the program example.

This section provides a review of all of the previous PostScript operators presented in a standard format. You will also find some new mathematical operators that will be useful. In addition, this section contains a number of program fragments using the operators. Working with these tools, including the operator summary, should give you a good understanding of the basic structure of PostScript before you proceed into the next chapter.

SAMPLE PROGRAM SEGMENTS

Having seen all of these operators in the abstract, you will now work with them in some program fragments.

ARITHMETIC SEGMENTS

Let us begin by reviewing some of the earlier exercises in the chapter, where we were developing this notation:

$$20 \quad 60 \quad \textbf{add} \quad \rightarrow \quad 80$$
$$20 \quad 60 \quad \textbf{sub} \quad \rightarrow \quad -40$$
$$2 \quad 6 \quad \textbf{mul} \quad \rightarrow \quad 12$$

You may also recall the problem presented in the discussion of the sequence

$$25 - (3 \times 4)$$

You saw that, to derive the correct result from this equation in PostScript, you had to write the following:

$$25 \quad 3 \quad 4 \quad \textbf{mul} \quad \textbf{sub} \quad \rightarrow \quad 13$$

The more natural sequence

$$3 \quad 4 \quad \textbf{mul} \quad 25 \quad \textbf{sub} \quad \rightarrow \quad -13$$

gives an incorrect result because the operands for the **sub** operator are not in the correct order. Using one of the new stack operators, **exch**, you can also obtain the correct result by writing the sequence as follows:

$$3 \quad 4 \quad \textbf{mul} \quad 25 \quad \textbf{exch} \quad \textbf{sub} \quad \rightarrow \quad 13$$

This sequence obtains the correct result by exchanging the 12 result of the **mul** and the 25 on the stack. The **exch** operator works by swapping the first two items on one stack, and this illustrates its use.

Note that you can also combine arithmetic operators with other operators on the same line of code. For example, the three statements below move the current point to exactly the same location:

> 108 648 **moveto**
>
> 108 612 36 **add** **moveto**
>
> 108 684 36 **sub** **moveto**

We also have the other mathematical operators, such as

> 2 3 **div** → 0.666

and

> 2 3 **div** **round** → 1

The **round** operator has one result that you might not expect until you think about it:

> −5.5 **round** → −5

(since −5 is mathematically greater than −6).

All in all, I think you will find the mathematical operators straight-forward.

TEXT-HANDLING SEGMENTS

You have already seen how to use the **show** operator to display a single line of text. As we discussed during the first exercise, the **show** operator positions the current point to the end of the string when it paints the string on the page. However, it can't move down to the next line auto-matically. You, as the programmer (or the application program), must provide the necessary up or down movement. This is generally done by issuing a **moveto** operator with appropriate new coordinates.

The next, obvious question is how to determine the new coordinates. Remember that you scaled the type you were using to a particular size by means of the **scalefont** operator. This size, the *point size,* governs the height of the characters; since you are using proportional fonts, the width of each character is scaled to the height but also varies in proportion to the nature of the character—the letter w, for example, is wider than the letter i. In this case, the minimum distance between two lines of type must be the point size; otherwise, letters would start to run into the type on the lines above and below them.

Generally, setting successive lines of type only the minimum distance apart makes a page look crowded and makes it difficult to read if there is much text. For this reason, typesetters usually space lines slightly farther apart than the point size of the type. This spacing is called *leading*. Leading is proportional to the size of the type being used; as a guide, for type in the 10- to 12-point range, leading would be one or two points. Therefore, if the type is 12-point (as in our example), the line spacing would be 13 or 14 points. This means that the y-coordinate would have to decrease (if you're moving down the page) by 13 or 14. To illustrate the effect of leading and to keep computation easy, the program example will use 12-point type with 14-point leading.

Like so many other elements of page design and makeup, the choice of type size and leading is essentially an aesthetic decision. The object, as always, is to have a page that is beautiful because it is clean in layout, easily legible, and pleasant to the eye. Factors that influence choice of point size and leading include the amount of text that needs to be set, the position and dimensions of the text block on the page, and so on.

Some of the books listed in the Bibliography contain valuable discussions of these and other issues of design and typography. You can also learn a great deal by carefully studying examples of work that you consider particularly good (effective and attractive) or bad (ineffective and unattractive). Once you start looking, you'll find these examples everywhere: books, newspapers, posters, advertisements, even restaurant menus. As you become more experienced (and start looking critically at your own work), you may find yourself developing an almost intuitive "sense of design."

PROGRAM EXAMPLE

Now you're ready to begin your third PostScript program. Once again, the program will display lines of text on the page, but this time the text will be set in two columns, as text and commentary might be in a textbook or in a translation. This is just a convenient format to illustrate two-column text being typeset without having to fill one column completely before starting the next. (After a few of these exercises, you will quickly understand why having a word-processing program that can produce PostScript output is so useful.)

Both columns will have sentences of several lines each to show you how multiline text can be set and to use some of the arithmetic operators you have learned in a typical situation. In addition, you will set two different type fonts: one for the body of the text and another for the commentary.

SETUP

Before you can begin the program, you must make some decisions regarding the layout of the output page. This page is relatively simple, and the layout parameters will be given in complete detail here. You should calculate each of the coordinates as we go through the setup; this will help you when you come to the program itself.

In this example, the output consists of a two-column page. The first column on this page will be the commentary. (Note that you may want to reverse the columns on facing pages, although we're not going to do that here; it would make the example too complex for now.) This column will be 2 inches wide with a 1-inch margin. There will be 1 inch between the first and the second column, to set the commentary well away from the body text. We will plan to leave half an inch for the right margin; this leaves 4 inches for the body-text column.

The example will be set in 12-point type with 14-point leading, as discussed above. The body text will be in Times-Roman again, but the commentary will be set in Times-Italic (the italic version of Times-Roman) to set it apart but keep it in the same type family. In addition, to enhance legibility and make the start of each paragraph quite evident, there will be 28-point spacing (two lines) between the paragraphs.

The text will begin 1.5 inches from the top of the page, which is 9.5 inches from the bottom of the page. This may sound foolish, but remember that PostScript is measuring from the bottom-left corner of the page in units of 1/72 inch. As a final touch, we will align the commentary paragraphs to begin at the same vertical point as the corresponding body-text paragraphs. In order to do that, you must know where the body-text paragraphs begin, which means that the body-text column (the second column physically) must be set first. The commentary column (the first physical column) can then be set to match, aligning each paragraph with the body text. In the example, there are only two paragraphs, but the principle is the same for multiple alignment points.

MULTILINE TEXT

Figure 1.6 is the text of the complete program. As you can see, it is a rather long but not really complex program.

```
/Times-Roman findfont 12 scalefont setfont          %1
288 684 moveto                                      %2
(The quick brown fox jumps over the lazy black) show %3
288                                                 %4
684 14 sub                                          %5
moveto                                              %6
(dog and then the quick brown fox jumps over that) show %7
288 684 28 sub moveto                               %8
(lazy dog again and again and again ... but the) show %9
288 684 42 sub moveto                               %10
(dog just doesn't pay any attention.) show          %11
%Now begin the second paragraph of the body text    %12
%Note the computation for use in the commentary section %13
288 684 70 sub moveto                               %14
(Here is the quick brown fox playing the same) show %15
288 684 84 sub moveto                               %16
(games again in a second text paragraph. You) show  %17
288 684 98 sub moveto                               %18
(can easily see how this could go on and on and ...) show %19
%
%
%Now we can set the commentary column               %20
%
%
/Times-Italic findfont 12 scalefont setfont         %21
72 684 moveto                                       %22
(This is a classic text) show                       %23
72 684 14 sub moveto                                %24
(and commentary layout;) show                       %25
%Now set the second commentary item
%  to match the second body paragraph
72 684 70 sub moveto                                %26
(using two fonts: ) show                            %27
72 684 84 sub moveto                                %28
((Times-Roman and Times-Italic)) show               %29
showpage                                            %30
quit                                                %31
```

Figure 1.6: Second exercise: text and commentary format

When complete, the program produces a page of output that looks just as you might have visualized it, as shown in Figure 1.7.

REVIEW OF EXAMPLE

This example provides several instructive points for your review. Let's go over it, line by line. The first three lines should be familiar from the first exercise. These lines set the font, establish the initial current point, and **show** the first line of text. You note that the x-coordinate of the **moveto** operator is 288, which is 4 inches from the left margin, while the y-coordinate is 684, which is 9.5 inches from the bottom of the paper. So far, so good.

Now look at lines %4 thru %6. You have completed the output of your first line of text in the second column; now you must move down one line. Since positive y is up, you have to subtract; and since you have

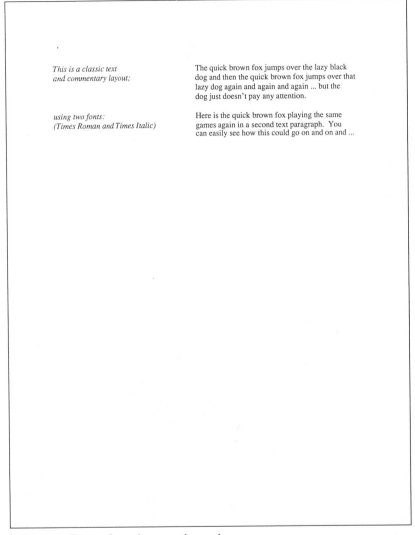

Figure 1.7: Output from the second exercise

decided on 14-point leading, you want to subtract 14 from the original y-value. First, you set the x-coordinate for the **moveto** at 288, just as in the previous line. Then you subtract 14 from 684, leaving the result (670) on the stack. Then you issue the **moveto** command. Since you had the foresight to put the x-coordinate on the stack before your calculations, the two required operands are on the stack for the operator.

Having reset the current point, you are now ready to **show** the next line of text. In line %8, you repeat the previous calculation, this time subtracting 28 (2 times 14, since you're on the second line) from the initial value of 684. As you may recall from our earlier discussion, all of these calculations can be placed on one line. That is easier to understand, since the **sub** simply replaces the y-coordinate. You follow this pattern for two more lines, down to line %12.

Now you have to set up to **show** the second text paragraph. This is really no different from the previous calculations, except that the value for subtraction must be increased by 28, as discussed earlier, in order to provide double-line spacing between paragraphs. The second paragraph continues, following the same sequence, down to line %19.

At this point, line %20, there is a block of comment lines that sets off the work on the commentary column from the work on the body text. The commentary section begins by establishing a new current font, Times-Italic, on line %21. Then there is the expected **moveto**. In this case, the x-coordinate value has been changed to 72 to reflect the 1-inch margin that was designated for the left edge of the paper. The y-coordinate, however, is set to the previously established value of 684; this will set the first line of the commentary at the same height as the first line of the text, as we wished.

The program proceeds to print two lines of commentary, using the same mechanisms that were used earlier in the program. At line %26, the second paragraph commentary begins by setting the y-coordinate to the same value as the y-coordinate that begins the second text paragraph. You can compare lines %14 and %26 to see how this was done; the essential point is to use the same value to be subtracted from the initial y-value.

Finally, the program concludes its page work by displaying two more lines of commentary. Note the use of parentheses within the string on line %99.

Now that the page is composed, you need to print it. You do this by means of the **showpage** operator, as in the first exercise. The last line, line %99, introduces you to a new operator: **quit**. This operator ends a PostScript session gracefully. You could end the session just by stopping your input and turning off the printer. That's not a graceful way to exit, but it works and it won't hurt anything if you use it. The preferable method, however, would be to use the **quit** operator, which allows you to leave all the equipment turned on and still terminate execution of the interpreter. It allows the interpreter to reset all states and clean up anything left over in the stack; the specific actions taken depend on the operating environment. I think it's the best way to end your session.

OPERATOR REVIEW

We will now review the operators presented in this chapter. You will be given some new operators when they fit in naturally and where use of the operator does not seem to require additional explanation. This same format will be used throughout subsequent chapters to summarize operators that have been used for the first time in that chapter. This will help you to recall the operators in each chapter, and it also forms an informal index for review of the topics covered in the chapter.

BASIC OPERATORS

Not every operator is presented in these reviews. As was noted earlier, the best way to work with a language is to learn the primary functions in the language well, and then to broaden your scope to include the more specialized operators. That is the rule followed here; only the major functions are presented or used. Some related functions or operators will only be noted; some will be omitted altogether. If you want to use these other operators, be sure to consult the *PostScript Language Reference Manual* for full specification of their requirements and results.

Let me emphasize that I am not discouraging you from using these other operators; they have a specific place in your PostScript work. In this book, however, the purpose is to keep to the basic operations. In my experience, you will understand the language better and achieve your objective of writing PostScript code more quickly by staying with a subset of the language that contains the operators most often used.

MATHEMATICAL OPERATORS

These are, without doubt, the most straightforward of all the operators. PostScript supports almost every mathematical operation that you may require for page processing; the following operators are those most useful in regular PostScript page descriptions.

The basic mathematical operators are the following:

Syntax	Function
num1 num2 **add** sum	adds *num1* to *num2*
num1 num2 **sub** result	subtracts *num2* from *num1*
num1 num2 **mul** product	multiplies *num1* by *num2*
num1 num2 **div** quotient	divides *num1* by *num2*

There are operators that affect the signs of results:

Syntax	Function
num **neg** −num	reverses the sign of *num*

There are operators that make integers of fractional results:

Syntax	Function
num1 **round** num2	rounds *num1* to the nearest integer. If *num1* is equally close to its two nearest integers, the result is the greater of the

GRAPHICS OPERATORS

The two following operators were introduced and explained in the examples. They are grouped here for review and convenience.

Syntax	Function
string **show** —	paints characters of *string* on the page at the current point
num1 num2 **moveto** —	sets the current point to x-coordinate *num1* and y-coordinate *num2*

OUTPUT OPERATORS

These two operators were used in the examples also.

Syntax	Function
— **copypage** —	prints out the current page onto the output device, and retains a copy of the current page and all current settings
— **showpage** —	prints a copy of the current page onto the output device and clears the page

STACK OPERATORS

The following operators directly access or manipulate the stack:

Syntax	Function
any1 any2 **exch** any2 any1	exchanges the top two elements on the stack
any **pop** —	discards the top element
any **dup** any any	duplicates the top element, and adds copy to the top of the stack
|– anyn **clear** |–	empties the stack

This last operator introduces a new conventional symbol, |–, which represents the bottom of the stack.

INTERACTIVE OPERATORS

This is the final group of operators to be discussed in this chapter; they are put here because I think you will want to know them, but they really don't fit anywhere. Two of these are operators that only work in the interactive mode; that is, they are inquiries that can be directed to the PostScript interpreter only from a terminal. As such, they can be extremely useful during the interactive work that you will be doing. However, they cannot be used in the batch mode.

Syntax	Function
= =	shows the top element of the stack and removes it
pstack	shows the entire contents of the stack, but does not remove any element

The final operator is one you have already met in the examples; it seems appropriate to end the chapter with

Syntax	Function
quit	ends operation of the PostScript interpreter

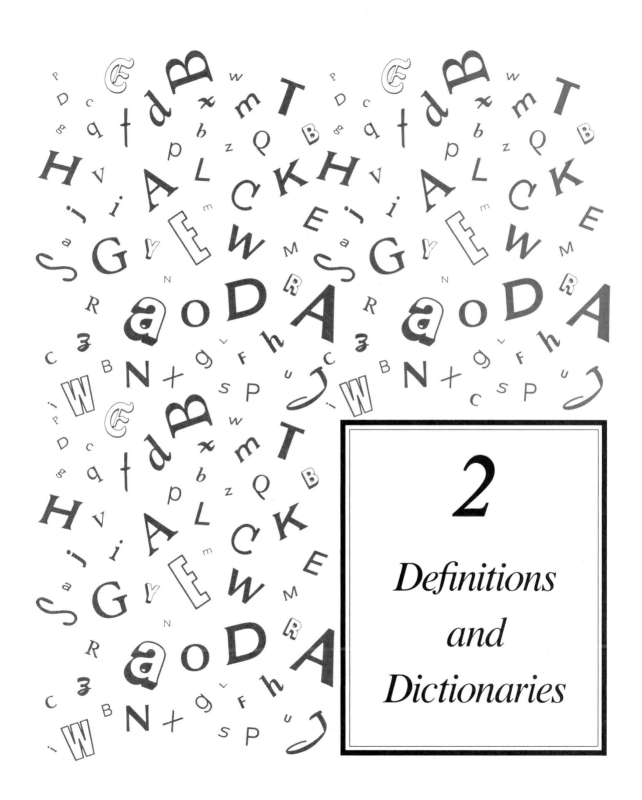

2

Definitions
and
Dictionaries

THIS CHAPTER IS CONCERNED WITH TWO BASIC ISSUES. THE FIRST ISSUE IS HOW YOU CAN ASSOCIATE LABELS with PostScript objects by using PostScript dictionaries. The second issue is how to create, name, and use PostScript procedures to build a PostScript program.

These are clearly critical issues in understanding and using any computer language. PostScript has some unique methods and unusual constructs in handling these points. In the preceding chapter, you learned the basics of PostScript structure and became familiar with the first group of PostScript operators. In this chapter we will build on this information to fashion programs that begin to take advantage of PostScript's capabilities, by using labels and procedures.

There are two main exercises in this chapter, as there were in Chapter 1. In this chapter, however, the exercises are not the major focus, but are primarily illustrations of the issues discussed in the various sections. For this reason, there is more discussion of page setup and problem analysis associated with these exercises than there has been previously.

The chapter begins with a discussion of PostScript dictionaries and of how to use the dictionary facilities to label various PostScript objects. The first section discusses what a PostScript dictionary is, what the various PostScript dictionaries do, and how to create and manipulate them. The second section describes how to use a dictionary and how the interpreter accesses and stores objects in a dictionary.

This discussion is followed by the third exercise. This exercise is a reworking of the last exercise in the preceding chapter, this time using variables and named constants to simplify and clarify the program text. The intention is to illustrate in a strong and clear way why you need to work with and exploit the facilities in the PostScript dictionaries.

The exercise is followed by a rather dry, but necessary technical discussion, defining and explaining PostScript objects. By now you will have familiarized yourself with many of the PostScript object types in various contexts, and possibly you will have wondered about an exact explanation for them. The discussion is also necessary to allow you to proceed into the next section on the definition and use of procedures in PostScript.

The section on PostScript procedures builds from the explanations of PostScript objects and the use of PostScript dictionaries. This section will allow you to start writing more natural—and more useful—PostScript code, and it introduces a number of new operators and some new syntax to expand your PostScript vocabulary.

This is followed by the major exercise of the chapter. This exercise is similar in design to the second and third exercises, but it is more realistic and produces a moderately complex page as output, with a format (if not content) that might be used in a production setting. There is a discussion to aid you in page setup; and as you work through the exercise, you will see how your PostScript program, with its procedures and variables, naturally grows out of this analytical process. As before, the exercise ends with a detailed analysis of the program so that you can review all the new procedures and techniques that are in the code.

This new exercise begins to exhibit the structure and complexity of a real computer program and so leads into the final major section of the chapter: a discussion of program structure and style in relation to PostScript coding.

The first issue, and one of the most important issues under structure and style, is the selection and use of names. How names are constructed, how they are used, and how naming conventions can aid you in choosing names that will contribute to the clarity and utility of your programs are all discussed. There are examples and also brief comments on the benefits of appropriate names drawn from personal experience.

The next topic describes and discusses an overall structural schema appropriate for a PostScript program. This is based on the specific and detailed requirements set forth by Adobe Systems as a standard Post-Script program structure. This global program structure is neither required by nor enforced by the PostScript interpreter and is not strictly part of the PostScript language. Nevertheless, if you are working with PostScript programs and files in specific environments, these issues will be vital. Even if you are using PostScript in a dedicated environment, you should still study and consider these issues and techniques, although you may decide to ignore them in the end.

The final section under structure and style is a brief explanation of programming style in a PostScript context. This includes points on indentation, line breaking, and similar issues that help make your Post-Script code more readable.

The chapter ends in the usual fashion, with a recap of the operators that have been introduced in the chapter. This provides both a reference and a review of the material that has been covered in the chapter.

DICTIONARIES

PostScript uses a dictionary mechanism to implement all of its processing functions. This makes the understanding and use of dictionaries in PostScript important in working with the language. Dictionaries and stack operations are two of the most important concepts in PostScript processing, not that either of these concepts is difficult to understand or to use. Of the two, stack operation, which you read about in the preceding chapter, is probably more difficult; but many computers and computer languages use stacks. The dictionary concept, of course, is familiar to all of us, but it is unusual in the context of a computer language. I think you will find the PostScript dictionaries both conceptually elegant and truly useful. As it does with stacks, PostScript implements multiple dictionaries to perform various functions; once you understand dictionary operations, you will use multiple dictionaries too.

DEFINITION

A dictionary, in English, French, Japanese, or any other language, is a book that associates words with their definitions. In PostScript, a *dictionary* is a table that associates a name, or *key,* with a *value.* More precisely, a PostScript dictionary associates a pair of PostScript objects; the first object is the key, which is usually a name literal, and the second object is the associated value.

As you probably have guessed, this dictionary mechanism is how we assign names to PostScript objects, particularly variables and procedures. By the end of the last chapter, the handling of program pieces was becoming unwieldy and difficult to follow; in fact, the previous exercises would have been improved by the substitution of variable names for some of the values. Here you will learn how to do this.

DICTIONARY STACK

PostScript uses its dictionary mechanism in a variety of important functions; for example, fonts are implemented through a series of dictionaries. However, the most important dictionaries are those provided for PostScript operations. PostScript maintains a *dictionary stack* where all PostScript operations are defined. As you read in the last chapter, all PostScript stacks work alike, and the dictionary stack works in the same fashion as the operand stack you have become familiar with. There are several operators, which will be described shortly, that specifically access and manipulate the dictionary stack.

Although the dictionary stack works like the operand stack, it is entirely distinct. You will have to keep this in mind as we begin working with user-created dictionaries.

DEFAULT DICTIONARIES

The PostScript system provides two default dictionaries on the dictionary stack: *systemdict* and *userdict*. These are the two bottommost entries on the dictionary stack; neither can be removed from the stack. The bottom entry is *systemdict* and *userdict* is right above it. These are the only two dictionaries on the stack when PostScript begins operations.

In all cases, the top entry on the dictionary stack is called the *current dictionary* and is referred to by the name *currentdict*. This means that, when PostScript begins operations, the current dictionary is *userdict,* and all references to the current dictionary refer to *userdict*. In fact, a substantial amount of work can be done using just the two default dictionaries. But creating and using additional dictionaries is easy, and it also adds to your PostScript vocabulary.

NAMES AND LITERALS

You must be wondering why I keep using the phrase "name literals" instead of just "names." The reason is that you have to distinguish between "names," which the PostScript interpreter looks up in the dictionaries, and "name literals," which are the literal values of the names and which the PostScript interpreter places on the stack as it would a string.

As you think about this, you will see that this is an essential distinction. Somehow, the interpreter has to distinguish the use of a name as a reference to an object already in the dictionaries, which is the ordinary usage of a name, from the use of the name as a literal to be enrolled into the current dictionary as a key or definition associated with some other object. This distinction is the reason for all the references to "name literal."

A *name* in PostScript can consist of almost any sequence of characters. All alphabetic and numeric characters are acceptable, as are most punctuation characters. There are ten special characters, which will be defined and discussed in the next section, that cannot be used in names. The most important of these is the space; valid names cannot contain spaces.

A *name literal* is any valid name preceded by the character /. As you might guess, the character / is one of the ten special characters; it is reserved to distinguish name literals from all other objects.

DICTIONARY CREATION

There is a good reason that PostScript provides two unremovable default dictionaries on the dictionary stack. Specific PostScript operators, and the interpreter, implicitly reference the current dictionary, which obviously requires that there be a dictionary to reference. However, you may sometimes need to create individual dictionaries that can then be referenced by the various PostScript operators. How you create a new dictionary is the subject of this section.

NOTATION FOR DICTIONARY REFERENCE

Before you plunge into dictionary creation, there are two points to be made about notation and capacity. We will use the notation *dict* to indicate a dictionary array in our discussion of operators. This is important because dictionary arrays have particular characteristics that distinguish them from other PostScript objects. Also, dictionaries are created with a specific capacity to hold pairs of objects. If you try to put more entries into the dictionary than the capacity specified at its creation, you will get an error—and more importantly, the *key,value* pair will not be entered.

DICTIONARY CAPACITY

Dictionaries are created by the use of the **dict** operator. This operator takes one operand, an integer that specifies the dictionary capacity, which is the maximum number of *key,value* pairs that can be placed in that dictionary. The operator returns an empty dictionary object with the specified capacity. Note that this dictionary object is returned to the operand stack; it is not placed on the dictionary stack. A dictionary is placed on the dictionary stack by the operator **begin** and is removed from the dictionary stack by the operator **end**. The **begin** operator requires a dictionary object on the operand stack, and it makes that object the current dictionary. The **end** operator does not affect the operand stack at all. These operators may be summarized as follows:

Syntax	**Function**
int **dict** dict	creates a dictionary *dict* with the capacity for *int* value pairs
dict **begin** —	pushes *dict* onto the dictionary stack and makes it the current dictionary
— **end** —	pops the current dictionary from the dictionary stack

Now that you know how to create dictionaries and move them on and off the dictionary stack, we need to discuss how to enroll objects into a dictionary and how to get access to them afterward.

Reference

In order to understand how to use dictionary entries, you need to know how the PostScript interpreter uses them. As the PostScript interpreter encounters an object, it takes one of two actions: either it places the object on the operand stack (as it would with a number or a name literal), or it looks the object up in the dictionary stack, using it as the key for the search. This is how the interpreter handles all names that are not name literals; that is, not preceded by the / character. Specifically, it is how the interpreter handles operator names, for example.

Operation

Until now, I have simply described the PostScript interpreter as executing the various operators we have discussed. This is a reasonable way to describe (and to think about) how the interpreter works; however, it is important for you to understand the overall process in greater detail. Operator names have no special significance to the interpreter; they are not "reserved" in the sense that operator names are in some other languages, such as COBOL and BASIC. Even in MS-DOS, certain names, such as CON and LPT1, are reserved to the operating system. In more ordinary languages, you must use reserved words or names correctly and for particular well-defined purposes; if you do not, you will generally receive an error message, and in any case, the code won't execute properly. In PostScript, however, operator names are simply keys into the *systemdict,* where they are associated with the actual built-in function that performs the action specified by the operator name. This makes PostScript different from other languages because you could re-define these names if you wanted to. The PostScript interpreter does not prevent you from using operator names for your own functions, although common sense dictates that you avoid such potentially confusing antics except under extraordinary circumstances. This explains why the *systemdict* is always on the dictionary stack and cannot be removed.

As discussed above, when the PostScript interpreter encounters a name that is not preceded by the special character / (which would make it a name literal, to be pushed onto the operand stack), it looks up the name as a key in the dictionary stack. The interpreter begins looking in the current dictionary. If it doesn't find the name as a key there, it continues to look down through the dictionary stack until it either finds a matching key or exhausts the stack. If there is no match, an error status is returned. When a match is found, the interpreter takes the appropriate action. If the value that matches the key is a procedure, the procedure is executed; if the value is not a procedure (in which case it's a string, literal, number, or so on), the value is placed on the operand stack. The interpreter continues in this way until it has dealt with all the PostScript objects presented to it (or until it encounters an error that forces it to stop).

SEARCH SEQUENCE

The sequence used by the interpreter to search for names should be clear from the discussion above. Dictionaries are searched down through the dictionary stack. This process begins with the current dictionary, continues through the *userdict* (which may be the current dictionary), and ends with the *systemdict* at the bottom of the stack.

There are two exceptions to this default search sequence. These occur with operators that specifically reference a particular dictionary. This may be required for two reasons. First, the operator by its nature may require a dictionary specification; font-manipulation operators are a good example of this (recall that fonts reside in a special set of dictionaries).

Second, the operator may be defined to provide specific access to dictionary values or operations. Generally, such operators fall outside of the scope of this book. In either case, it is important to remember that, while most PostScript operators deal with the current dictionary, there are operators that can be explicitly directed to work with a specific dictionary.

DICTIONARY ACCESS

The most frequently used PostScript dictionary operators are naturally the ones that expect to access the current dictionary. Certainly the most common dictionary operation is the act of enrolling a *key,value* pair in the current dictionary. This is done with the **def** operator, which is defined as follows:

Syntax   **Function**

key value   **def** —   associates *key* and *value* in the current dictionary

Let us consider a few examples that make use of this operator. Consider the example

/abc 123 **def**

This process will associate the name *abc* with the value *123* in the current dictionary. This means that, if you have placed the above definition earlier in a program, the following two statements will produce identical results, as shown:

123 456 **add** → 579

abc 456 **add** → 579

You see what the interpreter did here. In the second instance, the interpreter took the name *abc* and looked it up in the current dictionary, where it found the value *123*. It then took that value and pushed it onto the stack, just as it did in the first instance, when it encountered the value directly. Hence, the result of the **add** operator was the same in both cases. In other words, the dictionary behaves naturally, substituting a name for its associated value, just as if the value were inserted into the statement in place of the name.

A value is not limited to being a number; it can be any PostScript object. For example, we may write

/String1 (this is a string) **def**

as a definition in our current dictionary.

In addition to the **def** operator, which always refers to the current dictionary, there are several operators that reference the dictionary stack as a whole, in a fashion similar to the interpreter. These operators, **load**, **store**, and **where**, are like **def** in that they do not reference a specific dictionary; but unlike **def**, they do not stop with the current dictionary. Instead, they follow the interpreter's search process and search the entire dictionary stack, beginning with the current dictionary, until they find the key they have been given.

THIRD EXERCISE

This seems like an appropriate time for a brief exercise using variable names in a program. In order to give you a taste of what the use of variables does for a program, we will redo the second exercise using variables in the program instead of constants. I think you will find this version of the exercise cleaner and easier to understand.

PROGRAM EXAMPLE

Let's briefly review the structure of this example. This is a program for displaying multiple lines of text on a page in two columns. The two columns are set in a text-and-commentary format, with the commentary in italic type and the body text in regular type. There have been no alterations in the output, either in text or in spacing, so that you can compare one with the other to see how different approaches to a program may produce identical results.

As in our previous examples, a complete discussion of the program follows the listing. This discussion will cover the new issues that arise in using variables, and it will indicate some of the new choices facing you, as the programmer.

SETUP

The page layout remains identical to that of the previous example. The commentary column has a margin of 1 inch and is 2 inches wide. There is 1 inch of space between the first and second columns. The second, or body text, column begins 4 inches from the left edge of the page. The second column is 4 inches wide, with a ½-inch right margin. Both columns of text start 1.5 inches from the top of the page. Since PostScript is measuring from the bottom of the page, this is 9.5 inches from the origin.

Each column of text has two paragraphs of several lines each. The text is set in 12-point type on 14-point leading, with double-spacing between paragraphs. The commentary paragraphs are set to align with the text paragraphs, even though the text may be longer than the commentary.

MULTILINE TEXT REVISITED

Figure 2.1 shows the text of the original program, revised to use appropriate variable names in place of constants. The use of variables and named constants makes the program somewhat longer, but it emerges more comprehensible and still not really complex.

Altogether the exercise produces page output that looks identical to the previous page output; only the program has been changed. Refer to Figure 1.7 to compare your output with mine.

REVIEW OF EXAMPLE

The first thing you will notice about the revised example is that there are now two sections to the program. The first section begins with the comment line

%–––Setup Variables–––

and allows you to keep a particular type of program work in one place. There is a more extensive discussion of these structure and placement issues later in the chapter, under the heading "Program Structure and Style." You should notice, however, that there is a structure, and it has a point and a purpose.

```
%---------------Setup Variables-----------------------
% establish beginning x-coordinates for columns
/FirstColumnStart 72 def                                        %1
/SecondColumnStart 4 72 mul def                                 %2
% establish beginning y-coordinate for text
/VerticalStart 9.5 72 mul def                                   %3
% set up leading and paragraph spacing variables
/LineSpace 14 def                                               %4
/ParaSpace 28 def                                               %5
%---------------Begin Program-------------------------
/Times-Roman findfont 12 scalefont setfont                      %6
/NextLine VerticalStart def                                     %7
SecondColumnStart NextLine moveto                               %8
(The quick brown fox jumps over the lazy black) show            %9
/NextLine NextLine LineSpace sub def                            %10
SecondColumnStart NextLine moveto                               %11
(dog and then the quick brown fox jumps over that) show         %12
/NextLine NextLine LineSpace sub def
SecondColumnStart NextLine moveto
(lazy dog again and again and again ... but the) show      %13
/NextLine NextLine LineSpace sub def
SecondColumnStart NextLine moveto
(dog just doesn't pay any attention.) show
%Now begin the second paragraph of the body text
%Note the changes from the previous example
/NextLine NextLine ParaSpace sub  def                           %14
/SavePara NextLine def                                          %15
SecondColumnStart NextLine moveto                               %16
(Here is the quick brown fox playing the same) show
/NextLine NextLine LineSpace sub def
SecondColumnStart NextLine moveto
(games again in a second text paragraph. You) show
/NextLine NextLine LineSpace sub def
SecondColumnStart NextLine moveto
(can easily see how this could go on and on and ...) show
%
%
%Now we can set the commentary column
%
%
/Times-Italic findfont 12 scalefont setfont                     %20
/NextLine VerticalStart def                                     %21
FirstColumnStart NextLine moveto                                %22
(This is a classic text) show                                   %23
/NextLine NextLine LineSpace sub def
FirstColumnStart NextLine moveto
(and commentary layout;) show
%Now set the second commentary item
%  to match the second body paragraph
/NextLine SavePara def                                          %24
FirstColumnStart NextLine moveto
(using two fonts: ) show                                        %25
/NextLine NextLine LineSpace sub def
FirstColumnStart NextLine moveto
((Times Roman and Times Italic)) show                           %26
showpage                                                        %27
quit                                                            %28
```

Figure 2.1: Third exercise: text output with variables

This first program section is where the constants that you are going to use are first given names and initialized. These are constants in the sense that they will not change value within the program, although you might want to change them on a subsequent execution. That facility for change is one of the main reasons to use named constants within a procedure, rather than using straight numeric values as the previous exercises did.

It would be easier to adjust a structure like the one shown in this exercise simply by redefining the constant values.

There are five named constants set out in the start of the program. They are listed below with an explanation of what each one represents and how it was calculated.

Constant	Function
FirstColumnStart	The starting x-coordinate for the first column. The initial position is governed by the desired margin, in this case, 1 inch (72 points).
SecondColumnStart	The same calculation for the second column. In this case, the initial position is 4 inches from the left margin. Note that, unlike the first example, here you can simply insert the desired calculation (4 72 **mul**) within the definition.
VerticalStart	The same mechanism is used to calculate the y-coordinate for the top of the text.
LineSpace	The desired leading value, as discussed previously.
ParaSpace	The desired paragraph spacing. Note that you could have calculated this (by using 2 LineSpace **mul**) if you wanted to make it always a multiple of the line spacing. In this case, the decision was to make it a separate value, not necessarily related to the line-space value.

Now you begin the actual program. Most of this is familiar, so we won't repeat too much of the previous discussion. Line %6 again sets up the necessary font parameters for the **show**. Lines %7 and %8 are new, replacing a simple **moveto** that previously positioned the current point for the show. Line %7 defines and sets a variable, *NextLine,* to start at the point given by *VerticalStart.* Line %8 sets the current point to the coordinates given by *NextLine* and *SecondColumnStart.* Line %9—and all the subsequent **show** operations—is identical to the previous exercise. Lines %10 and %11 form the core of the change brought into the program by the use of variables. Line %10 resets the variable *NextLine* to its previous value less the *LineSpace* constant, while line %11 moves the current point to the newly calculated value. This identical operation is performed before each new line of text is output. This couldn't be done without a variable to save and store the current position of the line; and being able to repeat the operation in an identical fashion for each new line makes your programming both easier and clearer. So the program continues until the end of the paragraph.

At the end of the paragraph, line %14, you again recalculate *NextLine,* using the constant *ParaSpace* to give the correct spacing before the next line of text. Line %15 saves this position in a new variable, *SavePara,* for use in positioning the next column. The second paragraph of body text continues to be output in the same fashion as the first.

The output of the commentary column begins at line %20. (Don't worry if the numbers aren't in sequence; I restarted at 20 for this section.) Once again, the new font is set for the commentary output. Then line %21 resets *NextLine* to the beginning of the text position, and line %22 sets the current point to the coordinates given by *NextLine* and *FirstColumnStart.* The text output is a repetition of the command structures from the previous column, using *FirstColumnStart* instead of *SecondColumnStart.* At line %24, you change *NextLine* to the value you saved previously at line %15 to position the next line of output to the same vertical location as the beginning of the second paragraph of the body text.

The remainder of the example corresponds to what you have already learned. Once again, you terminate with a **quit** to clear the interpreter.

OBJECTS

Up to this point, we have dealt intuitively with the concept of PostScript objects. This easy and straightforward approach has worked well for us, primarily because the intuitive concept is fairly accurate. Now, however, you are ready for a complete and precise definition.

A PostScript *object* is any syntactic entity that can be recognized by the PostScript interpreter. All data in a PostScript program, as well as the procedures that form the program itself, consist of PostScript objects. Neither the PostScript language nor the PostScript interpreter makes any formal distinction between data and procedures. Any PostScript object may be either data or program; some objects may be treated as one thing one time and the other the next. This process is most noticeable in the handling of procedures, which are pushed onto the stack when they are first encountered, but are executed when they are subsequently processed. Procedures are discussed more completely below.

STATEMENT TYPES

In addition to becoming familiar with PostScript notation, there are a few format conventions you need to become comfortable with in order to read PostScript easily. PostScript programs use only the printable subset of the ASCII character set, plus the characters space, tab, and newline (return or linefeed). These three characters are referred to collectively as *white space characters*. These characters serve as separators for other objects, such as names and numbers. Any number of consecutive white space characters are treated as if they were just one. The only exception is within strings and comments where each of the white space characters has specific (and different) effects. In addition, there are ten special characters that serve as delimiters or markers for objects such as strings, procedures, name literals, and comments. These characters are the following:

Character(s)	Function
{ and }	begin and end a procedure
/	begins a name literal
%	begins a comment
(and)	begin and end a string
< and >	begin and end a hexadecimal string
[and]	begin and end an array

The most common of these are described more fully below.

PROCEDURES

Procedures are operators and objects grouped together within matched braces, { and }. Procedures are also known as executable arrays in PostScript. Some examples of procedures follow:

Syntax	Function
{Xpos 5 add}	This procedure would add 5 to the variable *Xpos*.
{add 5 div}	This procedure would add the top two operands on the stack and divide the result by 5.

Note that the procedures are not executed immediately when the interpreter reads them; they are stored and executed later. This issue is examined and discussed more fully in the next section of this chapter, which covers the creation and use of procedures.

NAME LITERALS

You were introduced to name literals, and their distinction from names, earlier in the chapter. Name literals are just what their name implies, names of objects, usually procedures or variables. All characters except special characters and white space characters can appear in a name literal. A name literal begins with / (slash). The slash is not part of the name itself and is not included when reference is made to the name. The special nature of the slash, like that of the braces that enclose procedures, is to notify the interpreter that what follows is a literal to be placed on the stack.

Some examples of valid names are the following:

/name

/NaMe   (note that this is different from **/name**)

/Paragraph_12

/Times-Roman   (a name you have already met)

/$@#&&8ˆ**   (a goofy name, but still valid)

There is no inherent limit on the length of a name, but remember that the newline character is a white space character and invalid within a name literal; therefore, a name literal cannot exceed one line in length.

COMMENTS

You have previously read about and used both comments and strings. However, the previous discussion only covered enough information to allow you to work comfortably with the exercises. This section and the next provide complete and precise definitions of comments and strings. As such, they duplicate to some extent information you already know.

Comments begin with the special character % (percent). The comment consists of every character from the %, including special characters, until the next newline character. PostScript treats a comment as if it were a single white space character. There are a few observations to be made about comments. First, since the comment begins with % and extends to the next newline character, it will always be the last element on a line or on a line by itself—which is where you would normally code while programming. Second, in multiple comment lines, each line must start with a %.

The ability to include special characters means that, once you begin a comment, the interpreter will not process anything until the next newline character. This can be valuable in providing documentation within the program itself. Some examples of comments are

```
/abc        %this is all comment (including {abc add xyz}
/abc%this is the same effect as the line above
        %this is %equally%%%[{] valid
12%is just '12' as far as the PS interpreter sees
        %and so on—you get the idea
```

The single exception to this use of % to introduce a comment is when the character % is included within a pair of string delimiters. In that case (and no other), it is included by the interpreter as part of the string.

STRINGS

A string in PostScript is a group of characters enclosed within matching parentheses, (and). Within a string, the only special characters are parentheses themselves and the \ (backslash) character. The following are examples of valid strings:

```
(this is a string)
(and so is !@#$%%ˆ&*−__= + this)
(and so is 1232 56677 45890)
(white space characters are NOT
        excluded from
a valid string)
```

Parentheses may also be included as long as they are balanced. For example,

```
(this is () a valid (0) string)
```

And you can create a null string with (), two parentheses with no intervening space.

The \ (backslash) character is a signal that there is a special requirement within the string. The character or characters immediately following the \ determine what interpretation is placed on the requirement. The valid combinations are as follows:

Character	Definition
\n	newline (linefeed)
\r	carriage return
\t	horizontal tab
\b	backspace
\f	form feed
****	backslash
\(	left parenthesis
\)	right parenthesis
\ddd	character code ddd (octal)
\newline	no character—both are ignored

Any other combination with \ is ignored.

The use of *ddd* has a special value in PostScript. Remember that PostScript is designed to use only the printable subset of the ASCII character set. This enhances both readability and portability, as we have discussed above. Thus the *ddd* notation provides a way to incorporate a character outside PostScript's normal range using notation that remains within the recommended subset. The *ddd* should be the octal value that corresponds to the character you want. The actual character represented may differ from font to font. See Appendix A of the *PostScript Language Reference Manual* for the octal values of characters in the standard fonts.

The *newline* provides a method to break a string into a number of lines for legibility or coding purposes without having the newline character actually become part of the string. This complements the use of *n* to force a new line in the string without adding one in the code. Some examples are as follows:

    (These three\
    lines will be combined\
    into one line)

    (This string will print
    on two lines)

    (And so will\n this one)

Finally, there is a special form of string, bracketed by < and >. A string within these two delimiters is a hexadecimal (base 16) string. The only valid characters are 0 to 9 and A (or a) to F (or f). Each pair of hexadecimal digits represents one character. Here are two examples of hexadecimal strings:

<1211a1f3>
<abCDef112290>

As you see, both upper- and lowercase letters within the correct range are equally acceptable. We can also illustrate the equivalence of pairs of hexadecimal digits to normal characters. Using the ASCII representation of characters, we can form the following example of a hexadecimal string:

<31355F4e616d65>

which is equivalent to the regular string

(15_Name)

OBJECT TYPES

The PostScript language has 13 distinct types of objects. These are as follows:

Numeric	Nominal	Composite	Special
integer	name	string	mark
real	operator	dictionary	null
boolean	file	array	save
			fontID

All syntactic entities recognized by the PostScript interpreter belong to one of these types.

Do not confuse this grouping of objects with the standard groups used by the *PostScript Language Reference Manual*. Even when the names of the groups are similar, the groups here are more inclusive and less precise, and are presented and used for conceptual organization and discussion.

All PostScript objects have certain common characteristics, which are type, attributes, and value. In general, when you deal with a PostScript object, you need only be concerned with its type and value. The attributes of an object are primarily of interest to the interpreter; if they interest you, you will find a full discussion in the *PostScript Language Reference Manual*. To deal with the combined issues of object type and value, we need to divide PostScript objects into two groups: simple objects and composite objects.

SIMPLE OBJECTS

Most PostScript objects are *simple* objects. This means that all their characteristics (type, attributes, and value) are inextricably linked together and cannot be individually changed. This is reasonable enough; you would hardly expect the object *123* to be the same as *456*. The only way to change the characteristics of a simple object is to copy it to a new object that has the desired characteristics.

COMPOSITE OBJECTS

Objects of the types *array, string,* and *dictionary,* however, are *composite* objects. This means that each of these types of objects has components and an internal substructure that is both visible and accessible. The substructure of each of these types is discussed more fully later in the chapter.

NUMERIC OBJECTS

There are two types of numeric objects in PostScript, *integer* and *real*. Integer objects consist only of integer numbers, between certain limits determined by the implementation. Real objects consist of real numbers within a wider range of limits. Real numbers generally are implemented as floating-point numbers and therefore have specific precision limitations. Numbers of both types may be intermixed freely in PostScript operations, except where an operator specifically requires an integer type (as some operators do). Where that requirement exists, you will find the notation *int* used in our description of the operator, to warn you that only an integer value is allowed.

Although they are not strictly numbers, we will also consider *boolean* objects as belonging to the numeric category. Boolean objects have only two possible values, true and false. As you will read later in this chapter, they are produced by the comparison operators and used by the conditional and logical operators. Although boolean objects are equivalent to the binary values, 0 and 1, which are often used in other computer contexts, these are distinct objects in PostScript, and 0 is not false nor is 1 true. For this reason, the specific objects *true* and *false* exist within PostScript for those occasions when you need a direct reference to those values.

NOMINAL OBJECTS

There are three types of PostScript objects that can be thought of as names or variants of names. These types are name objects, operator objects, and file objects.

A *name object* is an indivisible symbol uniquely defined by a set of characters. A name is a simple object; although it is referenced and identified by a string of characters, it is not the string of characters. The individual characters that make up the name are not in any sense elements of the name; they must be taken as a whole.

There are two important characteristics you need to notice about names. First, they must be unique. Any specific sequence of characters defines one, and only one, name object. Second, names do not have values in the same sense that they do in other programming languages. Instead, names in PostScript are associated with values through the use of the dictionary mechanism, as you have already seen.

Operator objects represent the built-in PostScript actions; when the operator is encountered, the built-in action is executed. As we already discussed, operator objects are the value half of the pairing in *systemdict* with the key of the operator name. For most purposes, you can simply regard operators as identical to their names. However, you should know that the operator and its name are not, in fact, precisely identical; and leave it at that.

A *file* is a readable or writable stream of characters that transfers information between PostScript and its environment. A *file object* refers to an associated, underlying file. PostScript provides two standard files: a standard input file and a standard output file. The standard input file is where the PostScript interpreter generally receives programs, commands, and data to be worked on; the standard output file is the destination of usual PostScript output, especially error and status messages and certain displays. Many PostScript programs can run satisfactorily with only the standard files. When these are not sufficient, however, PostScript provides a full set of file operators that allow you to open a file (the act that creates the file object) and to process the stream of characters in various ways. It is almost never necessary to refer directly to the standard files, but there are names and mechanisms for such reference if required. See the full discussion of file operators in the *PostScript Language Reference Manual* regarding these points.

SPECIAL OBJECTS

In addition to the object types described above, PostScript has four special types of objects, each of which exists for a specific purpose. All of these special types are simple objects.

The first special object is *null*. As its name implies, the null object is an object whose sole function is as a placeholder. PostScript uses null objects to fill empty or uninitialized positions in composite objects (such as a dictionary) when they are created. A null object can be referenced by the name, null. Most operators will return an error if they are given a null object as an operand.

The second object is *mark*. The mark is used to mark a position on the operand stack. There are several stack operators that use the mark object in stack manipulation.

The last two special objects are *save* and *fontID*. Both of these objects are used by the PostScript interpreter for its various operations; generally, you will not have to be concerned about them. As you would expect, the fontID object is associated with the creation and use of fonts; you will read more about this in the following chapters on fonts and graphics.

STRING OBJECTS

You are already familiar with the construction and use of strings in PostScript. A string object is simply a PostScript string. It is, as we said earlier, a composite object. Thus, any operation that copies a string, or part of a string, shares the string's value. String objects consist of a series of values, stored internally as integers from 0 to 255, and are conventionally used to store character data with one character being represented by each integer. Individual elements within a string can be accessed by means of an integer index.

DICTIONARY OBJECTS

Dictionaries were also discussed earlier. A dictionary object is simply a PostScript dictionary; like a string, it is a composite object. At the risk of sounding nonsensical, copying a dictionary to a new dictionary does not copy the values in the dictionary, it shares the values. Therefore, if you change a value in the old dictionary, you will retrieve the changed value in the new one. This issue becomes important in advanced text handling; it is covered in some detail in Chapter 6.

ARRAY OBJECTS

An array is an indexed collection of PostScript objects. PostScript arrays differ from arrays in most other computer languages in two respects. First, a PostScript array does not have to be composed of only one type of object. A PostScript array may contain, for example, numbers, strings, names, and even other arrays. The second difference is that PostScript arrays are one-dimensional. That means that access to individual elements in a PostScript array is always provided by a single index. Since elements of a PostScript array may consist of other arrays, you can construct the functional equivalent of multidimensional arrays if you require them.

The index to a PostScript array must be a nonnegative integer. PostScript indices begin at zero, so a PostScript array with n elements would be indexed by values from 0 to $n-1$. Any attempt to access an array with an index that is invalid will result in an error.

A typical PostScript array is created by bounding a collection of PostScript objects with brackets, [and]. When the PostScript interpreter encounters the [, it pushes a mark onto the operand stack and then pushes each following object onto the stack until it encounters the]. At that point, the interpreter removes everything down to the mark and creates an array from the objects taken off the stack. Some examples of PostScript arrays follow:

    [12 34 (abcd) 56 78]

This array consists of five elements: two integers, *12* and *34*, followed by a string, *abcd*, followed by two more integers, *56* and *78*.

    [/name (name) .125 34]

This array consists of four elements: a name literal, *name*, a string, *name*, followed by a real number, *.125*, and an integer, *34*. Remember that the name object *name* is not the same thing as the string *name*. A name object is a simple object and doesn't have component pieces as the string does.

Finally, the following array:

    [(div) 6 12 add]

is an interesting and instructive example. This array has only two elements, the string *div* and the integer result of adding 6 and *12*, 18. You should notice here that the array construction executes operators within it before creating the array itself. This is what distinguishes the [ ] pair from the { } set that defines a procedure. When the interpreter encounters [, it will continue to execute operators; when it encounters {, it will stop executing operators and instead place them onto the stack.

PROCEDURES

A procedure is an executable array of PostScript objects. As you have learned, procedures are enclosed in braces, { and }. This distinguishes them from other PostScript arrays, which are enclosed in brackets as described above. As you saw in the last example, this is an important distinction. You may find the concept of an "executable array" strange; if so, you may find it convenient to think of procedures as a separate type of PostScript object, belonging to its own class and having its own properties. The main point is that procedures are viewed by the interpreter as arrays that can be stored and executed.

The main difference between ordinary PostScript arrays and procedures is how each is handled by the interpreter. In an array, each object is processed by the interpreter in the same way that the object would be in ordinary execution: names are looked up in the dictionary and the appropriate value is substituted into the array; operators are executed in the ordinary fashion, taking operands from the stack and returning results that are inserted into the array definition; and so on. When a begin-procedure marker, {, is encountered, however, the interpreter stops executing the following objects and places everything onto the stack until the end-of-procedure marker, }, occurs. At this point, names are not looked up, and operators are not acted on; everything is placed onto the stack as one large object, almost as if it were a string. The actions specified within the procedure will only take place later in the program, when the entire procedure is executed by the interpreter.

Procedures are essentially small segments of PostScript programs. They are ordered collections, or arrays, of PostScript objects that accomplish a given task. These segments can be entered into a PostScript dictionary like any other PostScript object and referenced by name. In fact, most PostScript program analysis consists of identifying a hierarchy of required procedures.

TRANSFER OF CONTROL

Since PostScript is a programming language, it necessarily provides several mechanisms for changing the order of execution of operations. Some such mechanism is essential for any type of programming. Interestingly, PostScript does not provide a traditional "go to" or branch operator, nor does it have branch labels. In this sense, PostScript is a perfect example of a "structured" language. However, since most programmers have grown up with the notion of branching, you may find that you need to rethink your old habits.

Instead of branching, PostScript provides a variety of operators to perform procedures repeatedly or to execute them based on a particular condition. PostScript also provides a set of logical operators for creating, combining, and testing conditions. By using these facilities, a PostScript programmer can create complex procedural variations to accomplish any task. The essential requirement is to think of your task as a series of processes rather than as one complex flow. As we work through the examples in the following sections and chapters, I will try to show you some simple but effective methods for thinking about pages and processes to help generate good PostScript code.

PostScript operators that provide control of procedures can be divided into three groups, as follows:

- operators that execute a procedure repeatedly

- operators that execute a procedure conditionally, based on a test of an external object

- operators used by PostScript itself to control flow

These groups are somewhat arbitrary, and the first two groups, at least, will be common in your work. The first group is distinguished by being a simple, repeated operation. The operators in this group are the following:

Syntax	Function
{proc} **exec**	executes *proc*
int {proc} **repeat**	executes *proc int* times
init incr lim {proc} **for**	executes *proc* for values from *init* by steps of *incr* until reaching *lim*

The second group of operators is more complex, being dependent on the results of a conditional test, either outside and independent of the procedure being executed or within it. Here you will notice a new operand type, *bool*. This represents a boolean value, either true or false. These operators are

Syntax	Function
bool {proc} **if**	executes *proc* if *bool* is true
bool {proc1} {proc2} **ifelse**	executes *proc1* if *bool* is true and executes *proc2* otherwise

and also the pair of operators

Syntax	Function
{proc} **loop**	executes *proc* an indefinite number of times
exit	terminates the active loop

which are used together. This grouping of operators shows very clearly how easy and natural structured programming is in PostScript.

Structured programming is a method of developing program logic according to a specific set of rules. While this is not an appropriate place for a complete analysis of this subject, a brief discussion will help prepare you mentally to write PostScript code. One of the main rules of structured programming is that program logic should utilize only three control structures for maximum readability and logical clarity. These are the sequential control structure, the loop control structure, and the if-then-else control structure. Each of these structures is used as required to form a group of computer instructions that both conforms to strict structural requirements and performs a single logical function, which makes the code easy to read and understand.

The sequence control structure is just a fancy way of saying that the computer executes one instruction or operation after another; this is the ordinary sequential processing familiar to us all. The other two control structures, loop control and if-then-else control, correspond (more or less) to the first two groups of operators given above. The net result is that PostScript provides an ideal set of operators for creating a structured program.

We have already observed that the second group of control operators listed above depends on testing an external object and changing the control sequence based on the results of that test. PostScript provides the usual set of conditional operators to execute these tests. These operators are the following:

Syntax				**Function**
any1	any2	**eq**	bool	tests whether *any1* is equal to *any2*
any1	any2	**ne**	bool	tests whether *any1* is not equal to *any2*
num1 (str1)	num2 (str2)	**ge**	bool	tests whether *num1* or *str1* is greater than or equal to *num2* or *str2*
num1 (str1)	num2 (str2)	**gt**	bool	tests whether *num1* or *str1* is greater than *num2* or *str2*
num1 (str1)	num2 (str2)	**le**	bool	tests whether *num1* or *str1* is less than or equal to *num2* or *str2*
num1 (str1)	num2 (str2)	**lt**	bool	tests whether *num1* or *str1* is less than *num2* or *str2*

PostScript also provides a series of operators for combining conditions. These are the boolean operators and consist of the following:

Syntax				Function
int1	int2		int	
bool1	bool2	**and**	bool	logical or bitwise *and*
int1	int2		int	
bool1	bool2	**or**	bool	logical or bitwise inclusive *or*
int1	int2		int	
bool1	bool2	**xor**	bool	logical or bitwise exclusive *or*
int			int	
bool	**not**	bool		logical or bitwise *not*
—	**true**	bool		pushes the boolean value *true* onto the stack
—	**false**	bool		pushes the boolean value *false* onto the stack

The combination of these operators allows any form of test on a PostScript object.

PROCEDURES AND OPERATORS

The preceding section introduced you to the concept of procedures, as a part of the discussion of program control and related operators. Now you can begin to make more effective use of these operators, by putting names on procedures and using those names as part of the control and flow process. To illustrate this, let's revisit some of the procedural examples that you saw before. If you don't remember any of the operators, just go back to the end of the last chapter and look them up—or you can find them in the operator summary in Appendix A.

A procedure is named and entered into the current dictionary like any other PostScript object. For example,

    /average { **add** 2 **div** } **def**

defines a procedure, *average,* in exactly the same way that

/str (this is a string) **def**

defines the string *str.* All definitions are carried out in the same fashion. Procedure names can also be included in the definition of other procedures; for example, if you have defined *average* as shown above, then you might also define the procedure

/middlePage { 0 612 average } **def**

which would give you the average of the left and right edges of a standard page. Since the interpreter does not execute the procedure when the definition occurs, it is not necessary to have already defined *average* when you define *middlePage.* All that is required is that *average* be defined by the time you execute *middlePage.*

Notice that this procedural definition, *middlePage,* differs from the following definition of a named constant:

/MiddlePage 0 612 average **def**

It looks very similar, doesn't it? It is similar, and it would (in this case) accomplish the same goal as the preceding definition. In both cases, the final result would be to leave the value of the middle of the page on the stack. The difference is in how that result is obtained.

In the first definition, of a procedure, the calculation is carried out only at the moment the interpreter encounters the name *middlePage* in the program. In the second case, the calculation is carried out at the moment the definition is encountered, and the value of that calculation is stored under the name *MiddlePage.* These two cases have been constructed to illustrate how these procedures work; the judgement of when to use one or the other must be based on the requirements of each task or program. The point to note here is that, in the case of procedural definition, *average* does not have to be defined when the procedure is defined and the calculation of the value occurs at the moment of use. In the case of constant definition, the procedure *average* must be defined already, since it will be executed to compute the value to be stored, and that value, once computed, will be fixed and used whenever the named constant is invoked.

Using these techniques, we can now revisit some of the examples from the last chapter. Let's begin by defining the following procedure:

/inch { 72 **mul** } **def**

This small procedure allows you to translate inches into PostScript coordinates, which you will recall are 1/72 inch in each direction. Using this procedure, the following two program segments are identical in execution:

```
7.5 inch
7.5 72 mul
```

However, the first is, as you would expect, much easier to understand.

Now you might define a variable, *Xpos,* to measure movement across the page and a variable, *Ypos,* to measure movement down the page. Assume that you would like a 1-inch margin on both the left and right edges of the page, and that you also want to start printing 1 inch from the top of the page. Then you would define

```
/Xpos 1   inch def
/Ypos 7.5 inch def
```

to begin each variable at the appropriate margin. Remember that the PostScript vertical coordinate system is positive up the page, and so a larger number represents a position higher up the page; you will subtract from the *Ypos* variable to measure movement down the page. Then you could write the procedures

```
/rightMargin { 7 inch } def
/outsideMargin { rightMargin Xpos gt } def
```

The first procedure defines a position that we call *rightMargin* at 7 inches, and the second procedure defines a test, called *outsideMargin,* which checks the *Xpos* variable against the *rightMargin* position. Using these definitions, we can now test whether the *Xpos* variable has crossed the right margin by executing the procedure *outsideMargin.*

Let us suppose that you have determined that movement in the vertical direction will be at six lines per inch. Then you could define

```
/linespace { inch 6 div } def
```

and

```
/linedown { Ypos linespace sub } def
```

which defines the six-per-inch line spacing as *linespace* and creates a procedure, *linedown,* to subtract a *linespace* from the *Ypos* variable.

Now you can combine these procedures to accomplish in an easily understandable way the task of moving down one line if the position across the page has crossed the right margin. This could be written as

504 Xpos **gt** { Ypos 12 **sub** } **if**

but now you can write it as

outsideMargin linedown **if**

which is much more intelligible.

The important point here is that you have made an opaque piece of code understandable by the judicious choice of variable and procedure names. We will discuss this issue of names and procedures more thoroughly in the next section.

ERROR HANDLING

PostScript handles the errors that it discovers during operation in a uniform manner that takes advantage of various PostScript language facilities. You will find that an understanding of PostScript's default error handling and reporting will aid you in reading and modifying PostScript code.

PostScript default error processing works as follows. Every PostScript error has a unique name, which is also intended to describe the nature of the error encountered: for example, *stackoverflow, rangecheck, undefined,* and so on. Possible errors for each operator are clearly identified in the *PostScript Language Reference Manual.* When the PostScript interpreter discovers an error during its own operation or while executing an operator, it looks up the name of the error condition in a special dictionary called *errordict.* The interpreter then executes the procedure associated with that name in *errordict.* In all of this, you see that the handling follows standard PostScript procedures.

Each name in *errordict* has its own associated error procedure. All of the default error procedures operate in a standard way. They record information regarding the error in another special dictionary called *$error.* This special dictionary contains information about the cause of the error and about the state of the system and the interpreter at the time the error occurred. Then the procedures stop the execution of the PostScript program and invoke the generic error-handling procedure, **handleerror**.

This procedure accesses the error data stored in *$error* and prints a text message on the standard output file.

For the Apple LaserWriter, the text message generated by **handleerror** conforms to a standard status message format. This means that the text is bracketed by the strings *%%[* and *]%%* and consists of *key, value* pairs separated by semicolons. The standard format for an error message is the following:

    %%[Error: errorname; OffendingCommand: operator]%%

This rather formal structure allows user application programs to extract error messages (and other status messages) from other text or data being received over the communication channel and to provide additional processing if desired. Generally, it is considered good practice to screen errors and status information from the user of an application program; hence this method of reporting errors. If you are using the interpreter in the interactive mode, you will see the appropriate error message on your screen in the format shown above (assuming that you're using an Apple LaserWriter).

The PostScript default error processing provides better error diagnosis and messages than most computer languages, and you will generally find it sufficient for your needs. Because this entire process uses standard PostScript facilities, however, it is possible to alter the standard error-processing mechanism in various ways. Such advanced topics are outside the scope of this book; if you want further information, a full discussion of the possible alterations is presented in the *PostScript Language Reference Manual.*

FOURTH EXERCISE

To keep this exposition interesting and to help you assimilate all the material that you have been reading, let's try an additional exercise at this point. We will revisit some of the previous concepts and see how the use of procedures can both simplify and clarify them. I will leave it to you to review the third exercise and apply procedural definitions; if you will take the time, I think you will quickly see how all those repetitive blocks of two or three lines can easily be made into simple procedures.

For this section, you will program a similar but distinct page of output. It is similar in that it is set in two columns, in a text-and-commentary format; however, in this case it is text with marginal headings. The text represents a description of a company being analyzed; the marginal notations are subject headings.

Before you begin, however, there are several more points to be covered. You need to think more about how to analyze and then implement your page requirements in PostScript. The next section discusses some of the considerations that you must keep in mind as you design your PostScript program and introduces you to a few useful procedures.

STATEMENT FLOW

By now, you are probably becoming more familiar with PostScript's order of notation—operands followed by an operator—and are finding it easier to read more complex PostScript statements. Because of Post-Script's notational structure, complex PostScript statements are built up in concentric layers, somewhat like an onion.

The following example is a moderately complex PostScript statement, using operators you are familiar with, but not using any procedural definitions to simplify the structure of the statement. Please note that this style of programming is not recommended; it is presented here only to make a point and as an illustration of the concentric nature of typical PostScript code. For the purpose of the illustration, let us suppose that the following have been defined:

Variable	Definition
LeftMargin	left-margin position (in the x-direction)
RightMargin	right-margin position
StringSize	width of a string (in x-direction units)

Now suppose we wish to position the current point in the x-direction to display the string (the one whose width is given in *StringSize*) in the center of a line. The following code will accomplish that task:

```
LeftMargin                        %1
RightMargin LeftMargin sub        %2
2 div                             %3
StringSize 2 div                  %4
sub                               %5
add                               %6
```

In order to analyze this program fragment, first you need to think about how to determine the position, in the x-direction, where the string must begin to center it between the left and right margins. A quick analysis tells you that this point will be one-half the distance between the margins less one-half the size of the string. That's basically the same process most people would use to center a heading on a typewritten page: space to the center of the line and backspace once for every two characters in the heading. The above example follows the same process exactly, although it may not look like it at first reading. The difference is the "onionization" of the procedure; let's analyze it layer by layer.

The last thing you want to leave on the stack is the absolute x-coordinate for the display. We are assuming for now that movement to set the display operation will be invoked with the x-coordinate as an operand on the stack, as it would need to be for a **moveto**, for example. This x-coordinate will be the left margin plus some calculated displacement.

And so the last line, line %6, adds the result of the calculations performed in lines %2 to %5 to the variable *LeftMargin* in the first line, line %1. Here you see what I mean about the onion effect, with the last line being connected to the first. Moving inward, you see that line %2 calculates the distance between the left and right margins by subtracting the left margin from the right and leaving the result on the stack. Line %3 then divides that result by two, giving the displacement of the center of the line that now remains on the stack. Line %4 divides the length of the string, given by *StringSize,* by two to give one-half of the length and pushes that result onto the stack.

Now the stack contains three numbers: on top, one-half of the string length; next, the position of the center of the line; and finally, the left margin, still on the stack from line %1. All numbers are in x-axis units, and the top two are calculated from the left margin, as desired. Now line %5 subtracts the top operand from the one below it on the stack and returns the difference on the stack. This difference is precisely the calculated distance that we want to add to the left margin, which (not accidentally) is now the second operand on the stack. Line %6, as we discussed before, now adds the two remaining operands to provide the final, desired result. Thus, you can see how this small program consists of several layers, one inside the other.

PROGRAM FRAGMENTS

We have already mentioned PostScript's affinity for structured programming and how PostScript's control mechanisms fit naturally into the control concepts that build structured programs. At the same time, we discussed how structured programs are built of groups of instructions, or procedures, each of which performs a single logical function. In many ways, each of these procedures represents a program "fragment." When we discuss the overall considerations of program structure in the next section, you will see how these fragments are combined into pieces of a well-organized PostScript program. Because such pieces form an essential part of PostScript code, we are going to construct several fragments as a part of our exercises.

TEXT MANIPULATION

In many ways, the preceding example was a program fragment, although you may not have thought of it that way. In fact, as your first introduction to this concept, let's rework that example into a piece of code that might be used in a real PostScript program.

Begin by making the same assumptions as previously: that the three variables, *LeftMargin*, *RightMargin*, and *StringSize*, will be defined and set correctly independently of this procedure. For *LeftMargin* and *RightMargin*, this might be done in an initial section of the program, much as you set the named constants in the third exercise. The variable *StringSize*, of course, would have to be set after you have determined the string; therefore, it would most likely be set in the course of program execution, like the variables in the third exercise.

In any case, the procedural definition would look something like this:

```
/centerText
    {           LeftMargin
                RightMargin LeftMargin sub 2 div
                StringSize 2 div
                sub add }
    def
```

This is the same code you saw before, only now enclosed in braces { and } to make it a procedure and incorporated as part of the definition for the name *centerText*. How the procedure is broken up into lines is fairly arbitrary; you will read more on this issue later in the chapter.

In the same spirit, you can fashion a procedure to right-justify a string of text. In this case, suppose that you will be given a string of text on the operand stack, and the task is to create a procedure to display this string right-justified. Such a procedure will be less complex mathematically than the preceding example, but will have some additional elements in it.

The two additional elements will be, first, to determine the length of the string, and second, to display the string with the **show** operator. Such a procedure might look like this:

```
/rightJustifyText
    {        dup
             stringwidth pop
             RightMargin exch sub
             NextLine moveto
             show }
    def
```

This example raises several points. The first occurs immediately with the operator **dup**, which duplicates the value on the top of the stack. This is necessary because you need the string (which we are assuming is already placed on the stack for the call to the procedure) two times: once to measure it and once to display it. The second operation is taken care of by the last line in the procedure, the **show** operator. So, at that point, you must have the string you want to display on the top of the stack. The first operation, determining the size of the string, is performed by the **stringwidth** operator. Let's take a moment to look at this operator in the usual format:

Syntax			Function
(str1) **stringwidth**	wx	wy	calculates the width of the string *str1* in current units

Note that the operator returns two distinct values: one a width in the x-direction (*wx*) and the other a width in the y-direction (*wy*). These are necessary because some fonts—oriental languages such as Japanese and Chinese, primarily—have width in both directions. In the case of all English fonts, there is no y-direction width for a character, and hence the y-coordinate value will always be zero. The results come back with the y-value on the top of the stack and the x-value underneath it. This is convenient since you can now discard the unnecessary y-value by using the **pop** operator.

So the first two lines of the procedure duplicate the string that you were given initially and then determine the width of the string, leaving that calculated width on the top of the stack. Next you must subtract that width from the right margin to determine what x-coordinate value you need in order to display the string, ending at the right margin.

This little task is completed in the next line of the procedure. Since you want to subtract the calculated value already on the stack from the value for *RightMargin,* you need to use the operator **exch** after you place the constant *RightMargin* on the stack to swap the top two objects and to get the operands into the correct order for the **sub** operator. This leaves the correct x-coordinate for the starting point of the string on top of the stack, with the string itself immediately underneath. For the purposes of this exercise, let's assume that *NextLine* is the name of a variable that has been calculated to give the y-coordinate of the next line of text, as was done in the previous exercise. You push this variable onto the stack, which now (conveniently) is in the correct sequence to issue a **moveto**. This positions the current point at the x-coordinate that you calculated previously and at the y-coordinate, *NextLine,* ready for the **show** operator. And that's the next, and last, line of your procedure. It's easy, really, once you get the hang of it.

PROGRAM EXERCISE

This exercise has many of the features of the previous exercise, but it also introduces some new material. The task is to produce a page of output about a company, Acme Widget Corporation. The required format has a centered heading of two lines with the remainder of the page set in two columns of text. The first column has topic descriptions; the second column has the text itself. Once again, the topic headings are to be aligned with the beginning of the text paragraphs; this time, however, they are to be right-justified against a 2-inch margin. Now you need to analyze how such a page might be set up.

PAGE ANALYSIS AND SETUP

This exercise may be analyzed in several ways, all essentially correct and yet distinct. The approach given here is only one successful approach to the problem. You will develop your own methods as you become more familiar with page-layout problems.

You must now develop a layout of the page in sufficient detail so that you can program it. You can do this by working out the procedures that you will require to actually output the page. The process would proceed something like what follows.

The first output will be the heading. You will set this in Times-Bold, 16-point type on 20-point leading. There are two lines of heading, which are to be centered on the page. The left and right margins for this page will be ½ inch from either edge; this gives a left margin of ½ inch and a right margin of 8 inches, based on the left edge of the paper. This portion of the layout is shown in Figure 2.2.

The paragraph titles will be in the first column, as in the second and third exercises. This means that the second column will have to be set first, as before. The first column will be right-justified on a margin 2 inches from the left margin, which will be 2.5 inches from the left edge of the paper. There will be ½ inch between the paragraph titles and the text of the paragraphs. Therefore, the body text will begin at an offset of 3 inches from the left edge of the paper. The second column will be 4.5 inches in width to the right margin. These dimensions are illustrated in Figure 2.3.

You will use Times-Roman for the body of the text and Times-Bold (the bold version of Times-Roman) for the paragraph titles, both set in 12-point type on 14-point leading. Space between the paragraphs within the body text will again be two lines, or 28 points.

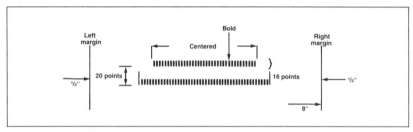

Figure 2.2: Heading layout for the fourth exercise

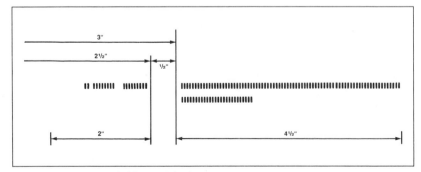

Figure 2.3: Layout of titles and body text

The heading on the page will begin 1.5 inches from the top of the paper, which is 9.5 inches from the bottom edge. The text and titles will begin 1 inch below that, which will be 8.5 inches from the bottom. All these numbers will be incorporated into named constants for the program. This final portion of the layout is shown in Figure 2.4.

Now that you have decided on the constants, you must develop the procedures. You will set the headings in the center of their respective lines with a procedure that will display text centered in a line. Next you will display the body text. You could move a line after each display within one procedure, but then you would have to make adjustments when you get to paragraph spacing. For this reason, you want to advance the line spacing independently of the text-handling and painting procedure. Finally, you must display the paragraph headings at the correct vertical positions to match the beginning of each paragraph, and you want to right-justify each of them.

This sequence identifies the following procedures:

Procedure	Function
centerText	takes a text string from the stack and centers it on the current line
bodyText	sets a text string from the stack for the body text of the page
rightJustifyText	sets a text string from the stack right-justified against a defined right margin

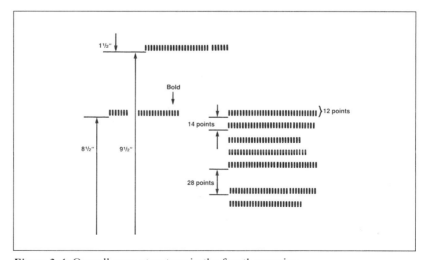

Figure 2.4: Overall page structure in the fourth exercise

And there are two additional procedures that will be required:

Procedure	Function
advanceLine	increments the current line position by the constant for leading
advancePara	increments the current line position by the amount of space between paragraphs

Based on these procedures and your previous analysis, you establish that the following named constants are required:

Constant	Definition
TopStart	starting point for the page titles; previously decided to be 9.5 inches from the bottom edge of the page
BodyStart	starting point for the text proper and for the paragraph titles; previously determined to be 8.5 inches from the page bottom
LineSpace	space between lines, or leading; determined to be 14 points
ParaSpace	space between paragraphs; determined to be 28 points (two lines)
LeftMargin	the absolute leftmost print position; intended to be ½ inch from the left page edge
RightMargin	the absolute rightmost print position; intended to be 8 inches from the left edge of the paper
SecondColumn	the horizontal beginning position of the body text; defined to be 3 inches from the left page edge
RightColumn	the horizontal right margin for the first column of paragraph titles; determined to be 2.5 inches from the left edge of the page

In addition, there will be several variables that will have to be defined dynamically as the program executes. The first is a vertical placekeeper: *NextLine*. The second is a group of variables, which you might name *SaveParaOne, SaveParaTwo,* and so on. These variables will store the required values of the vertical position for use in positioning the paragraph headings, as you did in the preceding examples.

PROGRAM

With this analysis and information, you can now proceed to develop the required procedures and program them. In this context, we will not spend time on development of each individual routine; both of the major routines mimic what has already been covered, with minor variations. A complete analysis of each routine and line of code will be presented after you have run the exercise. Figure 2.5 gives the full text of your program.

This program is significantly longer and more complex than your previous work, but it is more like real text output. The screen will scroll up again as you enter the program on your terminal. This produces the page of output shown in Figure 2.6.

There is one thing to notice about this program as you enter it. When a procedure is being defined, you do not get the PS> prompt back after a linefeed. Once you have entered the left brace, {, the interpreter waits to respond until it has received all of the input for the definition; in other words, it waits until it receives the matching right brace, }. This can be disconcerting the first time; don't worry, it's correct. Continue entering your procedure, and the interpreter will reappear at the end of the definition.

DISCUSSION AND REVIEW

The program begins with definitions of the procedures that you identified earlier. The first procedure is the little *inch* procedure, which will convert PostScript units into inches. Because the page layout was conceived entirely in inches, using this procedure will make your program much more readable.

The next two procedures are *advanceLine* and *advancePara*, which are essentially identical. The first moves the variable *NextLine* down by a distance given by the named constant *LineSpace*. The second procedure does the same, but it uses the named constant *ParaSpace*. The obvious intention is to use the variable *NextLine* as part of a **moveto** to position the text output as you have seen done in the smaller examples earlier in the chapter.

The constants *LineSpace* and *ParaSpace* have to be defined and set to the values that were determined as you set up the page. These constants could be defined here, since they are associated with these procedures. If you do that, however, and you come back later to modify these constants, you will have to go through all the procedural definitions to find

```
%-----------------------Procedures---------------------
/inch                           %create a procedure
    {    72 mul }               %to convert user units
    def                         %to use inch measurements

/advanceLine
    {    /NextLine
         NextLine LineSpace sub
         def   }
    def

/advancePara
    {    /NextLine
         NextLine ParaSpace sub
         def   }
    def

/centerText
    {    dup
         stringwidth pop
         2 div
         RightMargin LeftMargin sub 2 div
         exch sub
         LeftMargin add
         NextLine moveto
         show   }
    def

/bodyText
    {    SecondColumn NextLine moveto
         show   }
    def

/rightJustifyText
    {    dup
         stringwidth pop
         RightColumn exch sub
         NextLine moveto
         show   }
    def

%------------------------Named Constants----------------
/TopStart 9.5 inch def          %vertical start for head
/BodyStart 8.5 inch def         %vertical start for body

/LineSpace 14 def               %set line spacing (leading)
/ParaSpace 28 def               %set paragraph spacing

/LeftMargin .5 inch def         %set absolute left margin
/RightMargin 8 inch def         %set absolute right margin
/RightColumn 2.5 inch def       %set right edge of first column
/SecondColumn 3 inch def        %set left edge of second column

%-------------------Program (Title)----------------------
%Setup font for Title
/Times-Bold findfont 16 scalefont setfont              %1

%Move to selected position
/NextLine TopStart def                                 %2
(ACME WIDGETS INCORPORATED) centerText                 %3

/NextLine NextLine 20 sub def                          %4
(Fiscal Year 1986) centerText                          %5


%-------------------Program (Text Column)----------------
%Setup new font for Body Text
/Times-Roman findfont 12 scalefont setfont             %10
```

Figure 2.5: Fourth exercise: Acme Widgets program

```
/NextLine BodyStart def                                                 %11
(Acme Widgets was founded in 1952 by Dippy and Daffy Acme) bodyText      %12
advanceLine                                                             %13
(to produce high technology widgets for the booming aerospace) bodyText
advanceLine
(industry. Acme was quickly recognized as being the best) bodyText
advanceLine
(widget works in the country. Continued investment in new) bodyText
advanceLine
(technology and manufacturing methods has kept Acme Widgets) bodyText
advanceLine
(in the forefront of this industry.) bodyText

advancePara                                                             %14
/SaveParaOne NextLine def                                               %15

(Acme Widgets sells 72% of all widgets produced in the) bodyText
advanceLine
(United States; and it has 39% of the growing international) bodyText
advanceLine
(market.) bodyText

advancePara
/SaveParaTwo NextLine def

(Headquarters: Burbank, California) bodyText
advanceLine
(Domestic sales offices in Seattle, WA; Dallas, TX;) bodyText
advanceLine
(and Washington, D.C.) bodyText

advancePara
/SaveParaThree NextLine def

($223 million in gross sales for fiscal 1985;) bodyText
advanceLine
($248 million in gross sales projected for fiscal 1986.) bodyText
%-----------------------Program (Titles)------------------
%set font for Paragraph Titles
/Times-Bold findfont 12 scalefont setfont                              %20

/NextLine BodyStart def                                                 %21
(History:) rightJustifyText                                            %22

/NextLine SaveParaOne def                                               %23
(Market Position:) rightJustifyText

/NextLine SaveParaTwo def
(Offices:) rightJustifyText

/NextLine SaveParaThree def
(Financial Position:) rightJustifyText
showpage
quit
%all done
```

Figure 2.5 (cont.): Fourth exercise: Acme Widgets program

the appropriate constants. You will find that if you put all your named constants in one section of code, they will be easier to find and therefore easier to modify. So that's how it's done in this and all subsequent exercises.

Next you see the three procedures that form the heart of this exercise: *centerText, bodyText,* and *rightJustifyText.* Each of these procedures displays one type of the final output. The first procedure, *centerText,* will

ACME WIDGETS INCORPORATED
Fiscal Year 1986

History: Acme Widgets was founded in 1952 by Dippy and Daffy Acme
                  to produce high technology widgets for the growing aerospace
                  market. Acme was quickly recognized as being the best
                  widget works in the country. Continued investment in new
                  technology and manufacturing methods has kept Acme Widgets
                  in the forefront of this industry.

Market Position: Acme Widgets sells 72% of all widgets produced in the
                  United States; and it has 39% of the growing international
                  market.

Offices: Headquarters: Burbank, California
                  Domestic sales offices in Seattle, WA; Dallas, TX;
                  and Washington, D.C.

Financial Position: $223 million in gross sales for fiscal 1985;
                     $248 million in gross sales projected for fiscal 1986.

Figure 2.6: Output from the fourth exercise

be used to display the page titles. Note that the procedure itself will display any text centered between the two variables *LeftMargin* and *RightMargin*. This procedure is essentially identical to the one you created and analyzed earlier in the chapter. The difference is that *centerText* takes a text string (on the stack) as an operand and displays it after having calculated the center position; in this aspect, it is identical to the procedure *rightJustifyText*. *rightJustifyText* is the third, and last, procedure defined in the program; it is identical to the procedure created and analyzed earlier in the chapter and so needs no further explanation here.

The second procedure, *bodyText,* is straightforward. It simply moves to a specific position and shows a string of text. Like the two other procedures, it expects the text to be placed on the stack as an operand. Since this procedure sets the text for the body of the report, the position moved to is defined in the x-direction by the named constant *Second-Column* and in the y-direction by the calculated variable *NextLine.*

The structure of the program is now fairly clear. The main procedures are *centerText* to set the titles, *bodyText* to set the text for the body of the report, and *rightJustifyText* to set the marginal headings. The procedures *advanceLine* and *advancePara* will be used to calculate where the next line of body text will be output, depending on whether the next line continues the current paragraph or starts a new paragraph.

The next section of the program defines the named constants that are required for the program. Most of these are self-explanatory. They represent the values that were determined during the page-setup analysis. The names, of course, are arbitrary but not random or irrelevant. The choice of names is an important consideration that is discussed more fully in the next section. As in the third example, the paragraph spacing is defined independently of the line spacing, although the paragraph spacing is a multiple of the line.

The program itself is repetitive, and you will find that this is typical of PostScript programs generally. If you have done your analysis properly, the actual production of the page or pages of output becomes simply the repetition of the procedures using the appropriate text or data as operands.

As usual, the program begins by setting the font required for the first operation, in this case, for printing the page titles. Then the program initializes the variable *NextLine* to the position defined for the top line of the page, *TopStart.* Line %3 displays the first line of the titles, using the procedure *centerText* to center the line. Line %4 moves down one line. You can't use *advanceLine* here because the point size of the titles is 16 points, and the leading for the titles is 20 points, whereas *advanceLine* uses the *LineSpace* named constant as the leading. You could, of course, reset *LineSpace* to the desired 20 points for this portion of the program and reset it to 14 points when you get to the body of the text. If there were more than two or three lines of heading, that would be an efficient and clear way of doing the required movement; as it is, it is both easier and clearer to move the line directly, as line %4 does, by the desired amount—in this case, 20 points.

Line %5 finishes the titles by displaying the second line, also centered between the margins.

Line %10 sets the font for the body of the page, and line %11 sets the *NextLine* variable to position the body output. (As in the previous examples, line numbering is not continuous; don't think anything is missing.) The remainder of this section of the program sets the body text, using *bodyText* and *advanceLine* or *advancePara* as required. Note that the vertical position of each paragraph is recorded and saved in named variables. Line %15 gives an example of this. The current position, which is in the variable *NextLine,* is saved as the variable *SaveParaOne.* The starting position of each paragraph is saved for use in setting the marginal titles.

The next section of the program sets the marginal titles or comments. This section begins on line %20 by setting the font for the marginal titles. Line %21 moves back to the starting line for the first paragraph of the body. Note that this is not the variable *SaveParaOne,* because the first paragraph of the body begins on the line defined by the constant *BodyStart.* That's where *NextLine* is set to print the first marginal title, which is done by the *rightJustifyText* procedure in line %22. Now you move *NextLine* to *SaveParaOne,* in line %23, and then display the next marginal title, and so on, until all the titles have been produced. As usual, the last lines of the program produce the finished output by using **showpage** and then terminating the interpreter with the **quit** operator.

This program is not really difficult, yet it produces a page that is quite complex. Furthermore, you have now begun to develop a repertoire of PostScript routines that can be used in other circumstances and in other programs.

PROGRAM STRUCTURE AND STYLE

PostScript is a language that has a remarkable degree of flexibility combined with a large and powerful set of operators. But as a result of that flexibility and power, it has an equal potential to generate unsatisfactory, unworkable, and unintelligible code. PostScript, as we observed before, has no specific structural requirements; unlike most other computer languages, it has no reserved words and no enforced data structures. PostScript will allow any type of structure you find useful or entertaining—and it's the entertainment factor that you should worry about.

PostScript programs generally consist of a large series of procedures, or "program fragments," as we have called them. As you read in the preceding section, procedures can be—and most likely will be—used inside the definitions of other procedures. This process is called *nesting,* and it is both a natural outgrowth of the PostScript language and a powerful tool for helping you accomplish complex page description tasks. The net result is that every PostScript program that you are likely to encounter will consist of multiple levels of nested procedures, usually culminating in a few powerful procedural definitions that accomplish large parts of the final task.

However, if this process of nesting procedures in PostScript is both natural and powerful, it also can create a chaotic program when it is carried out in an undisciplined or uncoordinated way. You can easily imagine the difficulty and frustration in trying to discover the source of an error in a procedure when you need to trace through five or six or even more layers of nested definitions. The frustration level rises rapidly if the definitions are scattered throughout many pages of program text, and it will go into orbit if the names of the variables and procedures are short and cryptic or even completely nondescriptive. The only way to avoid most of these problems is to establish a style of programming and adhere to it tenaciously.

NAME SELECTION

Although the examples in the preceding section are somewhat complex and possibly difficult to follow, you can see that they would have been more opaque without the variable names that were used in them. Names like *LeftMargin* and *StringSize* are important in creating readable code because they aid you in understanding what function a program or program fragment is performing. In the example above, imagine how much more difficult it would have been to understand (or explain) if the variable names were replaced by numbers, as they might have been. Procedure names also need to describe what the procedure does, even more than variable names need to describe what the variable contains.

This brings up another useful point, particularly for naming variables, but also to a lesser extent, for naming procedures. Using named variables in the procedure above, rather than using the actual numbers, means that changes to the margins, for example, would not affect the procedure itself. By means of named variables, the procedure is independent of the actual margins that have been set for the page. This is a nontrivial benefit, which affects both independence and maintenance as well as readability.

PostScript is an unusually good language with regard to names, because there are virtually no limits on the length of a name or on the characters used in the name. This extraordinary flexibility is a great tool if you will take advantage of it. You should choose names that describe the function, not just to yourself, but also for others. If the names are too cryptic, so that only you know what they mean, you will discover that you will have forgotten your clever abbreviations and cryptic symbols when you look at the program again after a few weeks or months. So be warned.

There is also a tendency to reduce names to the smallest possible number of letters. This is particularly true for people who are accustomed to programming in languages where the maximum size of a name is only seven or eight characters. This habit is often rationalized by the programmer as reluctance to type out a long name, especially for a frequently used procedure or variable. There are several ways to use longer, more descriptive names and still avoid the repetitive typing. You will, in the long run, be glad you used the longer names even if it means additional work initially.

One thing to keep in mind is that output from applications that generate PostScript code, such as PageMaker, will not generate names that are of much illustrative use. The application, after all, has none of our mnemonic limitations; and conversely, it derives no benefit from meaningful associations. If you are going to do much modification of that type of output, I would strongly recommend that you use a good editor with a global search-and-replace function to modify the procedures and variables that you are working with into useful, descriptive names. This doesn't usually take long, since you will almost always be working with a small subset of the generated output.

NAME USAGE

Names are an important ingredient in creating order out of the potential chaos of any program. Names and conventions about names—how they may be constructed, what they should look like, and so on—form an important part of program structure and style.

If you are familiar with programming at all, you have probably wrestled with the pitfalls and advantages that are associated with names in a programming environment. Basically, there are two issues relating to names that you need to think about. We've already looked at the first: how to select names so that they will be meaningful in your particular environment. The second issue is the use of a set of practices, or conventions, to ensure that you use the same or similar structure for names of the same or similar type.

NAMING CONVENTIONS

Besides making individual procedure and variable names descriptive of their purpose, you will find it helpful to adopt some standard conventions for names in your programs. Development and use of naming conventions is a matter of your personal style of programming; it is an outgrowth of your experience and the requirements of the task at hand.

While no one else can define an appropriate set of conventions for you, there are two points to consider as you begin to establish your personal approach. First, PostScript treats uppercase and lowercase letters as distinct characters. This gives you the opportunity to use uppercase letters to help make your names both readable and distinctive. For example, you might decide to start every variable name with a capital letter and every procedure name with a lowercase letter, with subsequent words in both names being capitalized as appropriate. Then you would write

reEncodeFont	(a procedure)
StringSize	(a variable)
average	(a procedure)
Average	(a variable)
LeftMargin	(a variable)
testMargin	(a procedure)
outsideMargin?	(a procedure)

and so on. The two names, *average* and *Average,* also illustrate why you might want to use case to indicate purpose or use. Using a convention like the one outlined above, you know immediately which name is a procedure and which is a variable; if you are haphazard in your capitalization, the type of name would have to be clear from the context. The last name, *outsideMargin?,* also illustrates that you can use almost any character in PostScript names. Hence, the ? character is used to emphasize the test nature of the procedure.

The second point to keep in mind is the use of standard names throughout your procedures for specific variables or types of variables or procedures. There are particular variables that will reoccur throughout almost any PostScript program: a current line (vertical position), a current horizontal position, the margin settings, and so on. Similarly, there are types of variables that occur regularly: counters and strings, for example. In all such instances, using a standard set of names during your programming will provide enhanced portability and readability for your procedures. For common variables, you should establish common names, even recording the names in some place where they may be readily referenced—the best situation, of course, would be to keep them in a file that could be included at the beginning of each program. Some typical examples might be

Variable	Definition
Xpos	the current position in the x-direction (horizontally)
Yline	the current line position or position in the y-direction (vertically)

and some of the variables we have already seen (and some obvious relatives)

    LeftMargin
    RightMargin
    TopMargin
    BottomMargin

   For variable and procedure types, it is often useful to use prefixes or suffixes to indicate certain types. For example, using the prefix "test", we get

    testRightMargin
    testLeftMargin
    testTopMargin

or using the suffix "size", we have

    StringSize
    ArraySize
    DictSize

   These are only examples. In some of the exercises you will notice that I may not have followed these specific practices myself, and I'm not necessarily suggesting that you adopt them. You should be innovative and flexible and determine what works for you. Certainly you should consider carefully whatever standard names and naming conventions you do choose to adopt. As was said earlier, the choice and use of conventions is a personal decision that, ideally, will grow out of your experience and the requirements of the task to be accomplished.

PROGRAM STRUCTURE

There are two types of structure that are used in a program. One type is what might be called *local structure*. This is the type of structure that we have been discussing: naming conventions, and so on. This type also includes other issues such as spacing and indenting, use of comments, and similar issues that will be covered in the next section. The other type of structure is *global structure*. This is the overall structure of a program, and it is the subject of this section.

The global structure defines the sequence of major sections of your PostScript program and also defines what goes into each of those sections and how the sections are identified and separated from one another. The global structure of your program is completely independent of any local structure that you choose, but the use of a standard global approach to your programs will influence and motivate many of the choices you must make regarding style and conventions within your program. In particular, this is true when you follow the standard global structure recommended for PostScript programs.

There are compelling reasons for establishing and following some structural conventions for your PostScript programs. Some of the reasons are similar to the rationale for using naming conventions: enhanced readability, easier understanding, and improved overall clarity. Besides these common benefits, there are some additional benefits that can be gained by following a specific overall structure in the program. Unlike the naming conventions, however, recommended standards for overall program structure are published (like the operator definitions) in the *PostScript Language Reference Manual*.

There are two important additional benefits that you gain from following these recommended standard conventions. First, your program will be able to be processed by automatic processing programs, such as utility programs, that make use of these standards to identify portions of a PostScript program. An example of such a program would be a utility to extract and print specific pages of a document. Second, by following these structural recommendations, your program will have a common structural base with other PostScript programs, which could allow integration of code from other sources. Common structures are an essential ingredient for this type of flexibility.

DESIRABLE QUALITIES

Before we discuss specific recommendations for program structure and format, it will be worthwhile to establish what qualities we are attempting to create or enhance by the use of conventions. There are particular qualities that form the primary goals of structural conventions. The first and most obvious goal is one we have already mentioned: commonality. The establishment and use of common structures has several important benefits. To begin with, common structures will help you in understanding and analyzing new programs. Most of us find it easier to determine the differences between two basically similar structures than to establish common features between two very different structures. Next, common structures will help you when you want to integrate pieces from several programs into a new program. You will more easily and correctly identify the specific pieces that need to be taken from each old program to do what you want in the new one. Finally, the use of a common structure within a program will aid you in maintaining and modifying the program. This occurs for many of the same reasons that you can easily take out pieces of the program: common structures allow you to isolate problems in specific sections of code and to encapsulate functions in a specific place.

The second desirable quality of any structure to be established for PostScript is page independence. This means that each section of PostScript code that produces a page of output should be independent of all other pages in the document. This goal is less obviously desirable than the first goal of commonality, but it is equally important. PostScript is, after all, a page-description language, and as such, its primary function is to produce pages on an output device. Most documents consist of more than one page of output, and therefore most PostScript programs will be employed in generating multiple pages. This simple fact gives rise to several of the standard PostScript structural conventions (which will be described in detail below), all of which work to provide page independence within a PostScript program. By following these conventions, each page of output, as it is created in PostScript memory, will not depend on anything done by or output from the preceding pages. With some thought, you will see why this is desirable. Without this independence, pages could not be proofed or printed separately, and changing or maintaining individual pages would be almost impossible. Most of all, without it, unintended and undesired remnants from previous pages might carry forward and ruin your current page output. For these reasons, it is important that each page be an independent description.

The third desirable quality in program structure is ease of reading. This may seem trivial compared to the first two objectives. I can assure you, however, that working on a program that is difficult to read is like Chinese water torture—insidious and excruciatingly painful. When a program is not easy to read, you must go back over procedures, definitions, and sections repeatedly to try to figure out what is being done.

RECOMMENDED STRUCTURE

Adobe Systems, the designer of PostScript, recommends following a straightforward, standard structure that will aid in achieving these admirable and desirable goals. There are four basic components in the recommended structure: header, prologue, script, and trailer. Each of the components plays an important role in establishing the overall structure of a PostScript program.

However, it is important to remember that PostScript has no required program structure; that is, the PostScript interpreter does not require any particular global information to process PostScript statements correctly. The only requirements (if they can be called that) are intuitive and natural: that variables and procedures be defined before they're used, that fonts be enabled before they're used, and so on—basic, obvious conditions like that.

This recommended structure is defined and described in Appendix C of the *PostScript Language Reference Manual,* which establishes global structural conventions to be used by any PostScript program. Published conventions like these are particularly important in any complex environment, where there may be a number of PostScript users, perhaps connected over a network and sharing various system resources such as printers or typesetters. In these circumstances, having common structures is essential if jobs are to be processed correctly and efficiently and if electronic and physical output are going to be returned to the correct destinations.

One of the major differences between PostScript and other page-description languages is that many of them have enforced global structures, while PostScript does not. This means that as the programmer you have a choice. You may adopt and implement all of the PostScript conventions; you may choose to work with a smaller subset of the conventions; or you may ignore or adapt the published conventions to suit your own requirements and your own environment. In many cases, you will be working in a dedicated environment, using PostScript on a microprocessor with a single PostScript output device. In this case, much of the recommended structure will be superfluous, and you may choose to work with only a minimum of overall structure to your programs.

The only thing to be cautious about in this situation is that, if your PostScript programs don't follow the standards, they may not be suitable to the more complex environment we discussed, and they may not be able to be used with certain useful types of application programs. A simple example of such an application would be a program to reorder the printing sequence of a document. Many laser printers stack output face up, so that the first page printed ends up face up on the bottom of the output. This creates a problem in handling long documents, because someone usually has to resequence the output. If the PostScript file that created the output is properly structured—that is, follows the standard conventions—then you can use an application program that will print the pages so that they come out of the printer in their natural order with the last page on the bottom and the first page on top. This type of application can only work when there is a well defined structure within the PostScript document.

Another simple example is the issue of fonts and font changes within a PostScript document. PostScript supports many more fonts than are intially loaded on a typical PostScript printer. Therefore, many documents may need fonts that have to be loaded to the printer before the document can be printed. The PostScript structure allows you to specify which fonts are required by a document, or even a page, so that an application, like a print spooler, can identify whether these fonts need to be downloaded to the printer prior to sending your document.

Similarly, many of the structuring conventions that are cumbersome and unnecessary in a dedicated system become essential in the more complex, networked environment. Since it requires only a little extra effort to create a PostScript program that follows the conventional structure, I strongly recommend that you follow at least the minimum structural guidelines. Upward compatibility should not be sacrificed lightly.

There are four sections required in a properly structured PostScript program: header, prologue, script, and trailer. The header and trailer segments of the program are devoted primarily to providing specific global information about the program contained between them. The most important point about the header and trailer sections is that, from the viewpoint of the PostScript interpreter, they consist of comments only and do not contain any executable PostScript code.

The *header* section contains two types of information. The first type is what might be termed "creation data." This information covers who created the document, when it was created, and so forth, and is primarily required in a networked environment for routing and other identification purposes. The second type of information contained in the header is document information covering the fonts used and other technical information that is primarily used by utility programs.

The *prologue* contains procedures, named variables, and constants that will be used throughout the rest of the document. The prologue will generally have been written by a programmer and then will be included as the first part of every document (or script) that requires it. The prologue will usually be relatively complex, with a variety of variables and nested procedures defined within it. The *script* describes the specific elements to be produced on the output pages in terms of procedures and variables defined in the prologue, along with operand data as required. Each page description is expected to depend only on the prologue and to be independent of all the other pages. The intention here is to produce any page correctly, given only the prologue and the description of that page. When the process is done well, each page description within the script will be relatively short and probably quite repetitive, using the same procedures over and over.

This distinction between the prologue and the script portions of your program is probably the most important point to understand about document structure. You have noticed that all of the exercises and examples have been separated into these two components. This separation is not just good PostScript structure; it is good programming structure in general. As we have discussed, this method of organizing your procedures and definitions into one prologue section is essential for creating understandable and useful code.

When you follow this division, each section has its own unique responsibilities. The prologue contains all the procedures and definitions and should never contain any executable code. The script contains no procedures or definitions and has only executable code and operand data. The two sections are perfect mirror images; like Jack Spratt and his wife, they make a perfectly matched couple.

Finally, there is a *trailer,* which contains clean-up information. This is a place for document information that couldn't be easily generated in the header sections. This facility is provided for application programs that are directly generating PostScript output and would otherwise have a problem providing the required document information in the header. For example, one of the required data items in the header is a list of fonts used in the document. This information is particularly important if the document requires nonstandard fonts that need to be downloaded to the printer prior to processing the document. If the PostScript output is being created by an application, however, it may be difficult to generate this information in the header, before the document itself has been created. Therefore, the structural conventions allow the font information to be deferred to the end of the document and put in the trailer section. You will see how this works when we discuss each of the sections and their contents in detail below.

To review, you see that a PostScript program that follows the recommended structure will consist of four elements. A header and trailer provide global information and enclose the entire PostScript document. The document description contains the remaining two parts of the structure: a prologue that contains procedures and global variables, and a script that describes each of the pages to be output. These four sections will always be presented within the program in the following sequence:

Header

Prologue

Script

Trailer

In addition to dividing your PostScript program into these four sections, there is another practice you should follow within the script portion of the program to ensure page independence. Every PostScript program that generates a printable document should maintain its own indicators of the current status of the PostScript document output. When the document crosses a major structural boundary, such as a page, the PostScript program should take steps to ensure that the new page is independent from all preceding pages and does not interfere with any subsequent ones.

This can most easily be accomplished by invoking two PostScript operators: **save** and **restore**. These operators have the following format:

Syntax	**Function**
— **save** savestate	saves the current state of the PostScript virtual memory as *save state*
savestate **restore** —	restores PostScript virtual memory to the state indicated by *save state*

Since **restore** returns to the state presented to it as an operand, it is usually easiest and best to **save** the current state as a named variable and **restore** that specific variable. If a **save** is performed at the beginning of each page, and a **restore** is performed at the end of each page to the state saved at the beginning, then each page will necessarily be independent. If you have followed the recommended structure and placed all of your global variables and procedural definitions into the prologue, then each page will only be dependent on the prologue and the code between the **save** and the **restore** for that page. This practice is the fastest and most efficient method for ensuring page independence.

SPECIFIC FORMAT

In order to provide the necessary global information for structure, PostScript has established specific formats for items to be included within the header, trailer, and script portions of the program. Remember that there is nothing magic about these formats, nor is there anything in the PostScript interpreter that will complain if your program doesn't follow them. There may be other utility or application programs that handle PostScript programs that require this structure and these specific formats; PostScript itself does not.

These specific format conventions also may be subject to change. The conventions described here have been established by Adobe Systems and published, as mentioned earlier, in Appendix C of the *PostScript Language Reference Manual*. These conventions are specifically described as "PS-Adobe-1.0."

The important point in this sectioning process is that pieces of the PostScript program should be able to be handled and reordered, if necessary, without interpreting or executing the PostScript code itself. However, as you have already seen, the PostScript interpreter doesn't require or support any of this structure. The requirement, then, is for a method of indicating structure within a PostScript program that will be easily identifiable but transparent to the interpreter.

You can meet this objective by using a special form of comment to indicate sections and to provide structural information within a Post-Script program. You have already been introduced to comments within a PostScript program. The standard PostScript comment begins with the character % and ends with a new line. Structural information in a PostScript program is contained in lines that begin with the characters %% or %! and end with a new line. As you can immediately see, such lines will be treated by the PostScript interpreter as comment lines and hence ignored. However, because the lines of structural information begin with this combination of special characters, they are distinguishable from ordinary comment lines by any utility or other application program that needs the information to work on a PostScript document. They also are immediately recognizable when you view your own code.

A PostScript program does not have to provide all the structuring information in order to meet the requirement above, but there is a minimum amount of information that is required. Programs that provide this minimum amount of information are said to be *minimally conforming*. In the context of our previous discussion, this means that the program lacks the type of structural information required in a complex, networked environment, but it still provides the information required and retains the structural markers necessary for utility processing.

Thus, PostScript programs can be divided into three categories. First are programs that provide all the structural data and follow the entire set of conventions. These are the *conforming* programs. Next are the *minimally conforming* programs that provide the minimum of structural data. And finally, any program that does not meet at least the minimum set of conventions is *nonconforming*.

Very recently, Adobe Systems has announced a new release of these format conventions, numbered "PS-Adobe-2.0". This new release extends the 1.0 conventions to provide additional structure for PostScript documents and addresses some new issues that were not part of the earlier conventions. Note particularly that release 2.0 is an extension of version 1.0; all existing 1.0 conventions are included as an integral part of the 2.0 structure.

The 2.0 structure now establishes three sets of conventions, relating to three distinct areas:

- structure comments
- resource requirements
- query conventions

Each of these conventions addresses specific needs that may be present in a document-processing environment.

The *structure comments* are used to delimit the various components of a PostScript document. All of the 1.0 comments are part of this category. These comments break the PostScript document into the segments described below, and they have been expanded in version 2.0 to include two additional types of information. The first is document and page setup information. This includes information relating to output routing, addressing, printer setup, font handling and similar issues. These may be thought of as management concerns, which may affect the document as an entity or as individual pages. The second type of information is a kind of page- or document-markup convention, which establishes the beginning and ending of particular pieces that may require separate or special processing. This demarcation is particularly important for certain segments of the document, which may need to be removed or ignored in order to be processed successfully in specialized environments.

The *resource requirements* are a new type of comment that specifies resources that are required to produce the PostScript document, but which have not been included within the text. Such resources might include fonts, procedures, and other forms of files that may need to be accessed separately to create the final document. This type of comment is also used to specify other document requirements, which may be as varied as a particular form or paper stock or a particular paper color or collating sequence.

The *query conventions* are a new type of comment, used to enclose parts of a PostScript program that establish particular environmental parameters. They do this by executing certain operators, which query the output device to determine various characteristics or features available on the specific device and take appropriate action. A full discussion of these issues and operators is beyond the scope of this book, but an example of such concerns would be a query to the printer regarding available fonts, for example.

A complete discussion of the version 2.0 conventions is presented in Appendix B. For the remainder of this chapter, we will continue explaining and working with the 1.0 conventions. Remember that these conventions are still applicable in Version 2.0.

There is one major difference between 1.0 and 2.0 that you should be aware of. Beginning with version 2.0, the notion of *minimally conforming* programs no longer exists. Instead, a document is said to be *conforming* if it obeys a proper subset of the 2.0 conventions. Clearly, any document that is either conforming or minimally conforming under the 1.0 conventions is now a conforming document file. In version 2.0, a document need only use those conventions that are appropriate and consistent. To be a conforming program, however, a document must use those conventions it does implement in the correct manner and according to the syntax and conventions set out in Appendix B.

Now we are ready to discuss the exact format of the structure comments, as set out in version 1.0. Note that you must enter these comments exactly as shown; they are not like the regular PostScript comments, which are freeform. These comments must begin with the two characters %% followed by a key word. There is no space between the %% characters and the key word. As in all PostScript commands, upper- and lowercase letters are distinct, so you must enter key words exactly as shown. In comments that require data, the key word is followed by a colon and again there are no spaces. There may be one or more data values whose exact interpretation depends on the key word. The first value is separated from the colon by one space, and each subsequent value is separated from the following value by one space. A newline character must appear immediately after the last value, or after the key word if there is no data.

Adobe Systems recommends that all PostScript programs begin with a comment line that starts with the characters %!. This has advantages in specific environments (such as UNIX); you'll know if you are working in such an environment. In the typical micro-based environment, there is no advantage to following this recommendation if you're not going to follow the other structural conventions. In a conforming or minimally conforming program, this first line gives information regarding the structuring of the program and is called the *version identifier*. For a conforming program, the line must look like this:

    %!PS-Adobe-1.0

This identifies the PostScript program as being fully conforming to the structural conventions set out in the *PostScript Language Reference Manual*, Appendix C, which have been given version number 1.0. These are the same conventions presented in this section. For a minimally conforming program, the first line should begin with

    %!PS-Adobe-

followed by anything you want, except 1.0. A program that begins with any other line is presumed to be nonconforming.

The *header* comments begin immediately after the version identifier and end with *EndComments* or with any line that doesn't begin with %%. Where specific information can be postponed to the trailer section, as described earlier, the appropriate header key word must be followed by the value **(atend)** instead of the data value or values described below. The following are header comments:

Syntax	Function
%%DocumentFonts: font font font ...	Lists the fonts used in the document by their PostScript names. This comment is required for minimally conforming

Syntax	**Function**
	programs, and it can be deferred to a trailer by use of the **(atend)** specification.
%%Title: title	Gives the title of the document. This can be any text and is terminated only by a new line. The title is used for identifying documents; in some environments, this might be a file name or it might be formatted to be machine-readable.
%%Creator: name	The name of the person, user, or program (or maybe all three) who generated the PostScript document. This name may be different from the person or user designated to receive the document, which may be designated by the %%*For* comment (see below). The name consists of any arbitrary text, terminated by a new line.
%%CreationDate: text	Gives the date and time of the creation of the document. There is no specific format for this information; all that is expected is that the text will be able to be read as a date and a time by the user. Generally, this will come from the

Syntax	Function
	system in whatever the standard system format may be.
%%For: userid	This is the identification of the person or user who receives the output; if this comment is absent, the output destination is presumed to be the same as that indicated by as the %%Creator comment.
%%Pages: number	This is a nonnegative, decimal integer that represents the number of pages expected to be produced on the output device. If no pages will be output, the number 0 should be inserted. This comment also can be deferred to the trailer section by use of **(atend)**.
%%BoundingBox: llx lly urx ury	This gives the dimensions of the box that bounds all of the marks on a PostScript page. If the PostScript program produces more than one page, this is the largest box that bounds any page. The values are the x and y coordinates of the lower-left and upper-right corners of the page, given in the default user coordinate system. This comment may be

Syntax	**Function**
	deferred to the trailer section by means of **(atend)**.
%%EndComments	This comment explicitly ends the header section of the PostScript program. It is not required, since any line that does not begin with the characters %% or %! will terminate the header automatically, as explained above.

The body comments break up the executable portion of a PostScript program into the prologue and the individual pages of the script. If a utility program acts on a structured PostScript program, it must respect these markers and keep the structure intact as it operates on the program text. In particular, it must retain the prologue at the beginning (since the pages in the script portion depend on it), and it must retain any trailer information at the end.

The *prologue* starts either with the first line of the PostScript program that does not begin with the characters %% or %!, or with the first line after the *EndComments* statement that terminates the header section. The only comment in the prologue is the following:

Syntax	**Function**
%%EndProlog	Explicitly terminates the prologue section of the PostScript program. This comment is required in minimally conforming programs.

The *script* begins with the first line of the PostScript program following the *EndProlog*. The following comments are placed in the script code to mark page boundaries and to provide page information:

Syntax	**Function**
%%Page: label number	Marks the beginning of an individual page in the

Syntax

Function

document. The *label* and the *number* identify the page according to two methods. The *label* value is a text string that gives the page identification according to the document's internal-numbering or labeling scheme. For example, this might be page ix of the Introduction or page 2–4 (meaning the fourth page of Chapter 2, for example). The *number,* however, is a positive integer that gives the position of this page within the normal document output. This number begins at 1 and runs through *n* for an *n*-page document.

This information is intended to be useful to utility programs; using this, they can retrieve pages either by the internal page descriptions, that is, "pages 2–4 through 2–9," or by position, that is, "the last 10 pages." It also allows pages to be handled in nonsequential order; for example, if you wanted to produce pages in folio order for bookbinding.

Syntax	**Function**
	This comment is required in minimally conforming programs.
%%PageFonts: font font font	This comment lists the fonts required on the current page. These will be a subset of the fonts listed in the *%%DocumentFonts* header. Generally, this comment is only useful where there are many fonts being used within a document, and you (or an application or utility program) need to manage the fonts at the output device on a page level. This usually happens when the number of fonts in a document exceeds the memory capacity of the output device.

The script ends with the following comment:

Syntax	**Function**
%%Trailer	Ends the script portion of the program and marks the beginning of the trailer section (if any). This comment is required for minimally conforming programs. Any noncomment PostScript commands that follow this comment are presumed to be cleanup or otherwise not part of the page output.

The *trailer* section, like the header, contains only comments and begins immediately after the *Trailer* comment that terminates the script. The required portion of the trailer section consists of information that has been deferred from the header section by means of the **(atend)** parameter. The three pieces of information that can be deferred are *DocumentFonts*, *Page*, and *BoundingBox*. If none of these have been deferred, there is no trailer section required.

The order of the header and trailer comments is not generally significant. It becomes important only if there is more than one comment with the same key word. In that case, the data from the first header with the duplicated key word is retained and used; for a trailer, the data is taken from the *last* key word. This allows a utility program to modify the header and trailer information by placing the new header at the front of the PostScript program—after the version identifier, of course—and placing a new trailer at the end of the program, without having to delete any of the previous structural data. Remember, however, that the trailer data will be used only if there is a header with the same key word and the **(atend)** data specification.

In Version 2.0, the structure comments are divided up in a slightly different manner, as follows:

- header comments
- body comments
- page comments

The header comments serve the same functions as set out above, but the number and scope of the comments is greatly enlarged. The body comments provide structure for the document as a whole, or about multiple-page segments of the document. These comments include the **%% Trailer** comment and associated comments presented above. Finally, the page comments give information about structure within a given page and usually occur once for each output page.

In the next chapter, with the next exercise, we will begin following the 1.0 structural conventions explicitly so that you can see how they look in the context of a PostScript program.

PROGRAM STYLE

Everyone who writes programs has a programming style, just as anyone who writes a paragraph has a prose style; style is just your personal way of organizing your thoughts and expressing yourself in a language. It's easy enough to understand what "style" means in regard to natural language, but what does it mean when applied to writing programs, particularly in PostScript?

As we briefly discussed earlier in the chapter, there are two components to programming style. These may be thought of as global structure and local structure. Global structure includes where you put procedural definitions, how you name variables and constants and where you define them, and how you structure program flow. Local structure covers decisions regarding indentation, line breaks, and use of comments.

The preceding sections of this chapter have explained in detail how you might approach global structure for a PostScript program. Some of this structure is contained in the recommended (but not required) structural format using the comments previously described. Some of the global structure is inherent in the nature of the PostScript language itself, such as how you create and use procedures. Overall, at this point, you should have a clear understanding of these issues.

STRUCTURED DESIGN

There is one more point that you should know regarding PostScript program structure in the global sense. I would like to emphasize the elegance and strength of the PostScript language and how the structure of the language naturally and easily supports structured program design.

This is not an appropriate place for an extensive discussion of structured design—indeed, several good books and articles cover this topic. It is worthwhile to point out, however, that the structured approach to program design is accepted as one of the best and least error-prone of the approaches to analysis and implementation of complex program tasks. And, as you can see from the examples so far, to output even a simple page of text and graphics quickly becomes a complex task.

Program design is the part of the programming process that develops the structure and logic of a program. This involves two main steps: first, to identify the tasks that must be performed to produce the desired output, and second, to develop the logic to implement each of the required tasks. Typically, a programmer will spend a significant amount of time on program design. If the program design has been done correctly, the resulting code will be efficient, reliable, robust (meaning it won't fail under unusual circumstances), and maintainable.

All this emphasizes the importance of effective program design and the need for an approach to program design that will help ensure these qualities. The structured approach provides such a methodology.

This approach was first described by IBM computer scientists in 1974. Structured design is a methodology that breaks large and complex program tasks into many small groups of functions, called modules. Each module performs one and only one function within a program. A large and complex program is then built by combining many of these modules into a larger programming structure to accomplish the desired task.

You can see that this process fits naturally into the PostScript coding format. This is the "onionization" process that was described before and is built into PostScript structures. This is also the process that you will follow throughout the examples; it produces excellent results.

LOCAL STRUCTURE

Global structure has been the main focus and concern of this chapter until now, primarily because global structure has a much greater impact on the overall usefulness of a program than local structure. However, you will generally discover that good global structure is supported by good local structure, and vice versa. So there are some points to make regarding local structure in your PostScript code.

There are basically three decisions involved in local structure: where to break lines, how to indent code, and how to use comments. With the exception of the few rules about breaking lines in comments and so on, PostScript does not provide much guidance on issues of local structure. Essentially, in this area, as in the area of names and naming conventions, you are free to do whatever you decide based on your best judgement and experience. While it is your personal choice and style that will decide what conventions you use, I would offer you some advice and suggestions.

The first advice is in regard to indentation and line breaks. These should be used as tools to clarify the overall structure of your program, and there are three rules to follow for best results. First, use line breaks at every logical operation and try to keep one operator to a line; where you decide not to do this (for example, when setting fonts), at least keep one logical thought to a line. Second, use indentation to create an outline format for your procedures. This is particularly important and useful when you are doing logical tests. Finally, be consistent in your use of these tools. Don't put multiple operators together one time and then put them all on separate lines another time. If you look back at the previous exercises, you will see how I have chosen to structure procedures and variables.

Consistency is particularly important in PostScript. Of course, consistency within any program is essential; but with PostScript, you will find that you develop a library of common routines to accomplish certain functions. You will come to rely on these routines and to include them in many of your programs. As you do so, you will discover that such routines need to follow a common format for maintainability and utility in a wide variety of programs.

The use of comments is also a personal decision. Many program instruction books recommend using many comments for clarity and explanation. Personally, I find them less useful than good notes or other documentation, and I generally don't trust them—too often, someone has changed the code and not the comment. Nevertheless, they are useful and have a place in your local conventions. I would recommend that you use them in at least three places. First, use comments as full lines to break the prologue and script into useful sections. Second, use them at the beginning of procedures to describe what the procedure does, what it expects on the stack, and what (if anything) it returns to the stack. It is probably useful to establish some standard format for this information, particularly for your library routines. We will give an example of such a format with the next exercise. And, finally, use comments to annotate any portion of the program that is especially unusual or complex or otherwise out of the ordinary.

OPERATOR REVIEW

This section presents the same information given earlier in the chapter for a variety of operators. It is repeated here for your review and convenience.

DICTIONARY OPERATORS

Syntax	Function
int **dict** dict	creates a dictionary *dict* with the capacity for *int* value pairs
dict **begin** —	pushes *dict* onto the dictionary stack and makes it the current dictionary

Syntax	Function
— **end** —	pops the current dictionary from the dictionary stack
key value **def** —	associates *key* and *value* in the current dictionary

CONTROL OPERATORS

Syntax	Function
{proc} **exec**	executes *proc*
int {proc} **repeat**	executes *proc int* times
init incr lim {proc} **for**	executes *proc* for values from *init* by steps of *incr* until reaching *lim*
bool {proc} **if**	executes *proc* if *bool* is true
bool {proc1} {proc2} **ifelse**	executes *proc1* if *bool* is true and executes *proc2* otherwise
{proc} **loop**	executes *proc* an indefinite number of times
exit	terminates the active loop

RELATIONAL OPERATORS

Syntax	Function
any1 any2 **eq** bool	tests whether *any1* is equal to *any2*
any1 any2 **ne** bool	tests whether *any1* is not equal to *any2*

Syntax				Function
num1	num2			
(str1)	(str2)	**ge**	bool	tests whether *num1* or *str1* is greater than or equal to *num2* or *str2*
num1	num2			
(str1)	(str2)	**gt**	bool	tests whether *num1* or *str1* is greater than *num2* or *str2*
num1	num2			
(str1)	(str2)	**le**	bool	tests whether *num1* or *str1* is less than or equal to *num2* or *str2*
num1	num2			
(str1)	(str2)	**lt**	bool	tests whether *num1* or *str1* is less than *num2* or *str2*

LOGICAL OPERATORS

Syntax				Function
int1	int2		lint	
bool1	bool2	**and**	bool	logical or bitwise and
int1	int2		int	
bool1	bool2	**or**	bool	logical or bitwise inclusive or
int1	int2		int	
bool1	bool2	**xor**	bool	logical or bitwise exclusive or
int		int		
bool	**not**	bool		logical or bitwise not
—	**true**	bool		pushes the boolean value *true* onto the stack
—	**false**	bool		pushes the boolean value *false* onto the stack

STATE OPERATORS

Syntax	Function
— **save** savestate	saves the current state of the PostScript virtual memory as *save state*
savestate **restore** —	restores PostScript virtual memory to the state indicated by *save state*

3

*Introduction
to Fonts
and Graphics*

THIS CHAPTER INTRODUCES A VARIETY OF POSTSCRIPT GRAPHICS CONCEPTS AND OPERATORS. IT ALSO PROVIDES a formal introduction to and discussion of PostScript fonts, which you have been using informally so far.

The chapter begins with a section on basic PostScript graphics concepts. Most of this section is an expanded discussion of PostScript page layout and an introduction to PostScript graphics. The section leads into these topics by examining the nature of PostScript graphic images. This nature is precisely defined by and primarily a function of PostScript's target output devices, which are examined in detail.

The exploration of page layout revives issues that were discussed in Chapter 1 in a less formal and detailed manner. After this review, you are introduced to simple PostScript graphics constructions. There are several examples using straight-line segments to illustrate both the old concepts and new operational issues. The examples proceed from straight-line segments to the creation of closed figures made from straight lines. Then the figures are filled with shades of gray. The examples proceed naturally, each building on the previous work so that you can easily follow the structure.

The examples also illustrate how to create procedures that generate standard shapes and how such procedures can best be structured to be useful on a variety of pages and in a range of formats. These issues of flexibility and independence, which are tightly connected, will remain with us throughout the chapter.

The next section is concerned with fonts and PostScript font machinery and also recapitulates some of the earlier material about text and text output. The section starts with some observations and definitions regarding fonts generally and proceeds to the specifics of PostScript fonts. This is an important topic. The section does not require any operators other than the ones you are already familiar with; however, the actual function of each of the operators is discussed in detail, whereas before you were only given minimal information for practical application.

Because PostScript treats fonts and text as graphics objects, you need to have some insight into the PostScript font machinery to establish real control over text output. The ultimate objective is to understand the process and be able to manipulate text and graphics output comfortably on a PostScript page.

The third section of the chapter continues the previous discussion of the use of graphics. It adds curved-line segments to straight lines and produces a series of examples similar to the examples developed around straight lines. This work leads into an examination of the PostScript coordinate structure and PostScript methods for transforming an ideal page—which is what you are working on—into a concrete page of output on a specific device. This PostScript facility, which is inherent in the PostScript design objective of device independence, can also be used advantageously by the PostScript programmer to adjust the page. The three most common adjustments are translation, rotation, and scaling of coordinates. Each of these is discussed in detail, with examples.

But coordinate adjustment is only part of the story. The section continues by returning to the issues of procedure construction that were raised earlier in the chapter. Now you have all the concepts and tools to make independent and flexible graphics procedures. This portion of the chapter shows you, by discussion and example, how to do that.

The chapter ends with a fifth exercise that uses all the preceding work and integrates the techniques that you have been reading about and practicing. In this exercise you will create a simple, stylized logo for an imaginary company. The logo is reasonably complex and yet simple to create with the tools you have been learning. This exercise also leads into the next chapter, which uses the logo as a graphics element in a simple document.

GRAPHICS CONCEPTS AND BASICS

PostScript was designed from its inception as a language with powerful graphics capabilities. The PostScript language has many features in common with other computer languages, since it addresses the same or similar tasks and must overcome the same problems as they do. But PostScript goes far beyond traditional computer-language tasks to provide the ability to handle and output graphics images of all types. In many ways, all the other features of PostScript are centered on and support this unique capacity to describe graphics objects.

You have already been introduced to the PostScript graphics concept of "painting onto a page"; that is, rendering an image or other graphic onto an output device. This is a natural and intuitive way to think about graphics; and this conceptual model of graphic output is satisfactory because, to a great extent, it approximates what graphic artists actually do as they work. However, the computer and its associated output devices do not work in that way; they require their instructions in mathematical forms.

I make this point simply to explain the necessary intrusion of certain mathematical concepts into portions of this chapter. By their design, PostScript graphics operators insulate the user from most mathematical considerations. There is, however, an irreducible minimum of mathematical information that is involved in particular graphics objects. Take a circle as a good, simple example. When a graphic artist wishes to put a specific circle on a specific page, he or she need only pick the place and draw the circle. To create a circle on a laser printer, however, requires two mathematical data: a radius (or diameter) and a center. This is what I mean by the "irreducible minimum" of mathematics that will intrude upon us as we proceed through the chapter.

To continue with the circle as an example, PostScript does not have a simple operator that produces a circle. Instead, PostScript has operators that produce arcs, arbitrary portions of a circle. These operators can then be used, with the proper operands, to create a new procedure that will generate a circle. In fact, you will create and use such a procedure in the last exercise in this chapter. By combining PostScript graphics operators into such procedures, you will be able to generate a wide array of graphics objects for your use. This chapter will show you the basics of the creation and use of such procedures.

GRAPHIC IMAGES

Human beings have a strong visual orientation. Our languages are full of visual imagery. In English, we say "I see" when we mean that we understand something, and the saying "a picture is worth a thousand words" has become a cliché. It is this visual orientation that inspires the need to render images into a permanent and concrete form, through pictures or other graphics.

A variety of means is available to create images. The most ancient, surely, is to apply paint or some other opaque medium to a prepared surface. By this method we get paintings and drawings of all types: oil, watercolor, acrylic, enamel, and so forth; and by extension we have collage and similar assemblies. Another method of capturing or creating images is through photography, by using light to create chemical changes on special media, which can then be translated into images. This happens because the images are captured by millions of tiny dots on the photographic surface. All methods of rendering images involve one or another of these techniques, or a combination of both.

Printing, if you think about it in these terms, is painting with ink. With text, each character on a printed page is a continuous line of ink, just like a line in a drawing. When it comes to reproducing pictures or graphic images that don't involve lines, however, modern printing technology, on high-speed presses, becomes more like the photographic process. An image is broken down into a set of dots, which are then grouped together to render the image onto paper. This process of grouping dots to recreate an image is called *screening,* and it plays in important role in PostScript image handling.

RASTER OUTPUT DEVICES

The PostScript language is designed to work with a general class of output devices, known as *raster output devices.* You may be surprised to learn that the television is the original and prototypical raster output device; in fact, that's where the term "raster" comes from. Raster devices are characterized by having a number of dots that are activated in some manner to make up an image. On a television screen, these dots are composed of phosphorescent material activated by a beam of electrons, but the dots may be created by any mechanism. Essentially, the image is created by using dots and a screening process, just like the printing process described above. Unlike printing, however, raster output devices render text characters as a series of dots; there is no such thing as a continuous line on these devices.

Each dot on a raster output device represents one picture element, or *pixel.* Although these elements are also conventionally called "dots," this is a generic term and doesn't necessarily represent the actual pixel shape. Pixels may be round, square, oval, or rectangular—whatever shape is most appropriate and convenient for the specific output device manufacturer. Generally, pixels, like binary numbers, are either off or on, zero or one. You can immediately understand how well this concept fits into a digital-processing framework.

Some devices have pixels that can be varied in intensity by various methods. This translates into more than binary values for each dot. Even in devices with a single intensity, pixels may be grouped together by the screening process to create the effect of varying intensity.

As so often in life, there are advantages and disadvantages to this process of composing in dots. The advantage is that this mechanism produces both text and graphics without distinction. Each character or image is simply a set of pixels to be set appropriately. The disadvantage is that there is not a continuous boundary for a character or other graphic, so that, at the finest and smallest level, all objects look ragged and uneven.

RESOLUTION

Naturally, the intention is to produce text or graphics that appear continuous to the eye, although ultimately they are composed of dots. This illusion of continuity is created by having a large number of dots, or pixels, in a given area. The number of pixels per unit area is called the *device resolution*.

Because resolution is measured by area, it has both horizontal and vertical components. Many devices have identical resolution in both directions; such devices generally provide resolution measurements as *dots per inch,* or dpi. Where the resolution is different in the horizontal and vertical directions, each resolution must be expressed separately, such as 240 by 300 dpi.

Obviously, the greater the device resolution, the better it can fool the eye into seeing a continuous line instead of a string of dots. But even on devices of high resolution, there is still the issue of how to define the boundary of an image. This process is particularly critical for text characters because quick recognition of the distinctive shapes of characters has a major impact on speed and ease of reading. This issue of adjustment of pixels at image boundaries is called *tuning,* and although it is important, it is also extremely device dependent. This is just one reason to choose an intermediary language like PostScript, which provides both flexibility and control without requiring concern about specific device characteristics.

DEVICE CLASSIFICATION

It should be clear from this discussion that all typewriters and similar devices are not raster output devices. This includes old-style "letter quality" printers, which are essentially based on typewriter technology. Such devices rely on preformed letters or shapes, and ink onto paper transfer to produce their results. They have no screen facilities and so cannot successfully represent generalized images.

Dot matrix printers, even though they are impact printers, are raster output devices, with resolutions typically between 100 and 200 dpi. Most page printers—laser printers, ink-jet printers, and so on—have resolutions between 300 and 600 dpi. Typesetting machines, using photographic techniques to create pixels, achieve resolutions between 1000 and 2800 dpi; some very high resolution systems go even higher.

Obviously, higher resolution devices have more information per unit of area and so impose significantly greater demands on system resources, such as computational power. All of this is reflected in higher costs for using such devices.

Displays on computer terminals are also raster output devices. These generally have the lowest resolution of the raster output devices, ranging between 50 and 100 dpi. At such low resolutions, tuning becomes most important and poor tuning is most noticeable. For this reason, text characters and graphics figures may appear ragged on the terminal, although they will appear smooth enough on a higher resolution device, such as a laser printer.

POSTSCRIPT GRAPHICS CONCEPTS

At this point you are familiar with PostScript page structure and the PostScript page coordinate system both from your previous reading and from the exercises. Let's quickly review these key concepts now to set the stage for further discussion.

PostScript operates on an ideal page, called the current page. Positions on the page are given by x and y coordinates that work like mathematical coordinate systems. The origin, point (0, 0), is in the bottom-left corner of the page; movement in the x-coordinate is horizontal with positive movement toward the right of the page, while positive movement in the vertical, or y-coordinate, direction is up the page. The default coordinate units are 1/72 inch.

LINE CONCEPTS

PostScript creates images on the page by tracing a current path, which can then be "painted" to become visible. There are several methods of painting the current path. The end of the current path is the current point. So far, you have not actually dealt with the current path; you have only moved the current point around on the page to govern the location for text output. Working with a specific current path wasn't necessary because the **show** operator, which is used for text output, handles those issues automatically. Now that you are starting to produce graphics, however, you need additional information, along with more operators, to deal with the current path.

The current path can be composed of both straight- and curved-line segments, and it can also have multiple, discontinuous segments. The path may close or cross itself, creating enclosed areas or figures on the page. Remember that the current path itself is not visible; it is only made visible on the page by painting operators, which have various properties that will be explained later. Finally, after all the desired areas have been painted onto the page, the page must be output on the device by specific commands.

OPERATOR REVIEW

You have already used several of the most basic PostScript operators that relate to the current page. The **moveto** operator sets the current point to the given coordinates, and **show** paints a given text string onto the current page at the current point. The **show** operator also sets the current point to the position following the last character of the output string. Finally, you have used both the **showpage** and the **copypage** operators to create output on the printer.

SIMPLE LINES

Not all output is text, however; and if text was all you wanted to output, you could find many ways other than PostScript to produce it. You will begin to develop your PostScript graphics vocabulary in this section by learning to draw simple, straight lines. All of the examples in this chapter will assume that you are already in the interactive mode, at the PS> prompt, and ready to proceed.

For the first example, create two lines, 2 inches long and each beginning at a point 3 inches from the left edge of the paper and 6 inches from the bottom edge. This can be done with the code in Figure 3.1. This produces the page of output in Figure 3.2.

From here on, for simple examples like this, I won't show you the entire page, but just the relevant figure output. By now you understand the PostScript coordinate system and can reasonably picture the location of these figures on the page.

This short program introduces several new operators. The **inch** procedure, on line %1, is already an old friend; you will see it again and again in these examples. Line %2 moves to the position designated as the beginning of the lines, 3 inches from the left side and 6 inches from the bottom of the page. The next line contains the first new operator, **lineto**. This operator takes x and y coordinates as its operands and draws the current line from the current point to the designated point. The designated point then becomes the current point. The effect is just

```
%Begin simple line example
/inch                                              %1
     {       72 mul   }
     def
3 inch 6 inch moveto                               %2
5 inch 6 inch lineto                               %3
stroke                                             %4
newpath                                            %5
.1 inch setlinewidth                               %6
3 inch 6 inch moveto                               %7
3 inch 8 inch lineto                               %8
stroke                                             %9
showpage                                           %10
%all done
```

Figure 3.1: A simple line example

like that of putting your pencil down on the current point and moving it up to a designated spot on the page. The **lineto** operator doesn't actually make a mark on the current page; remember, that is done by the **stroke** operator in line %4.

That completes the first line, which is 2 inches horizontally. You know it is because the coordinates of the end of the line, given to **lineto** in line %3, are 2 inches further in the x-direction than the current point, which was set in line %2; and the coordinates are the same in the y-direction. The next line will be 2 inches vertically, because the coordinates will be 2 inches greater in the y-direction and the same in the x-direction.

Line %5 presents another new operator, **newpath**. This operator does just what you would expect: it clears the current path. Note that it doesn't erase the line you have already painted onto the page; it only eliminates any segments of the current path that have not been painted.

This is followed by another new operator, **setlinewidth**. This operator sets the width of the current line to the given number. Here, you have defined a line 0.1 inches wide. The default width of a line is 1 unit, or 1/72 inch, which is what the first line was. Then lines %7 through %9 repeat the actions of lines %2 to %4 and create another line; however, this time it's a thicker, vertical line instead of a horizontal one.

Finally, line %10 outputs the entire page with a **showpage** in the usual fashion. This is a simple procedure, and yet it illustrates several important PostScript graphics commands.

The next example is a variation on the theme. Let's mark two X's on the page, along the same line, 5 inches from the bottom of the page. The first X will be on the left side of the page, 3 inches from the left edge; the second will be on the right, 6 inches from the left edge. Each X will be 1 inch high and 1 inch wide.

Before you begin coding, briefly review Figure 3.3 with me. This figure lays out the coordinates for the first X in inches. Note the coordinates of the ends of the crossed lines that form the X. As you can see, we need to draw two lines to make up the figure: one, from the lower left (3, 5) to the upper right (4, 6); and the second, from the lower right (4, 5) to the upper left (3, 6). Of course, which end of the line you choose to start from is arbitrary; either line could just as well be drawn in the opposite direction. I will leave it to you to work out the coordinates of the second X.

Figure 3.2: First example output: a vertical and a horizontal line

The second example is shown in Figure 3.4. Note two points about the coding before you begin. First, if you are continuing from the previous example without exiting from PostScript, you don't need to define the **inch** procedure again; but it won't hurt anything if you do. Second, if you have just started the PostScript interpreter, the **newpath** command is not strictly necessary since nothing is in the current path; but again, it can't hurt anything, and it is a good habit to get into. As you would expect, the program produces two X's on a line, as in Figure 3.5.

There are no new operators in this short program, and nothing should come as a surprise. We have already discussed lines %1 and %2; whether you need them depends on whether you are starting PostScript fresh or

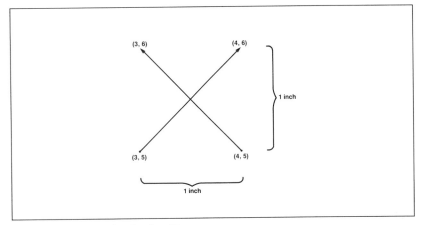

Figure 3.3: Layout for the first X

```
%Begin second example
newpath                            %1
/inch                              %2
     { 72 mul }
       def
%Do first X at (3, 5)
3 inch 5 inch moveto               %3
4 inch 6 inch lineto               %4
4 inch 5 inch moveto               %5
3 inch 6 inch lineto               %6
stroke                             %7
%Do second X at (6, 5)
6 inch 5 inch moveto               %8
7 inch 6 inch lineto               %9
7 inch 5 inch moveto               %10
6 inch 6 inch lineto               %11
stroke                             %12
%Now to show the output
showpage                           %13
quit                               %14
```

Figure 3.4: Second example: two X's on a line

Figure 3.5: Second example output

are continuing from previous work. In either case, you are familiar with these operators. We have already discussed the endpoint coordinates of the first X; in lines %3 and %4 you see how the first line of the X is constructed. Then you move your electronic "pencil" to the opposite corner of the X and make the second line. Finally, you ink in the two lines with the **stroke** command in line %7. The second X is constructed in an identical fashion, but starting, as defined, at the point (6, 5). Then the entire page is printed, and you're done.

To finish this section on simple lines, let's review the operators that have been introduced here and put them in our conventional format.

Syntax	Function
num1 num2 **lineto** —	Adds a straight-line segment to the current path. The line segment extends from the current point to the *num1* x-coordinate and the *num2* y-coordinate. The new current point is (*num1, num2*).
num **setlinewidth** —	Sets the current line width to *num*. This controls the thickness of the lines painted by subsequent **stroke** operators.
— **stroke** —	Paints a line following the current path and using the current color.
— **newpath** —	Initializes the current path to be empty and causes the current point to be undefined.

CLOSED FIGURES

Now that you can draw straight lines, let's use those lines to make some figures. Closed figures are just a collection of lines (straight or otherwise) that finish at the point where they began. Figures of this type are certainly some of the most typical graphics elements, and PostScript has several operators to help you construct and display them.

The first two examples of this section will draw squares at various points on the page; and all dimensions, as before, will be in inches. These two examples will have similar features, but will be positioned at different places on the page so that you can do them in one session with the interpreter, if you want to.

In the first example of the set, you will draw a 1-inch square with its bottom-left corner at the point (3, 5); that is, 3 inches from the left edge of the page and 5 inches from the bottom edge. Then you will move to the point (6, 5) and draw a box that is tilted to the left, so that the bottom of the box is a line from (6, 5) to the point (7, 6), like the first line of the X in the last example. The layout of these two squares is shown in Figure 3.6.

The essence of any closed figure is that the original line returns to its starting point. PostScript provides a special operator to close a figure, the **closepath** operator. There is a particular reason to use this operator to finish a figure, which is not entirely obvious. As you saw in the earlier examples, PostScript lines have an actual width, like the stroke of a brush or of a calligraphic pen. Since a line begins and ends precisely at the designated points, which are in the middle of the stroke, if you return the line to the starting point using most PostScript operators, you will have a small space at the end of the line—where it joins the original line—that is not filled in. This is illustrated in Figure 3.7.

This problem can be avoided by using the **closepath** operator. If you use **lineto** or any other PostScript operator to finish the figure and close the path, the interpreter doesn't register that this last junction of lines is anything special; when you use **closepath**, it will finish the figure and fill in the resulting join for you automatically.

The program for these first two figures is shown in Figure 3.8. It produces the output in Figure 3.9.

This example is really straightforward and only has one new operator, **closepath**, which has already been discussed. Each box is begun by moving to the desired location. Then each side of the square is put in by drawing a line to the next corner of the box, as in Figure 3.6. The **close-path** operator returns the line to the starting point from the last corner,

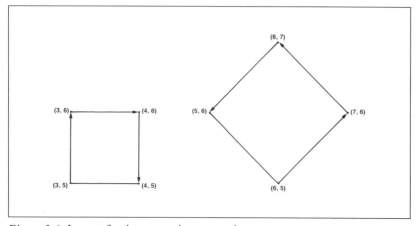

Figure 3.6: Layout for the square box example

finishing the four sides. Finally, the **stroke** operator inks the four sides of the box. The only possible surprise here may be the use of **copypage** for output; I did that so both this example and the next example will show on the next page. If you want, you can use **showpage** instead and leave these boxes off the next page of output.

The next example produces two boxes identical to the first two, but it uses some new operators to create them *relative* to a starting point—in this case, the first coordinate, the lower-left corner of the first box.

These two new operators are **rmoveto** and **rlineto**. These are identical to the two matching operators, **moveto** and **lineto**, with which you are already acquainted, except that the operands these new operators use are relative to the current point rather than absolute page coordinates. Let's use the first square as an example.

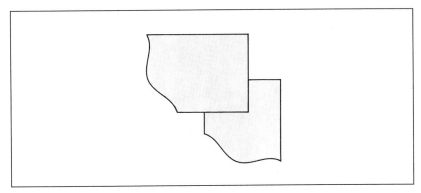

Figure 3.7: Line join

```
%Begin square box example
/inch                                          %1
      { 72 mul }
      def
newpath                                        %2
%Do first square
3 inch   5 inch   moveto                        %3
3 inch   6 inch   lineto                        %4
4 inch   6 inch   lineto                        %5
4 inch   5 inch   lineto                        %6
closepath                                      %7
stroke                                         %8
%Do second square
6 inch   5 inch   moveto                        %9
7 inch   6 inch   lineto                        %10
6 inch   7 inch   lineto                        %11
5 inch   6 inch   lineto                        %12
closepath                                      %13
stroke                                         %14
%Now see what was done
copypage                                       %15
```

Figure 3.8: Square box example

This square is 1 inch on each side. Using **lineto**, you must calculate the coordinates of each corner of the square to use as operands. Thus you start at (3, 5), make a line up to (3, 6), go across to (4, 6) and down to (4, 5), and then close the path back to the starting point. Using **rlineto** instead, you can code this as starting at (3, 5)—just as before—but then moving 1 inch on the y-axis and 0 units on the x-axis, relative to the current point. This takes you to the next corner, just as before, and from there you proceed 1 inch in the x-direction and 0 units in the y-direction

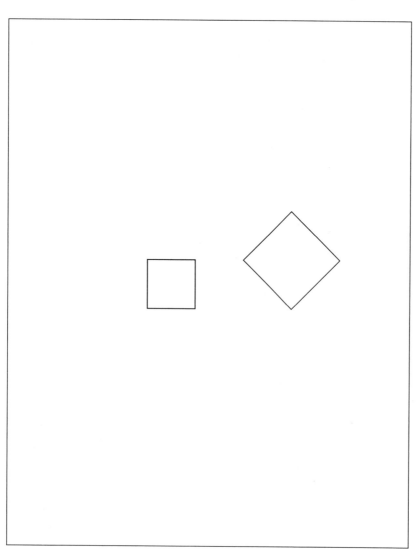

Figure 3.9: Square box example output

to the next corner, and so on. All of this is shown in Figure 3.10.

In the first example, after you finished the first square, you moved the current point to the corner of the next box, (6, 5). Now you can move the current point relative to the corner of the first box to start the second box. This distance, as shown in Figure 3.10, is 3 inches in the x-direction and 0 units in the y-direction. These new commands are valuable precisely because they do not require that you know where on the page you began; they simply allow you to create movement and lines relative to where you are at this moment on the page. When we construct graphics procedures, you will see how useful this facility is.

The program for our new boxes is given in Figure 3.11. Note that the set of boxes now begins at the point (3, 2) rather than (3, 5). This allows

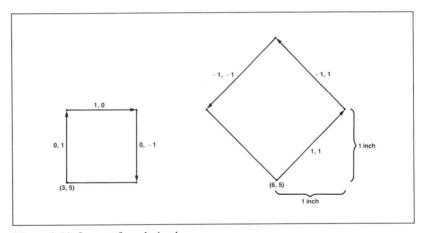

Figure 3.10: Layout for relative boxes

```
%Begin second square box example
/inch                                           %1
        { 72 mul }
        def
newpath                                         %2
%Do first square
3 inch  2 inch  moveto                          %3
0   1 inch   rlineto                            %4
1 inch  0  rlineto                              %5
0  -1 inch   rlineto                            %6
closepath                                       %7
%Do second square
3 inch  0 inch  rmoveto                         %8
1 inch   1 inch   rlineto                       %9
-1 inch  1 inch  rlineto                        %10
-1 inch  -1 inch  rlineto                       %11
closepath                                       %12
stroke                                          %13
%Now see what was done
showpage                                        %14
```

Figure 3.11: Relative boxes example

you to print both sets of boxes on one page, if you used **copypage** before, and compare them. You may find this instructive. The program produces the output in Figure 3.12, which is indistinguishable from that produced by the first example, shown above it in the figure.

The output from this program was designed to be identical to that from the previous example. When you look at the two programs, you will immediately notice that they are almost identical as well, except that the

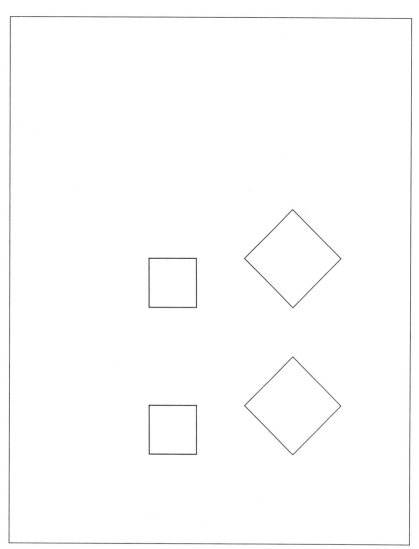

Figure 3.12: Relative box example output

equivalent relative commands have been substituted for the prior operators and there is only one **stroke** operator. The only absolute coordinates in the program are in line %3, which is the first **moveto**. This must have an absolute coordinate. The previous **newpath** command has cleared the current path, and consequently, no current point is defined. Therefore, there is nothing to move relative to, and the use of any relative operator (or any operator that requires a current point to work from, such as **lineto**) would give you an error.

You also notice that, in this example, you have drawn both boxes before you issue the painting command, **stroke**. The previous example could have been done in the same way, using one painting command, if you wanted to. However, in this example, it is essential to paint the figures only once because **stroke** erases the current path as it works, having the same effect as a **newpath**. If you painted the first box at the same point in the program as in the preceding exercise, before moving on to the second box, you would get an error in this program, because the **rmoveto** command would have no current point to move from. Therefore, you only stroke the path once, at the end of the procedure.

It is important to note that this program will work at any point on the page, once you have changed the coordinates in line %3. Thus, if you set line %3 to point (3, 5), as in the first example, none of the remaining code would have to be altered to produce the two boxes at exactly the same points. In contrast, if you tried to reuse the code from the previous example, you would have to change every coordinate, which means almost every line. You can see how you can use these relative commands to great advantage in creating procedures. You will put this knowledge to use in the next section as you continue to develop graphics.

Before you leave this section, let's recap in the standard format the operators that have been introduced here.

Syntax	Function
num1 num2 **rmoveto** —	(relative moveto) starts a new segment of the current path in the same manner as **moveto**. However, the new current point is defined from the current point (x, y) to x + *num1* as an x-coordinate and y + *num2* as a y-coordinate. The new

Syntax	**Function**
	current point is (x + *num1*, y + *num2*).
num1 num2 **rlineto** —	(relative lineto) adds a straight-line segment to the current path in the same manner as **lineto**. However, the line segment extends from the current point (x, y) to x + *num1* as an x-coordinate and y + *num2* as a y-coordinate. The new current point is (x + *num1*, y + *num2*).
— **closepath** —	Closes the segment of the current path by appending a straight line from the current point to the segment's starting point (generally the point specified in the most recent **moveto** or **rmoveto**).

SHADING

Not all figures are simply line drawings. You might want to fill in the figure with a color or pattern. PostScript has a wide variety of operators that will help you accomplish such tasks. As an introduction to these operators, let's begin with the simplest and most obvious operation: filling a figure with black.

By this time, you are probably getting tired of drawing boxes; this exercise will draw two triangles, instead, and color them black. The dimensions and other data for these triangles are given in Figure 3.13.

This example will also introduce procedures to create these figures. As you see from the figure, these are two triangles: one is a right triangle, and the other is an isosceles triangle. You will define two procedures, one for each triangle, which will need to be positioned with the current

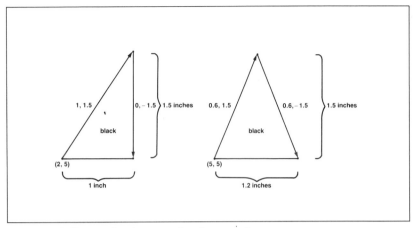

Figure 3.13: Layout for the two-triangle example

point at the left corner of the triangle and with the base (or bottom dimension) and the height of the triangle on the stack. Let's call these two procedures **rightTriangle** and **isoTriangle**.

Remember to take the operands off the stack in the reverse order that you put them on when you called the procedure. In this case, you will call the procedure like this:

      height   *base*   **rightTriangle**

Then you will take *base* off the stack first, since it will be on top, and take *height* off next. Since these procedures are your creations, and not PostScript operators, the order of operands is completely arbitrary. For the example, I have chosen to put *height* on the stack followed by *base*.

With that preliminary out of the way, let's go on to the example in Figure 3.14, which produces the output in Figure 3.15.

There are several instructive points to this example. The example is set up into the prologue and script format that you read about in the last chapter. The previous examples in this chapter haven't contained any procedures other than **inch**; now that you are beginning to code procedures, you should follow the standard format. You remember that, in the standard format discussed in the last chapter, a PostScript program will consist of four sections: a header, a prologue, a script, and a trailer. We are still not including the header and trailer sections because to do so would make these short procedural examples too formal and bulky—and it wouldn't add to the clarity or readability of the examples. When you begin to code complete exercises in the next chapter, we will use the full structuring conventions.

```
%Begin triangle procedure example
%---------------------Procedures---------------------
/inch                                          %1
       { 72 mul }
       def
%define graphic procedure for right triangle
/rightTriangle                                 %2
%called as: height base rightTriangle          %2.1
       {    /Base exch def                      %2.2
            /Hgt exch def                       %2.3
            Base Hgt rlineto                    %2.4
            0 Hgt neg rlineto                   %2.5
            closepath }                         %2.6
       def                                      %2.7
%define graphic procedure for isosceles triangle
/isoTriangle                                   %3
%called as: height base isoTriangle             %3.1
       {    /Base exch def                      %3.2
            /Hgt exch def                       %3.3
            /HalfBase Base 2 div def            %3.4
            HalfBase Hgt rlineto               %3.5
            HalfBase Hgt neg rlineto           %3.6
            closepath }                         %3.7
       def                                      %3.8
%---------------------Program---------------------
newpath                                        %4
2 inch 5 inch moveto                           %5
1.5 inch 1 inch rightTriangle                  %6
fill                                           %7
5 inch 5 inch moveto                           %8
1.5 inch 1.2 inch isoTriangle                  %9
fill                                           %10
showpage                                       %11
%all done
```

Figure 3.14: Triangle procedure example

The prologue contains three procedures: **inch**, **rightTriangle**, and **isoTriangle**. The basic requirements of the two triangle procedures were discussed before you started the coding, but there are several points you should note about the actual code of each procedure. Let's take them in order.

The **rightTriangle** procedure begins by defining two variables: *Base* and *Hgt*. These two variables represent the base and height, respectively, that are on the stack when the procedure is called. The comment line at %2.1 shows what operands are expected on the stack and in what order. In this case, the base is on the top of the stack (and was the last of the operands, remember). To define *Base*, you push the name literal, */Base*, onto the stack, and then you exchange the literal and the desired number and execute the **def** operator. The exchange is necessary because **def** requires the value to be defined on top of the stack and the name literal to be associated with that value next. You will see this technique used often in PostScript procedures.

Base and *Hgt* are each defined in the same manner, removing the value from the stack as they are defined. Once the variables are safely stored, you can begin to draw the lines. Line %2.4 draws the first line from the

Figure 3.15: Triangle procedure output

current point to the point defined by base, height. Now you want to move straight down to the second corner of the triangle to form the right angle. To do this, however, you must move in a negative direction on the y-axis. The natural thought would be simply to put a minus in front of *Hgt,* but that won't work. *Hgt* is a name in the dictionary that represents a number; it is not a number itself. It becomes a number again as soon as it is retrieved from the dictionary; therefore, you must retrieve it (by using its name), store it on the stack, and then negate the number on the stack by means of the **neg** operator. That's what was done in line %2.5. Then **closepath** finishes the figure.

The isosceles triangle is constructed in much the same way. The only difference is that, in this case, you need to calculate the displacement for the top of the triangle, since the second side does not equal the height and the third side does not equal the base as in the right triangle. This calculation is performed in line %3.4, which divides the base value in half. Since the two sides of an isosceles triangle are equal, the top point must have an x-displacement that is one half the base. This value is calculated as the variable _HalfBase_ in line %3.4, and it is used as the x-displacement in the remainder of the procedure, which is straightforward.

Now that the procedures are finished, the prologue is complete and the script portion of the program can begin. As you were promised, the script is relatively short and repetitive. Line %4 clears any path debris, and line %5 moves to the bottom-left corner of the first triangle. The **rightTriangle** procedure is then called with operands of a height of 1.5 inches and a base of 1 inch.

The resulting figure is not stroked, however. This time, you use the **fill** operator to fill the figure completely with black. If you had wanted another line figure, you could have used **stroke** instead; nothing in the procedure constrains you. This is a positive feature of the PostScript concept of creating a current path and then filling it using whatever painting operator you wish.

Next you move the current point to the left corner of the second triangle and repeat the process, using the **isoTriangle** procedure and the height and base of 1.5 inches and 1.2 inches, respectively. After filling in the triangle, the resulting page is printed.

There is no **quit** operator at the end of the above example because you may want to continue these short exercises. For this reason, we will not repeat the **inch**, **rightTriangle**, or **isoTriangle** procedure. Let us assume that you are continuing directly on to the next example. (If you don't, just reenter those procedures from the previous example.)

This example will define a **squareBox** procedure, to complement the previous triangle procedures. This box will be used in conjunction with the triangles to illustrate the use of shades of gray in filling a figure—all the way up to white. It will also demonstrate what happens when one figure overlays another.

Let us begin by drawing two square boxes and an overlapping isosceles triangle, as laid out in Figure 3.16. You will notice several things about this figure. First, it gives all the essential dimensions for the program. Second, it assumes that you will define the **squareBox** procedure to take a size parameter as an operand from the stack. The figure shows the starting point of each of the figures: (2, 5) for the first box, (2.5, 5) for

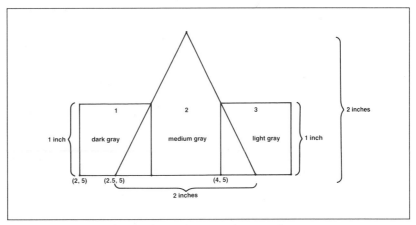

Figure 3.16: Layout for overlap and gray-scale example

the triangle, and (4, 5) for the second box. Both boxes have 1-inch sides, and the triangle is 2 inches along the base and 2 inches high. Each of the figures is filled with gray: dark gray for the first box, medium gray for the triangle, and light gray for the last box. The figures will be produced in order, left to right: box, triangle, and box.

You will adjust the gray value that fills in each figure by means of a new operator, **setgray**. This operator takes an operand between 0 and 1, with 0 being *black* and 1 being *white*. Any number outside the range 0 to 1 is an error. For this example, you will use 0.25, 0.5, and 0.75 to set the gray level for each figure.

The use of 0 for black and 1 for white may seem confusing. The analogy is to light rather than to ink on a page. With light, 0 represents no light, or black, and 1 represents full light, or white. Thinking of 0 and 1 as light may help you remember the two values.

The example code is given in Figure 3.17. This generates the output in Figure 3.18.

You will notice that each of the figures completely overlays the preceding one, even though the preceding figure was darker. This would remain true no matter what colors were used. The effect is that of opaque paint or of a solid piece of paper. There is no mixing or bleeding of colors in the electronic world, nor are the colors transparent.

This effect can be handy, and we will end this section with one last example to illustrate this point graphically. In this example, you will generate a square box and fill it with black. Then you will generate a right triangle at the same origin and color it white. The dimensions, coordinates, and design of the output are given in Figure 3.19.

```
%Begin overlap and gray scale example
%----------------------Additional Procedure--------------
/squareBox
        {       /Dim exch def
                0 Dim rlineto
                Dim 0 rlineto
                0 Dim neg rlineto
                closepath }
        def
%----------------------Program----------------------------
newpath
%Do first box
2 inch 5 inch moveto
1 inch squareBox
.25 setgray
fill
%Do triangle
2.5 inch 5 inch moveto
2 inch 2 inch isoTriangle
.5 setgray
fill
%Do last box
4 inch 5 inch moveto
1 inch squareBox
.75 setgray
fill
%Now show the results
showpage
```

Figure 3.17: Example of overlapping figures and gray scale

I will assume again that you are continuing from the preceding exercise, and will not include the procedures. With that caution, the program
is shown in Figure 3.20. It provides the interesting output shown in
Figure 3.21.

This output should reinforce the previous discussion; you see how the
white triangle has overlaid the black square to give the effect of a single,
reversed black triangle. This overlay process can be used to good effect
as you will see in the exercise later in this chapter.

We will end this section with a recap in the standard format of the two
new operators.

Syntax	Function
num **setgray** —	sets the current color to a shade of gray corresponding to *num*. *num* must be between 0, corresponding to black, and 1, corresponding to white, with intermediate values corresponding to intermediate shades of gray.

Figure 3.18: Overlap and gray-scale output

Syntax	Function
— **fill** —	paints the area enclosed by the current path with the current color; clears path.

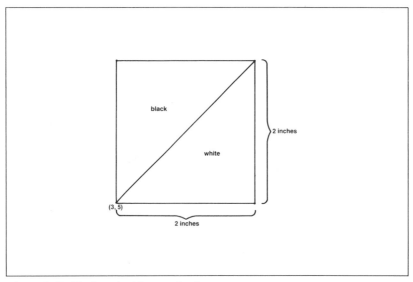

Figure 3.19: Black-and-white overlap layout

```
%Do box and triangle
newpath
%First do box in black
3 inch 5 inch moveto
2 inch squareBox
0 setgray
fill
%Then do triangle at same origin in white
3 inch 5 inch moveto
2 inch 2 inch rightTriangle
1 setgray
fill
showpage
```

Figure 3.20: Black-and-white overlap example

FONTS

You have already been informally introduced to fonts in the exercises
and examples in Chapters 1 and 2. Up to this point, you have been given
font commands for the exercises without much explanation, since you
were concentrating on character placement, string handling, and similar

Figure 3.21: Black-and-white overlap output

basic operations. You also needed some basic graphics concepts and operations before beginning serious work with PostScript fonts. Now you are ready to proceed to a broader discussion of fonts and their management and use in PostScript.

This approach has meant that we have skipped over, but not ignored, PostScript font operations. You probably feel comfortable with the font operators you have worked with so far, and you may have an intuitive feeling for how they operate. PostScript font operators offer a natural approach to font access and use, and you have probably not found this informal approach either difficult or disconcerting.

However, you will want to make more extensive use of fonts as the exercises become more complex, and you will need to understand more about the choices and operations that are available working with Post-Script fonts. In this section, you will begin to explore these issues. This does not require introducing any new PostScript operators. Instead, it requires a fuller discussion of fonts generally and a more detailed and systematic look at PostScript font operations specifically.

FONT DEFINITION

A *font* is defined as a set of type—meaning a complete collection of characters and punctuation—in one style and size. Perhaps a font can be most easily understood if you think of it as being like the type ball in your typewriter, which gives a specific form and size to each letter or character that you type. For example, most people are familiar with the Courier type style, which is a standard office typewriter font. Just as a typewriter can't type without a type ball or element, the PostScript interpreter can't create letter images without an active font.

This section and the next discuss general font issues. Many of these topics apply to all fonts in any environment; some apply only to raster output devices; none, however, are limited to PostScript alone. These general issues involve the use of fonts, font construction on raster devices, families of fonts, and font names. Later we will discuss font issues that specifically relate to PostScript. These include access to and scaling of fonts, types of PostScript fonts, and font operators.

TYPE AS GRAPHICS

Before we examine all the technical aspects of fonts, let's discuss type as a graphic object. The form of letters is one of the most ancient of graphic elements. As soon as humans began to write, they began to think about and modify the shapes that were used to convey language. Indeed, many languages, ranging from ancient Egyptian to modern Chinese, use stylized pictures to represent words and concepts. The design of modern print typefaces grew out of the formal writing of medieval times, as printing tried to imitate calligraphy. Each letter in a good typeface is a small work of art; each is an object of intricate graphic design.

Aesthetics and utility are merged in perfect harmony in the best type designs. The beauty of a typeface is directly related to how well it performs its utilitarian functions of clarity, emphasis, and legibility. Each style of type is designed to enhance these qualities in various settings. Each style fulfills these functions in a way that is complementary to specific page environments or design requirements.

FONTS FOR RASTER OUTPUT

Typefaces were originally designed for printing applications, and as we observed earlier, type in such applications consists of solid and continuous lines of ink. The task, then, is to translate these beautiful and essential objects from continuous lines into dots, for display on a raster output device. This task is neither easy nor trivial, particularly for devices with low or medium resolution.

The essential problem is to carry over all the fine nuances of the typeface design into the series of dots that form an image on the raster output device. The process of converting the outline of a character on a font into pixels is a special case of the process known as *scan conversion*. In many cases, fonts are further enhanced when human judgement is applied to adjusting the pixels to create the most harmonious and attractive characters at a given font size. This process is known as *font tuning*. Obviously, the rendering of a typeface by conversion to pixels is going to be most noticeable at very small type sizes, where the features of individual letters may be only a few pixels. In this case, the characters may appear ragged or uneven; in extreme cases of small type on low-resolution devices, certain characters may become indistinguishable.

FONT USE

Fonts are changed within a document for many reasons. Sometimes it may be only for fun, to show off the variety of fonts available with a laser printer. Usually, however, there is a more serious reason. In some cases— for example, on insurance policies—there is a legal requirement regarding the text. Sometimes font changes are necessary to make a point stand out or to differentiate certain portions of the text, such as instructions from data on a form or headings from body text. In any case, the requirements for fonts generally fall into one or another or a combination of three categories.

First, fonts are used for legibility. This is probably the most obvious, but also the most overlooked requirement. The object of printing anything is to have it read with a minimum of strain and a maximum of ease. Many fonts have been designed specifically for clarity and readability, particularly where space is limited. The use of a crisp, clear font helps pack the maximum amount of information into a small space while retaining reading ease. Thus, readability is the first thing to think about when evaluating fonts.

Fonts are also used to emphasize a point or to make a statement. Sometimes this objective clashes with the issue of legibility, as in some of the fonts that imitate handwritten script or Gothic lettering. Generally, however, emphasis is provided by the use of either bold or italic fonts or by increasing the size of the font used, or sometimes both. This use is especially important to divide one type of information from another on a page; for example, instructions on a form are often printed in italic type to make them stand out from the information requested.

Finally, fonts are used to enhance the quality of the finished output. A typeset page certainly has more impact, and possibly more credibility, than one that is typewritten. Typeset-quality fonts provide immediate letter recogition to the eye. This clarity of shape is an essential element of a fine font.

Overall, the selection of a correct font for a given task is an important part of creating an acceptable page. The font or fonts selected will help you make a clear, readable document. You can use them to emphasize specific items and to distinguish certain portions of the page from others, and they will provide you with output that can be immediately and easily understood by you and your readers.

Font Families and Font Names

There are a variety of ways to group fonts. The simplest and most obvious is by design, or *typeface*. Most of these typefaces have names, which represent a complete range of fonts with a common design but in different sizes and styles. Such a set of fonts is called a *font family*. Remember that a font, properly speaking, is only one size in a particular style of typeface design. You may have noticed that I have been using the term "font" for what we have now defined as a font family; for convenience, I will continue to use "font" in this way whenever there will be no confusion.

These font families can be classified into three categories by distinct design elements. The first category comprises the *serif* fonts. Serif fonts have small lines that finish off the major strokes of each letter, similar to the effect of a chisel on stone or of a calligraphic pen on paper. The Times font family, which you have been using for text output so far, is a serif font family. The second category is called *sans-serif*. As you might guess, these fonts are distinguished by the absence of the serif lines. The Helvetica font family is a sans-serif font family. Generally, serif fonts look more traditional, while sans-serif fonts have a more modern appearance. Finally, some fonts don't fall easily into either of these two groups; one such font is Courier, which, as we discussed before, is primarily used for typewritten output. Fonts such as Courier are *typewriter* fonts.

FONT SIZES

Fonts vary in size within a family as well as in design between families. Every character in a font has a height and a width. The width of a character within a font is called the *pitch*. All characters in a typewriter font have a single width. Such fonts are called *fixed pitch* or *monospaced* fonts. Characters in most fonts, however, have different widths depending on the shape of the individual character; these are called *variable pitch* or *proportional* fonts. Thus, in a typewriter font like Courier, the letter i takes up as much space as the letter w—just as it would on your type-writer—while in a proportional font like Helvetica, the w will be much wider than the i.

To say that the width of characters in a font is proportional is not to say that there is a fixed mathematical relationship between them. Type-faces are designed so that all their characters will fit together aestheti-cally, and proportions that seem to be mathematically correct may look ungainly when the letters are put together on the page. Arriving at "optically correct" proportions is a long process of trial and error, and one of the advantages of using traditional typefaces is that you have the benefit of many other people's experience.

Font height is generally given in points, just like the spacing on the page. The most usual size for reading type is 10-point. Smaller point sizes indicate smaller type, with 4 to 6 points being about the smallest type that most of us can read. You remember that there are 72 points in an inch, so that 36-point type, for example, is ½-inch from the top of the ascender of any character in that font to the bottom of any descender (for example, from the top of the k to the bottom of the p, with capital letters and x-height letters appearing smaller). Type size is often varied for much the same reasons that type styles are varied: to achieve an effect or to mark off special sections of text, and so forth, as required.

FONT ACCESS

All fonts must be made available to the interpreter before they can be used by PostScript operators. To begin with, every PostScript output device has some fonts that come with it, or are *built-in*. At a minimum, all PostScript-equipped devices have the Times family, the Helvetica family, and the Courier family. Some PostScript devices have more than these three families, but all have at least these. All the fonts that you will use in this book are from this minimum set of built-in fonts.

Apart from the fonts that always reside in your printer, there are two methods of making fonts available. One method is by sending a copy of the font from your PC or Mac to the printer to be stored in the printer's electronic memory. This process is called *downloading*. The other method is to create a new font using PostScript operators. This requires, as you may expect, some fairly complex PostScript code; it will be covered, along with some other complex font procedures in Chapter 5.

Each copy of a font requires memory within the printer controller, and each make and model of printer can hold a different number of fonts in its memory. Sometimes there is a trade-off between the number and size of the fonts and the size and complexity of the pages that can be handled by the printer. We will examine some techniques to deal with such trade-offs in Chapter 6, on advanced text handling.

FONT SOURCES AND OWNERSHIP

If you are not familiar with the world of printing and typesetting, it may surprise you to find out that not all fonts are public property. In fact, almost all the high-quality, elegant fonts are private property; the designs are licensed to companies that want to incorporate the fonts into various devices. Adobe Systems, the developer of PostScript, has licensed a wide variety of classic fonts for use with PostScript; for example, Times-Roman and Helvetica are licensed fonts.

POSTSCRIPT FONTS

PostScript treats text characters as general graphic objects subject to appropriate operators just like any other graphic; a box or a triangle is conceptually no different to the interpreter than a g or an R, and vice versa. Because PostScript makes no distinction between text and other graphics, it has no problem combining text and graphics on a page. In a real sense, all pages are graphic images to the PostScript interpreter. You could actually draw every character of a font on a page using PostScript operators, but that would be tedious and difficult. Instead, PostScript provides a variety of high-level operators to handle text conveniently and efficiently.

PostScript describes fonts through the use of a *font dictionary*. Each font dictionary is referenced by a PostScript name literal and provides information and procedures for building all the characters in that font. You have already seen the PostScript font mechanism at work in the exercises. The name of a PostScript font is used as a key into a special dictionary that returns the associated value, which is a font dictionary. This font dictionary is then used by the PostScript interpreter to define the process for rendering characters in a string onto the current page. The interpreter uses each character as an index to select the correct definition process.

There are two important points to remember here. First, PostScript actually does draw each character, using appropriate graphics operations; and second, the PostScript interpreter creates characters through the use of a font dictionary that contains all the information required to produce a given font, including appropriate procedures for rendering each character.

TYPES OF FONTS

Most PostScript fonts contain characters that are defined as outlines in the font dictionary and are then processed by the interpreter and filled in to make the character. By using this process to create characters, PostScript can render all sizes of text with a minimum of distortion and can perform many other graphics operations on the characters or using the characters. Both Times and Helvetica are defined as outline fonts.

Some PostScript fonts contain characters that are defined as lines to be stroked rather than outlines to be filled. Courier is such a font.

It is also possible to create PostScript fonts directly, as images that are rendered by the interpreter as a series of pixels. Such fonts are called *bit-mapped* fonts. PostScript has no built-in fonts of this type, but it is possible for a PostScript user to create and work with these fonts. We will discuss all these issues—graphics operations with fonts, changing fonts, and creation of new fonts—in Chapter 5.

Because the characters in PostScript fonts can be stroked or filled as required, they can also be modified by means of the **setgray** operator to show on the page in the usual range of black to white, depending on the **setgray** operand. This provides an easy and effective way to show white lettering against a dark or patterned background, for example.

FONT METRICS

Earlier we discussed how all characters have height and width. In PostScript fonts, each character's width is given as an (x, y) displacement. This pair of numbers makes up the value that represents the distance from the beginning of the present character to the point where the next character can begin; essentially these are the coordinates for a relative move command. Most Indo-European alphabets have a positive x-component and a zero y-component for this value; other alphabets may differ, having negative x-components or nonzero y-components. The values returned by the **stringwidth** operator are the sum of these (x, y) coordinates for all the characters in the string under evaluation.

Characters in PostScript fonts also have height. A font specifies the shape of the characters in one standard height. This size is defined as the minimum vertical separation necessary to ensure that two successive lines of text do not interfere with one another; that is, that the top of an f in one line doesn't run over the bottom of a g in the line above it. All PostScript fonts are set up so that this height is 1 unit. In the default coordinate system that you have been using, that would be 1-point high.

Such type would be too small to read, and it also would be difficult to convert into dots. In order to get the type size you want on the output page, you must expand the type to the correct size in both the x and y dimensions. This process is called *scaling* the font.

FONT MANIPULATION

Now you have covered all the basic considerations in dealing with PostScript fonts. In order to use a PostScript font, the following three steps are required:

1. The font name must be looked up to retrieve the font dictionary.

2. The characters in the font must be scaled to the correct size for output.

3. The scaled font must be identified to the interpreter as the font to be used for text output.

Each of these tasks has its own operator, and each operator performs its job in such a way as to leave the information for the next task's operator on the stack. In this way, the operations can be invoked naturally in the sequence above.

This is what you've been doing in the earlier exercises. The first operator, **findfont**, identifies the font dictionary by its name, taking a name literal as an operand, looks it up in the special dictionary, and returns the associated font dictionary onto the stack. If you should give it a name it doesn't find, it will return an error; on the Apple LaserWriter, it issues the error message and uses a default font dictionary (Courier). The **scalefont** operator performs the second task. This operator requires two operands: a number that represents the scaling factor and a font dictionary that is to be scaled. You provide the scale number, and the font dictionary is usually on the stack already as a result of a previous **findfont**. The operator returns a properly scaled font dictionary to the stack, where it is used as an operand by the next operator in the series, **setfont**. This operator, as its name suggests, makes a font dictionary on the stack into the *current font*. This is the name for the dictionary that the interpreter uses for all subsequent text output.

At this point, we have returned to our original definition of a font as a set of type in one style and one size. Now you know both how to go about setting up and using a PostScript font and how PostScript itself treats and works with fonts.

Let's recap these font operators in our standard format.

Syntax	Function
name **findfont** font	obtains a font dictionary specified by *name* and puts it onto the operand stack
font scale **scalefont** newfont	applies *scale* to *font* to create *newfont*, whose characters are enlarged in both the x and y directions by the given scaling factor when they are printed
font **setfont** —	establishes *font* as the font dictionary to be the current font for all subsequent character operators

GRAPHIC EXTENSIONS

So far in this chapter you have read about and worked with straight lines and characters from fonts as graphic objects. You have built a variety of shapes and figures, both stroked and filled, and you should be familiar and comfortable with basic PostScript operations.

With this background, you are now ready to extend your graphics vocabulary in two directions. First you will work with arcs, circular shapes, and figures composed of both curved- and straight-line segments. Second, you will become acquainted with PostScript measurement and coordinates in more detail.

This will prepare you for a final summary of PostScript graphics, which will explain the conceptual and practical framework of all PostScript graphics operations. This summary will also provide insight into PostScript graphics procedures. You will learn how to formulate, define, and use PostScript procedures that are independent of page structure and that will not affect or be affected by other graphics operations.

CURVES

Most interesting shapes and figures are not composed of straight lines alone. Curved lines are generally an important part of dynamic and visually attractive designs. Operations to create and use curved-line segments are therefore essential in any comprehensive set of tools for rendering graphic objects.

By their nature, curved lines present more problems in a computer environment. By now you are used to PostScript's ability to describe any point on a page as a pair of numbers (x, y) that give measurements from a specific point on the page. These coordinates are called *rectangular* coordinates, because the two dimensions, measured by x and y, are at right angles to one another. Straight lines are natural in rectangular coordinates, which you have been using to move around the PostScript page. Curved lines, however, require more work to define and more information to use; unfortunately, they also require additional mathematics. We will begin with the easiest form of curved lines: circular arcs.

CIRCULAR ARCS

Even in rectangular coordinates, the mathematics necessary to describe a circle precisely are relatively simple. You needed two pieces of information, or *parameters,* to place a square box on the page, although you may not have thought of it this way. In order to use the **squareBox** procedure, you needed to set the current point to the position for the bottom-left corner of the box and you needed to give a dimension for the box. The circle also requires two parameters in order to be positioned on the page. These two parameters are the location of the center of the circle, which is equivalent to the corner of the box, and the radius of the circle, which is equivalent to the dimensions of the box.

Circular arcs are just portions of a circle. To define a circular arc requires two additional parameters: the points that form the beginning and the end of the arc. While there are various ways to specify the endpoints of an arc, PostScript uses a simple and straightforward method, specifying the two angles that measure the beginning and ending radii of the arc, taken counterclockwise from the horizontal axis. This measurement process is illustrated in Figure 3.22.

In this figure, the center of the circle is at point *(x, y)* and the radius is *r*. The arc of the circle to be drawn begins at *angle1* and runs counterclockwise to end at *angle2*. These five values (two for the center point and one each for the radius and two angles) are the operands that are required for the PostScript **arc** operator.

The **arc** operator takes these five values and creates a circular line segment that begins at the point specified by *angle1* and ends at that given by *angle2*. This endpoint becomes the new current point. The **arc** operator may perform one additional step. If the current point is undefined when you call **arc**, it just draws the circular segment as described above. If, however, the current point is defined, **arc** draws a straight-line segment from the current point to the beginning point of the arc and then constructs the arc.

Let's try an example to help you practice these operations using **arc**. Like the early examples with straight lines, this won't be visually exciting, but it will illustrate the possibilities.

This example will produce a page with three arcs, one above the other and each demonstrating the use of the operator. The three figures and

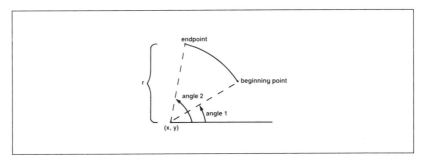

Figure 3.22: Measurement of circular arcs

their relevant dimensions are shown in Figure 3.23. The solid lines on each figure will be stroked onto the output page; the dotted lines and the angular measurements are inserted for reference.

The example program looks like Figure 3.24, and the output page is shown in Figure 3.25.

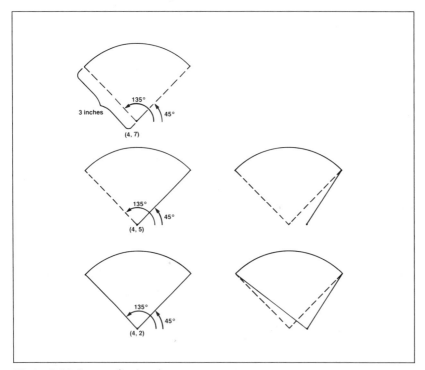

Figure 3.23: Layout for drawing arcs

```
%Begin arc examples
/inch
        { 72 mul }                              %1
        def
newpath                                         %2
4 inch  7 inch  3 inch  45 135 arc              %3
stroke                                          %4
5 inch  5 inch  moveto                          %5
4 inch  5 inch  3 inch  45 135 arc              %6
stroke                                          %7
5 inch  2 inch  moveto                          %8
4 inch  2 inch  3 inch  45 135 arc              %9
closepath                                       %10
stroke
showpage
```

Figure 3.24: Example of multiple arcs

The program consists essentially of three **arc** operators. The first **arc**, you notice, begins right after a **newpath**, which means that the current point is undefined. The **arc** operator is invoked in line %3 with the operands that were defined before: center at (4, 7), radius of 3 inches, and beginning and ending angles of 45° and 135°, respectively. This segment is then stroked. Since **stroke** performs an implicit **newpath**, there is once again no current point. Therefore, the program performs a

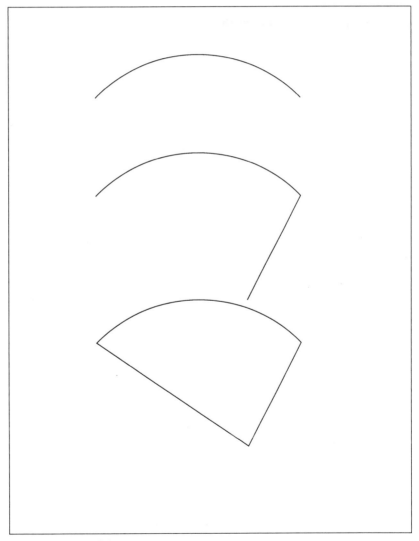

Figure 3.25: Multiple arc output

moveto to the point (5, 5), making it the current point. In line %6, **arc** is called again with the same operands except that the center is shifted to the point (4, 5). This generates a straight line from the current point (5, 5) to the beginning of the arc and then generates an arc identical to the preceding one. This path is stroked. Finally, in lines %8 and %9, the same sequence is repeated with the points (5, 2) and (4, 2); but the result is closed by **closepath** in line %10 before being stroked.

PostScript has a matching operator, **arcn**, which performs the same functions as **arc** and requires the same operands, except that **arcn** draws the arc clockwise. That means that, if you wanted to reproduce the first arc presented in the program using **arcn**, you would code the operator as

    4 inch 7 inch 3 inch 135 45 arcn

If you reversed the angles back to 45 135,

    4 inch 7 inch 3 inch 45 135 arcn

you would get an arc like the one in Figure 3.26, which forms an arc from the part of the circle not painted by the first arc by moving clockwise from 45° to 135°.

CLOSED CURVES

Now let us proceed to closed figures that combine circular arcs and straight lines. You will see that all the techniques you applied to straight-sided figures can be used with circular ones as well.

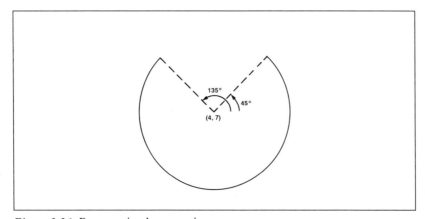

Figure 3.26: Reverse circular arc using **arcn**

As you saw in the last example, adding straight-line segments to a circular arc is easy. Therefore, as a change of pace, the next example will draw and shade a circle. This example will first draw a circle and fill it with a dark (0.25) shade of gray. Then it will move down the page and draw a square of the same dimensions and shading as the circle and place a circle, colored white, within it. The program is shown in Figure 3.27. This produces the expected output, shown in Figure 3.28.

This example is clear by itself, and we won't spend much time on explanations. The **inch** and **squareBox** procedures are familiar to you; the new procedure, **circle**, is just the **arc** operator, moving from 0° to 360° to complete the circle. The **circle** procedure requires the other three operands to be on the stack when it executes.

The only other point that may give you pause is how to establish the coordinates for the center of the circle that is overlaid onto the square. In this case, the dimensions of each of the figures were chosen to make the calculation easy; these dimensions are shown in Figure 3.29.

The next example is a little more interesting, and it introduces you to a new operator, **arcto**. This operator draws arcs connecting two lines, rather than using a center and a radius. In this example you will use **arcto** to draw a square with rounded corners; it looks a bit like a television screen, so we will call the procedure **screenBox**. The example uses the procedure twice: once to draw the box and stroke it, and then again to

```
%Begin circle and square example
%--------------------Procedures------------------
/inch
      {       72 mul }
      def
/squareBox
      {       /Dim exch def
              0 Dim rlineto
              Dim 0 rlineto
              0 Dim neg rlineto
              closepath }
      def
/circle
      {       0 360 arc }
      def
%--------------------Program--------------------
newpath
%Do first circle
4 inch  7 inch  2 inch circle
.25 setgray
fill
%Move down and do box
3 inch  2 inch moveto
2 inch squareBox
fill
%Then add circle in center
4 inch  3 inch  1 inch circle
1 setgray
fill
showpage
```

Figure 3.27: Circle and square example

Figure 3.28: Circle and square output

draw the box inside a square. The square is filled with gray (0.25) and the screen is filled with light gray (0.8).

Before we begin the example, let's look at the operator **arcto**, which forms the heart of the program. In order to follow this discussion, look at Figure 3.30. This operator, like **arc** and **arcn**, adds the arc of a circle to the current path, possibly including a straight line. In this case, however, the arc drawn is defined by the radius *r* and two tangent lines.

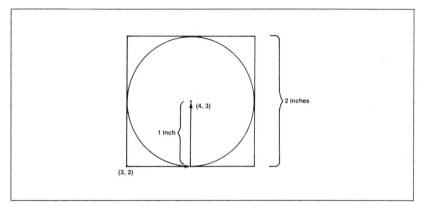

Figure 3.29: Layout for overlapping circle and square

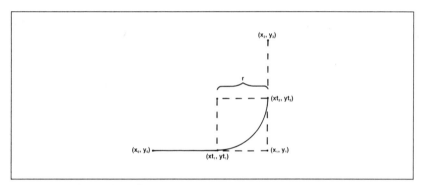

Figure 3.30: Operation of **arcto**

The tangent lines are from the current point—(x_0, y_0) in the diagram—to the point (x_1, y_1) and from (x_1, y_1) to the point (x_2, y_2). Unlike the previous arc operators, **arcto** requires a current point to start from.

The center of the arc is located at the intersection of the two lines that are perpendicular to the tangent lines at the distance r. (If you remember geometry, you will remember that there is only one such point.) The center lies inside the inner angle formed by the two lines. The arc begins at the first tangent point, (xt_1, yt_1) on the first line from (x_0, y_0) to (x_1, y_1), and ends at the second tangent point, (xt_2, yt_2) on the line from (x_1, y_1) to (x_2, y_2). Before constructing the arc, **arcto** adds a straight-line segment from the current point (x_0, y_0) to the first tangent point (xt_1, yt_1), unless the two are the same point. At the completion of the operation, the point (xt_2, yt_2) becomes the current point.

Finally, the **arcto** operator, unlike other line-drawing operators, returns the coordinates of the two tangent points on the stack: xt_1, yt_1, xt_2, yt_2.

I don't know what use this operation is; every program or example that I know of using **arcto** throws away this information by executing four **pop** operators to clean up the stack after the operation. The complication is annoying, but hardly onerous.

Let's design the **screenBox** procedure to see how **arcto** works in a concrete example. Suppose that you want to create a procedure that will work like **squareBox** but produce a square with rounded corners. This means that the current point will be positioned at the lower-left corner of the box when the procedure is invoked, and the desired size of the box should be on the stack. For this exercise, assume that the radius on the corners (the one additional piece of information that you will need) is fixed at 0.25 inches; in the next section you will see how to scale the corners to the size of the box.

Now look at Figure 3.31. If the current point is (x, y), then the four corners of a square with width *d* will be the points (x, y), (x + d, y), (x + d, y + d), and (x, y + d). Because you want rounded corners tangent to the lines connecting these points, they represent the operands required for the **arcto** operator.

Since you want all the corners rounded, you must save the current point and then move some distance down the first side before you start the **arcto** commands. If you didn't do this, the first **arcto** would draw a straight line beginning at the current point, which is also a corner of the box; and a small portion of the line would stick out when the corner was rounded on the finished figure. The result would have a bottom-left corner that looks like Figure 3.32.

Here is the design of the **screenBox** procedure:

- Save the width value (d) off the stack.
- Save the current point values.
- Move some distance in the x-direction to start the lines.
- Perform four **arcto**s using the following pairs of points:

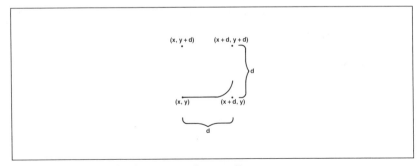

Figure 3.31: Layout for the corner of **screenBox**

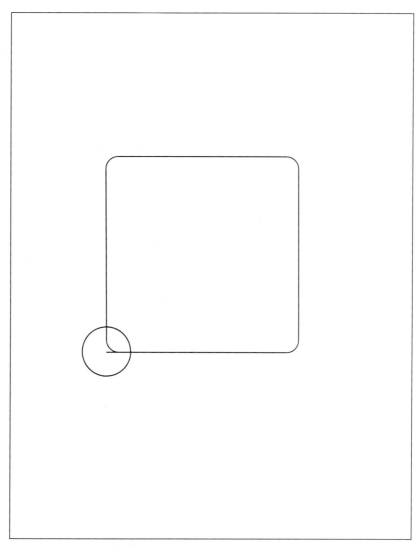

Figure 3.32: Example of **screenBox** without move

1. $(x+d, y)$, $(x+d, y+d)$
2. $(x+d, y+d)$, $(x, y+d)$
3. $(x, y+d)$, (x, y)
4. (x, y), $(x+d, y)$

- Finish by closing the figure to ensure that the end of the last **arcto** meets the starting point.

Having outlined what the procedure should look like, you can now design the page. In this case, you have two figures to create: a simple, stroked **screenBox** and a filled **screenBox** inside a **squareBox**. The first of these is easily set up; you simply decide where to position the bottom-left corner of the screen, move there, and call the procedure with an appropriate width argument. In this case, the corner is placed at (3, 7) and the width is set as 2 inches.

For the second figure, you can position the **squareBox** in the same way you did the preceding **screenBox**, but you need to calculate where to position the **screenBox** that you want to place within it. Consider the layout in Figure 3.33, which gives all the necessary dimensions to execute the program. Note that, in choosing (3, 3) as the bottom corner for the square, you will have 2 inches between the bottom of the preceding figure—at (3, 7)—and the top of this box at (3, 5). In addition, notice that you can center the screen inside the square by leaving 0.25 inches on each side, which makes the point (3.25, 3.25) the starting point for the screen and makes the width 1.5 inches.

Having discussed **arcto**, the design of **screenBox**, and the precise layout of the figures, let's put all this to use. The program is given in Figure 3.34. This program produces the output in Figure 3.35.

This program begins with a prologue that contains three procedures. The first and second procedures, at lines %1 and %2, are already familiar. The **screenBox** procedure begins at line %3. You have already analyzed the requirements for this procedure above; the only points to be discussed here are how to implement the design requirements.

Line %3.2 takes the width operand off the stack and saves it as the variable *Dim*. This is exactly like **squareBox**. Line %3.3 introduces a new operator, **currentpoint**, which does what you might expect and pushes the x and y values of the current point onto the stack. Remember from the design of **screenBox** that you need to save the current point to

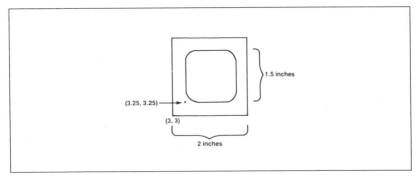

Figure 3.33: Layout for overlapping screen and box

```
%Begin rounded corner example
%--------------------Procedures-------------------
/inch                                                %1
       {      72 mul }
       def
/squareBox                                           %2
       {      /Dim exch def
              0 Dim rlineto
              Dim 0 rlineto
              0 Dim neg rlineto
              closepath }
       def
/screenBox                                           %3
       %expect stack: width                          %3.1
       {      /Dim exch def                          %3.2
              currentpoint                           %3.3
              /Ypos exch def                         %3.4
              /Xpos exch def                         %3.5
              .5 inch 0 rmoveto                      %3.6
       %first side                                   %3.7
              Xpos Dim add  Ypos                     %3.8
              Xpos Dim add  Ypos Dim add             %3.9
              .25 inch arcto                         %3.10
              4 {pop} repeat                         %3.11
       %second side                                  %3.12
              Xpos Dim add  Ypos Dim add
              Xpos          Ypos Dim add
              .25 inch arcto
              4 {pop} repeat
       %third side                                   %3.13
              Xpos          Ypos Dim add
              Xpos          Ypos
              .25 inch arcto
              4 {pop} repeat
       %last side and corner                         %3.14
              Xpos          Ypos
              Xpos Dim add  Ypos
              .25 inch arcto
              4 {pop} repeat
       %and close up the figure
              closepath }                            %3.15
       def
%------------------------Program----------------------
newpath                                              %4
3 inch  7 inch moveto                                %5
2 inch screenBox                                     %6
stroke                                               %7
3 inch  3 inch moveto                                %8
2 inch squareBox                                     %9
.25 setgray                                          %10
fill                                                 %11
3.25 inch  3.25 inch moveto                          %12
1.5 inch screenBox                                   %13
.8 setgray                                           %14
fill                                                 %15
showpage                                             %16
```

Figure 3.34: Example of screen and box

calculate the points for the four **arcto**s. This takes place in lines %3.4 and %3.5, where the current values of x and y are stored as *Xpos* and *Ypos*. Next you have to move away from the corner, as described in the design. This is done in line %3.6 by an **rmoveto**, moving 0.5 inches along the x-axis. You could move any distance greater than 0.25 inches, but you must move at least the radius of the arc (in this case 0.25 inches) to

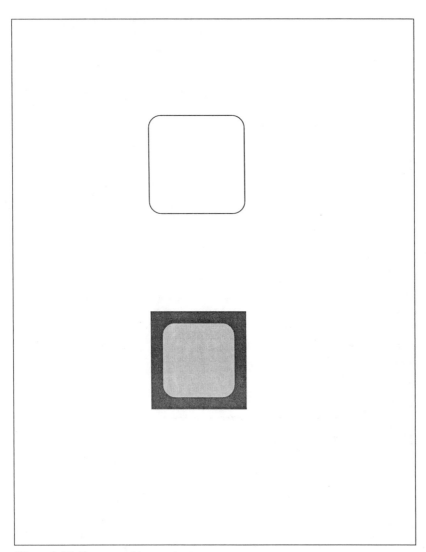

Figure 3.35: Screen and box output

be sure that you won't have a bit of line sticking out. If you look back at Figure 3.33, you will see how that works.

Line %3.7 begins the first side of the screen. Line %3.8 calculates the first point (x + d, y), using *Xpos*, *Dim*, and *Ypos*. Line %3.9 calculates the second point for the first side, (x + d, y + d). Then line %3.10 sets the radius of the arc at 0.25 inches and calls **arcto**. Finally, line %3.11 executes **pop** four times to throw away the extraneous coordinates that **arcto** leaves on the stack.

The remaining three sides of the figure are done in the same manner, each pair of points being calculated according to the setup design. The resulting figure is finished in line %3.15 by a **closepath** to fill in the small segment of line that would otherwise remain between the end of the fourth **arcto** and the point that the figure started.

The script portion is, as always, simple and easy to follow; all the hard work has been done in the prologue. Line %4 clears any path debris so that you start with an empty page. Lines %5 and %6 create the first figure, an outlined screen, with the dimensions laid out earlier. Lines %8 to %11 create the desired square and fill it with 0.25 gray. Line %12 moves the desired distance into the square to set up for the screen. Lines %13 to %15 create the screen figure and fill it with a light (0.8) gray. Finally, on line %16 the entire page is output.

This example shows more complex procedures than the earlier ones. With the **screenBox** procedure, you are getting near to what you want graphics procedures to look like. However, before you can go on to completely independent graphics procedures, there are two issues that still must be covered: measurement and its relation to coordinates, and PostScript graphics machinery. These are the subjects of the next two sections.

Before proceeding to those topics, however, here are the three new operators for drawing circular arcs in our standard format.

Syntax	**Function**
x y r ang1 ang2 **arc** —	adds a counterclockwise arc of a circle to the current path, possibly preceded by a straight-line segment. The arc has radius *r* and the point *(x, y)* as a center. *ang1* is the angle of a line from *(x, y)* with length *r* to the beginning of the arc, and *ang2* is the angle of a vector from *(x, y)* with length *r* to the end of the arc. If the current point is defined, the **arc** operator will construct a line from the current point to the beginning of the arc.

Syntax	Function
x y r ang1 ang2 **arcn** —	performs the same function as **arc**, except in a clockwise direction.
x₁ y₁ x₂ y₂ r **arcto** xt1 yt1 xt2 yt2	creates a circular arc of radius *r*, tangent to the two lines defined from the current point to *(x1, y1)* and from *(x1, y1)* to *(x2, y2)*. Returns the values of the coordinates of the two tangent points *(xt1, yt1)* and *(xt2, yt2)*. The **arcto** operator also adds a straight-line segment to the current line, if the current point is not the same as the starting point of the arc.

MEASUREMENT AND COORDINATES

PostScript provides a number of facilities to control and adjust coordinates. These operators make PostScript coordinate systems both flexible and independent. The flexibility allows, for example, coordinates to be different on different parts of the same page; and PostScript coordinates, which are independent of the device, can also become largely independent of the nominal page coordinates. This flexibility and independence come about because PostScript maintains a coordinate system, the *user space*, which is separate from the coordinates used by the specific output device, called the *device space*.

You will remember that we defined and discussed the *default user space* in Chapter 1. This is the coordinate system that you have been working in for all of the procedures and programs until now. This is the entire set of coordinate parameters—(0, 0) origin at the bottom-left corner of the page and the x and y dimensions of 1/72 inch—that you are familiar with. This system is satisfactory for most of your PostScript coding, and you will continue to use it to the end of the book. It is not, however, the necessary or only coordinate system for PostScript. It is simply the *default* system: what you get when you start a fresh page.

DEVICE SPACE

Let me emphasize again that this coordinate framework (the user space) bears no intrinsic relationship to the physical output device (the device space). As discussed earlier, raster output devices vary greatly in their individual ability to resolve images. At current technological levels, for example, a typical laser printer has a resolution of 300 dpi both vertically and horizontally. Moreover, each output device has an individual addressing system to identify points on the output page. The specific addressing mechanism for the device is what forms the basis for the device space.

Individual devices use a wide range of methods to address points in their output area. Each device can vary from others in a number of ways: paper path, resolution, scanning direction, and so on. Each of these variables may influence the coordinate system native to the device. Some devices, such as terminals, even have differing resolutions in the vertical and horizontal directions. All of these limitations must be avoided to obtain device independence. For those circumstances in which it is essential to know specific information about the output device, PostScript provides operators that can access this information.

USER SPACE

We have defined the user space as the coordinate system that programs use to specify points on the current page. We also have discussed a default set of values that allow a program to work on the page. These default values offer both simplicity and convenience, and thus represent an excellent starting point. They are, nevertheless, completely arbitrary and can be changed at will. Both unit size and orientation are not constrained in any way. Specifically, they are not tied to the resolution or coordinate system of the output device; and generally, they are not fixed to any particular page structure.

This admittedly arbitrary set of default coordinates does provide the PostScript program with a consistent place to start page construction. As the process of page composition continues, the PostScript program may need to modify the user space to accommodate specific requirements. This is done by means of coordinate transformation operators, powerful operators that provide much procedural flexibility. At this point, keep in mind that the coordinates in the user space are not rigid, like a sheet of graph paper. Instead, the coordinates are on a kind of rubberized sheet that can be shrunk, expanded, or twisted as necessary.

Thus, there are two key points to remember about coordinates in user space:

- They are independent of the output device.

- They can be transformed into any orientation on the current page.

TRANSFORMATION OF COORDINATES

This ability to transform coordinates in user space into any form that you want is a direct outgrowth of the need to transform user coordinates into device coordinates. This process is performed by the *current transformation matrix, or CTM.* A transformation matrix is a mathematical device that changes one set of (x, y) coordinates into another set in a uniform way. You don't have to be concerned here with how this works; you should just understand that it is happening.

Since the PostScript interpreter needs to make this transformation from user space to device space in any case, it turns out that adding an additional transformation, or even several transformations, is easy. This means that you can map an infinite variety of changes onto the default user space.

PostScript provides operators that will perform the most common transformations in a natural way. There are three coordinate changes that are most often needed and used, and each of these transformations has a special PostScript operator. They are the following:

Operator	Function
translate	moves the user-space origin (0, 0) to a new position with respect to the current page, while leaving the orientation of the axes and the unit length along each axis unchanged.
rotate	turns the user-space axes about the current origin by a particular angle, leaving the origin and the unit length along each axis unchanged.
scale	modifies the unit lengths independently along the current x and y axes, leaving the origin and the orientation of the axes unchanged.

These powerful modifications can be performed individually or in sequence to provide a wide variety of effects on the coordinate system. Let's look at some of the previous examples, using these operators to demonstrate what they can do and how they might be used in a program environment.

TRANSLATION

Translation is simply moving the coordinates around on the page. An example might look like Figure 3.36. In this case, the coordinates are translated to (7, 5). After the translation, the same code that produced the square at (2, 1) would produce a square at (2, 1) in the new coordinates, which would be (9, 6) in the old coordinates. Both the old and new coordinates and the two boxes are shown in Figure 3.36.

This translation process wouldn't be of much use for drawing boxes. After all, the **squareBox** procedure works from the current point, which can be set by a simple **moveto**. A translation would take as much coding and work as a move, perhaps more. Nevertheless, while this observation is correct for the square, let's consider the effect of using a translation with **screenBox**. You remember that you had to save the current point during this procedure, and you used the x and y values in a number of calculations to create the screen. Look at how the use of translation simplifies this procedure in Figure 3.37.

Note that all the labor and confusion of getting and saving the current point and adding up the various corners is now gone. This screen starts at the point (0, 0) and therefore has its corners at the points—for **arcto** purposes—of (0, 0), (d, 0), (d, d), and (0, d). Note also that the **rmoveto**

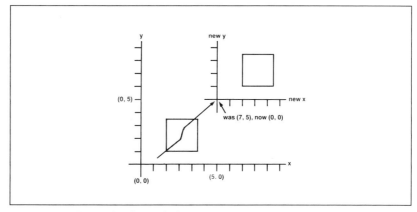

Figure 3.36: Example of translation

```
/screenBox
     {     /Dim exch def
           .5 inch 0 moveto
           Dim 0    Dim Dim .25 inch  arcto
           4 {pop} repeat
           Dim Dim   0 Dim .25 inch  arcto
           4 {pop} repeat
           0 Dim     0 0    .25 inch  arcto
           4 {pop} repeat
           0 0      Dim 0   .25 inch  arcto
           4 {pop} repeat
           closepath }
     def
```

Figure 3.37: Revised **screenBox** procedure

```
%Begin translation example
-----------------------Procedures----------------------
/inch
     {     72 mul }
     def
/screenBox
     {     /Dim exch def
           .5 inch 0 moveto
           Dim 0    Dim Dim .25 inch  arcto
           4 {pop} repeat
           Dim Dim   0 Dim .25 inch  arcto
           4 {pop} repeat
           0 Dim     0 0    .25 inch  arcto
           4 {pop} repeat
           0 0      Dim 0   .25 inch  arcto
           4 {pop} repeat
           closepath }
     def
-----------------------Program----------------------
newpath
.25 setgray
1 inch  1 inch translate
1.5 inch screenBox
fill
2 inch  2 inch translate
1.5 inch screenBox
fill
2 inch  2 inch translate
1.5 inch screenBox
stroke
showpage
```

Figure 3.38: Example of translated figures

is now changed to a straight **moveto**, since you begin the procedure at
(0, 0). Of course, this series of instructions will only execute correctly
if the bottom-left corner of the screen is point (0, 0); otherwise, it will
produce strange results or fail entirely.

Translation will take care of that problem, however. Look at the example
in Figure 3.38, which produces the page of output shown in Figure 3.39.

There are two points to note about this example. The first one is the
use of the **translate** operator. As you see, this operator takes two operands: the x and y coordinates of the point on the current page where you

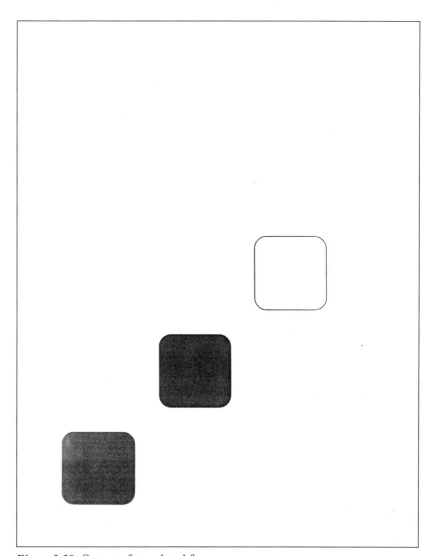

Figure 3.39: Output of translated figures

want the new origin. In this example, the screen has been moved around
the page without any concern about the location of the current point. For
the **screenBox** procedure, the current point is always the origin (0, 0).
The second point to note is that the **translate**s are cumulative; that is,
each one is a movement relative to the current origin, not the original
origin, as would be the case with a **moveto**. Once you understand the
operation of the **translate**, the rest of the program is easy for you to read.

The one point that may raise a question is the first translation of (0, 0) to (1, 1). This was necessary because point (0, 0) in the device space on the LaserWriter is not within the imageable area of the printer; that is, a spot at (0, 0), while it's correct, won't print. The *imageable area* of a device is the actual area that is visible for reproduction. The dimensions of the imageable area of the LaserWriter are given in the *PostScript Language Reference Manual*, Appendix D.4. The imageable area of a default, letter-size page is 8.0 by 10.92 inches, centered on an 8.5 by 11.0-inch sheet; that is, there are left and right margins of 0.25 inches and top and bottom margins of 0.04 inches. Anything you attempt to print outside these boundaries will not be printed on this device, although the coordinates are valid and may produce output on another PostScript device.

ROTATION

Rotation is much like translation, except that it turns the coordinates around the current origin rather than moving them laterally. This is illustrated in Figure 3.40.

Rotation can be used independently or combined with other operators like translation. Consider the example in Figure 3.41. This produces the page of output in Figure 3.42.

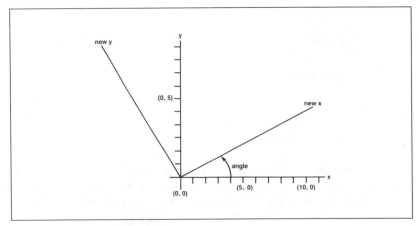

Figure 3.40: Example of rotation

This program example was given to you without the usual preliminaries; if you are unclear about how anything in the example works, go back for a moment and reread it.

You will notice that this example has been treated, like some of the previous examples, as a continuation of other work. It assumes that the procedures, which are quite familiar to you, have already been defined; there are no changes in the procedures for this example.

As with most of the recent examples, the example begins with a **newpath** in line %1 to give the current path a fresh start. Line %2 translates the origin to (1, 1) in current coordinates, while line %3 rotates the coordinates 30° counterclockwise. Then lines %4 and %5 create the screen figure and stroke it. Line %6 moves the coordinates again, this time to point (4, 2) in current coordinates. Remember that this movement is cumulative and relative to the current (not the original) coordinates; as a result, the new origin has been moved to a point at an angle to the original coordinate system. You may have noticed that the second screen figure is not where you would have thought it would be. It is farther away on the y-axis than on the x-axis, although the translate moved farther on the x than on the y-axis. This happens because the coordinates are tilted. Figure 3.43 gives you a graphic picture of what has happened.

Lines %7 and %8 stroke another screen figure. Then line %9 moves the current point to (2, 2) in the current coordinates. The axes are rotated a further 15°, making a tilt of 45° in all. The program draws and strokes a 2-inch square in lines %11 and %12, and the page is output in line %13 to finish the example.

This program illustrates again the cumulative effect on the coordinate transformation operators. It also demonstrates that these operators can be used together, as in lines %2 and %3, for example, or they can be used separately, as in line %11.

```
%Begin rotation example
newpath                          %1
1 inch  1 inch translate         %2
30 rotate                        %3
1.5 inch screenBox               %4
stroke                           %5
4 inch  2 inch translate         %6
1.5 inch screenBox               %7
stroke                           %8
2 inch  2 inch moveto            %9
15 rotate                        %10
2 inch squareBox                 %11
stroke                           %12
showpage                         %13
```

Figure 3.41: Example of rotated figures

SCALING

The last transformation operator that you are going to work with here is the **scale** operator. This operator changes the size of the x and y dimensions of the user space; that is, by means of the **scale** operator,

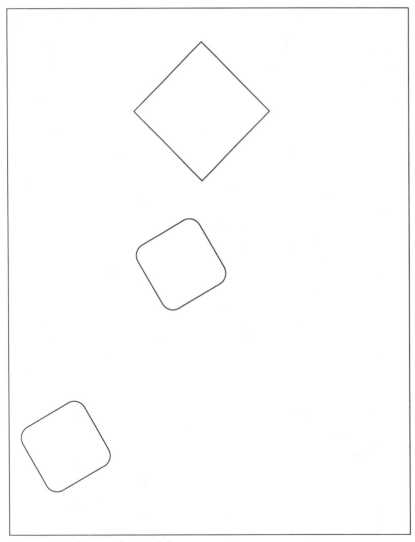

Figure 3.42: Output of rotated figures

you could make 1 inch (in our default coordinates) into ½ or 2 or 12 (or whatever) inches. More important, you could eliminate the **inch** procedure entirely.

Look at the example in Figure 3.44. This program produces the output in Figure 3.45.

This program is interesting for what it *doesn't* have; namely, it doesn't have any references to **inch** except in the **scale** operator. These references

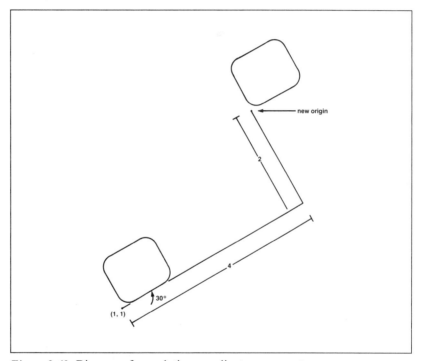

Figure 3.43: Diagram of cumulative coordinate movement

```
%Begin scaling example
newpath                                              %1
1 inch  1 inch scale                                 %2
2 2 moveto                                           %3
2 squareBox                                          %4
fill                                                 %5
4 6 moveto                                           %6
.5  2 scale                                          %7
2 squareBox                                          %8
.25 setgray                                          %9
fill                                                 %10
showpage                                             %11
```

Figure 3.44: Example of scaled figures

Figure 3.45: Output of scaled figures

have been retained for convenience and clarity; but they too could have been eliminated by replacing *1 inch* with 72, and so on, using the actual scale in the default coordinates. If you had done that, there would be no reference, and hence no need, for **inch** at all.

Because you have scaled all the axes to units of 1 inch, all the coordinate values are automatically inches. So lines %3 and %4, for example, produce the same results as the following lines of code within the default coordinate system:

```
3 inch 5 inch moveto
2 inch squareBox
```

At line %7, the coordinates are scaled to ½ inch by 2 inches, and then the same size square as is coded on line %4 is drawn again on line %8. Remember that you have already scaled the coordinates to 1 inch and that all transformations are cumulative; hence, you only need the simple numeric values to rescale the coordinates. Normally, you would have had to include the **inch** procedure after the numbers to rescale the coordinates.

The sides of the figure are the same size in the procedure; but as you can see, they are not the same size on the output. The result isn't even a square anymore, it's a rectangle. This results from the rescaling of the axes in a nonuniform manner. In particular, the x-axis has been shortened to ½ inch, while the y-axis has been lengthened to 2 inches. The net transformation is that one unit along the x-axis is one quarter the size of a unit along the y-axis, the ratio of ½ to 2; therefore, what was previously a 2-unit square becomes a 1-unit by 4-unit rectangle. These two figures provide an excellent example of the **scale** operator in action.

To end this section properly, let us list these three new operators in the standard notation.

Syntax	Function
tx ty **translate** —	moves the origin of the user space to *(tx, ty)* in the previous coordinate system
angle **rotate** —	rotates the user space around the origin by *angle* degrees
sx sy **scale** —	scales the user space by the factor *sx* in the x-dimension and by the factor *sy* in the y-dimension

GRAPHICS PROCEDURES

You have now been introduced to a number of "current" settings. You know how to manipulate the current path, set text or draw figures from the current point, and fill in figures or stroke lines in the current color. In the previous section, you learned how to transform the current PostScript coordinate structure into virtually any shape you want. As you have seen, these transformations are cumulative and can be combined. This creates a powerful tool that can generate multiple shapes out of a simple graphic object, but it also raises some questions and problems.

The very power and persistence of these operators causes some concern. How can you be sure that the page structure is what you wanted, or thought it would be, when you designed a procedure? You have already been using operators like **newpath** to ensure that you don't get unexpected results. And in the original **screenBox** procedure, you saw how you needed to access the value of the current point for the procedure to function correctly. As these current state variables increase—and there will be more in this book—we need to develop a method of controlling these values in a unified manner. Luckily, the PostScript interpreter faces a similar problem and provides a solution.

GRAPHICS STATE

There are a number of other implicit arguments that are necessary for the painting operators to function properly. These consist of objects such as current color, current line width, current font, and so forth. All of these parameters, which together are necessary for the correct operation of the painting operators, are contained in a PostScript data structure called the *graphics state*. This structure defines the context, or background, for each of the painting operators. Most of the time, as you work on a page, you will want the same context for your graphics operations; therefore, setting these once as a global structure makes writing PostScript easier and more straightforward than if you had to specify these arguments for each operation.

The graphics state is not itself a PostScript object, nor can it be directly accessed or modified. It is, rather, a collection of objects that form the control parameters, and these can be both read and altered by various graphics operators. In this way the current context can be changed as necessary to produce the output you want.

The graphics state is a data structure and is maintained by PostScript in a separate graphics stack. PostScript provides a **gsave** operator to push the current graphics state (or context) onto the graphics stack and a **grestore** operator to pop the topmost state on the stack and make it the current graphics state. This provides a valuable and necessary mechanism for controlling the current context for graphics operations.

INDEPENDENCE

So the graphics state is the place where these current values, including the current transformation matrix, are stored. You can control the status of the graphics state, to some extent, by explicitly saving and restoring it. This is not just one more thing to worry about; on the contrary, this is the means of your liberation—or at least of the liberation of your PostScript procedures.

In the previous section, you saw several examples of how procedures were partially freed from specific page position and coordinate measures. These same techniques, coupled with **gsave** and **grestore**, can create procedures that are entirely free from the page structure in their design. The procedures can be constructed, as it were, in their own coordinate system and then placed onto a page when and where you want them, in the size and shape that you decide, and need not disturb the remainder of the page in any way. Such independence is important when you want to develop a library of procedures that you can use repeatedly in different documents and with varied page designs. The best demonstration of this is to take some of the previous examples and rework them into independent procedures of the type just described.

EXAMPLES

In this section we will rewrite one of the procedures used in previous examples in a completely independent format. The object will be to illustrate how to create procedures that can be moved anywhere on the page and used at any size you wish. This requires a change, not only within the procedure itself, but also in how you invoke it within a program, or script. As you designed each procedure, you had to establish a context for its operation and had to determine what operands would be required for its execution. These context and operand requirements have not changed; but your ability, via transformation operators, to shape and modify the environment has changed. The net result is that each procedure must be rethought and reworked, and each program using the procedure will require the same type of effort.

Let's use the **screenBox** procedure as our illustration. This procedure was already partially modified for independence in the previous section. I say "partially" because it still contains references to the **inch** procedure in two important places. That means it still assumes that the default coordinate units are in effect—that one unit on the axes is 1/72 inch.

You will remember from our earlier discussion that the arc of the curved corner should be proportional to the length of a side; if you were to use the previous procedure to make a screen figure with a very short side, for example 0.5 inches, the round arc would take up almost all of the side; conversely, if the figure had a large side, say 8 inches, the rounding at the corners would hardly be noticeable. Similarly, you had to move some distance along the base of the figure to avoid having an extraneous line segment, and that distance was also proportional to the radius of the arc at the corners.

Now all these considerations and limitations can be removed and all the dimensions scaled to the figure itself, without any outside references. Look at the revised procedure in Figure 3.46.

See how much simpler the procedure has become. This new **screenBox** is designed to be called after two things have taken place. First, the coordinate system has to be translated to the point on the page where you want to position the bottom-left corner of the screen figure. This is the same technique that was used in the previous example; you saw how it worked there. Second, this new procedure requires that the coordinates have been scaled to the correct size to create the figure you want. In the default coordinate system, this procedure would create a box 1 unit (1/72 inch) on a side—hardly big enough to see. However, by means of scaling you can draw the box any size you require. You can even make it a rectangle rather than a square.

Let's see a concrete example of independent procedures in use. First, you will put a 1-inch square screen at the point (3, 8)—all dimensions here are in inches, as always. Then you will put a rectangular screen, 1-inch wide by 2-inches high, at point (5, 8). Finally, you will both outline (stroke) and fill a 2-inch high, square screen at (3, 3). The example is given in Figure 3.47, which produces the page shown in Figure 3.48.

This example illustrates how you have to create programs and procedures that work together. Let's review it, line by line. The prologue

```
/screenBox
        {       .5  0  moveto
                1 0   1 1 .25 arcto
                4 {pop} repeat
                1 1   0 1 .25 arcto
                4 {pop} repeat
                0 1   0 0 .25 arcto
                4 {pop} repeat
                0 0   1 0 .25 arcto
                4 {pop} repeat
                closepath }
        def
```

Figure 3.46: Coordinate-independent **screenBox**

consists of the two procedures, **inch** and **screenBox**. The **screenBox** procedure is as presented above; **inch** is included to make coordinate movement easier and more intelligible.

The script, or program section, begins with **newpath** for the usual reasons. Then, on line %1, there is the first of several sets of **gsave**, **grestore** pairs. Remember that all coordinate transformations are cumulative, and so you need to keep track of them. The best and easiest way to do this is to preserve the original, default graphics state, make the needed transformations, and then restore the original state saved earlier. In this way, each transformation begins from the same basic condition, and each change will have the anticipated result.

The first **gsave**, on line %1, is matched by a **grestore** at the end of the first screen figure, on line %1.6. Line %1.1 moves the origin to the

```
%Begin procedure independence example
%----------------------Prologue--------------------
/inch
        {       72 mul }
        def
/screenBox
        {       .5 0 moveto
                1 0   1 1 .25 arcto
                4 {pop} repeat
                1 1   0 1 .25 arcto
                4 {pop} repeat
                0 1   0 0 .25 arcto
                4 {pop} repeat
                0 0   1 0 .25 arcto
                4 {pop} repeat
                closepath }
        def
%----------------------Script----------------------
newpath
gsave                                                   %1
        3 inch  8 inch translate                        %1.1
        1 inch  1 inch scale                            %1.2
        screenBox                                       %1.3
        .25 setgray                                     %1.4
        fill                                            %1.5
grestore                                                %1.6
gsave                                                   %2
        5 inch  8 inch translate                        %2.1
        2 inch  1 inch scale                            %2.2
        screenBox                                       %2.3
        fill                                            %2.5
grestore                                                %2.6
gsave                                                   %3
        3 inch  3 inch translate                        %3.1
        2 inch  2 inch scale                            %3.2
        screenBox                                       %3.3
        gsave                                           %3.4
            .5 setgray                                  %3.4.1
              fill                                      %3.4.2
        grestore                                        %3.4.3
        1  2 inch div  setlinewidth                     %3.5
        stroke                                          %3.6
grestore                                                %3.7
showpage
```

Figure 3.47: Example of independent procedures in use

Figure 3.48: Output of independent procedures

desired location at (3, 8). Line %1.2 scales the x and y axes uniformly to 1-inch units. Then lines %1.3 to %1.5 create the figure and fill it with dark (0.25) gray.

The next **gsave, grestore** pair is in lines %2 through %2.6. This time, the x and y axes are scaled nonuniformly, so that 1 unit on the x-axis is 2 inches, while 1 unit on the y-axis is 1 inch. Note here that the corners of the figure are "rounded" in the same proportions as the axes are scaled; hence the corners are no longer really round, but rather elliptical. Also notice that the box is black, since you don't set the gray scale. This occurs without regard to the **setgray** that you executed within the preceding segment, because the gray value set there was reset by the **grestore** at %1.6 to the default value (black).

The last set of **gsave**, **grestore** is in lines %3 to %3.7. See how the save and restore functions are paired on the portion of the example. Remember that the graphics state is maintained by the interpreter on a separate, but otherwise usual, PostScript stack mechanism, just like the operation stack or the dictionary stack. Each **grestore** puts back the state saved by the last **gsave**. Here you have one **gsave**, **grestore** pair within another. Note that the use of indentation here provides a visual clue to the effect and relationships of the paired operators.

Now that you know what is being done, why is there a **gsave** on line %3.4? To answer that, you must consider the effect of the **stroke** and **fill** operators. Both of these require a current path to work on, and both erase the current path after they have executed. Since you want to *both* stroke and fill the last screen figure, you need to preserve the current path while also using it for each operator in turn. Also, you want the line stroked to be black, while the interior of the figure should be lighter. For these reasons, you want to save the graphics state, including the current color and the current path, after you have created the figure but before you fill it with gray. This allows you to restore everything with the **grestore** in line %3.4.3.

You are probably wondering why line %3.5 exists. Line %3.5 restores the line width to the default unit coordinate, one point. It does this by taking the reciprocal of the current scaling factor, 2 inches, and making that the current line width. This is necessary because the **stroke** operator would paint a line 2 inches wide otherwise. You will remember that **stroke**, by default, always paints a line 1-unit wide in the current coordinate units. Actually, in the earlier discussion, no mention was made of coordinate units; we just said the line was 1 unit and left it at that, or adjusted it to multiple units. However, the line is 1 unit in the current coordinates; if you have scaled those coordinates, the line will take on the size of the scale factor. In this case, the scale factor has been set to 2 inches on line %3.2. If you just issued a **stroke**, without any adjustment, you would get a line 2-inches wide all around the figure—which is not what you want. Note that the adjustment of the line width does not affect the portions of the current path already drawn; it will only affect subsequent operations like the **stroke** on line %3.6, which is what you want.

Now that you've seen how all these concepts fit together in a small example, let's put them into a larger context. The next section will show you how to combine these techniques to create a larger figure.

FIFTH EXERCISE

This exercise will build on and make concrete the set of concepts that you have been reading about, thinking about, and working with throughout this chapter. Although the examples have illustrated the concepts presented and many of them have built on preceding work, this exercise is intended to integrate much of this material and allow you to see many of these ideas in a practical setting.

This exercise builds a logo for an imaginary sporting goods company, which will be called Mountain Sports, Ltd. The logo consists of a simple, stylized figure of three mountains, one behind the other two, with the sun overhead. The mountains are represented by triangles shaded in gray and the sun, by an uncolored circle. All the elements of this design are easily constructed with the tools you have at this point. Figure 3.49 shows the layout and dimensions of the logo design.

You will note some differences between this figure and previous figures that you have worked with. First, the dimensions are given in units, not inches. The dimensions here are all relative dimensions; they represent the sizing and placement of the various elements in space and in relation to one another. For this exercise, the actual output will be scaled with ½ inch being 1 unit on the figure. Since the figure has an overall width of 17 units, or 8.5 inches at the scaled dimensions, you will display the

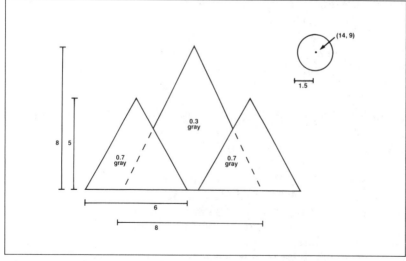

Figure 3.49: Layout for the logo graphic

figure along the length of the paper. This orientation of the paper—printing along the length instead of the width—is called *landscape* orientation. The normal print direction, printing across the page, is called *portrait*.

You are, by now, quite able to analyze such layouts for yourself and to work out the necessary operations to create the figure presented. Let me just suggest that there is room here for four procedures. Two of them will draw the two figure elements: one for the hill and one for the sun. Following the principle of clarity for procedure names, these will be called **hill** and **sun** in the exercise.

The third procedure will be **halfInch**, which is the desired measure and scaling factor. The fourth procedure in the exercise is called **landscape**, and it reorients the coordinates for the landscape mode of printing. This procedure is only invoked once during the program, and so you may wonder why it should be a procedure at all. There are two reasons. First, when you are working in the interactive mode, you may want to play with the figures you've created—to try out various positions, for example, or various shadings. You may have an error in your code or in your typing and have to redo the page several times to correct it. In any case, making such transformations in a procedural form ensures that they are the same for each exercise or variation. The second reason is one that we have touched on before: you will probably want to develop a library of PostScript routines for use in your environment. A procedure such as this is an excellent candidate for inclusion in that library.

Let me encourage you to take a few moments to work out your own approach for this figure and to write down a few notes on how you might code the program itself. Remember that any approach that produces the desired output is correct. The program that follows is just one way to get the output; there are certainly others. In any case, it will prove valuable for you to try some coding on your own and then check it against the program provided in Figure 3.50. This program produces the expected output, shown in Figure 3.51.

Let's review this exercise in detail. The exercise begins with two general procedures. The first, **halfInch**, is a variant of the **inch** procedure that you are familiar with. It simply multiplies by 36 instead of 72. The second procedure is the **landscape** procedure that we discussed above. This procedure does three things. First, it scales the coordinates to ½ inch, using the **halfInch** procedure. Then it translates the coordinates to the bottom-right corner of the page, in preparation for changing to landscape orientation. This may surprise you; you have to visualize the coordinates on the page, and when you do, you will see that the bottom-left corner of the page in the landscape mode is the same as

```
%------------------------Set Exercise--------------------
%!PS-Adobe-1.0
%%Title: Exercise 5
%%Creator: David Holzgang
%%CreationDate: 18 January 1987  17:30:00
%%For: Understanding PostScript Programming
%%Pages: 1
%%EndComments
%------------------------Prologue----------------------
/halfInch                           %create a procedure
    { 36 mul }                      %to convert user units
    def                             %to use halfinches

/landscape                          %create a procedure to
    { 1 halfInch 1 halfInch scale   %print landscape
      17 0 translate                %format
      90 rotate  }
                                    def

/sun
    { /Radius exch def
      0  0  Radius  0  360 arc }
    def

/hill
    { /Base exch def
      /Hgt  exch def
      /HalfBase
          Base 2 div def
      0 0 moveto
      HalfBase Hgt lineto
      Base  0 lineto  }
    def


%%EndProlog
%%Page: i 1
%------------------------Script-----------------------
%set up unit measures
landscape                                        %1
1 1 halfInch div setlinewidth                    %2
2  4  translate                                  %3
%begin logo
%do background mountain
gsave                                            %4
    3  0  translate                              %5
    8  8  hill                                   %6
    .3 setgray                                   %7
    fill                                         %8
grestore                                         %9
%do left and right hills
gsave                                            %10
    %left hill
    5  6  hill                                   %11
    .7 setgray                                   %12
    fill                                         %13
    %right hill
    7  0  translate                              %14
    5  6  hill                                   %15
    fill                                         %16
grestore                                         %17
%do sun
gsave                                            %18
    14   9    translate                          %19
    1.5  sun                                     %20
    stroke                                       %21
grestore                                         %22
%logo finished
%look at output
showpage                                         %23
%%Trailer
%all done
```

Figure 3.50: Example of the logo graphic

Figure 3.51: Logo graphic output

the bottom-right corner in portrait mode. After the translation, the co-ordinates are rotated 90° to set up the landscape orientation. Note that the bottom-left corner of the page is still the origin.

The next two procedures in the prologue are specific to the task at hand: **hill** and **sun**. The **sun** procedure is simply a circle procedure, assuming that the center of the circle is at the origin and that the radius of the circle is on the stack. The **hill** procedure is similar to the procedure you used earlier to construct an isoceles triangle, except that the corner of the triangle is assumed to be at the origin and there is no **closepath** to finish the bottom side (since you might want to use the figure stroked rather than filled and not want a baseline). You don't need to be concerned about using **fill** under such circumstances since the **fill** operator will perform an implicit **closepath** before it fills in the figure. Note that the procedure must start with a **moveto** to the origin, so that the **lineto** (or **rlineto**, for that matter) will have a place to start.

Lines %1 to %3 of the script set up the coordinates on the page by means of **landscape** and then correct the current line width to a 1-point size to compensate for the scaling, as you did in the last example, and move the initial origin inside the imageable area of the page. Lines %4 to %9 form the first figure. This is the background hill, which must be constructed first so that the hills in the foreground will overlay this image. Position, size, and coloring are as specified in the layout. The **grestore** in line %9 resets all the coordinates to what was in effect at line %4, when the **gsave** was done. In particular, the origin returns to the point (2, 4) in the user coordinates; that is, to a position 1 inch from the left edge of the paper and 2 inches from the bottom edge when the paper is held sideways. You can see here the power of the save and restore combination.

The second set of **gsave** and **grestore** runs from line %10 to line %17. This set builds the left and right hills, which will overlap the background hill in the correct way. Again, the layout specifies all the required dimensions and the coloring. The final set of **gsave** and **grestore** in lines %18 to %22 creates the sun over the mountains. The only point to note here is the earlier setting of the line width, which is essential to ensure that the **stroke** operator in line %21 will work as you expect. The page is then output.

You also see that this exercise conforms to the structuring conventions laid out previously. In this regard, it is a good example of how to code and implement these conventions.

This exercise concludes the substantive portion of the chapter. This chapter is full of material that needs digestion and thought, whereas the next chapter will keep you busier. You will construct a complete invoice form for Mountain Sports, Ltd., using a variant of the logo that you have just finished.

OPERATOR REVIEW

This section recapitulates all the operators from this chapter. As before, there is nothing new here; this section is a review and reference.

DRAWING OPERATORS

Syntax	Function
num1 num2 **lineto** —	adds a straight-line segment to the current path. The line segment extends from the current point to the *num1* x-coordinate and the *num2* y-coordinate. The new current point is (*num1*, *num2*).
num1 num2 **rmoveto** —	(relative moveto) starts a new segment of the current path in the same manner as **moveto**. However, the new current point is defined from the current point (x, y) to x + *num1* as an x-coordinate and y + *num2* as a y-coordinate. The new current point is (x + *num1*, y + *num2*).
num1 num2 **rlineto** —	(relative lineto) adds a straight-line segment to the current path in the same manner as **lineto**. However, the line segment extends from the current point (x, y) to x + *num1* as an x-coordinate and y + *num2* as a y-coordinate. The new current point is (x + *num1*, y + *num2*).

Syntax	**Function**
x y r ang1 ang2 **arc** —	adds a counterclockwise arc of a circle to the current path, possibly preceded by a straight-line segment. The arc has radius *r* and the point *(x, y)* as a center. *ang1* is the angle of a line from *(x, y)* with length *r* to the beginning of the arc; and *ang2* is the angle of a vector from *(x, y)* with length *r* to the end of the arc. If the current point is defined, the **arc** operator will construct a line from the current point to the beginning of the arc.
x y r ang1 ang2 **arcn** —	performs the same function as **arc**, except in a clockwise direction.
x_1 y_1 x_2 y_2 r **arcto** xt_1 yt_1 xt_2 yt_2	creates a circular arc of radius *r*, tangent to the two lines defined from the current point to (x_1, y_1) and from (x_1, y_1) to (x_2, y_2). Returns the values of the coordinates of the two tangent points (xt_1, yt_1) and (xt_2, yt_2). The **arcto** operator also adds a straight-line segment to the current line, if the current point is not the same as the starting point of the arc.

GRAPHICS OPERATORS

Syntax	Function
— **stroke** —	paints a line following the current path and using the current color.
— **fill** —	paints the area enclosed by the current path with the current color.
— **newpath** —	initializes the current path to be empty and causes the current point to be undefined.
— **closepath** —	closes the segment of the current path by appending a straight line from the current point to the path's starting point (generally the point specified in the most recent **moveto**).
num **setlinewidth** —	sets the current line width to *num*. This controls the thickness of lines painted by subsequent **stroke** operators.
num **setgray** —	sets the current color to a shade of gray corresponding to *num*. *num* must be between 0, corresponding to black, and 1, corresponding to white, with intermediate values corresponding to intermediate shades of gray.
— **gsave** —	saves a copy of the current graphics state

Syntax	Function
	on the graphics state stack.
— **grestore** —	resets the graphics state by restoring the state on the top of the graphics state stack and pops the stack.

COORDINATE TRANSFORMATION OPERATORS

Syntax	Function
tx ty **translate** —	moves the origin of the user space to (*tx, ty*) in the previous coordinate system.
angle **rotate** —	rotates the user space around the origin by *angle* degrees.
sx sy **scale** —	scales the user space by the factor *sx* in the x-dimension and the factor *sy* in the y-dimension.

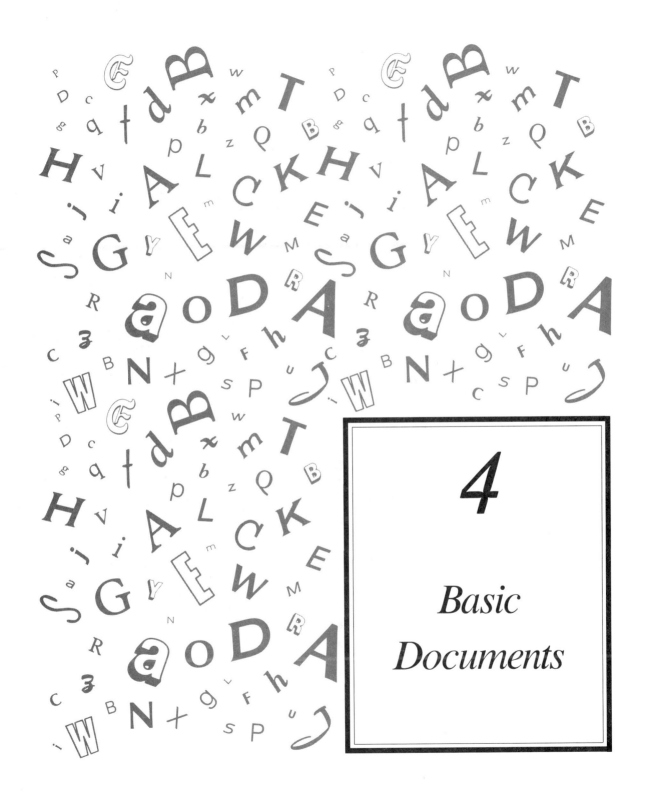

4

Basic Documents

THIS CHAPTER IS INTENDED TO INTEGRATE THE TECH-NIQUES AND PROCEDURES THAT YOU HAVE BEEN learning, by means of a long and detailed exercise. The purpose of this exercise is to produce a basic document that uses both text and graphics on one page.

The basic document in this exercise is an invoice form for our imaginary company, Mountain Sports, Ltd. You developed a graphic element at the end of the last chapter that will form the basis for a company logo. In addition, to add realism to your work, you will take the data from a typical spreadsheet application—in this case, Lotus 1-2-3—and place it on the invoice form. The product will be a completed invoice form, filled out with data generated by a spreadsheet application.

This process requires consideration of both the form and the data; it cannot be carried out by considering one or the other separately. This exercise accurately reflects the real task of designing data display and capture mechanisms in actual companies. Some trial and error, both in design and in processing, is inevitable. For obvious reasons, most of that has been eliminated here, but the flow from the form design to the data structure and back is still evident.

The chapter begins with an overview of the current task. The first part of the chapter discusses the conceptual problem of how to merge form and data onto one page. Then you will begin the rough design of the form and start setting up the common elements necessary for a successful merger of data and form. As the form design progresses, the need for more definition of the data elements becomes evident. We will then cover the nature of the data, its size and positioning in relation to the form design, and how it will need to be treated on the page. This section ends with a consideration of how you will adapt standard application output to fit into the data structure you have laid out and how it can be placed on the form.

The second section of the chapter deals with the form itself. This follows the pattern of previous exercises, which should be familiar to you. With the information about the data that was developed in the previous section, you can finish the detail layout of the form. After you finish the layout, you will design and program the necessary procedures.

Here you will analyze procedures in a way that you might actually use. For PostScript in particular, the process of design from the topmost level down to the simplest level is a useful technique. This process of "top down" design helps you quickly identify the procedures that are required to create this relatively complex form.

The section continues with the creation of discrete parts of the form, which were identified in the first section. Each of these parts is programmed and printed, and finally, the completed blank form is printed by combining the discrete sections.

The third section of the chapter performs the same task for the data output. First, it analyzes the requirements for the Lotus spreadsheet and shows you what the spreadsheet looks like. This is simple and not limited to Lotus; any spreadsheet program would be adequate for this task. Then the usual process of analysis and design begins. First, you will create the data output that is required for integration onto the form, and then you will develop and program the procedures that will reproduce that output on a PostScript page. This process results in an intermediate output, like the earlier blank form, which is a page with only variable data.

The section continues by combining these two pages of output into one unit, thus producing a complete form that includes variable data generated by the spreadsheet application. This is accomplished using the previously developed procedures combined into a single program. You will find this exercise illuminating.

The chapter ends with a short section on the use of these techniques in the "real world." The section also discusses how additional data can be integrated into the form and how you might change the design if you were going to produce multiple forms using the same or similar data.

SIXTH EXERCISE: A BASIC DOCUMENT

In this exercise, you will design and create a basic document, one that might be used in real-life circumstances. This document is a single-page form, an invoice, and will be designed to work with the output from a typical application program—in this case, the spreadsheet program Lotus 1-2-3. This exercise addresses a common concern that occurs in many situations: how to create and fill out a form. Such tasks are typical in everyday business operations, and sometimes in personal life as well, and this exercise is a useful illustration of ordinary complexity in handling page output.

Forms are particularly illuminating not only because they are a regular part of ordinary life, but also because they are conceived and used as complete pages. In this respect, they differ from text output or most computer-generated reports for example, where the page structure is a way to organize a continuous stream of output into a readable unit. Since PostScript is a page-description language, in this exercise you will see how the PostScript page concepts fit naturally into the design and use of forms.

This is also an exercise that can be accomplished with the tools that you have developed so far. You may be surprised, but think of all the points you have covered. You have worked with text as captions, as labels, and as individual lines making up small paragraphs. You have centered and right-justified text output in different fonts. You have also worked with graphic figures of various shapes and sizes; and you finished the last chapter by designing and printing a simple logo as a graphic unit. These tools are ready to be combined and used in the task of creating and filling in a simple form.

EXERCISE STRUCTURE

Before you can proceed to any other problems in designing and creating this exercise, you must consider the overall structure of the task at hand; that is, to create an invoice form and fill it with data produced by an application program. A number of points must be resolved before you can complete this job successfully. This section of the chapter presents a simple but elegant approach to structuring this or any similar task.

The page in this exercise needs to be structured to accommodate both the fixed-form information and the variable data provided by the application. Both the fixed and the variable parts of the page have their own requirements and impose constraints on the page design, and yet each must fit into the other. The solution is to consider the design of each part of the page separately.

Actually, the exercise is designed as two separate pages. The pages are complementary, so that the final output is created by overlaying one page with the other. You might think of each page as transparent, with the fixed data, the form, on one sheet and the data to be filled in on another. The two sheets are complementary in the sense that the fill-in sheet is constructed so that the location of the data matches the places on the form that require data. The technique is to place one image onto the output device, lay the other image over the first without erasing or disturbing anything, and then output both as one unit.

We will use this method to create the output in this exercise. Each page will be designed individually, with all the required procedures and variables placed in the prologue. Then each page will be created (but not printed out) by a script enclosed by the **save** and **restore** operators, so that each page is essentially independent of anything except the prologue. The end of the program will print the finished document, which will consist of both pages, superimposed, like a double exposure in film.

You can see how much depends on the design of the form and the fill-in sheet. Yet this is no different from, and no more laborious than, the considerations that must be made when designing a form initially and when designing output from an application to match the preprinted form. Since the natural sequence would be to design a form and then set up the application output to match, we will follow that sequence here.

FORM

The first page to consider is the form itself. You may think of this as just an ordinary blank form. In this case, however, you will only print a test version of the blank form; once the form is correctly programmed, it will be printed with the associated data page as described above.

The first consideration is what information is required on the form for it to perform its function. In this case, the form is an invoice for the imaginary company, Mountain Sports, Ltd. The basic information on any invoice will be a list of items purchased and a total for the entire list. Therefore, the body of the form will consist of lines for the ordered items with a total at the bottom.

As a step toward designing this form, you may consider the information requirements as a series of blocks; for now, you may treat these blocks as units for positioning and analysis. The first block has already been identified as the list of items purchased. This block will occupy the center of the page, taking up most of the space; its size will depend on the other blocks of information that need to be fitted around it.

The second block will contain the total of the items above and any additional information related to that total, such as shipping or handling charges, sales tax, and so on. There might also be a trailer block to finish the page; this would be optional information that might be variable, for example, a company motto or a variable sales message of a line or two. In this exercise, for the sake of simplicity and clarity, a trailer block will not be included; but you should keep the possibility in mind for use if you need it. That completes the information at the foot of the page.

Above the major data block there will also be two blocks of information: a header block and a logo block. The header block will contain variable information such as the name and address of the customer, the date of the invoice, and perhaps other pertinent data such as terms, delivery date, and so on. The logo block will consist of the graphic logo plus the name and address of the company. Presumably these elements would have been designed as a unit and would be used as such; but each element (the graphic and the pieces of the name and address) could be handled separately for specific effects. In this exercise, the logo will be treated as a unit, with some alternative treatments discussed at the end of the chapter.

The entire set of blocks will come together on the page in something like the block diagram in Figure 4.1. The order of the blocks is natural and derives directly from the analysis of the information on each block. You began with the body block in the center of the page; the totals block, by its nature, must follow directly below the main data block, and any optional trailer block would come below the totals. On the top, the logo would naturally come first, with the heading data immediately preceding the main body.

Before you can define a final layout for this form, you must perform several more steps as follows:

1. Identify specific information (data elements) to be included in each box.

2. Decide on the size and placement of data elements in each box.

3. Determine the overall size of each box.

4. Position and scale each box onto the final form layout.

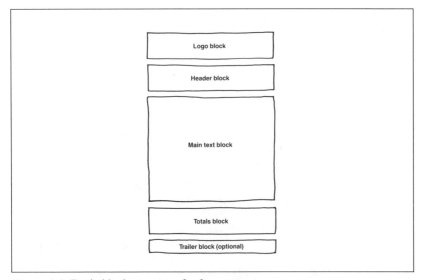

Figure 4.1: Basic block structure for form output

Although you are still working with the blank form, you can see that the nature of the data that will fill in the form is becoming important, and you can't effectively finish the design of the blank form without considering the data to be on it.

FILL-IN

The data that will fill in the invoice form will be generated by a Lotus 1-2-3 spreadsheet, although any spreadsheet application would be adequate here. This application needs to perform the following tasks:

- provide an entry method for those data elements that must be entered
- calculate specific data elements
- display information and titles on the screen for editing and review
- output data elements in a consistent format for integration onto the final form output.

Now you need to decide what data elements belong in each block. In a real systems analysis, you would need to identify what data was required for processing the invoice and what data was required on the invoice to tie back into the inventory and order-processing methods in use at the store. For the exercise, data elements used in each section will represent an arbitrary, but fairly typical, selection of data that may be required on a standard invoice.

As before, let's start with the main or body block. In this case, a line of body data will consist of the following data elements:

1. item number
2. item description
3. quantity ordered
4. quantity delivered
5. unit price
6. extended price

Of these six data elements, the first five will have to be entered on the spreadsheet, while the sixth, extended price, can be calculated as quantity delivered multiplied by unit price.

This leads to a consideration of the second block of data, which contains the totals. In this section there will be four data elements, as follows:

1. item total
2. sales tax
3. shipping and handling charge
4. invoice total

Only one of these elements, the shipping and handling charge, needs to be entered. Each of the remaining elements can be calculated. The first element, item total, is the sum of the extended prices of the lines above. The sales tax is a percentage of the item total; in the California county where I live, this would be 6½ percent. Finally, the invoice total is the sum of the three preceding fields. This completes the bottom of the spreadsheet.

Data in the header block is more complex and generally has a wider variation in required elements than in the body or totals sections. For simplicity of design and ease of programming, the data elements selected for this exercise will be kept to a minimum set of commonly used elements. These will be the following:

1. name and address
2. invoice number
3. date

The name and address data will have to be entered. You will enter it as a block of four lines of text in the spreadsheet that will be transferred as a unit to the form. The invoice number could be generated or entered; in this case, it will be entered, to keep our operation as simple as possible. The date is commonly available from most computer systems, and in this case the date will be generated automatically by the spreadsheet application. Of course, you could make it an entry field if you wanted to process invoices with multiple dates or for a date other than the current date, for example.

You have finished identifying the required data elements in each box. Now you need to determine the size—the length and width—and the placement of these data elements within each box.

Remember that the form and the fill-in sheet are complementary, designed so that the application data will fall into the proper spaces on the form. In this process, it is easiest to design "backwards" so to speak, at least partially working out the size and placement of the data elements and then designing the form around them. This approach is effective because the data is the essential information being presented; the form is just a method of organizing the data.

The approach is also effective because the length and width measures for the data are easier to determine. The form might be constructed in a variety of formats and use different typefaces; however, the data has some constraints on presentation that will help you determine the length and width of the elements. In this exercise, and in most cases of form construction and fill-in like this, you want to make the data appear to be typed. This differentiates the data from the form and corresponds to the most common presentation of data on forms. Because Courier is a common typewriter font and is available in PostScript, data output for the application will be in Courier. Most typewriter fonts are monospaced fonts, typically 10 or 12 characters per inch. PostScript Courier is also monospaced, and you can select a point size to give the desired character spacing—in this case, you select a 10-point font to give a spacing of 12 characters per inch.

Line spacing is also fairly rigid for this type of output, usually 6 or 8 lines per inch. Both 6 and 8 divide evenly into 72 (which is the number of PostScript units per inch), giving 12- and 9-point spacing respectively. Nine-point spacing will not work with the 10-point type that you have chosen; however, 12-point spacing will work well. This provides 10-point type on 12-point leading, which you already recognize from our previous discussions as acceptable spacing for normal reading purposes.

You may be wondering why 10-point type will give you 12 characters per inch. If the type is 10 points, doesn't that imply that there will be about 7 characters per inch? Or if you want 12 characters per inch and an inch is 72 points, shouldn't you use 6-point type? The calculations ($72 / 10 = 7$ and $12 \times 6 = 72$) are certainly correct; the confusion stems from the concept of point size. From our previous discussion of point size and font metrics, you may remember that point size was the size necessary to ensure that two lines of type didn't run into one another, and that the width (for proportional fonts) varied according to the character. Here you are using a monospaced font, so the width is the same for each character; but the point size still fulfills the same function of providing clearance between lines. As you may recall, the vertical measurement to ensure adequate spacing must include both ascenders and descenders. These are the parts of letters that extend above and below the line of type, like the top of the letter b or the bottom of the letter y. If you look at Figure 4.2, you will see how these are measured.

Because point size is a vertical measurement, the width of the characters is always less than the point size; in effect, a box that fits around

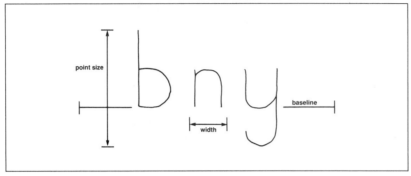

Figure 4.2: Character measurements

every character in a font would always be taller than it would be wide. Therefore, about seven lines of 10-point type will fit in a vertical inch, but the characters (in a monospaced font) will come out 12 to an inch. Of course, in a proportional font, the width of each character, and hence the number of characters per inch, will be variable.

Using these measures of 12 characters per inch and 6 lines per inch, you can work out the space required for the data in each of the lines. In this section you will work with the data elements only, as you might do for printing onto blank paper. The form measurements and layout will come later in the chapter, after you have worked out the data layout.

To begin with, the physical page is 8½ inches wide. You have to allow for margins on all sides, both for printing and aesthetic reasons, and allow room for the form to be printed. In this case, suppose that you establish 1-inch margins on both sides of the page. This leaves a maximum of 6½ inches for each line of data. The logo block at the top of the page is part of the form, and you will want it to print as close as possible to the top of the page. At the bottom, however, you should leave a margin of about 1 inch so that the data doesn't appear to run off the page.

The maximum line width is primarily a concern in the main block, which contains the list of purchased items. At 12 characters per inch, there will be a maximum of 78 characters across a 6½-inch line, including all spaces and punctuation. Using the previous list of data elements, you might allocate the spacing as follows:

Data Element	No. of Characters	Type
item number	8	alphanumeric characters
	5	spaces

item description	25	alphanumeric characters
	3	spaces
quantity ordered	5	four digits and sign (-9999)
	3	spaces
quantity shipped	5	four digits and sign (-9999)
	3	spaces
unit price	6	three digits, decimal, and two digits (999.99)
	3	spaces
	2	spaces
extended price	10	$-99,999.99$
	78	characters

Notice that you must provide room for a sign in several of the fields and for appropriate punctuation in the currency fields. The signs will be required for processing credits and returned items. You will also notice that the spaces between unit price and extended price have been divided into two parts: 3 spaces and 2 spaces. The 2-space section is provided to allow room for aligning the totals (which will be larger than any individual price) under the extended-price column.

The totals block contains four short data elements, which will be aligned under the extended-price column from the main text block. Nothing in the totals block is going to approach the maximum line width, and spacing can be allocated as follows:

Data Element	No. of Characters	Type
item total	11	$-999,999.99$
sales tax	9	$-9,999.99$
shipping and handling	10	$-99,999.99$
invoice total	11	$-999,999.99$

Similarly, nothing in the header block will be maximum width, either. The name and address data will consist of four lines, one below the other, while the invoice number and date are relatively short numeric items.

Space might be allocated as follows:

Data Element	No. of Characters	Type
name and address (4 lines)	30	alphanumeric characters
invoice number	6	digits (999999)
date	9	DD-MMM-YY

You have now completed width allocation for all the data elements that have been identified. But you still must determine how many lines each block will require, which can best be done after discussing how you are going to merge the form and the data into one document.

INTEGRATION

You have already worked out the method for producing a completed form by overlaying the blank form and the data onto a single output sheet. The data will be placed over the form, and both will be printed out together. The form clearly has to be designed and built like any other PostScript page, using the techniques that you have practiced in earlier chapters. You might, however, think that the application output could be printed onto the form without further processing, using whatever printing method the application provides.

Unfortunately, that is not possible for two reasons. First, output for your PostScript printer usually must be in PostScript; and most applications do not produce PostScript output, although this may change. Lotus 1-2-3, which we are using for this exercise, does not produce any laser-printer output. But PostScript-equipped printers often may be able to emulate another printer—for example, the Apple LaserWriter will emulate the Diablo 630—or perhaps you have an application that will produce PostScript output. Even in such cases, there is a second reason not to use the application output directly. The procedures used to create the data output are not "transparent"; that is, they may erase or otherwise damage the form that will already be generated and painted onto the output device, waiting to be printed along with the data. So you will expect to modify whatever output is provided by your application. However, you should note that you could easily work with PostScript output, if the application provided it, and tailor it to the requirement for processing the combined form and data.

It is not difficult to adapt standard output to the PostScript environment. The problem is to insert the necessary PostScript procedures into the application output so that the data will go onto the page with the structure required to match the form. You can do this easily by following these steps:

1. Print the application output to a disk file.
2. Edit the disk file to add PostScript procedures.
3. Send the revised file to the printer.

Later in the chapter, you will read about other methods of working with application output, but the method presented here is easy to understand and to work with.

As you have already discovered, PostScript structure is best used by creating powerful procedures to handle large segments of the desired page. You can use such procedures to process large pieces of the application output, treating output elements as strings and positioning an entire group on the page as required for the result you want. Knowing this, you can see that only modest editing will be necessary to prepare the application output for printing.

We have completed the initial analysis that was necessary before you could begin detailed layout and programming. Let's review what you have accomplished so far. You have structured the output page, both form and data, into major output blocks. You have also identified and positioned data elements for each block. The size of each data element and the horizontal spacing of elements within a line in the main text block—which is the largest portion of the form and contains the most data—have all been established. Finally, the minimum line spacing will be six lines per inch; however, the overall vertical spacing remains to be finalized because it depends on the detailed structure of the form itself.

FORM

You are ready to begin the detailed layout and design of the form. Because both parts of the final output must fit together exactly to work properly, this section frequently refers to the location of data elements on the other part of the output; and the same thing will happen in reverse when you design the data output in the next section. This natural back-and-forth should not be a surprise and would be equally necessary if you were designing a form to be printed and used on a typewriter or on a computer printer. In all cases, the form and the associated data make up a single output unit and ultimately must be considered and designed as such.

LAYOUT

Let's consider how to structure and lay out the form. You know that the minimum desirable spacing between lines is 6 lines per inch, or 12 points per line. This information provides a basis for starting the final layout. In addition, there are several design elements that are important considerations.

In laying out any page, there are a number of issues regarding form design and data placement that need to be resolved on aesthetic grounds or that may involve arbitrary choices. Such decisions are usually arrived at by a process of trial and error, making each judgement based on how the output looks—which is why WYSIWYG ("What You See Is What You Get") is so important in page-composition software. To avoid making this exercise tedious and repetitive, this trial-and-error process has already taken place, and the layout shown in Figure 4.3 is the result. As before, this layout contains design elements, such as the box around the purchased items and the totals, and the marks around the name and address, that are purely arbitrary; the same applies to some of the spacing decisions that are incorporated into the layout. Nevertheless, all these elements are taken from actual forms and are commonly used.

All vertical dimensions are given in inches or lines, or both, using the previously established basis of 6 lines per inch for the output. One of the first things you notice about this design is that the main text and totals have both been enclosed in a box, similar to the figure produced by the **screenBox** procedure that you worked on in the previous chapters.

Let's analyze this layout, working from the bottom up and starting with this box. Working from the bottom of each of the elements and blocks makes sense. This position represents the baseline for the text and defines a precise y-coordinate to be used for positioning both text and graphic elements. In keeping with standard PostScript measurement, all the lines are numbered from the bottom of the page. This means that there are 66 lines on the page (11 inches at 6 lines per inch) with line 66 being the top of the page. With this housekeeping out of the way, let's review the form layout in detail.

The bottom of the data box is at line 4, leaving a 2/3-inch margin at the bottom of the page. The data elements within the totals block are

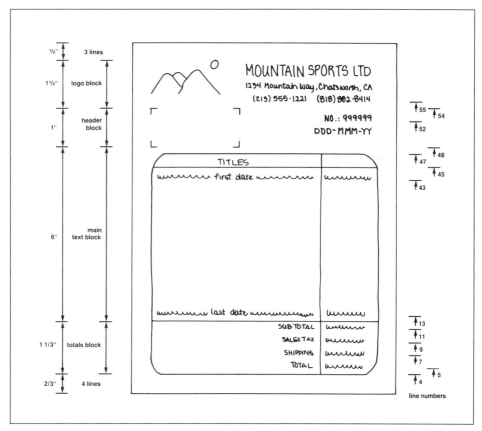

Figure 4.3: Form layout

double-spaced and located as follows:

Data Element	Location
item total	line 11
sales tax	line 9
shipping and handling	line 7
invoice total	line 5

This portion of the data box represents the totals block that was discussed earlier. The box is designed to enclose both the main text block and the totals block; but before you can determine the position for the top of the box, you need to position the top two blocks on the form.

The base of the topmost block, the logo block, is at line 55. This leaves 12 lines, or 2 inches, to the top of the physical page. The detail of the logo has not been designed yet, but you can estimate, based on the work in the last chapter, that you will require 1½ inches for the logo, leaving ½ inch as a top margin. Since the top of the logo is jagged and not uniform across the page, this top margin is not precise, but the estimate gives you a rough box to work with that is 1½ inches high and 7½ inches wide—a convenient ratio of 1:5.

The base of the header block is at line 48. You will note that the name and address information, which is 4 lines of data, is enclosed in an area set off by a series of graphic elements that look like corner tabs. This element is common in many forms and is designed (so I'm told) to help align the name and address space for window envelopes. In any case, the data elements in the header block are positioned as follows:

Data Element	Location
name and address (4 lines)	lines 52 to 49
invoice number	line 52
date	line 50

The top two "corners" are located on line 54, while the bottom two are on line 48. The word "Invoice" and the title "No. :" are also on line 52, before the position for the invoice number.

Now that these two top blocks are positioned, the remaining area is available for the main text block. The data box, which encloses both the main text and the totals, will have its top line on line 47. You will need titles for the data within the box, so set aside the top two lines of the box for title information and start the first data line two lines below that, on line 43. The last data item that will fit into the main text block should also be double-spaced from the totals. That places it two lines higher than the item total; therefore, it would be located at line 13.

You have now established the overall vertical spacing of the form as follows:

Data Element	Location
logo block	top at line 63
	baseline 55
header block	top at line 54
	baseline 48

main text block   top at line 47

                       baseline 13

totals block   top at line 11

                       baseline 4

In addition, the main text block and the totals block have been combined by means of a box that surrounds all the data elements from both blocks, combining them into a single graphic unit.

MAIN TEXT AND TOTALS

Now you need to set up and program each of the blocks in detail. You can begin with the box that encloses both the data items and the totals. Remember that you are not concerned with the positioning of the data or the totals themselves, but are creating the places on the form where those items will appear after they are output by the application. The top of the box will look like Figure 4.4.

This figure shows you the detail of the top of the box, along with the title information and the first line of the item list. The outer edge of the box will consist of a 2-point line, double the usual line width. A horizontal line of 1 point will be used to separate the title information from the data, and vertical lines of 1 point will be used to separate data elements down the page into columns. The positioning of these lines is shown in Figure 4.5, along with the x-coordinate required to position each of

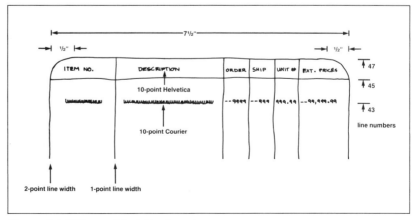

Figure 4.4: Titles and first-line layout

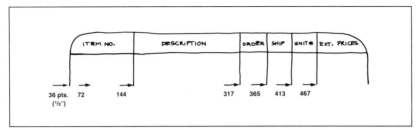

Figure 4.5: Column positioning

them. These coordinates were calculated using the character spacing for the data that will be below them; you remember that the data will be spaced 12 characters to the inch, which means that each character is 6 points wide.

The titles themselves will be in 10-point Helvetica and based 6 points (a half line) above the horizontal line that divides the title area from the data. This will approximately center the titles in the boxed area formed by this line and the top of the large data box, allowing 8 points above and 6 points below the title text. As discussed earlier, there is a double space down to the first line of data, on line 43. The data, the list of items purchased, will be entered from the spreadsheet, and that spacing will be discussed when we design the application output in the next section. In any case, the last data item that can be printed will be on line 13.

The setup information for the bottom of the box, which is the bottom of the form, is presented in Figure 4.6. This figure starts at the last data item and continues to the end of the form. This portion of the form contains totals information from the spreadsheet, which is placed next to appropriate labels, double-spaced in lines 11 to 5. The last data line is set off from the totals by a 1-point line positioned 6 points (half a line) below line 13; this will be line 12.5. The bottom of the box that encloses the data and totals is on line 4; as before, the line that forms the entire box is 2 points wide. The vertical line that divides the extended prices on the data portion of the form is brought down through the totals section to divide the numeric values from the labels; there is room enough for the larger totals fields because you allowed an extra two spaces in the extended-price column just for this purpose. The rest of the vertical lines end at the horizontal line that divides the data section from the totals.

The labels for the totals are in 10-point Helvetica-Bold and are right-justified at a position 4 points to the left of the vertical line.

You are ready to develop the procedures that will be required to produce the main data block and the totals block. You will develop these procedures together because you have enclosed these two blocks with

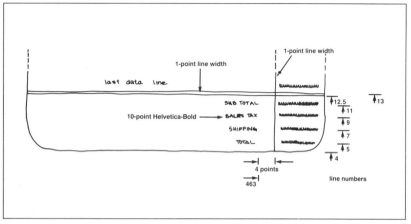

Figure 4.6: Last line and totals layout

the data box, effectively making them into one graphic unit. There isn't much overlap between this portion of the form and the other blocks, so you may as well make the procedures specific. When you have produced the final version of the program, it should follow the conventions discussed earlier; for now, you can break the program into prologue and script sections that can be integrated into a completely structured PostScript program later.

The major procedures for this part are as follows:

Syntax	Function
screenBox	produces the box that encloses the data and totals sections. This procedure differs from the earlier version in that it requires two operands for height and width (because this box is not a square).
dataTitles	produces the title information at the top of the data box, including both the titles and the horizontal line underneath them.
footTitles	produces the titles for the totals and the horizontal line above them; also produces the vertical line that separates the titles from the data.
verticalLines	produces the vertical lines that divide the columns of data. The lines extend from the top of the data box to the horizontal line that divides the last data line from the totals area.

Each of these procedures will use additional procedures. In real PostScript programming, you might begin to write the program using these procedures at this point. Let's look at Figure 4.7 to see what the program (that is, the script) portion might look like.

The program flow follows what has been discussed previously. You will notice that, first, the entire script section is enclosed in a **save**, **restore** pairing of operands on lines %1 and %11. This is good PostScript practice, as you learned when these operators were introduced. Second, you will notice that the **screenBox** procedure does not stroke the box, but leaves that outside the procedure. This is done so that you can set the line width at line %5 before stroking the figure in line %6. Also notice that the entire procedure is enclosed in a **gsave**, **grestore** pair on lines %2 and %7, in order to avoid missetting the other elements elsewhere on the page.

This program also identifies two more procedures that you will want to write: **inch** and **line**. You can see that the measurements on the page are given both in inches and lines; whichever is easiest and most natural has been used. The net result is that most y-coordinates are in lines, while the x-coordinates are either in inches or just in the native x-values. For this reason it is easier to use two procedures to help position items, instead of trying to convert one into the other.

Now you are ready to write the procedures. The figures that follow give each of the procedures identified so far, along with a short discussion.

Figure 4.8 gives the familiar **screenBox** procedure as you finally developed it in Chapter 3. The only difference is that there are now two dimensions required to develop the box, rather than one, which leads to the definition of two variables. If you don't remember the **arcto** operator, you should review it in the operator summary at the end of Chapter 3. The choice of the starting point (0.5 inch) and the size of the radius (0.25 inch) are arbitrary; you may adjust them to any values you find satisfactory.

```
%-------------------Program Script (Form) ------------------
%-------------------------Data Box -------------------------
/Page save def                                          %1
gsave                                                   %2
     .5 inch  4 line  translate                         %3
     7.5 inch  43 line  screenBox                       %4
     2 setlinewidth                                     %5
     stroke                                             %6
grestore                                                %7
verticalLines                                           %8
dataTitles                                              %9
footTitles                                              %10
Page restore                                            %11
copypage                                                %12
```

Figure 4.7: First draft of the form script

Now you can move on to the next procedure, **verticalLines**, in Figure 4.9. This procedure moves to the top of each of the columns identified in Figure 4.5 and rules a line from the top of the box, at line 47, to the bottom of the data area, at line 12.5. It doesn't stop at line 13, which is the last data line, because there is a horizontal line 6 points (a half line) below the data and it would look best to run the vertical lines into the horizontal one.

The next procedure is **dataTitles**, in Figure 4.10. This procedure is also straightforward; but it creates a need for an additional procedure to support it. The **dataTitles** procedure starts by moving to the point identified for the horizontal line dividing the data from the titles and draws that line. Then it moves to the position for the title text, which is 6 points, or a half line, above the horizontal line at line 45.5.

At this point, you realize that you must decide where to display the title headings. You have already established the location of the vertical

```
%---------------------Prologue (Form) --------------------
/screenBox
%expects translate origin to bottom-left box corner
%called as:    X-size Y-size screenBox
        {    newpath
             /DimY exch def
             /DimX exch def
             .5 inch 0 moveto
             DimX 0   DimX DimY .25 inch arcto
             4 {pop} repeat
             DimX DimY  0 DimY .25 inch arcto
             4 {pop} repeat
             0 DimY      0 0      .25 inch arcto
             4 {pop} repeat
             0 0        DimX 0    .25 inch arcto
             4 {pop} repeat
             closepath }
        def
```

Figure 4.8: Revised **screenBox** procedure

```
/verticalLines
        {    newpath
             144 47 line moveto
             144 12.5 line lineto
             317 47 line moveto
             317 12.5 line lineto
             365 47 line moveto
             365 12.5 line lineto
             413 47 line moveto
             413 12.5 line lineto
             467 47 line moveto
             467 12.5 line lineto
             stroke    }
        def
```

Figure 4.9: The **verticalLines** procedure

lines that divide the data elements into columns; an obvious solution is to center the titles between the columns. This is performed by the new procedure, **centerText**, which takes three operands: the string to be displayed, and the left and right positions between which the string is to be centered. The procedure will need to set the current point for the **show**, so you define the variable *Line* to hold the y-coordinate position. This is similar to the previous procedure for centering text that you developed in Chapter 1. That procedure, however, centered a text string between predefined margins; this one centers it between arbitrary x-coordinates.

The positions chosen for the centering are derived from the column positions shown in Figure 4.5. The first column begins at position 72, or 1 inch from the edge of the paper. No vertical line is ruled here as it would be redundant; the line at the edge of the box is sufficient to create a column for the data. The second and subsequent columns are used as positioned, except that the starting position for the centering has been moved right 1 point to allow for the width of the line that creates the column.

The final procedure that was identified initially is **footTitles**, shown in Figure 4.11. This procedure also requires a newly identified helper, **rightJustifyText**, which will take a string and an x-coordinate position and right-justify the string against the x-coordinate.

The basic procedure begins by creating the necessary horizontal and vertical lines that were previously identified. Then the titles of the totals are each positioned and right-justified. The process is identical for each title: first, the variable *Line* is set to provide the necessary y-coordinate

```
/dataTitles
    {    newline
        .5 inch 45 line moveto
        7.5 inch 0 rlineto
        stroke
        .5 inch 45.5 line moveto
        /Helvetica findfont 10 scalefont setfont
        /Line 45.5 line def
        (ITEM NO.)
        72 144 centerText
        (DESCRIPTION     )
        144 317 centerText
        (ORDER)
        318 365 centerText
        (SHIP)
        366 413 centerText
        (UNIT #)
        414 467 centerText
        (EXT. PRICE)
        468 540 centerText   }
    def
```

Figure 4.10: The **dataTitles** procedure

for the **show**, as you did in the **centerText** procedure above. Then the **rightJustifyText** procedure is invoked to set the desired string.

Now that these major procedures are defined, you need to turn your attention to the supporting ones in Figure 4.12. Each of these procedures sufficiently resembles the procedures used previously for these same functions that no further explanation is needed. If you have any questions, reread the appropriate sections of Chapter 2.

```
/footTitles
       {    newpath
            .5 inch 12.5 line moveto
            7.5 inch 0 rlineto
            stroke
            467 12.5 line moveto
            467 4 line lineto
            stroke
            /Helvetica-Bold findfont 10 scalefont setfont
            /Line 11 line def
            (SUBTOTAL)
            463 rightJustifyText
            /Line 9 line def
            (SALES TAX)
            463 rightJustifyText
            /Line 7 line def
            (SHIPPING)
            463 rightJustifyText
            /Line 5 line def
            (TOTAL)
            463 rightJustifyText        }
       def
```

Figure 4.11: The **footTitles** procedure

```
/inch
       {    72 mul    } def

/line
       {    12 mul    } def

/centerText
       {    /Right exch def
            /Left exch def
            dup
            stringwidth pop
            2 div
            Right Left sub 2 div
            exch sub
            Left add
            Line moveto
            show }
       def

/rightJustifyText
       {    /RightColumn exch def
            dup
            stringwidth pop
            RightColumn exch sub
            Line moveto
            show }
       def
```

Figure 4.12: Auxiliary procedures for the form

The entire data box can now be produced by running the procedures and the script as previously identified. The program so far looks like Figure 4.13. All of this is familiar territory for you. This program produces the page of output in Figure 4.14—not our full form yet, but a good start.

You will notice that a **copypage** appears at the end of this program segment. It was placed there so that you can proceed directly to the next portion of the form without rerunning the program to get both elements together. This saves a bit of time and effort; as you can see, the actual

```
%---------------------Prologue (Form) ----------------------
%---------------------Support Procedures ------------------
/inch
        {      72 mul    } def

/line
        {      12 mul    } def

/centerText
        {      /Right exch def
               /Left exch def
               dup
               stringwidth pop
               2 div
               Right Left sub 2 div
               exch sub
               Left add
               Line moveto
               show }
        def

/rightJustifyText
        {      /RightColumn exch def
               dup
               stringwidth pop
               RightColumn exch sub
               Line moveto
               show }
        def
%-----------------------Major Procedures -------------------
/screenBox
%expects translate origin to bottom-left box corner
%called as:   X-size Y-size screenBox
        {      newpath
               /DimY exch def
               /DimX exch def
               .5 inch 0 moveto
               DimX 0   DimX DimY .25 inch arcto
               4 {pop} repeat
               DimX DimY   0 DimY .25 inch arcto
               4 {pop} repeat
               0 DimY      0 0      .25 inch arcto
               4 {pop} repeat
               0 0        DimX 0    .25 inch arcto
               4 {pop} repeat
               closepath }
        def

/verticalLines
        {      newpath
               144 47 line moveto
               144 12.5 line lineto
```

Figure 4.13: Program for the data block

```
                317 47 line moveto
                317 12.5 line lineto
                365 47 line moveto
                365 12.5 line lineto
                413 47 line moveto
                413 12.5 line lineto
                467 47 line moveto
                467 12.5 line lineto
                stroke      }
        def

/dataTitles
        {       newline
                .5 inch 45 line moveto
                7.5 inch 0 rlineto
                stroke
                .5 inch 45.5 line moveto
                /Helvetica findfont 10 scalefont setfont
                /Line 45.5 line def
                (ITEM NO.)
                72 144 centerText
                (DESCRIPTION    )
                144 317 centerText
                (ORDER)
                318 365 centerText
                (SHIP)
                366 413 centerText
                (UNIT #)
                414 467 centerText
                (EXT. PRICE)
                468 540 centerText    }
        def

/footTitles
        {       newpath
                .5 inch 12.5 line moveto
                7.5 inch 0 rlineto
                stroke
                467 12.5 line moveto
                467 4 line lineto
                stroke
                /Helvetica-Bold findfont 10 scalefont setfont
                /Line 11 line def
                (SUBTOTAL)
                463 rightJustifyText
                /Line 9 line def
                (SALES TAX)
                463 rightJustifyText
                /Line 7 line def
                (SHIPPING)
                463 rightJustifyText
                /Line 5 line def
                (TOTAL)
                463 rightJustifyText      }
        def
%-------------------Script (Form) --------------------
%-------------------Data Box -------------------------
/Page save def                                %1
gsave                                         %2
        .5 inch  4 line  translate            %3
        7.5 inch  43 line  screenBox          %4
        2 setlinewidth                        %5
        stroke                                %6
grestore                                      %7
verticalLines                                 %8
dataTitles                                    %9
footTitles                                    %10
Page restore                                  %11
copypage                                      %12
```

Figure 4.13 (cont.): Program for the data block

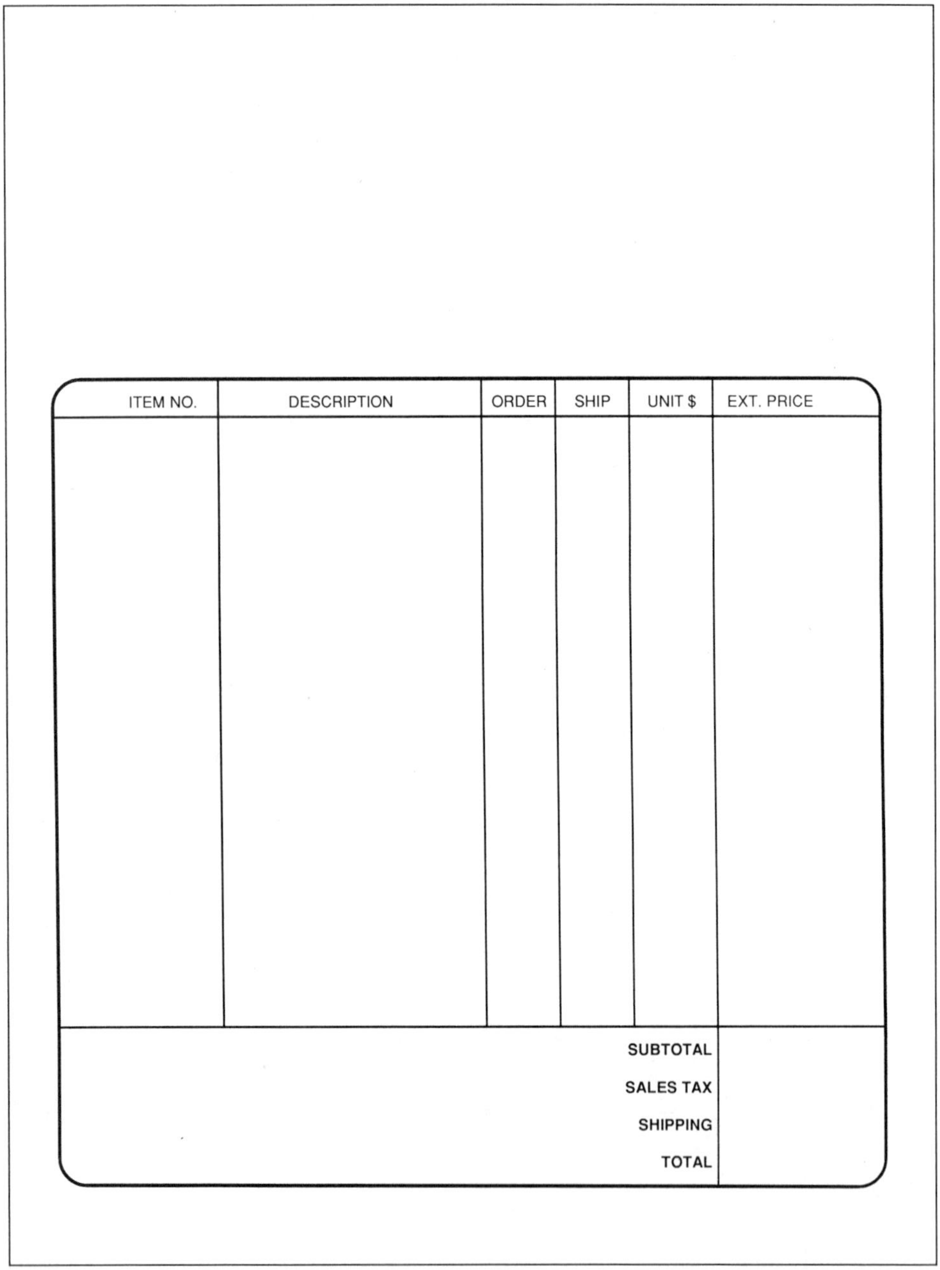

ITEM NO.	DESCRIPTION	ORDER	SHIP	UNIT $	EXT. PRICE
				SUBTOTAL	
				SALES TAX	
				SHIPPING	
				TOTAL	

Figure 4.14: Main text block and totals block

program is compact and would be easy to rerun if you needed to do so.

You will notice that you are reusing procedures that were developed earlier in the book, either in the same or in a slightly modified form. This is characteristic of PostScript and illustrates what has been said before about developing a library of PostScript procedures to work from. With such a library of tested procedures, you will find that you can produce a variety of relatively complex pages in a short time. We will discuss this in more detail later in the chapter.

HEADER

Now you can move on to set up and program the header block in detail. In this case, the setup is fairly easy because you have already done most of the required work.

There are three data elements in this block: name and address, invoice number, and date. Of these, only the invoice number has any impact on the setup of the header block within the form. You have already allocated space inside the small graphic "corners" for the name and address, and the date will be on a line by itself. Only the label for the invoice number needs to be positioned and integrated with the data output. The easiest way to do this is to set an arbitrary margin on the right side of the page that leaves enough room for the invoice number and then right-justify the label against that margin. If you wanted to be fancier, you could use the string for the invoice number to calculate the position for the label; but for this exercise, using a margin will suffice.

This procedure produces a setup for the title information within the header block, as shown in Figure 4.15. This figure shows you both of the labels necessary in the header block and their respective positions and sizing. The "INVOICE" label will be centered between the page

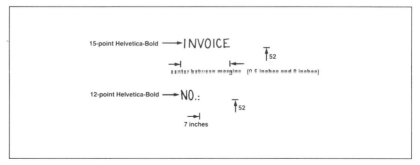

Figure 4.15: Header title information

margins of 0.5 inch and 8 inches and set in 15-point Helvetica-Bold at line 52, as set on the original form design. The "NO. :" label, for the invoice number, is set in 12-point Helvetica-Bold and also is located at line 52. In this case, the label is right-justified against an arbitrary 7-inch margin, which leaves 1 inch for the number itself.

The setup for the "corners" is equally easy and is shown in Figure 4.16. The box bounded by these "corners" is 6 lines, or 1 inch, high and must fit 25 characters across. As discussed earlier, there will be 12 characters to the inch, so allowing for spacing and position adjustment, you can make this box 2.5 inches, or 30 characters, wide. The "corners" themselves are 12 points in each direction, and the baseline of the entire figure is at line 48.

In this case, you can see that the following two procedures will make up the header block:

Syntax	Function
headTitles	produces the title information for the header
cornerBox	produces the box made out of the small "corner" graphic elements

Following the same methods used before, you can work out what a script using such procedures might look like:

```
%—————————Header Block———————
headTitles
gsave
       .5 inch 48 line translate
       2.5 inch 1 inch cornerBox
grestore
```

This section of the program looks, unsurprisingly, much like the preceding section for the data block. Once again, the graphic portion of the figure, which is produced by the **cornerBox** procedure, is enclosed in a **gsave, grestore** pair so that the changes made within the procedure don't affect anything else in the program. In particular, the effect of the **translate** that you use to move the origin to the bottom-left corner of the box is confined to the procedure itself. The titles stand by themselves, since they are positioned by lines relative to the original coordinate system on the page and don't require any special movement to work correctly.

This only leaves you the task of working out these procedures. Taking both together, you have the code in Figure 4.17. You will notice that the

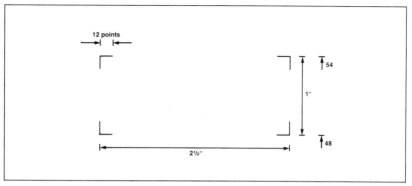

Figure 4.16: Name and address box in header

```
/headTitles
    {
        %first set invoice title
        /Helvetica-Bold findfont 15 scalefont setfont
        /Line 52 line def
        (INVOICE)
        .5 inch  8 inch  centerText
        %now set number title
        /Helvetica-Bold findfont 12 scalefont setfont
        (NO. :)
        7 inch rightJustifyText}
    def

/cornerBox
%expects translate origin to bottom-left box corner
%called as:    X-size Y-size cornerBox
    {    newpath
        /DimY exch def
        /DimX exch def
        %bottom-left corner
        0    0    moveto
        0   12    rlineto
        0    0    moveto
       12    0    rlineto
        %bottom-right corner
       DimX 0    moveto
        0   12    rlineto
       DimX 0    moveto
       -12 0     rlineto
        %top-left corner
       0 DimY    moveto
       0 -12     rlineto
       0 DimY    moveto
       12    0   rlineto
        %top-right corner
       DimX DimY moveto
        0 -12       rlineto
       DimX DimY moveto
       -12  0      rlineto
       stroke    }
    def
```

Figure 4.17: Header block procedures

headTitles procedure makes use of the previously developed supporting procedures, **centerText** and **rightJustifyText**. This illustrates how you need to think about procedure structure as you're working through a PostScript program; often you will find that there are common supporting procedures that you can use throughout the program. When you find such procedures in several programs, as you have here with these two procedures, they become strong candidates for inclusion in your library of PostScript routines.

The **cornerBox** procedure is long, but simple. It is easy to see how this procedure operates. It begins at the bottom-left corner, which is the origin for the figure, and produces two 12-point lines: one line in the x-direction and one in the y-direction. The **moveto** between the two **rlineto**s is required because the **rlineto** will move the current point as it executes, leaving you positioned at the end of the line. Because each part of the line needs to start from the common vertex, you need to move the current point back there explicitly. Notice that this is done for each of the box corners.

After creating the bottom-left corner, you move over to the bottom-right corner with an explicit **moveto** command and create the next corner. Here the lines extend up the page in the y-direction, but go back across the page in the x-direction; hence, the negative sign is required on the **rmoveto** for the line in the x-coordinate. The rest of the corners function in exactly the same way; only the negative signs change to indicate the proper motion for each **rlineto**.

The final result is a program that is a combination of the previous elements and looks like Figure 4.18. This program produces the output in Figure 4.19.

There are a couple of points to note here. First, this portion of the program assumes that you are continuing your work from the preceding segment; therefore, the necessary support procedures should already be defined. If they were not, you would get an error as you tried to execute the procedures that depend on them. This assumption is made to save space here; if you need to redo the procedures, go back to the preceding section and copy them again.

The second point is that the preceding section, like this portion of the form, ended with a **copypage**. If you have continued from the previous exercise, then you will see both elements of the form on your output, because **copypage** will have left the output generated by the earlier segment still on the page. Figure 4.19 shows only the output generated by the current program segment; therefore, don't think it's an error if the output from the previous segment is also present.

```
%-------------------Major Procedures (Header) -----------
/headTitles
        {
            %first set invoice title
            /Helvetica-Bold findfont 15 scalefont setfont
            /Line 52 line def
            (INVOICE)
            .5 inch  8 inch  centerText
            %now set number title
            /Helvetica-Bold findfont 12 scalefont setfont
            (NO. :)
            7 inch rightJustifyText}
    def
/cornerBox
%expects translate origin to bottom-left box corner
%called as:     X-size Y-size cornerBox
        {   newpath
            /DimY exch def
            /DimX exch def
            %bottom-left corner
            0   0   moveto
            0  12   rlineto
            0   0   moveto
           12   0   rlineto
            %bottom-right corner
           DimX 0   moveto
            0  12   rlineto
           DimX 0   moveto
          -12   0   rlineto
            %top-left corner
            0 DimY   moveto
            0  -12   rlineto
            0 DimY   moveto
           12   0   rlineto
            %top-right corner
           DimX DimY moveto
            0  -12   rlineto
           DimX DimY moveto
          -12   0   rlineto
           stroke      }
    def
%-----------------------Header Block -------------------
headTitles
gsave
    .5 inch 48 line translate
    2.5 inch 1 inch cornerBox
grestore
copypage
```

Figure 4.18: Header block program

LOGO

The logo block is the one block that remains to be set up and programmed. This block will use the graphic element that you developed at the end of Chapter 3 as a logo graphic and will integrate the name of the company and its address information to make a complete logo for the form.

The setup of the logo block has to begin with consideration of the graphic element, which needs to be sized and positioned before you can

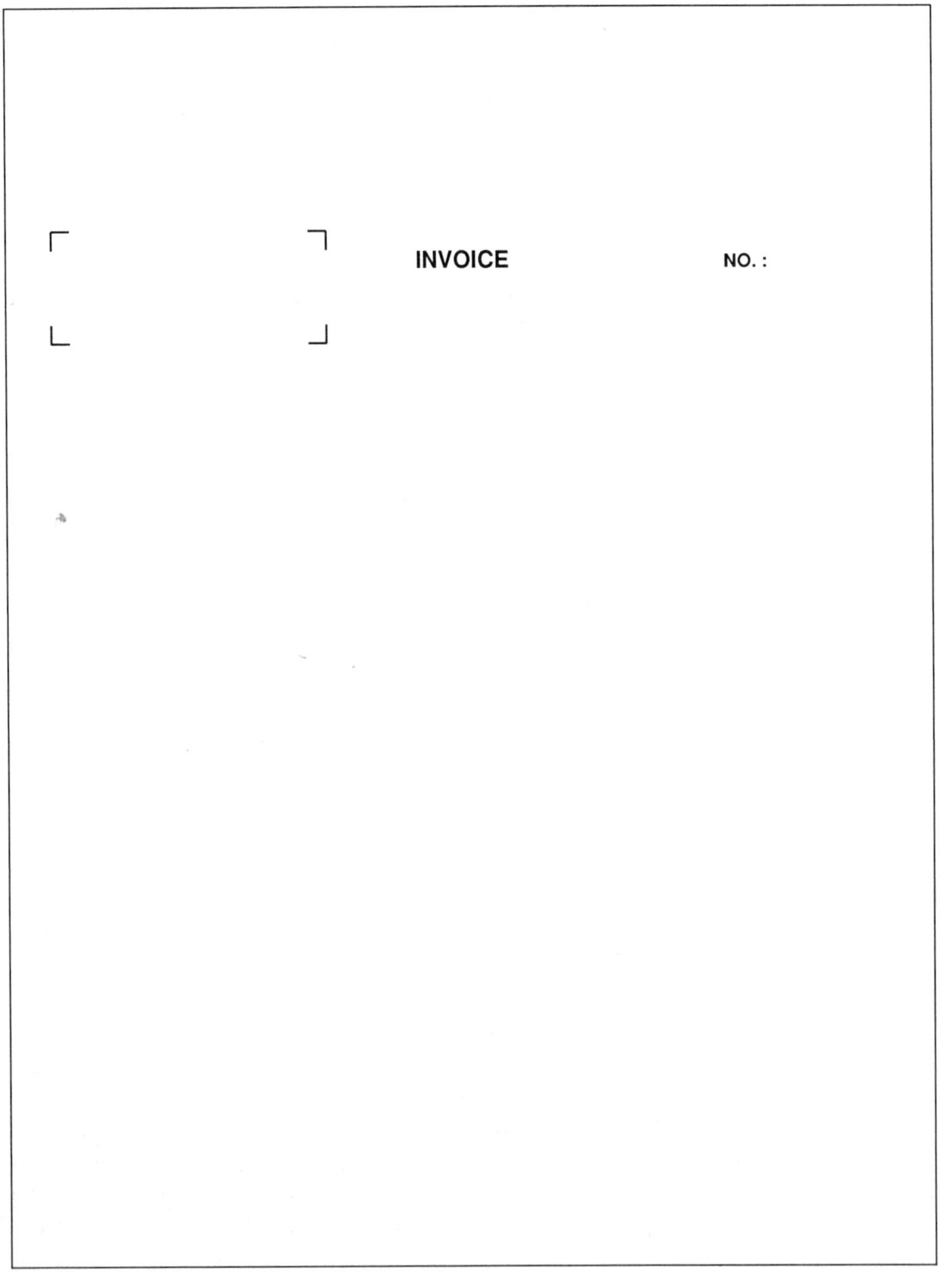

Figure 4.19: Header block

do anything with the text elements. When you built the graphic in the last chapter, you created an element that was 17 units wide by 11 units high and produced the output graphic using ½ inch as a unit. Now you must fit the graphic into a defined space: the space that you left at the top of the form for the logo block. Here is where the power and elegance of the PostScript language become evident. The graphic is not a particular size; it is 11 by 17 *units*. Since you want the height of the graphic to be about 1½ inches, you need to divide 1½ inches by 11 to get the appropriate scaling factor. In this case, cursory examination shows that 1½ inches is an inappropriate measure for this division, so you quickly convert that into 108 points; dividing 108 by 11 gives 9.8 points per unit. For convenience, that number has been rounded down to 9.5 units; you don't want to round up, since that would push the graphic into the top of the page.

Using that factor, and doing some arithmetic, you can figure out that the horizontal dimension of the graphic will be approximately 2¼ inches (17 × 9.5 / 72). Now you can leave an open square of that dimension on the detail setup for the logo and proceed to lay out the text elements as shown in Figure 4.20.

All measurement on this figure starts from the bottom-left corner of the box that will contain the graphic element; in other words, unlike the previous blocks, the logo block is self-contained. The entire logo, graphic and all, forms a complete aesthetic unit, which can be moved or adjusted as required without reference to any other element on the page. In addition, this block can be reused in other contexts.

The name of the company, Mountain Sports, Ltd., is set uppercase in 18-point Helvetica-BoldOblique type. As the name implies, this type style is both bold and slanted and serves to emphasize the name in the logo. The name is based on a line that is 0.75 inch above the logo baseline, which will be about halfway up the graphic. The name and address lines

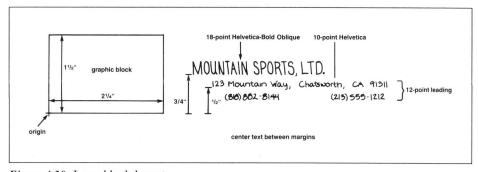

Figure 4.20: Logo block layout

are all centered between the margins. The address lines begin 0.5 inches from the logo baseline, making them 18 points (a half inch) below the name. This means that they are set the same distance from the name text as the name is high. Since the address lines are set in 10-point type, this is a good distance, and it sets them off enough from the name to be easily legible. The two address lines are set in 10-point Helvetica with 12-point leading.

This analysis suggests two procedures: one for the graphic and one for the text. These can be defined as follows:

Syntax	**Function**
logoTitles	sets the company name and address text for the logo
graphic	produces the graphic element for the logo

However, the entire logo is measured and located as a unit. That means you need to create a third procedure to connect one procedure with the other. In this case, the best method will be to define a new procedure, **logo**, that will contain both **logoTitles** and **graphic** along with the required scaling for the graphic.

This procedure simplifies the body of the program, which now must contain only the following lines to generate the logo block:

```
%————————Logo Block————————
gsave
        .5 inch 55 line translate
        logo
grestore
```

Let's look at the procedures individually. You can begin with the titles, shown in Figure 4.21, because they will be the most straightforward. As before, the auxiliary procedures for centering and right-justifying text strings are important. With those available, however, the rest of the procedure is easy. Note that the measurements are, as discussed earlier, all based on the logo origin and not the page origin as in the previous procedures for the header and data text.

The procedure for the graphic element is an adaptation of the fifth exercise in the preceding chapter, making it into a procedure instead of a program. It looks like Figure 4.22. This uses the same supporting procedures that were required in the fifth exercise: **sun** and **hill**. These procedures are shown in Figure 4.23.

```
/logoTitles
        {
            /Helvetica-BoldOblique findfont 18 scalefont setfont
            /Line .75 inch def
            (MOUNTAIN SPORTS, LTD.)
            0 8 inch centerText
            /Helvetica findfont 10 scalefont setfont
            /Line .5 inch def
            (123 Mountain Way,  Chatsworth, CA  91311)
            0 8 inch centerText
            /Line .5 inch 12 sub def
            ((818) 882-8144                    (213) 555-1212)
            0 8 inch centerText }
        def
```

Figure 4.21: The **logoTitles** procedure

```
/graphic
        {    newpath
             %begin logo
             %do background mountain
             gsave
                 3   0   translate
                 8   8   hill
                 .3 setgray
                 fill
             grestore
             %do left and right hills
             gsave
                 %left hill
                 5   6   hill
                 .7 setgray
                 fill
                 %right hill
                 7   0   translate
                 5   6   hill
                 fill
             grestore
             %do sun
             gsave
                 14    9     translate
                 1.5 sun
                 stroke
             grestore
             %logo finished
                 }
        def
```

Figure 4.22: The **graphic** procedure

This only leaves the **logo** procedure to be defined, as follows:

```
/logo
        {    logoTitles
             9.5 9.5 scale
             1 9.5 div setlinewidth
             graphic    }
        def
```

This procedure does just what is required and no more. It calls the procedure **logoTitles**; then it scales the coordinates for the graphic, resets the line width to 1 point, and calls **graphic**. All saving and restoring of the graphic state and any translation of the coordinates is left for the main line program; in fact, both of those actions will be required to invoke **logo**, as you saw earlier.

To finish the final block, before you proceed to the completed form, the short program for the logo by itself is shown in Figure 4.24. This procedure, by itself, produces the output in Figure 4.25.

```
/sun
    {     /Radius exch def
          0  0  Radius  0  360 arc }
    def

/hill
    {   /Base exch def
        /Hgt   exch def
        /HalfBase
        Base 2 div def
        0 0 moveto
        HalfBase Hgt lineto
        Base  0 lineto  }
    def
```

Figure 4.23: Auxiliary procedures for **graphic**

```
%---------------------Support Procedures ------------------
/sun
    {     /Radius exch def
          0  0  Radius  0  360 arc }
    def

/hill
    {   /Base exch def
        /Hgt   exch def
        /HalfBase
        Base 2 div def
        0 0 moveto
        HalfBase Hgt lineto
        Base  0 lineto  }
    def
%-------------------Major Procedures (Logo) --------------
/logoTitles
    {
        /Helvetica-BoldOblique findfont 18 scalefont setfont
        /Line .75 inch def
        (MOUNTAIN SPORTS, LTD.)
        0 8 inch centerText
        /Helvetica findfont 10 scalefont setfont
        /Line .5 inch def
        (123 Mountain Way,   Chatsworth, CA  91311)
        0 8 inch centerText
        /Line .5 inch 12 sub def
        ((818) 882-8144              (213) 555-1212)
        0 8 inch centerText }
    def
```

Figure 4.24: Logo block program

```
/graphic
    {    newpath
         %begin logo
         %do background mountain
         gsave
              3   0   translate
              8   8   hill
              .3 setgray
              fill
         grestore
         %do left and right hills
         gsave
              %left hill
              5   6   hill
              .7 setgray
              fill
              %right hill
              7   0   translate
              5   6   hill
              fill
         grestore
         %do sun
         gsave
              14    9     translate
              1.5 sun
              stroke
         grestore
         %logo finished
                   }
    def

/logo
    {    logoTitles
         9.5 9.5 scale
         1 9.5 div setlinewidth
         graphic    }
    def
%-----------------------Logo Block --------------------
gsave
    .5 inch 55 line translate
    logo
grestore
showpage
```

Figure 4.24 (cont.): Logo block program

You will notice that the program doesn't use **copypage** this time. If you have been working continuously, now you will see the entire form on your output; in either case, you need to clear the page for the final form output, which comes in the next section.

ENTIRE FORM AS A UNIT

Even though you have built each of the blocks individually, some work is still necessary to make them all into a single form output. You should establish the full PostScript structure around your program; until now, the structure has been minimal. You also need to set up the various procedures and establish the order of creation for each block. None of this is difficult; it just takes a few moments to work out.

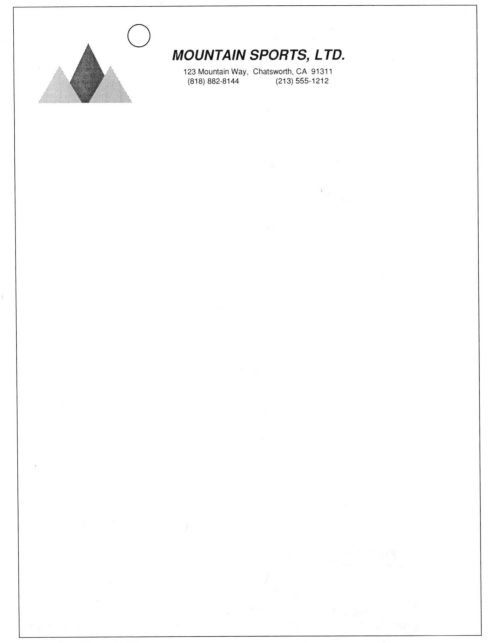

Figure 4.25: Logo block

The structure is familiar to you by now; it will repeat what you have seen in the previous examples. The order of the blocks is not critical; you only need to take the necessary **save** and **restore** functions into account and make sure that the elements are all located properly. In this exercise, you can start at the top of the page with the logo block and work down.

With this housekeeping out of the way, the final form program is shown in Figure 4.26. Once again, you notice how short and simple the body of the program is compared to the prologue. Properly constructed and defined, the procedures do all the work in PostScript. This exercise produces the page of output in Figure 4.27.

```
%----------------------------Exercise Six-----------------------------
%!PS-Adobe-1.0
%%DocumentFonts Helvetica Helvetica-Bold Helvetica-BoldOblique
%%Title: Exercise 6 (Form)
%%Creator: David Holzgang
%%CreationDate: 16 February 1987 10:30:00
%%For: Understanding PostScript Programming
%%Pages: 1
%%EndComments
%-----------------------Prologue-----------------------------
%----------------------Support Procedures -----------------------
/inch
        {      72 mul    } def
/line
        {      12 mul    } def

/centerText
        {      /Right exch def
               /Left exch def
               dup
               stringwidth pop
               2 div
               Right Left sub 2 div
               exch sub
               Left add
               Line moveto
               show }
        def

/rightJustifyText
        {      /RightColumn exch def
               dup
               stringwidth pop
               RightColumn exch sub
               Line moveto
               show }
        def

      /sun
        {            /Radius exch def
               0   0   Radius   0   360 arc }
        def

      /hill
        {      /Base exch def
               /Hgt  exch def
               /HalfBase
               Base 2 div def
```

Figure 4.26: Completed form program

```
              0 0 moveto
              HalfBase Hgt lineto
              Base  0 lineto  }
      def
%---------------------Major Procedures (Logo) -------------------
/logoTitles
      {
              /Helvetica-BoldOblique findfont 18 scalefont setfont
              /Line .75 inch def
              (MOUNTAIN SPORTS, LTD.)
              0 8 inch centerText
              /Helvetica findfont 10 scalefont setfont
              /Line .5 inch def
              (123 Mountain Way,  Chatsworth, CA  91311)
              0 8 inch centerText
              /Line .5 inch 12 sub def
              ((818) 882-8144                  (213) 555-1212)
              0 8 inch centerText }
      def

/graphic
      {     newpath
            %begin logo
            %do background mountain
            gsave
                  3   0   translate
                  8   8   hill
                  .3 setgray
                  fill
            grestore
            %do left and right hills
            gsave
                  %left hill
                  5   6   hill
                  .7 setgray
                  fill
                  %right hill
                  7   0   translate
                  5   6   hill
                  fill
            grestore
            %do sun
            gsave
                  14    9      translate
                  1.5 sun
                  stroke
            grestore
            %logo finished
                  }
      def

/logo
      {     logoTitles
            9.5 9.5 scale
            1 9.5 div setlinewidth
            graphic   }
      def
%------------------Major Procedures (Header) --------------------
/headTitles
      {
              %first set invoice title
              /Helvetica-Bold findfont 15 scalefont setfont
              /Line 52 line def
              (INVOICE)
              .5 inch 8 inch centerText
              %now set number title
              /Helvetica-Bold findfont 12 scalefont setfont
              (No. :)
              7 inch rightJustifyText  )
```

Figure 4.26 (cont.): Completed form program

```
        def
/cornerBox
        %expects translate origin to bottom-left box corner
        %called as:      X-size Y-size cornerBox
        {     newpath
              /DimY exch def
              /DimX exch def
              %bottom-left corner
              0    0   moveto
              0    12  rlineto
              0    0   moveto
              12   0   rlineto
              %bottom-right corner
              DimX 0 moveto
              0   12 rlineto
              DimX 0 moveto
              -12  0   rlineto
              %top-left corner
              0 DimY  moveto
              0   -12  rlineto
              0 DimY  moveto
              12   0   rlineto
              %top-right corner
              DimX DimY moveto
              0   -12  rlineto
              DimX DimY moveto
              -12  0   rlineto
              stroke    }
        def
%------------------Major Procedures (Data Box) ------------------
/screenBox
        {     newpath
              /DimY exch def
              /DimX exch def
              .5 inch 0 moveto
              DimX 0   DimX DimY .25 inch arcto
              4 {pop} repeat
              DimX DimY  0 DimY .25 inch arcto
              4 {pop} repeat
              0 DimY     0 0      .25 inch arcto
              4 {pop} repeat
              0 0        DimX 0   .25 inch arcto
              4 {pop} repeat
              closepath }
        def
/verticalLines
        {     newpath
              144 47 line moveto
              144 12.5 line lineto
              317 47 line moveto
              317 12.5 line lineto
              365 47 line moveto
              365 12.5 line lineto
              413 47 line moveto
              413 12.5 line lineto
              467 47 line moveto
              467 12.5 line lineto
              stroke    }
        def

/dataTitles
        {     newpath
              .5 inch 45 line moveto
              7.5 inch 0 rlineto
              stroke
              .5 inch 45.5 line moveto
              /Helvetica findfont 10 scalefont setfont
              /Line 45.5 line def
```

Figure 4.26 (cont.): Completed form program

```
                (ITEM NO.)
                72 144 centerText
                (DESCRIPTION     )
                144 317 centerText
                (ORDER)
                318 365 centerText
                (SHIP)
                366 413 centerText
                (UNIT $)
                414 467 centerText
                (EXT. PRICE)
                468 540 centerText    }
        def

/footTitles
        {       newpath
                .5 inch 12.5 line moveto
                7.5 inch 0 rlineto
                stroke
                467 12.5 line moveto
                467 4 line lineto
                stroke
                /Helvetica-Bold findfont 10 scalefont setfont
                /Line 11 line def
                (SUBTOTAL)
                463 rightJustifyText
                /Line 9 line def
                (SALES TAX)
                463 rightJustifyText
                /Line 7 line def
                (SHIPPING)
                463 rightJustifyText
                /Line 5 line def
                (TOTAL)
                463 rightJustifyText      }
        def
%%EndProlog
%%Page: i 1
%---------------------------Script (Form) ---------------
/Page save def
%produce logo box
gsave
        .5 inch   55 line translate
        logo
grestore
%produce header block
headTitles
gsave
        .5 inch   48 line translate
        2.5 inch   1 inch cornerBox
grestore
%produce data box (main text & totals blocks)
gsave
        .5 inch   4 line   translate
        7.5 inch  43 line   screenBox
        2 setlinewidth
        stroke
grestore
verticalLines
dataTitles
footTitles
%form page finished
Page restore
showpage
%%Trailer
%all done
```

Figure 4.26 (cont.): Completed form program

MOUNTAIN SPORTS, LTD.

123 Mountain Way, Chatsworth, CA 91311
(818) 882-8144   (213) 555-1212

INVOICE   NO. :

ITEM NO.	DESCRIPTION	ORDER	SHIP	UNIT $	EXT. PRICE
				SUBTOTAL	
				SALES TAX	
				SHIPPING	
				TOTAL	

Figure 4.27: Complete blank form

This blank form is a fairly complex page, but it is only half of what we set out to accomplish. Now you must turn your attention to the other half of the desired output, the data that comes from the spreadsheet application.

FILL-IN

Now that the form has been completed, you are ready to begin work on the application information that will provide the data to fill in the blank form. You have already done quite a bit of work on the application, so this stage will go quickly.

One of the main issues regarding any application is the number and size of the data fields that will be required. You established this information earlier in the chapter, when you were designing the form. Let's recap here all the data items that need to be on the form and the sizes that were selected for each of them.

Data Element	No. of Characters	Type
name and address (4 lines)	30	alphanumeric characters
invoice number	6	digits (999999)
date	9	DD-MMM-YY
item number	8	alphanumeric characters
	5	spaces
item description	25	alphanumeric characters
	3	spaces
quantity ordered	5	four digits and sign (-9999)
	3	spaces
quantity shipped	5	four digits and sign (-9999)
	3	spaces

unit price	6	three digits, decimal, and two digits (999.99)
	3	spaces
	2	spaces
extended price	10	− 99,999.99
items total	11	− 999,999.99
sales tax	9	− 9,999.99
shipping and handling	10	− 99,999.99
invoice total	11	− 999,999.99

The spacing information for each line item has been retained in this list because it will play an important part in setting up the spreadsheet.

Early in the chapter, you also laid out the sequence of steps that you need to take to place the data on the form. These steps were as follows:

1. Output completed data from the spreadsheet to the disk file.
2. Edit the disk file to add the required PostScript commands and procedures.
3. Copy the disk file to the printer to create PostScript output.

This leaves two areas that must be addressed before you can take the steps outlined above. First, you must create the application itself; that is, you have to create a Lotus spreadsheet with the necessary data items and structure to integrate with the form. Second, you have to design PostScript procedures that will take the disk output file from the application and merge it onto the form you have already produced.

APPLICATION CONSIDERATIONS

This section covers the design of the spreadsheet to provide data for the form. We are not going to describe in detail how to accomplish what has to be done. Several excellent Lotus books are available; and in any case, the specific spreadsheet program that is used to prepare the data is not the issue here. The object is to produce output from a standard application package and integrate it with a predesigned and preprogrammed PostScript form.

We will specify what you need to be aware of and what adjustments you need to make in the spreadsheet to have the output mesh correctly into the blank form. As you will see, in many ways these considerations and adjustments are identical to those you would make for printing on a blank form using a typical impact printer.

The horizontal spacing has already been set by having chosen a monospaced font and then by having set the sizes for each of the data items. As you may recall, that was the reason for establishing the spacing to go along with the data. You may not have realized it at the time that you were doing this horizontal layout, but the spacing is inherent in the nature of the data and the font. The data line is fixed at 78 characters long. This translates into 6½ inches, as you will remember from the earlier calculations. Since each character will take up a fixed width (because you are using a monospaced font), the horizontal spacing across the line is also fixed; you know precisely where each character of each data item will appear on the fill-in.

However, the vertical spacing is not fixed yet. The form has been designed with a vertical spacing of 6 lines to the inch, but that covers the form text and does not limit the data. The form has a basic space for the data items that begins at line 43 and ends at line 13, inclusive. Therefore, there are 31 lines (at 6 lines per inch) for data items. At 6 lines per inch, the spacing is 12 points; this spacing is the minimum for a 10-point font, which is what you will be using for data. Furthermore, 31 lines is probably more data items than you want on a form; and it is certainly more than will fit on a screen. Therefore, you choose a spacing of 1½ lines, or 18 points, for each data line. This provides space for 16 line items (since the first and last lines still hold data), which is enough for our purpose and will fit comfortably on the screen.

Figure 4.28 shows the screen designed for input of the invoice data onto a Lotus spreadsheet. There are several points to notice about this screen. First, the data flows down the screen in a natural way, with the invoice number at the top, followed by the name and address and the date. A line of titles follows, to help identify the data line items, and this is followed by 16 lines for the data. Finally, there are the four totals items, each aligned under the extended-price column, just as you had them on the form.

The first column on the right holds the titles for each area. These titles are kept on the side so that you can exclude them when you print; they are unnecessary on the form. The second column is intentionally blank to provide a spacing mechanism; the data to be entered starts in the third

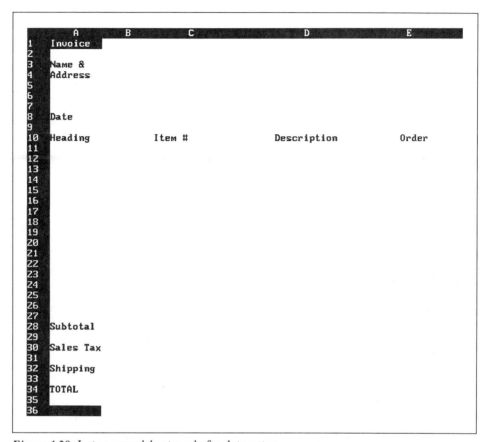

Figure 4.28: Lotus spreadsheet ready for data entry

column. Each column is sized to match the size of the data on the line items. There is no need to worry about the sizing for the name and address or for the other single data items, because Lotus will allow you to enter and display data of any size in a field as long as the adjacent cells are blank. Since these items are alone on a line, this presents no problem. The data in the line items, however, is positioned as it is on the form, one item beside another. For these items, column size is important.

Now that you have seen the blank form, let's put some data into it. Figure 4.29 shows the spreadsheet filled out with the sample data to be applied ultimately to the form you've designed. This data is wide enough and long enough to require several screens to display it all. Notice that the totals are located below and in line with the extended-price column.

	A	B	C	D	E	F	G	H
1	Invoice		10423					
2								
3	Name &		David Holzgang					
4	Address		22621 Penfield Ave.					
5			Chatsworth, CA 91311					
6								
7								
8	Date		20-Feb-87					
9								
10	Heading		Item #	Description	Order	Ship	Unit $	Ext. Price
11			12-456	Backpack - Blue	1	1	28.95	$28.95
12			28-145	Wool Socks - Size 10	4	4	3.95	$15.80
13			95-004	Strawberries	10	10	1.45	$14.50
14			95-010	Apricots	5	5	1.29	$6.45
15			96-148	Chicken Cacciatore	4	4	2.95	$11.80
16			96-104	Beef Stew	4	3	2.95	$8.85
17			96-107	Spaghetti with Meat Sauce	2	2	2.95	$5.90
18			96-242	Trail Mix	4	4	0.98	$3.92
19			35-129	First Aid Kit	1	1	9.49	$9.49
20								
21								
22								
23								
24								
25								
26								
27	Subtotal							$105.66
28								
29	Sales Tax							$6.87
30								
31	Shipping							$3.42
32								
33								
34	TOTAL							$115.95
35								
36								

Figure 4.29: Lotus spreadsheet with data

Several fields are computed by standard Lotus functions; these were discussed above, but let's review them here.

Field	**Definition**
date	comes from the operating system and is formatted into the form shown here
ext. price	the unit price times the number of units shipped
subtotal	the sum of the extended prices above
sales tax	6.5% of the subtotal
total	the sum of the subtotal, the sales tax, and the shipping

That completes the creation of and data entry onto the application spread-sheet. This is really a simple data screen, using functions or facilities available in most spreadsheet programs.

APPLICATION OUTPUT

You need to set up the output from the application that will be edited into PostScript format. Each application program differs in this area; what is presented here is what works for a Lotus application.

The general task is to output the appropriate data from the spreadsheet to a disk file instead of a printer. On Lotus, the choice of disk or printer output is made when the Print function is selected; but the spreadsheet needs to be given additional parameters before it will print the data. First of all, you need to specify a range for the Print function. In this case, the spreadsheet has been set up so that the required range begins at cell C1 with the invoice number and extends to cell H33 (those being the top-left and bottom-right corners of the range, respectively), which contains the invoice total amount. This makes specification of the range quite natural.

Second, you need to reset the default margins; the correct margins are 0 on the left and 80 on the right. If you don't reset the margins, Lotus will break the page at column 76, with a left margin of 4. Since the data lines are 78 characters long, they would be split into two, putting the extended prices on a separate line. Therefore, you need to reset the margins to ensure that all the data on each line comes out on one line rather than two lines.

Now you can print the selected data to a disk file. If you printed it to a printer, it would look like Figure 4.30.

INTERFACE TO FORM

You are ready to edit the output data file, but first you must decide what you're going to do. You want to be able to print the data onto a page using PostScript procedures. Now that you have the necessary data, you need the procedures.

The identification of the procedures follows from the work you have already invested in the design of the form and data. The data has been written to a disk file as a series of output lines. You need to take these output lines, make them PostScript strings, and display them on the page at the correct locations. You will also need to do some further setup work in PostScript before you can output the strings: for example, you need to set the current font.

The procedures will be concerned primarily with the placement and display of strings. As you think about this issue, you will see that there are two different approaches you might take to the problem of displaying

```
      10423

David Holzgang
22621 Penfield Ave.
Chatsworth, CA  91311


   31-Dec-86

Item #              Description       Order    Ship    Unit $     Ext. Price
12-456      Backpack - Blue              1       1      28.95         $28.95
28-145      Wool socks - Size 10         4       4       3.95         $15.80
95-004      Strawberries                10      10       1.45         $14.50
95-010      Apricots                     5       5       1.29          $6.45
96-148      Chicken Cacciatore           4       4       2.95         $11.80
96-104      Beef Stew                    4       3       2.95          $8.85
96-107      Spaghetti with Meat Sauce    2       2       2.95          $5.90
96-242      Trail Mix                    4       4       0.98          $3.92
35-129      First Aid Kit                1       1       9.49          $9.49




                                                                   $105.66

                                                                     $6.87

                                                                     $3.42

                                                                   $115.95
```

Figure 4.30: Application output before editing

the data on the form. The first would be to position and display each element of the data individually. If you did this, you might place and display the name, then the first line of the address, the second, and so on. In particular, if you follow this method, you would place and display each item number, each description, each price, and so on throughout the entire range of data.

Alternatively, you could display the data in groups, with the name and address data as one group and each line of item data as a single string. This is the approach that has been taken here. It is simpler than the first approach, and it will involve much less editing of the output; however, it has limitations. The first, and most obvious, limitation is that this method depends upon display in a monospaced font. If the display font were not monospaced, you could not be sure that each line was the same length; worse yet, you could not be sure that the data was aligned from one line to the next. That would clearly be unacceptable. Since the display font is monospaced, however, you need have no concern on that score. Another limit is that the relative positions of data elements within a group cannot be changed. This is not an issue here, but it might become an issue if you were displaying a group of forms or moving the same data from one output to another.

Once you have chosen to display the data as groups, the composition of the groups comes easily. The natural groups follow the blocks that you have already structured and will look like this:

Data Group	Composition
name and address	all four lines of name and address data (or less if all four lines are not present). Each element will be a separate string.
invoice number	a single number, treated by itself.
date	the date as a string, positioned by itself.
data item	each data line, treated as an individual string.
totals	all the totals elements treated as a uniform set; all four must be present, at least as zeros.

With these groups, you can identify the procedures required to create the desired output as follows:

Syntax	Function
address	takes four strings on the operand stack and places them as the name and address on the output page

Syntax	Function
invNumber	sets the invoice number in the correct font onto the output page
date	sets the date element in the correct font and positions it onto the page
totals	sets each of the totals on the correct line; must right-justify them to match the positioning of the extended price in the data items

Finally, there will be two procedures for the data items, as follows:

Syntax	Function
lineOne	sets the first line of data, and then positions that line at line 13 and sets up a line variable for use by all subsequent data lines
nextLine	increments the line variable for the next line of output, and then sets the next string of data from the stack on that line

These procedures are not difficult; however, they are complex enough to deal with various possibilities in the application output. Let's look at all of them in Figure 4.31 and then discuss each individually. Some of these will probably surprise you a little, but you will quickly see why each step was taken when we discuss each procedure.

Let's begin with the first procedure, **address**. This procedure has several qualities that may surprise you, and it introduces a new operator, **count**. The basic issue here is that you want to allow for name and address groups that have less than four lines of data; and you have a related, but distinct, problem in that the data will come to you—as you know from other PostScript procedures—in the reverse order from the one it had as it went onto the stack. The order onto the stack will normally be the name followed by each address line; so the name will be at the bottom of the stack with the address lines above it. However, you want the name always to appear on the top line provided on the form; and conversely, you want the address lines to appear below the name with blank lines at the bottom when there are less than four lines of data.

How do you tell what line the top string on the stack goes on, if it's the last of a variable number of lines? You do what you naturally would do and count the number of lines you have to print. That's where **count**

```
/address
       {       .6 inch 49 line moveto
               count 3 gt
               {show} if
               .6 inch 50 line moveto
               count 2 gt
               {show} if
               .6 inch 51 line moveto
               count 1 gt
               {show} if
               .6 inch 52 line moveto
               count 0 gt
               {show} if        }
       def

/invNumber
       {       /Line 52 line def
               8 inch rightJustifyText     }
       def

/date
       {       /Line 50 line def
               8 inch rightJustifyText     }
       def

/totals
       {       /Line 5 line def
               7.5 inch rightJustifyText
               /Line 7 line def
               7.5 inch rightJustifyText
               /Line 9 line def
               7.5 inch rightJustifyText
               /Line 11 line def
               7.5 inch rightJustifyText      }
       def

/lineOne
       {       1 inch 43 line moveto
               show
               /NowLine 43 line def        }
       def

/nextLine
       {       /NowLine NowLine 18 sub def
               1 inch NowLine moveto
               show }
       def
```

Figure 4.31: Fill-in procedures

comes in. This operator counts the number of items on the stack and returns that number to the top of the stack, without affecting anything underneath. Now you can count the items on the stack, which will be the number of lines you have to print. If the number is equal to or greater than the relative number of lines remaining to be printed on, then you **show** the string; otherwise, you don't. The **if** operator does this for you. The conditional **gt** tests the current count from the stack against one less than the current line number. If the count is greater than that number, the boolean value **true** is pushed onto the stack; otherwise, the value **false** is pushed. The **if** operator tests that value and executes the **show** procedure if it is true, but does not execute it if the value is false. The net result is that each line is positioned as you want it to be, and all four lines are used only if there are four lines to be displayed.

The next two procedures, **invNumber** and **date**, are virtually identical. They both assume that there is an appropriate string on the stack and display it at the correct line number, right-justified against the 8-inch margin. The margin to be justified against is shown in Figure 4.3, which gives the complete form layout. Notice that the invoice number and date line up against the same margin as the right side of the data box, which is ½ inch from the right edge of the paper, hence, 8 inches from the left edge. The correct line numbers also are shown in Figure 4.3.

The next procedure is **totals**, which displays the totals information on the form. This procedure assumes that there are four strings on the stack and that they have been placed on the stack in order from subtotal to total. As before, this means that you will have to remove them from the stack and place them in reverse order; in other words, the total first, followed by the other items up the page to the subtotal. You already specified that all four items are required, even if they are zero, so you don't need any conditional testing.

You want to align these totals under the extended prices on the data section of the form. In order to do so, you need to look back at Figures 4.4 and 4.6. Figure 4.6 shows the line numbers for the totals, and it also shows the relation of the totals block to the last data line. You see there that the decimal position of the totals should align with the decimal position for the extended-price column. Figure 4.4 gives detailed spacing information for the data line; in this case, you want to notice the spacing for the extended-price column. This data column ends ½ inch from the right side of the data box, or 1 inch from the right edge of the page. Using the usual PostScript coordinates, that is 7.5 inches from the left edge of the page. Now the totals are larger than the extended price, but they can be lined up using the right margin, since all of these numbers have a decimal point followed by two digits. Therefore, you must right-justify the totals against the 7.5-inch margin to align them under the extended price.

The last two procedures are **lineOne** and **nextLine**. These two procedures display the data lines for the main text block. The first procedure, **lineOne**, sets the first data item on line 43 and then sets a variable, *NowLine*, for use in printing subsequent lines. The other procedure, **nextLine**, prints all other data lines on the page. It subtracts 18 points from the current value of *NowLine* to move down the page the prescribed distance, moves the current point to that line, and prints the data item. Both procedures use an x-coordinate margin of 1 inch, which is the correct value, based on Figure 4.4, for the starting point of the data line.

The assumption here is that the data line is exactly 78 characters wide. You have ensured that by setting the column widths to the correct values in the spreadsheet application and then by setting the alignment within those columns as you wanted it to show on the output page. No additional spacing or placement of the data is being done. If the columns of data were aligned correctly on the spreadsheet, they will be aligned correctly on the page. This is a miniature WYSIWYG.

Finally, notice that there is no font selection or setting within these procedures, unlike some of the procedures used for the form output. These procedures are more like the support procedures you identified before; they have some potential for wider applicability. I don't want to mislead you: these procedures are somewhat dependent upon the font used to output the strings. In particular, they depend on having a mono-spaced font to ensure alignment. Nevertheless, it improves both flexibility and control to keep the setting of fonts outside the procedures themselves.

EDITED OUTPUT

Now that you have the output in a disk file and you have defined the procedures for printing the data, you need to combine the two by editing the disk file. In doing this, you need to take two steps. First, you need to add the procedure definitions to the beginning of the file as a prologue. Second, you need to edit the output data itself to put it into PostScript form.

There is no good way to explain in detail how to edit the output file, because each editor works differently and each has its own idiosyncrasies. You want to edit the output from the application in the same mode and with the same techniques that you would use to create and edit a program text—not surprising, since that's what you are essentially creating. Use whatever editor you prefer and work on the output file.

One small point might make your work easier: I find it helpful to build the procedures (the prologue) as a separate file and then copy it into the data file as a unit. This allows the procedures to be changed easily and helps ensure that mistakes in one file don't affect the other.

The procedures for the prologue have been discussed above; but what needs to be done to the output data to put it into PostScript form? Actually, not much. Refer back to Figure 4.30 for a view of the output as it appears before editing.

First, you need to set the fonts for the invoice number and for the display. In this case, the invoice number will be set in the same type font and size as the literal "NO. :" in the header block; and the rest of the text will be in 10-point Courier, as discussed earlier. Then you need to transform all the data output into strings by enclosing them in ( ). Finally, you need to add the appropriate procedure calls after each string or set of strings.

After you have finished that, however you do it with your editor, your output file should look like Figure 4.32.

DRAFT PAGE

Now you should be able to put together the PostScript program in Figure 4.33. This is the compilation of the two pieces that you have just built, the procedure definitions and the edited page output, into one program. The **save** at the beginning of the program and the matching **restore** at the end are all that have been added to the previous work;

```
%application output converted to PostScript format
/Helvetica-Bold findfont 12 scalefont setfont
(10423)
invNumber

/Courier findfont 10 scalefont setfont

(David Holzgang)
(22621 Penfield Ave.)
(Chatsworth, CA  91311)
address

(20-Feb-87)
date

( 12-456     Backpack - Blue           1     1    28.95     $28.95)
lineOne
( 28-145     Wool socks - Size 10      4     4     3.95     $15.80)
nextLine
( 95-004     Strawberries             10    10     1.45     $14.50)
nextLine
( 95-010     Apricots                  5     5     1.29      $6.45)
nextLine
( 96-148     Chicken Cacciatore        4     4     2.95     $11.80)
nextLine
( 96-104     Beef Stew                 4     3     2.95      $8.85)
nextLine
( 96-107     Spaghetti with Meat Sauce 2     2     2.95      $5.90)
nextLine
( 96-242     Trail Mix                 4     4     0.98      $3.92)
nextLine
( 35-129     First Aid Kit             1     1     9.49      $9.49)
nextLine

($105.66)
($6.87)
($3.42)
($115.95)
totals
```

Figure 4.32: Edited application output

```
%-----------------------Prologue (Form data) --------------
/address
        {       .6 inch 49 line moveto
                count 3 gt
                {show} if
                .6 inch 50 line moveto
                count 2 gt
                {show} if
                .6 inch 51 line moveto
                count 1 gt
                {show} if
                .6 inch 52 line moveto
                count 0 gt
                {show} if        }
        def

/invNumber
        {       /Line 52 line def
                8 inch rightJustifyText      }
        def

/date
        {       /Line 50 line def
                8 inch rightJustifyText      }
        def

/totals
        {       /Line 5 line def
                7.5 inch rightJustifyText
                /Line 7 line def
                7.5 inch rightJustifyText
                /Line 9 line def
                7.5 inch rightJustifyText
                /Line 11 line def
                7.5 inch rightJustifyText      }
        def

/lineOne
        {       1 inch 43 line moveto
                show
                /NowLine 43 line def       }
        def

/nextLine
        {       /NowLine NowLine 18 sub def
                1 inch NowLine moveto
                show }
        def
%-----------------------Script (Form data) ---------------
/DataSave save def
/Helvetica-Bold findfont 12 scalefont setfont
%application output converted to PostScript format
(10423)
invNumber
/Courier findfont 10 scalefont setfont
(David Holzgang)
(22621 Penfield Ave.)
(Chatsworth, CA  91311)
address
(20-Feb-87)
date
( 12-456       Backpack - Blue          1      1     28.95       $28.95)
lineOne
( 28-145       Wool socks - Size 10     4      4     3.95        $15.80)
nextLine
( 95-004       Strawberries            10     10     1.45        $14.50)
nextLine
( 95-010       Apricots                 5      5     1.29         $6.45)
nextLine
```

Figure 4.33: Completed fill-in program

```
( 96-148        Chicken Cacciatore          4    4    2.95      $11.80)
nextLine
( 96-104        Beef Stew                   4    3    2.95       $8.85)
nextLine
( 96-107        Spaghetti with Meat Sauce   2    2    2.95       $5.90)
nextLine
( 96-242        Trail Mix                   4    4    0.98       $3.92)
nextLine
( 35-129        First Aid Kit               1    1    9.49       $9.49)
nextLine
($105.66)
($6.87)
($3.42)
($115.95)
totals
DataSave restore
```

Figure 4.33 (cont.): Completed fill-in program

they ensure that this page does not cause changes to any subsequent pages and are, as you have read before, an important element in good PostScript code. There are no surprises in this program, and unsurprisingly, it produces a page of text that looks like Figure 4.34.

This is essentially the same output that you would have received by printing the page on a line printer directly from the spreadsheet application. The spacing is somewhat different, since you have moved the output around the page, and of course, the fonts are fancier than most applications will support; nevertheless, this is generally what the application output is supposed to look like.

However, if you hold both Figure 4.34 and Figure 4.27 up to a strong light, you will see that they fit over one another perfectly. You have now created, as individual pages, each of the parts of the completed form that you want to print as a unit. The remaining task is to perform, within the printer, the same action you just took by holding the two pages together. Essentially, you are going to create each page on the printer, as though they were transparent, and then print the pair together.

FORM AND FILL-IN

The process of printing each of these pages together, one overlaying the other, is easy. You could just take the two finished programs above and run them, one after the other, as long as you didn't issue a **showpage** between them. Although this would work, it is hardly a satisfactory solution for a serious program; the correct method is to integrate the two pieces into one program.

```
David Holzgang                                              10423
22621 Penfield Ave.
Chatsworth, CA  91311                                     20-Feb-87


          12-456     Backpack - Blue              1    1    28.95      $28.95
          28-145     Wool socks - Size 10         4    4     3.95      $15.80
          95-004     Strawberries               10   10     1.45      $14.50
          95-010     Apricots                    5    5     1.29       $6.45
          96-148     Chicken Cacciatore           4    4     2.95      $11.80
          96-104     Beef Stew                   4    3     2.95       $8.85
          96-107     Spaghetti with Meat Sauce   2    2     2.95       $5.90
          96-242     Trail Mix                   4    4     0.98       $3.92
          35-129     First Aid Kit               1    1     9.49       $9.49




                                                                     $105.66

                                                                       $6.87

                                                                       $3.42

                                                                     $115.95
```

Figure 4.34: PostScript output from the edited application data file

It may surprise you to learn that you can run either of the two programs first, without affecting the other page output. First, the page descriptions for each page are enclosed with **save**, **restore** operators, which serve to prevent any interference by the first page on the second—no matter in which order they are produced. In addition, you might expect that printing the strings of data over the form would wipe out the lines on the form. That would happen if you had a graphic element, filled with white, and displayed it over the form. Because PostScript colors are opaque, the white would overlay and obliterate the black lines. With text, however, the situation is different. Text spaces are not graphics, as the letters are, but rather are true spaces. Therefore, they don't affect the black lines printed by the form even if those lines were painted before the **show** command for the text line.

The two pages are integrated by encapsulating one of the pages into a single procedure and including that procedure within the other program at an appropriate point. The obvious candidate for this process is the form, since you are likely to want to use the form with different data items.

Following the previous discussions on naming conventions, you might choose to name this procedure something like **formInvoice**. This leaves open the possibility of developing additional forms—packing lists, purchase orders, "pick lists," and so forth—that could all start with the uniform identifier "form" and then continue with an appropriate label.

The **formInvoice** procedure is the body of the form program enclosed in procedure brackets, and it is set out in the complete program in Figure 4.35. It is included in its own section of the prologue, entitled "Major Procedures (Complete Form)".

Once this new procedure has been included in the prologue for the data program, you will have to add a line to the program to produce the form. This can be done either at the beginning or the end of the program, as we discussed before. In this case, it will be done at the beginning. In either case, you can visualize the data being printed onto a blank form that has been drawn onto the output device.

The completed program, with all support procedures and with the complete PostScript structure, is shown in Figure 4.35. After all this, you finally have the two pages combined onto one output page, as in Figure 4.36.

There is nothing new in this program; only the packaging has changed. You are familiar with all the procedures and are accustomed to the structuring conventions as well. As before, the actual program (script) is relatively short, and most of the real work is done in the design and testing of the procedural components. You will notice that the only data

```
%--------------------------Exercise Six---------------------------
%!PS-Adobe-1.0
%%DocumentFonts Helvetica Helvetica-Bold Helvetica-BoldOblique
%%Title: Exercise 6 (Form & Fill-in)
%%Creator: David Holzgang
%%CreationDate: 17 February 1987 11:45:00
%%For: Understanding PostScript Programming
%%Pages: 1
%%EndComments
%--------------------------Prologue---------------------------
%----------------------Support Procedures ----------------------
/inch
        {     72 mul    } def

/line
        {     12 mul    } def

/centerText
        {     /Right exch def
              /Left exch def
              dup
              stringwidth pop
              2 div
              Right Left sub 2 div
              exch sub
              Left add
              Line moveto
              show }
        def

/rightJustifyText
        {     /RightColumn exch def
              dup
              stringwidth pop
              RightColumn exch sub
              Line moveto
              show }
        def

  /sun
        {     /Radius exch def
              0  0  Radius  0  360 arc }
        def

  /hill
        {     /Base exch def
              /Hgt  exch def
              /HalfBase
              Base 2 div def
              0 0 moveto
              HalfBase Hgt lineto
              Base  0 lineto  }
        def
%---------------------Major Procedures (Logo) -------------------
/logoTitles
        {
              /Helvetica-BoldOblique findfont 18 scalefont setfont
              /Line .75 inch def
              (MOUNTAIN SPORTS, LTD.)
              0 8 inch centerText
              /Helvetica findfont 10 scalefont setfont
              /Line .5 inch def
              (123 Mountain Way,  Chatsworth, CA  91311)
              0 8 inch centerText
              /Line .5 inch 12 sub def
              ((818) 882-8144                (213) 555-1212)
              0 8 inch centerText }
        def
```

Figure 4.35: Program for completed form with data

```
/graphic
    {   newpath
        %begin logo
        %do background mountain
        gsave
            3  0  translate
            8  8  hill
            .3 setgray
            fill
        grestore
        %do left and right hills
        gsave
            %left hill
            5  6  hill
            .7 setgray
            fill
            %right hill
            7  0  translate
            5  6  hill
            fill
        grestore
        %do sun
        gsave
            14   9   translate
            1.5 sun
            stroke
        grestore
        %logo finished
        }
    def

/logo
    {   logoTitles
        9.5 9.5 scale
        1 9.5 div setlinewidth
        graphic   }
    def
%------------------Major Procedures (Header) --------------------
/headTitles
    {
        %first set invoice title
        /Helvetica-Bold findfont 15 scalefont setfont
        /Line 52 line def
        (INVOICE)
        .5 inch  8 inch centerText
        %now set number title
        /Helvetica-Bold findfont 12 scalefont setfont
        (No. :)
        7 inch rightJustifyText  }
    def

/cornerBox
    %expects translate origin to bottom-left box corner
    %called as:    X-size Y-size cornerBox
    {   newpath
        /DimY exch def
        /DimX exch def
        %bottom-left corner
        0   0   moveto
        0   12  rlineto
        0   0   moveto
        12  0   rlineto
        %bottom-right corner
        DimX 0 moveto
        0  12 rlineto
        DimX 0 moveto
        -12  0  rlineto
        %top-left corner
        0 DimY  moveto
```

Figure 4.35 (cont.): Program for completed form with data

```
                   0  -12  rlineto
                   0 DimY  moveto
                   12   0  rlineto
                   %top-right corner
                   DimX  DimY  moveto
                   0  -12  rlineto
                   DimX  DimY  moveto
                   -12  0  rlineto
                   stroke    }
        def
%------------------Major Procedures (Data Box) ------------------
/screenBox
        {    newpath
                   /DimY exch def
                   /DimX exch def
                   .5 inch 0 moveto
                   DimX 0   DimX DimY .25 inch arcto
                   4 {pop} repeat
                   DimX DimY  0 DimY .25 inch arcto
                   4 {pop} repeat
                   0 DimY     0 0    .25 inch arcto
                   4 {pop} repeat
                   0 0      DimX 0   .25 inch arcto
                   4 {pop} repeat
                   closepath }
        def

/verticalLines
        {    newpath
                   144 47 line moveto
                   144 12.5 line lineto
                   317 47 line moveto
                   317 12.5 line lineto
                   365 47 line moveto
                   365 12.5 line lineto
                   413 47 line moveto
                   413 12.5 line lineto
                   467 47 line moveto
                   467 12.5 line lineto
                   stroke    }
        def

/dataTitles
        {    newpath
                   .5 inch 45 line moveto
                   7.5 inch 0 rlineto
                   stroke
                   .5 inch 45.5 line moveto
                   /Helvetica findfont 10 scalefont setfont
                   /Line 45.5 line def
                   (ITEM NO.)
                   72 144 centerText
                   (DESCRIPTION    )
                   144 317 centerText
                   (ORDER)
                   318 365 centerText
                   (SHIP)
                   366 413 centerText
                   (UNIT $)
                   414 467 centerText
                   (EXT. PRICE)
                   468 540 centerText   }
        def

/footTitles
        {    newpath
                   .5 inch 12.5 line moveto
                   7.5 inch 0 rlineto
                   stroke
```

Figure 4.35 (cont.): Program for completed form with data

```
                467 12.5 line moveto
                467 4 line lineto
                stroke
                /Helvetica-Bold findfont 10 scalefont setfont
                /Line 11 line def
                (SUBTOTAL)
                463 rightJustifyText
                /Line 9 line def
                (SALES TAX)
                463 rightJustifyText
                /Line 7 line def
                (SHIPPING)
                463 rightJustifyText
                /Line 5 line def
                (TOTAL)
                463 rightJustifyText        }
        def
%------------------Major Procedures (Complete Form) --------
/formInvoice
        {       /FormPage save def
                %produce logo box
                gsave
                    .5 inch  55 line translate
                    logo
                grestore
                %produce header block
                headTitles
                gsave
                    .5 inch  48 line translate
                    2.5 inch  1 inch cornerBox
                grestore
                %produce data box (main text & totals blocks)
                gsave
                    .5 inch  4 line  translate
                    7.5 inch  43 line  screenBox
                    2 setlinewidth
                    stroke
                grestore
                verticalLines
                dataTitles
                footTitles
                %form page finished
                FormPage restore    }
        def
%%EndProlog
%%Page: i 1
%---------------------------Script (Form) -----------------
formInvoice
/DataPage save def
/Helvetica-Bold findfont 12 scalefont setfont
%application output converted to PostScript format
(10423)
invNumber
/Courier findfont 10 scalefont setfont
(David Holzgang)
(22621 Penfield Ave.)
(Chatsworth, CA  91311)
address
(20-Feb-87)
date
( 12-456      Backpack - Blue         1     1    28.95     $28.95)
lineOne
( 28-145      Wool socks - Size 10    4     4     3.95     $15.80)
nextLine
( 95-004      Strawberries           10    10     1.45     $14.50)
nextLine
( 95-010      Apricots                5     5     1.29      $6.45)
nextLine
( 96-148      Chicken Cacciatore      4     4     2.95     $11.80)
```

Figure 4.35 (cont.): Program for completed form with data

```
nextLine
( 96-104      Beef Stew                    4     3     2.95      $8.85)
nextLine
( 96-107      Spaghetti with Meat Sauce    2     2     2.95      $5.90)
nextLine
( 96-242      Trail Mix                    4     4     0.98      $3.92)
nextLine
( 35-129      First Aid Kit                1     1     9.49      $9.49)
nextLine
($105.66)
($6.87)
($3.42)
($115.95)
totals
DataPage restore
showpage
%%Trailer
%all done
```

Figure 4.35 (cont.): Program for completed form with data

in the script is the data that was supplied by the application. All the other information—titles, fonts, spacing, and so on—is contained in the procedures themselves.

WRAP-UP

The entire program is presented in Figure 4.35 as one piece, because that is the best way to read the program and because, if you want to run the program, you need to present it to the interpreter in more or less that order. In practice, however, you may prefer to split the prologue and the script into two files. In that way you could send the prologue to the printer first, and then send the page of data. You will then have the ability to send multiple pages of data to the printer. The next section of the chapter focuses on this and similar topics.

RECAP AND REVIEW

Before we look at alternative ways to use the skills and the procedures you have worked on so diligently, we should discuss the intention of this exercise. The exercise was done for illustrative purposes, to demonstrate what can be done with the amount of PostScript that you now know. This is not, and was not intended to be, a practical method of filling data onto a form. Obviously, you don't want to have to hand-code every set of data that comes out of your application program. There are other more

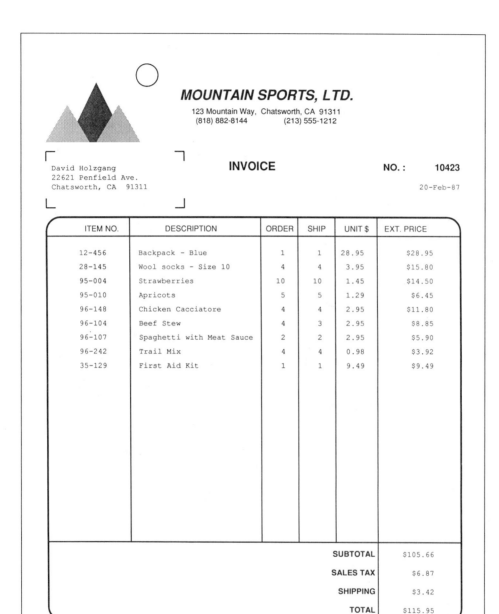

MOUNTAIN SPORTS, LTD.

123 Mountain Way, Chatsworth, CA 91311
(818) 882-8144   (213) 555-1212

David Holzgang
22621 Penfield Ave.
Chatsworth, CA 91311

INVOICE

NO. :   **10423**

20-Feb-87

ITEM NO.	DESCRIPTION	ORDER	SHIP	UNIT $	EXT. PRICE
12-456	Backpack - Blue	1	1	28.95	$28.95
28-145	Wool socks - Size 10	4	4	3.95	$15.80
95-004	Strawberries	10	10	1.45	$14.50
95-010	Apricots	5	5	1.29	$6.45
96-148	Chicken Cacciatore	4	4	2.95	$11.80
96-104	Beef Stew	4	3	2.95	$8.85
96-107	Spaghetti with Meat Sauce	2	2	2.95	$5.90
96-242	Trail Mix	4	4	0.98	$3.92
35-129	First Aid Kit	1	1	9.49	$9.49
				SUBTOTAL	$105.66
				SALES TAX	$6.87
				SHIPPING	$3.42
				TOTAL	$115.95

Figure 4.36: Completed form with data

effective and sophisticated methods for accomplishing the same type of link between PostScript code and an application program. Although we cannot give you a detailed discussion that covers every possible application, we will discuss the general problems and some possible solutions in Chapter 6, when we have developed additional PostScript operations that will be useful for such work. Nevertheless, the exercise here is useful because it shows two points clearly.

First, PostScript is a language of remarkable power and flexibility. Using a relatively small set of the PostScript operators, you have created an invoice form that looks professionally produced—if not professionally designed. If you look around, you will discover how many corporate logos and forms can be precisely reproduced with basic PostScript operations. Limitations of point size, graphic shape, and so on, which may be imposed for many reasons by applications that produce PostScript output, are in no way inherent in the language itself.

Along the same lines, I hope you have noticed how efficient PostScript can be at generating such pages. Although we began the chapter calling this a basic document, that does not imply that the page is simple to produce: a significant number of bits are on this page. If you were to try to reproduce this page using straight bit-mapped patterns, it would require a large amount of printer memory and transmission time, and you would have lost the flexibility inherent in building common, reusable procedures for handling such documents.

Second, the structure of this exercise begins to show you how application output may be modified to generate practical results. The process of producing a prologue to be preloaded into the printer, and following that with the actual document data, is precisely the format followed by most of the applications that produce PostScript. Once you understand PostScript structure, the process itself becomes transparent. Although such work is outside the scope of this book, you don't have to be a programming whiz to see how you might write a small program to take output like the file from Lotus and turn it into PostScript data.

ADDING NEW DATA

You would not have to do anything difficult if you did want to use this form with other data. You would repeat the same process that you used above: namely, write the Lotus output to a disk file, edit the output into PostScript, add the procedure calls, and send the file to the printer. The only problem with this as a practical solution is that the task of editing the data is tedious and repetitive, and probably prone to error. For all these reasons, the exercise is more for practice than for practical use.

FORM SETS AND DATA

Notice that these procedures have all been debugged and tested. They make up a reliable set of building blocks to use with this form and to create other forms. If you did want to create other forms within this same family, there are some issues to consider.

To begin with, the procedures are well designed for this purpose. Procedures like **logo**, for example, could be transferred to any other form. The procedure has been deliberately constructed to be able to be placed and scaled anywhere onto a page with minimum fuss. Many of the other procedures are equally portable, especially the supporting procedures.

However, the issue of the data must be considered. If you were going to produce a set of forms, you might want to create or input common data, such as name and address, only once. If you did that, you would need additional techniques to manage the data within your PostScript program. You would also have to reconsider the decision to display the line data as a single unit. You might want to display individual items of data, so that you could identify them and carry them forward to other pages for output. As this exercise is structured, you would either have to take the entire line of data or use none of it. Nevertheless, none of these issues is exceptionally difficult to resolve, and for the ability to produce a matched set of forms—for example, an invoice, a packing slip, and a statement—you might be willing to invest in the necessary effort.

Overall, I hope that you are pleased with what you have accomplished so far. Beginning with the simplest PostScript output, you have developed and built a fairly complex form and integrated that with output from a spreadsheet program. This is not trivial; there are few software packages that can do the same task. You also have developed a small but useful and growing library of PostScript techniques that you can use repeatedly to generate more complex pages. Finally, you are developing a grasp of PostScript programs and structure that will enable you to make full use of the resources that the PostScript language places at your disposal.

5

Creating and Modifying Fonts

THIS CHAPTER PROVIDES ADDITIONAL INFORMATION ON HOW FONTS WORK IN POSTSCRIPT AND ON HOW YOU CAN control and affect the font machinery. It includes information on how to modify fonts and how to add additional fonts to your PostScript output device, either by downloading more fonts or by creating new ones.

The chapter starts with a detailed discussion of PostScript font mechanics. The detail is necessary if you are going to adjust the fonts in the ways that we are going to discuss, but the detail will also aid you in using PostScript fonts efficiently. The first topic covered is the font dictionary, which is where PostScript stores all the information related to a given font. The second topic is how the interpreter uses the dictionary to create characters and how those characters are treated when you place them on an output page.

With this information as a guide, you proceed to the first task: modification of a PostScript font. The purpose of the first exercise is to access some of the accented characters that are available in most PostScript fonts. This exercise introduces you to code such as you might find in an actual application prologue. The exercise is complex, and therefore each step is examined in detail. The final result is your complete understanding of an important PostScript technique. Then you proceed to the modification of a font to create characters that are outlines, rather than solid shapes. As you will discover, this is easier, but it is still a valuable way to modify characters.

The next section deals with two related but different topics. The first topic is the global modification of fonts. Up to this point in the chapter, all the modifications have been done character by character; now you will modify all the characters in the font at once. The most common, and the most useful, global change that you can make to fonts is in the size of the characters. This is the related second topic of this section: font measurement, or metrics. You will learn how to make size changes in two different ways; then you will use the techniques you have read about in an example where you create and display both condensed and expanded versions of a PostScript font.

The last section in the chapter is a short discussion about adding fonts to your PostScript device. The two ways of adding fonts to PostScript are downloading additional fonts and creating new fonts. The focus in this section is on understanding the process and the options available, rather than on actually performing the task. This is done because the task is inherently complex and because the actual process depends somewhat upon your environment. It is important to understand the process, however, so that you can make informed choices about font sources and font use; and there is a careful discussion of things you should be aware of in using additional fonts in your PostScript document.

The chapter ends with an operator review similar to the ones in Chapters 2 and 3. Like them, this final section is intended as both a review and a reference; it provides in one place and in one standard format all the PostScript operators that have been introduced in this chapter.

FONT MECHANICS

Until now, you have been using the PostScript fonts that are supplied with every PostScript device. Moreover, you have been using these fonts in the most natural way; that is, setting text in the font and then displaying that text on a page. All of the work that you have done so far with fonts has been oriented toward this type of text output. Text output is the most typical use of fonts generally, whether in PostScript or in any other reproduction technology. There have been enough challenges in producing typeset-quality documents without adding complexity by altering the type itself.

You have mastered the basic font operations and should be comfortable with positioning and displaying text on an output page. This enables you to move beyond simple text and use PostScript fonts in a more creative way.

PostScript is a powerful language, oriented toward page description on raster-output devices. It is also, as we discussed earlier, a language with a natural affinity for graphics. In particular, PostScript treats characters in fonts as graphic objects. This concept allows you to make interesting and useful modifications to PostScript fonts, and indeed, even to create your own fonts.

Your first response to that idea may be to wonder why you would ever want to modify or create a font. After all, the fonts are already provided, and they work well. There are two reasons. First, PostScript fonts contain more characters than can be accessed from the keyboard. There are 256 characters available in a PostScript font, while there are less than 100 keys on your keyboard. Obviously, the keyboard contains the most frequently used characters: the alphabet, both uppercase and lowercase; numbers; and common punctuation. But there are additional characters, less frequently used, that are still included in the standard PostScript fonts. These characters include the tilde, the symbols for the British pound and the Japanese yen, the cents sign, the upside-down exclamation point and question mark (used as punctuation in Spanish), and many others. All the additional characters that are included in the standard PostScript fonts are clearly set forth in the "Codes and Names" section of Appendix A of the *PostScript Language Reference Manual*.

These additional characters are referenced by using the *ddd* notation, which was mentioned when we discussed strings in Chapter 2. Let's expand on that notation. The form *ddd* is used within a string to indicate to the PostScript interpreter that you wish to reference the character indicated by the octal value *ddd*. If you look in Appendix A of the *PostScript Language Reference Manual*, you will see that each character has an octal code assigned to it. When you want to include a character that isn't on the keyboard in your string, you can look up the octal code in this table and use that code, in the form *ddd*, to reference the character. For example, the tilde is shown as code 176; that means you would code *176* to insert a tilde into a string. An entire string including the code would look like this:

(This string has a tilde, \176, included in it)

When you perform a **show** on that string, the tilde character would appear between the commas. Because every character has a code, you could use all octal numbers to create a string, but that would be a waste of time for keyboard characters. Every character can be referenced by number if you choose; for the interpreter, there isn't any difference between the letter *a* and the code *141*.

You may think this an embarrassment of riches, but PostScript doesn't stop there. When you use the techniques presented in this chapter, you will have an additional 56 characters available for special work. These special characters make up all accented characters that are used in various languages. On your command, PostScript creates them by combining the required accent and the normal letter. However, it doesn't do that by backing up and overstriking, as some printers must do; instead, it creates the two objects together.

This is different from the process of referring to characters not on the keyboard that we outlined above. In that case you don't have to do anything special to the font to access the characters; in this case, you must modify the font to make PostScript create the characters that you want. You are going to learn the techniques for font modification in this chapter.

You might want to modify fonts for a second reason. Fonts have their own measurements, called *metrics*, included within them. You can access and change these metrics in several ways to produce new fonts, with valuable properties. Techniques for doing this are also part of the chapter.

You can also create your own fonts; however, the PostScript fonts supplied by Adobe Systems generally will satisfy even the most demanding graphic artist. The fonts themselves are of good quality, and there is an extensive selection, with more fonts being added almost every month. More important, the fonts have been tuned and formed to present a satisfactory graphic image on the output devices. As discussed above, Adobe Systems has taken great care to license fonts with long histories and excellent reputations. This aspect of quality is not easily acquired nor is it something to trifle with.

The creation of even adequate fonts is not an easy or a quick job. The task is complex and requires a good understanding of PostScript font machinery. In addition, aesthetic quality is an essential but indescribable requirement. Nevertheless, a particular application, or even an unusual document, sometimes requires a created font. Actual creation of a new font is beyond the scope of this book, but we will discuss font concepts and machinery in sufficient detail that you will be well-equipped to undertake such a task.

In this chapter you will acquire a detailed understanding of the workings of PostScript fonts. Effective and efficient use of PostScript fonts requires that you have a good, working knowledge of font structure and font mechanics. Even if you never modify a font—much less create a new one—you will find this knowledge invaluable in creating PostScript documents. Whether you are programming PostScript directly or using an application program, you will be able to understand good font-handling practices and distinguish them from those that are poorly conceived and poorly executed. You will apply these techniques here; you will understand why you are applying them; and you will be able to distinguish them in other PostScript programs as well.

OPERATIONS REVIEW

Before you start working on the new material, there are two types of PostScript operations that we should review here: font operations and dictionary operations. The font operations are clearly important, but you may wonder why dictionary operations should be included. The answer is that PostScript fonts are implemented by means of dictionaries. In all aspects of using fonts, you will constantly work with dictionary objects. The fonts themselves are dictionaries; and as you will see, they contain subsidiary dictionaries as well.

FONT OPERATIONS

PostScript provides a simple method for accessing and using fonts. This is the method that you have been working with during the previous examples and exercises. The first task is to identify the font to be used, by putting the name of the font onto the stack and invoking the **findfont** operator. Next, the font must be set to the correct point size that you want to use. This is done by the **scalefont** operator, which requires the desired size on the stack as a numeric operand. Finally, the font must be identified to the PostScript interpreter as the current font, that is, the font to be used for all subsequent text operations. The **setfont** operator does this. After the font is made the current font, operators such as the **show** operator can be invoked to use that font to display strings onto the output device.

This simple sequence normally looks like this in the code that you have been using:

```
/Helvetica findfont 12 scalefont setfont
```

If you remember the first time you used this sequence, you will remember that these are three separate and independent, but related, operators. Each one has a place and a purpose, and they sometimes must be separated to perform particular tasks. The entire PostScript font machinery is complex, and this sequence of operations is deceptively simple. The details of this process will be presented below; for now, you just need to refresh your memory on each of the three distinct operations.

DICTIONARY OPERATIONS

Dictionaries are an essential component of PostScript generally and are the major implementation mechanism for fonts in particular. Most of the dictionary work that you have done up to now has been defining and retrieving objects from the default **userdict**. But because PostScript fonts are themselves dictionaries, you now have to refresh your memory about general dictionary operations and learn some new operators that will help you access and use the font dictionaries.

This refresher isn't intended to be a full recapitulation of things you already know; instead, it will be more like a series of one-liners, recalling certain aspects of dictionary operations. If any of this isn't clear or doesn't come back to you, don't hesitate to review the topic in Chapter 2 and return here when you are ready. You're under no compulsion to forge ahead before you feel comfortable. The new material, of course, will be fully covered and presented in the usual way.

To review, a dictionary is a PostScript object that contains *key,value* pairs. The key is used to access the value from the dictionary. There are two standard dictionaries that are always present: the **systemdict** and the **userdict**. PostScript works with a dictionary stack, and you may have more dictionaries than just these two. The topmost dictionary is called the current dictionary; in your work so far, the current dictionary has been **userdict**. The normal search method for dictionaries is for the interpreter to take a key, usually a name, and search down through the dictionary stack until it finds a match for the key. The interpreter then retrieves the value associated with the key and returns that to the stack or executes it, as appropriate.

Values are associated with keys, and entered into the current dictionary, by means of the **def** operator. No special operator is required to retrieve a value from the dictionary. When the interpreter receives a name, it looks up that name in the dictionary stack. Operators are no different from any other PostScript name in this respect; the main difference is that operators are defined in the **systemdict**.

As we said before, fonts themselves are PostScript dictionaries and can be handled and accessed with the appropriate dictionary operators. Each font dictionary also contains additional internal dictionaries, making up a set in a hierarchical order. All of this will become clearer when you begin to work with the font dictionaries. The list of all the available fonts is maintained in a master dictionary, called the **FontDirectory**. Each font has its own dictionary and is referred to by its name, like Helvetica or Times-Roman, which is the key for that font in the font directory.

Until now, you have been using the default **userdict** for your definitions, and you have not had to add any other dictionaries to the dictionary stack or worry about using them. The font handlers take care of most of the manipulation of the font dictionaries for you, but for investigative and debugging purposes, you will need to know how to add a new dictionary to the dictionary stack and how to stop using it. These two operations require two new operators as follows:

Syntax	Function
dict **begin** —	pushes *dict* onto the dictionary stack and makes it the current dictionary

— **end** —		pops the current dictionary off the dictionary stack and makes the dictionary that was immediately below it the current dictionary

As mentioned earlier, the dictionaries **systemdict** and **userdict** are installed permanently on the dictionary stack. Any attempt to pop them, for example, by using an **end** operator without having issued a **begin**, will cause an error.

FONT DICTIONARY

Every PostScript font dictionary follows a set format. This means that specific keys must be present in the dictionary and other keys may be present. The values associated with each of these keys may vary, but the type of object associated with a specific key is invariable. This makes perfect sense, because the PostScript font machinery cannot work without some specific information.

Other than the set format, there is nothing special about a font dictionary. It is created and manipulated by the same operators that work on regular dictionaries. The only special handling comes when you want to identify a specific dictionary as a font dictionary. For this, you use the **definefont** operator, which checks the new dictionary for the correct format and then enrolls the name that you give the dictionary into the master font directory, **FontDirectory**. The **definefont** operator also adds a special fontID object with the name **FID** to the new directory. All of these required and optional keys are listed below.

REQUIRED ENTRIES

There are five required entries in a font directory; four of them are supplied by you, and the fifth is created by the **definefont** operator. These keys and their associated meanings are listed here:

Key	Type	Definition
FontMatrix	array	an array that converts character coordinates into user coordinates.

		The characters are built in their own coordinate system (called the *character-coordinate system*) that is independent of the user-coordinate system; the size of each character is initially one unit high in the user coordinates.
FontType	integer	a number that indicates where the information for character descriptions is to be found and how it is represented.
FontBBox	array	an array of four numbers in the character-coordinate system that gives lower-left x, lower-left y, upper-right x, and upper-right y for the box that encloses all characters in the font, called the *font-bounding box*. This box is just large enough to enclose all marks made by any character in the font, if all the characters were printed one on top of the other at the same point.
Encoding	array	an array of 256 names that maps the character codes (the numeric values) to a set of character names. This process and what is included in this array are described more fully in the section on font encoding later in this chapter.
FID	fontID	an entry that serves internal purposes in the font machinery and that is automatically created by the **definefont** operator.

OPTIONAL ENTRIES

In addition to these five required entries, there are a number of optional entries. PostScript built-in fonts contain the following additional keys with associated values:

Key	Type	Definition
FontName	name	contains the font's PostScript name. This is for information only; it is not used by the font machinery.
PaintType	integer	a code that indicates how the characters in the font are to be painted. The valid codes are as follows:

    0 characters are filled

    1 characters are stroked

    2 characters are outlined

    3 characters fill or stroke (or a combination of these) themselves.

Arbitrary changes in this value will most likely have poor results; the only reasonable change is from 0 to 2 (filled to outlined).

Key	Type	Definition
StrokeWidth	number	the stroke width in character-coordinate units for outlined fonts. This field is not initially present in filled fonts and must be created when making an outlined font from a filled font.
UniqueID	integer	an integer identifier for this font; it must be unique to the font. Every different font, no matter how slight its difference may be from another font, should have its own **UniqueID** value. This entry is not required; but if it is present, it will be used by the font-cache mechanism to help the cache run more efficiently.
CharStrings	dictionary	associates character names (from **Encoding**) with shape

		descriptions in a proprietary, protected format.
Private	dictionary	contains protected information about the font.
Metrics	dictionary	may contain width and side-bearing information for any character in the font. This entry is not normally present in built-in fonts; if it is present, it will override the widths and side bearings encoded in the character description of whatever characters are included here.
FontInfo	dictionary	contains optional information about the font. This information is entirely for the benefit of PostScript programs that use the font; the PostScript font machinery ignores this information. Figure 5.1 shows what is contained in this dictionary.

That completes the list of keys in a font dictionary and the types of objects associated with each key.

USES FOR THE FONT INFORMATION

Most of this information has little or nothing to do with the average PostScript programmer; it is useful to know, some of it is interesting, but generally it doesn't affect how you handle the PostScript fonts. Some of the entries must be modified to create certain effects or to change the font's characteristics. Most of the time, such manipulation is dangerous and potentially disastrous.

There are two components that do lend themselves to modifications, however. These are the font's **Encoding** and the **FontMatrix**. Both of these components provide you with powerful change mechanisms that can be used advantageously. We will discuss these changes in the rest of this chapter.

In addition, you might want to change the font's **PaintType**. This is one way to derive outlined fonts, although we will discuss and work with

Key	Type	Definition
Notice	string	the trademark or copyright notice (if applicable).
FullName	string	the full text name of the font. Note that this and the three following entries are primarily for documentation; these names are not organized in any systematic way and have no effect on the font keys used with **findfont** and **definefont**.
FamilyName	string	the name of the font family to which this font belongs.
Weight	string	the weight of the font: for example, Bold, Italic, Light, Ultra.
version	string	the font's version number.
ItalicAngle	number	the angle in degrees counterclockwise from 90° of the dominant vertical strokes of the font.
isFixedPitch	boolean	a value that, if *true*, indicates that the font is a fixed-pitch (monospaced) font.
UnderlinePosition	number	the distance in character-coordinate units from the baseline of the characters to the underline.
UnderlineThickness	number	the stroke width in character-coordinate units for the underline.

Figure 5.1: The contents of the **FontInfo** dictionary

an alternative method for showing strings in outline format later in the chapter. The general process of font modification is discussed in detail in the corresponding section of this chapter, and some examples of common modifications are given. After you have completed the examples in that section, you should be able to make other changes, such as from filled to outlined, without difficulty.

MECHANISM OF NORMAL OPERATION

The normal operation of PostScript fonts uses the information in the font dictionary to create the images of the characters that are to be painted onto the output device. Let's consider exactly how this operates in detail.

You begin the process by putting a name literal, which represents a font name, onto the operand stack and invoking the **findfont** operator, as follows:

/Helvetica **findfont**

This operator takes the name literal off the operand stack and looks it up in the **FontDirectory**. If it doesn't find the name, it will return an error, as we discussed in Chapter 3, in the section on PostScript fonts. If it finds the name, it returns the associated value to the operand stack. This value is a pointer to the named font dictionary.

It may surprise you that you get a pointer back and not the object itself. Remember that a dictionary is a composite object and that values of composite objects are shared, not duplicated, as we discussed in Chapter 2. This sharing is done by using pointers to the objects, instead of moving the objects themselves. Therefore, what you get back on the operand stack is a pointer. If you display the stack by using the **pstack** or = = operators, you will see something like this:

PS>/Helvetica findfont
PS>pstack
— dictionary —
PS>

This is what you expect, and it shows you what type of object the pointer on the stack points to.

Next you would issue the command to set the point size for the font, like this:

12 **scalefont**

This operator, **scalefont**, takes the value on the operand stack and uses it to scale **FontMatrix** from one unit to the number of units given. The

result is stored back into a new **FontMatrix**, and the pointer to the
modified font is returned to the stack. Now you issue the **setfont** operator.
This takes the pointer off the operand stack and stores it into the graphics
state as the *current font*. Once that has been done, the modified font can
be retrieved from the graphics state by executing the **currentfont** operator. Remember that all of this has been done using pointers, not the
actual objects themselves. Using pointers is quicker and more efficient
than manipulating entire dictionaries.

HOW TO ACCESS AND READ FONT INFORMATION

You can't retrieve the font information listed above simply by executing
the name of the desired object and then looking on the stack, as you
might with a typical object. The information is unavailable because the
font dictionary is not on the dictionary stack, where the interpreter is
looking for the information. To retrieve the information, you must move
the desired font dictionary to the dictionary stack and make it the current
dictionary.

The explanation that follows depends more heavily on the interactive
mode than any of the previous examples; consequently, we will stop at
several points between prompts for explanations. Before going on each
time, let the interpreter come back to the PS> prompt. Also, note that
we are not discussing how to access the font as a font; we are talking
about accessing the font information in the font dictionary as listed above,
which is a different matter. You already know how to access the font in
a normal way; what you want to learn is how to examine items in the
font dictionary, for example, the **FontName**.

Let's look at the built-in Helvetica font first. This is a good example
of how you can access PostScript font information. You would start like
this:

```
PS> /Helvetica findfont
PS> pstack
— dictionary —
```

These lines tell you that you have retrieved the Helvetica font dictionary
and that the pointer (for our purposes, the dictionary) is on the operand
stack. Normally, you would continue with **scalefont** and **setfont**, but not
this time. Instead, you continue as follows:

```
PS> begin
```

This line takes the dictionary off the stack, puts it on the dictionary stack, and makes it the current dictionary. That's what we previously said would be necessary for you to retrieve information from the font dictionary as though it were a regular dictionary. Let's make sure that the dictionary is there, like this:

```
PS> FontName
PS> = =
/Helvetica
```

This process assures you that the Helvetica font dictionary is now on the dictionary stack, since you can retrieve information from it by giving the interpreter the name, or key, and getting the associated value back on the operand stack.

You will notice that you used the = = operator, instead of the **pstack** operator that was used above. The **pstack** operator shows you the entire stack without disturbing or altering the stack in any way; however, the = = operator shows you only the topmost item on the stack, and it pops that item. In the first instance, you saw the dictionary on the stack and left it there, since you wanted to use it; whereas in this case, you popped the name literal because there was no reason to leave it on the stack.

Going down another level is just the same technique applied again. For example, suppose you want to access the **FontInfo** dictionary. You would do it like this:

```
PS> FontInfo
PS> pstack  .
—  dictionary  —
PS> begin
PS> Notice
PS> = =
(Helvetica is a registered trademark of Allied Corporation)
PS> end
```

Here you have used the **end** operator to pop the **FontInfo** dictionary off the dictionary stack when you were through with it. Remember that you can't access the **FontInfo** dictionary until you have performed the earlier step of getting a font dictionary and putting it on the dictionary stack. If you try to access **FontInfo** before that, you will receive an error; the **FontInfo** dictionary is included within the font dictionary, just like the other font information.

FONT ENCODING

The preceding section discussed and reviewed the operations required to select a font and put it into use. Now you are going to explore, in the same detail, the operations that place a character on a page using a font. In *font encoding,* the process that actually paints characters on the page, you can have a marked effect on the efficiency of PostScript programs. This is also the first process that we will modify (slightly) to revise an existing font.

THE ENCODING PROCESS

We will use the **show** operator as our example because this is the operator that you have worked with so far, but the same process applies to all the character operators. In the ordinary course of work in Post-Script, **show** is called with a string as an operand. Let's use (abcd) as the example; then you would write

   (abcd) show

to paint the string onto the output page. The example assumes that the **currentfont** is set as you want it. For the rest of this section, we will assume that a current font is already provided.

The **show** operator is going to work on each character in the string in an identical fashion, so we will only look at the process for one character. The **show** takes the first character and uses the character code, which is the numeric value of the character as given in Appendix A of the *PostScript Language Reference Manual,* as a key into the **Encoding** array. This array matches the value of the character with a name. This is the reverse of the normal dictionary process, where a key is a name and returns a numeric value; in this case, the index, or key, is the numeric value and the associated element is the name literal. Names of simple alphabetic characters in the **Encoding** array are single letters, but other characters have names that are complete words, such as "plus", "comma", and "cent". The names of all the characters are given in the "Codes and Names" section of Appendix A of the *PostScript Language Reference Manual,* alongside the octal codes. Notice particularly that the numbers also have word names, like "one", "three", and so on.

The name of the character is then used as a key into the **CharStrings** dictionary for the current font. **CharStrings** tells the interpreter how to construct the given character using normal PostScript graphics operations, just as you might draw a character using PostScript procedures. When the character is fully formed at the correct size, it is output onto the page at the current point. Then the current point is moved the appropriate distance for positioning the next character.

The formed character is also stored in the *font cache*. The font cache is an area that is set aside to help speed the process of rendering characters. Once a character has been used on a page, it will stay in the font cache for a period of time. As a result, the next occurrence of that same character doesn't have to go through the entire process outlined above; instead, the interpreter uses the image of the character that already has been created and stored in the font cache. This makes the process of printing the character on the order of a thousand times faster than executing the entire procedure again.

You have had a detailed look at the complete process of handling fonts and rendering characters in fonts. You can see several points where you might change font operations to create useful effects. The first example in the next section discusses the simplest of these changes.

TYPES OF FONTS

You can create three types of fonts, corresponding to the three types of graphic images that PostScript can represent. These are as follows:

- outlined fonts
- stroked fonts
- bit-mapped fonts

Outlined fonts may be rendered onto the page either as outlines, or more commonly, as filled shapes. In either case, they behave like a box or a circle on a page. Stroked fonts, however, are made up of lines rather than shapes; they resemble the straight lines you produced in earlier examples. Just as you could not fill a line, you cannot fill a stroked font. You can use a technique we will mention in the next section to change a stroked font into a fillable shape. Both of these types of fonts use PostScript operations to render the fonts onto a page.

The third type of font, bit-mapped, is somewhat different. We are not going to discuss bit-mapped fonts in detail, but I want to mention them for the sake of completing the list and because you will probably hear them mentioned as you read about computers and graphics. Bit-mapped fonts are direct pictures, as it were, of a letter. They are a series of dots (the bits) that are turned on to make up a letter—similar to the pictures of Christmas trees produced in computer departments by printing zeros and ones on a page. Generally, such fonts do not provide the best typeset quality for your output. These fonts require a lot of coding and design, and extensive discussions or examples of bit-mapped fonts are beyond the scope of this book.

ADVANTAGES OF POSTSCRIPT FONTS

Characters in PostScript fonts generally are created by the equivalent of the path construction and painting operations. This is consistent with the design of PostScript and the notion of type as a graphic object. This approach provides several benefits for the user that may not be obvious at first glance.

First, this approach to creating characters preserves the quality of the fonts. In fine (and expensive) typesetting, each letter of each font is handcrafted to give the look and feel that the type designer had in mind. This may mean, for example, that the stroke widths or relative sizes of letters within the same font group but at different point sizes are subtly different. While PostScript can't go that far, it comes closer to this careful craftsmanship than any alternative I am aware of. In particular, since PostScript capably draws each character at the correct point size, it preserves the relative size and weight relationships down to the finest resolution available to it. Many electronic fonts, however, are simply reductions or enlargements of a fixed character size; thus, the font becomes coarse and unappealing at sizes quite different from the design size. This doesn't happen with PostScript fonts.

In addition, this process of drawing the characters forms an important part of the device independence that PostScript provides. Because PostScript is independent of device-specific qualities such as resolution, it must have a way to represent characters in which it can place the characters in the same relative positions on different devices and yet allow the maximum resolution that each device is capable of producing. After all, you wouldn't be interested in using, and paying for, a high-resolution device if it did not provide output of a higher quality.

FONT MODIFICATION

Now that you have covered the operation of PostScript fonts in detail, it's time to use this knowledge to help you change the available fonts. This section of the chapter will show you how to modify fonts and characters within fonts to provide effects that you may not be able to achieve in any other way.

Remember that the font machinery is complex, for all its ease of use, and that you must be careful when working with the fonts. Arbitrary or unplanned changes are likely to result in poor-quality output at best and a disaster at worst. Be sure to read the exercises carefully before you begin, and follow the explanations so that you know what is intended. With that small caution, you will find that the modification of characters and fonts is both useful and fun.

CHARACTER MODIFICATION

The first type of modifications that you will work with are modifications of individual characters. These modifications are both the easiest to make and the most common. You will find this work interesting, because it allows you additional freedom to use characters as graphic objects.

All modifications to a font ultimately are modifications of characters. What character modification means here is modification to individual characters within a font, rather than global modifications to a font that change all the characters uniformly. Such global modifications will be covered in the next section.

The first character modifications that you will work on are those that change the font encoding to allow you to access characters that are otherwise unavailable to your program.

REENCODING FONTS

The use of the **Encoding** array to output a character onto a page may have seemed indirect. So it is, but it offers substantial benefits. One of these benefits is the ability to render characters that are not in the standard encoding; another is the ability to rearrange standard characters into an alternative encoding scheme if necessary. In this example, you will modify the standard encoding to add characters. The characters that are available are listed under "Unencoded Text Characters" in Appendix A of the *PostScript Language Reference Manual.*

You now have enough information to understand where these characters come from. These are characters that have names and procedures in the **CharStrings** dictionary for the built-in fonts, but that do not have names in the standard **Encoding** array. You have to make entries for those characters that you want to use in a new **Encoding** array with the names of the characters at the desired positions. Let's try an example.

This example is a portion of a menu for a fancy dinner, which presents some interesting combinations of food and wine. You want to produce a menu with correctly accented letters where required. After reviewing the names of the food and wine, you make a list of the additional letters, with accents, that you will need for the wording on the menu. Now you look in Appendix A of the *PostScript Language Reference Manual* to determine the correct name for each of these letters. The complete list of the letters that you will use, along with the correct name for each letter, is shown in Figure 5.2.

Executing these names in **CharStrings** will cause the interpreter to create the accented characters as shown in the appendix. The task now is to include these character names in an encoding vector so that you can use them in your menu.

First of all, you have to decide what character codes you want to use to make these letters. Theoretically, you may choose any character between the codes of 0 and 255; however, that isn't practical. Your document is already using ordinary text and punctuation, so you don't want to substitute any of these special characters for the regular ones. The special characters aren't on the keyboard, but we have already discussed how you can use the octal codes to call out these characters. You need to determine what octal codes you want to use.

You have identified seven accented characters that you want to use on the menu. Look at the "Encoding Vectors" section of Appendix A of the *PostScript Language Reference Manual*. This section gives the standard

Character	Name
â	acircumflex
à	agrave
è	egrave
é	eacute
û	ucircumflex
ü	udieresis
ó	oacute

Figure 5.2: Accented letters for the menu example

encoding vectors; the first vector shown is for the normal text fonts, and the second is for the symbol font. Look at the first vector, which is the one you will be working with. You will see two shades of gray on the table, marking empty spaces in the encoding vector. The darker shade shows where there is a potential conflict with the normal control characters that your computer might send, but the lighter shade indicates codes that are unused. You can see that there is a continuous block of unused codes from \330 to \336; these are the codes you will use for your additional letters.

Before you get to the example, there is one more point to discuss: the choice of font for the menu and the method of changing the encoding vector for that font. In this example, you will use 10-point Times-Roman font for all the type. You certainly don't want to modify the encoding vector for Times-Roman permanently. Therefore, the correct way to produce a small modification of the encoding vector is to duplicate the font before you modify it.

Here are the steps that you need to take in the program to produce the menu output:

1. Duplicate the Times-Roman font.

2. Reset the encoding vector to include the new codes and the associated character names.

3. Set the menu text using the appropriate octal codes for the accented characters.

The program necessary to perform this example is given in Figure 5.3, which produces the results pictured in Figure 5.4.

This is not an easy program to follow, so we will discuss each part of it in detail. The program begins by defining the two variables, *Ps* and *Lead*. These two will be used in the program to determine the point size for the output and the line leading. They have been made variables to provide an easy method for changing and adjusting the output.

Next, in line %3, the program defines an array, **MenuVec**, which has the revised encoding in it. Specifically, this array consists of pairs of entries: an octal number specifying the code, and the name of a character from the list in Figure 5.2. This array introduces you to the use of brackets, [and], as delimiters for arrays, as mentioned in Chapter 2; the use of brackets is precisely like the use of braces, { and }, for procedures. The array itself consists of lines %4 to %10. Each line contains a pair of objects: a number and a name literal. The number is an octal number, denoted by the prefix 8#, followed by the three digits of the character position. In this case, the positions are those chosen earlier, 330 to 336.

```
%-----------------------Variables-----------------------
/Ps 12 def              %set point size                    %1
/Lead 14 def            %set leading                       %2

%---------------------Modified Encoding Vector------------
/MenuVec [                                                 %3
   8#330 /acircumflex                                      %4
   8#331 /agrave                                           %5
   8#332 /egrave                                           %6
   8#333 /eacute                                           %7
   8#334 /ucircumflex                                      %8
   8#335 /udieresis                                        %9
   8#336 /oacute                                           %10
 ] def                                                     %11

%---------------------Procedures-------------------------
/inch
      {     72 mul   }   def
/ss                                                        %12
      {    Xpos Line moveto show
           /Line Line Lead sub def }
      def

/nextblock                                                 %13
      {    /Line Line 40 sub def }
      def

%---------------------Re Encode Font---------------------
/ReEncodeDict 12 dict def                                  %14
begin                                                      %15
    /BasefontDict /Times-Roman findfont def                %16
    /NewfontDict BasefontDict maxlength dict def           %17
    BasefontDict                                           %18
    { exch dup /FID ne                                     %19
      { dup /Encoding eq                                   %20
        { exch dup length array copy                       %21
           NewfontDict 3 1 roll put }                      %22
        { exch NewfontDict 3 1 roll put }                  %23
        ifelse                                             %24
      }                                                    %25
      { pop pop }                                          %26
      ifelse                                               %27
    } forall                                               %28

    NewfontDict /FontName /Times-Roman-Menu put            %29

    MenuVec aload                                          %30
    length 2 idiv                                          %31
    { NewfontDict /Encoding get 3 1 roll put }             %32
    repeat                                                 %33
    /Times-Roman-Menu NewfontDict definefont pop           %34
end                                                        %35
%---------------------Program (Wines)--------------------
%Setup reencoded font as current font
/Times-Roman-Menu findfont Ps scalefont setfont           %36
%Position and show wines
/Xpos  5.5 inch def                                        %37
/Line 8.5 inch def                                         %38
(Louis Roederer Cristal  1979 ) ss                         %39
(      Brut ) ss
nextblock                                                  %40
(Ch\330teau Clerc Milon  1970) ss                          %41
(Ch\330teau La Gaffli\332re  1970) ss                      %42
nextblock                                                  %43
(Ch\330teau Cheval Blanc  1970) ss
(Ch\330teau Haut-Brion  1970) ss
( ) ss
nextblock
(Ch\330teau Les Forts de Latour  1970) ss
(         (en magnum) ) ss
nextblock
```

Figure 5.3: Menu example

```
%----------------------Program (Food)--------------------
%Position and show courses
/Xpos  1 inch def
/Line 8.5 inch def
(Oxtail Rillettes) ss
(  with Catalan-style Tomato Bread) ss
nextblock
(6-Lily Risotto) ss
(  with Black Sesame Seeds) ss
nextblock
(Saffron-flavored Rago\334t of Chicken,) ss
(  Chicken-of-the-Forest Mushrooms,) ss
(  and Parsnips) ss
nextblock
(Roast Triangle Tip of Beef with Bordeaux Basil Butter,) ss
(  Pencil-thin Asparagus,) ss
(  and Stuffed Baby White Eggplant) ss
nextblock
%Move toward center of the page
/Xpos 3.5 inch def
(Assorted Cheeses \331 la Red Smith) ss
nextblock
(Marc de Gew\335rztraminer (Gilbert Miclo),) ss
(Marc Mascar\336, and other alcohols) ss
nextblock
(Caf\333 Demi-decaf\333in\333) ss
```

Figure 5.3 (cont.): Menu example

The name is the name for the character that you want to print when you invoke that character code; the names are taken from Figure 5.2. These names must correspond to the keys in the font's **CharStrings**.

Two simple, short procedures follow. The first, **ss**, shows a given string at the point specified by the *Xpos* and *Line* variables and moves down the page by the size of the *Lead* variable. The second procedure, **nextblock**, moves the vertical place variable, *Line*, down the page by a fixed distance, 40 units. These procedures will be used to display the text on the page at appropriate locations.

Line %14 begins the portion of the program that is most interesting: the part that reencodes the font. The section begins by defining a working dictionary, so that nothing you define here will be contingent on or affect the permanent dictionaries. The new operator, **dict**, takes an integer operand and creates an empty dictionary, big enough to hold the number of entries equal to the integer value of the operand, and returns the new dictionary to the stack.

Line %15 issues a **begin** to push the new dictionary, *ReEncodeDict*, onto the dictionary stack and to make it the current dictionary. Line %16 defines the variable *BasefontDict* to contain a copy of the Times-Roman font dictionary, which was retrieved by the **findfont** operator. You will use this dictionary everywhere in the following code. Line %17 uses another new operator, **maxlength**, to determine the maximum size of *BasefontDict*. This number is used as an operand by another **dict**, and the resulting dictionary—which is still empty—is defined as *NewfontDict*. This dictionary will become your new font. Notice that *NewfontDict* is exactly the same size as the original font dictionary.

Lines %18 through %28 fill in the new font dictionary with entries from the original font dictionary, represented by *BasefontDict*. The **forall** operator on line %28 executes the procedure defined in lines %19 through %27 for every element in the *BasefontDict* dictionary.

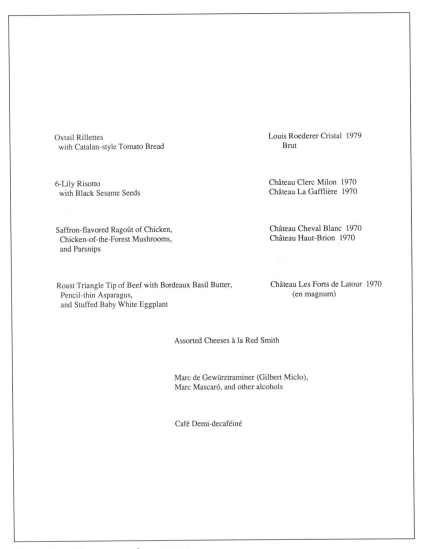

Oxtail Rillettes
  with Catalan-style Tomato Bread

Louis Roederer Cristal 1979
  Brut

6-Lily Risotto
  with Black Sesame Seeds

Château Clerc Milon 1970
Château La Gafflière 1970

Saffron-flavored Ragoût of Chicken,
  Chicken-of-the-Forest Mushrooms,
  and Parsnips

Château Cheval Blanc 1970
Château Haut-Brion 1970

Roast Triangle Tip of Beef with Bordeaux Basil Butter,
  Pencil-thin Asparagus,
  and Stuffed Baby White Eggplant

Château Les Forts de Latour 1970
  (en magnum)

Assorted Cheeses à la Red Smith

Marc de Gewürztraminer (Gilbert Miclo),
Marc Mascaró, and other alcohols

Café Demi-decaféiné

Figure 5.4: Menu example output

Fundamentally, the procedure in these lines copies each element of *BasefontDict* into the new *NewfontDict*. This is done by a clever use of two new operators, **put** and **roll**. To begin with, you want to insert key, value pairs into a dictionary that is not on the dictionary stack. You can do this by means of the **put** operator. This operator takes three operands: a dictionary, a key, and a value. The value must be on top of the stack, followed by the key, followed by the dictionary. Remember this order, as it is the key to what you have to do next. You will retrieve each entry from the *BasefontDict*, and the key for each entry will be put onto the stack by the **forall** operator followed by the value—except that somehow you need to get the *NewfontDict* dictionary onto the stack below the key. You can do this trick with the **roll** operator. Let's look at the stack after **forall** has done its work; for this example, we'll use the *FontName* entry, but remember that **forall** is going to get each and every entry in the dictionary. The stack at this point is shown in Figure 5.5.

Now you push the dictionary, *NewfontDict*, that you want to work with onto the stack, which now looks like Figure 5.6. Note the small numbers to the right; these are not part of the stack, but they are essential for understanding how **roll** works.

Now you invoke the **roll** operator, which takes two more operands, 3 and 1. These two numbers tell **roll** that you want to affect the top three operands on the stack and that you want to move them all up one position. That means that the key, in this case the name literal */FontName*, at

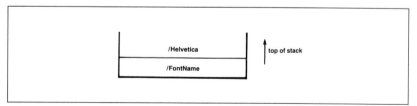

Figure 5.5: Stack entries after **forall**

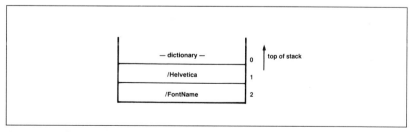

Figure 5.6: Stack entries after *NewfontDict*

position 2, will roll up to position 1; and the value, at position 1, will roll up to position 0. Of course, that action can't be continued because the dictionary, at position 0, has no position above it to go to. So **roll** does what you may have suspected from its name and places the top element, the dictionary, marked 0 in Figure 5.6, after the lowest element that you moved, */FontName,* marked 2. This rolls all the operands into the new positions shown in Figure 5.7, which is what you need for the **put**. When you execute the **put**, you will get an entry into the dictionary *NewfontDict* that matches the original entry from *BasefontDict*.

You want exactly the same entries, but with two exceptions. (Naturally, nothing could be that simple.) These two exceptions are handled by a pair of **ifelse** conditions within the larger procedure.

The first exception is the original **FID** entry. You may remember from our previous discussion that this entry will be created by the **definefont** operator; therefore, you can't copy it onto the new font. This exclusion is handled by the first **ifelse**, which has the conditional test on line %19 matching the **ifelse** on line %27. Let's analyze this process.

First of all, you have to identify the **FID** entry. You could do that by testing for the key, the name */FID*, except that you know the key went onto the stack first, followed by the value. Therefore, you must reverse the order on the stack by using an **exch** before you can do the test. You do that first on line %19. Then you need to test for the name literal */FID*. When you perform the test, using the **ne** operator, it will consume the two objects on the stack used for the test and return a boolean value **true** or **false**. Because you will use up the key by doing the test, first you must use a **dup** operator to make an extra copy. Then you push the name literal, */FID*, onto the stack and make the comparison. If the comparison is **true**, the **ifelse** operator executes the first procedure, from lines %20 to %25; if it is **false**, it executes the second procedure, given on line %26. Since the test is whether the entry is not equal to */FID*, it will execute line %26 if the key is */FID*, and it will execute lines %20 to %25 for all other keys. That works, since line %26 consists of two **pop**

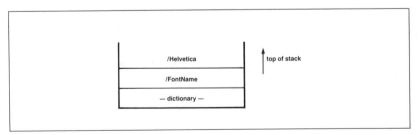

Figure 5.7: Stack after **roll**

operators, which simply throw away the /FID entry from the original dictionary. Notice that this leaves one unused entry in the new dictionary, since the new dictionary was created to hold the same number of entries as the old one. This space will be used by **definefont** for the new **FID**.

Lines %20 to %25 form the second **ifelse** test. In this case, you are looking for the **Encoding** array. You may want to know why you can't copy the original **Encoding** array and then modify it. For the answer, recall the discussion of composite objects in Chapter 2. An array is a composite object, and when you duplicate a composite object, you share the values between both copies. If you were to **put** the old encoding array into the new font dictionary, the two arrays would be sharing the same values. Thus, when you modify the encoding array, you would affect the old array as well as the new one, and you don't want to do that. Instead, you want a new version of **Encoding** with the same values.

PostScript provides one operator, **copy**, that will copy values from one composite object to another. You will use the **copy** operator to generate the new encoding array to go into *NewfontDict*.

First, you have to test for the **Encoding** entry. This test is just like the one for the **FID**, except that you don't have to swap the top two operands on the stack first, because you already did that for the previous test. You will duplicate the key on top of the stack and test whether it is equal to the name literal /Encoding. If it is not equal, then the **ifelse** on line %24 executes the second procedure, on line %23. This procedure is basically the routine that we analyzed earlier, using the **put** and **roll** operators. However, it must be preceded by another **exch** operator. This is necessary because you took the key and the value from the original dictionary and reversed them to perform the **ifelse** tests on lines %19 and %20. Now you must put these back the way they came from *BasefontDict* originally.

If the test is true and the entry is the encoding array, **ifelse** executes the procedure on lines %21 and %22. This procedure starts out by swapping the operands on the stack again, for the same reasons the procedure on line %23 had to—namely, to put the key and value back in the order they were in originally. This also, not coincidentally, places the actual encoding array on top of the stack for further work.

The last part of the procedure is also familiar, since it consists of the same sequence of **put** and **roll**. The new part is on line %21, where you have to provide a new copy of the encoding array. You begin this task by duplicating the array on the stack and then using the **length** operator to determine how many entries it has. The **length** takes the array and returns an integer value, the size of the array, to the top of the stack. This value is the operand for the **array** operator, which generates an empty array of the given size. The operand stack now contains the following items, from the top down: an empty array that is exactly equal in size to the original encoding array, the original encoding array, and the *Encoding* name literal. Now you can apply the **copy** operator, which moves the values from the original array to the empty array, one by one, and returns the new, filled array to the top of the stack. This leaves the new array, followed by the name literal, on the stack. You perform the same exercise to enroll this object into the new font dictionary.

You have created a new font dictionary, *NewfontDict*, which has an independent copy of the original encoding vector and does not yet have an **FID** entry, but has room for one. Having enough room is essential, because when you eventually issue the **definefont** command in line %34, there must be a place to enter the new **FID** entry in the font dictionary. In line %29, you change the **FontName** entry in the new font to the name that you want to use—in this case, */Times-Roman-Menu*.

Now you must modify the encoding vector to add the entries for the additional characters you want to use. This is done in lines %30 to %33. This piece of code is also tricky, but it is similar to the preceding task, in lines %18 to %28. First you put *MenuVec* on the stack. *MenuVec* has seven pairs of entries that must be added to the encoding vector inside the new font dictionary; your first task is to unravel *MenuVec* into its component parts so that they can be placed into the new encoding array in the correct locations. This can be done by the **aload** operator, which takes an array on the operand stack and converts it into all its parts. It places all the parts on the stack in order, with the last element on the top. Finally, **aload** pushes a copy of the original array onto the stack. Applying this operator to *MenuVec* results in the stack looking like Figure 5.8.

Now you have to insert these values into the encoding array in the *NewfontDict* dictionary. This task is done by the **repeat** operator in line %33, which needs to execute the procedure on line %32 once for each pair of entries in the new vector. The number of times to execute the procedure is calculated on line %31. First, the **length** operator is used to determine how many entries there are in the array, which was on the top of the stack after the **aload** operator as shown in Figure 5.8 and is now replaced by the results of **length**. This number is twice the correct number, because the entries come in pairs. Therefore, you divide the number by two (well, almost). The **repeat** operator requires an integer on the operand stack; the **div** operator returns a real number in all cases, even if the actual numbers used in the division are integers. The answer here is to use a variant of divide, **idiv**, that solves this problem. This operator returns only an integer result; any remainder is discarded. Using this, the integer 7 is pushed onto the stack as a result of the operations on line %31.

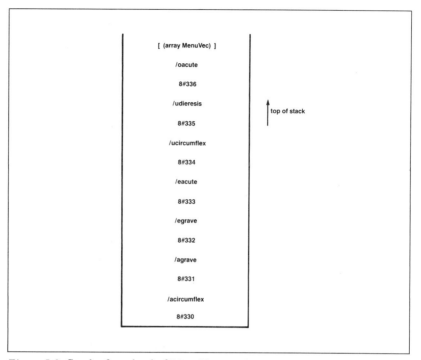

Figure 5.8: Stack after aload of *MenuVec*

Look at the procedure in line %32. This uses the familiar **roll** and **put** sequence to insert the entries in *MenuVec* into the new encoding vector. The process is the same as the earlier sequence that you used, but here you are working on an array instead of a dictionary. Actually, **put** will work on three types of objects: arrays, strings, and dictionaries. All of these objects can be indexed and thus used with the **put** operator. This use of **put** is discussed more fully in the "Operator Review" section at the end of the chapter.

The procedure retrieves the new encoding vector from the new font dictionary, *NewfontDict*, by executing the **get** operator. This operator takes two operands: first, a string, an array, or—in this case—a dictionary; next, an index (for a string or array) or a key (for a dictionary). Here you give it the dictionary *NewfontDict* and the key, the name literal */Encoding*, and it returns the value associated with the key in the dictionary, the encoding array itself, on the operand stack.

This is what is required for the insertion of the new encoding values. Now you **roll** an index and a value from *MenuVec* into position, and the **put** operator adds the key,value pair to the */Encoding* array. When the

repeat is finished, all the new values have been transferred from *MenuVec* to the new **Encoding** entry in *NewfontDict*.

You may wonder why you don't have to issue a **put** to match the **get** and restore the encoding array to the font dictionary. Again, this is a situation created by the shared values of composite objects. As we observed earlier, an array is a composite object, and therefore two duplicate arrays share values. In this case, the array on the stack that you are working with is a duplicate of the actual array in the font dictionary, and the two copies share values. When you change the values in the copy on the stack, you are simultaneously changing the values for the copy in the font dictionary.

Now you have constructed a well-formed font dictionary in *NewfontDict* and are ready to put it to use. It is enrolled in **FontDirectory** by the **definefont** operator in line %34, using the name */Times-Roman-Menu* that you inserted into the dictionary before. That definition does not automatically affect the name that you use here; it's up to you to keep the two names the same. Finally, the whole set of definitions is cleaned up by popping the temporary dictionary, *ReEncodeDict*, from the dictionary stack.

The rest of the program follows the usual form and is straightforward. The new font is used, like any other font, in a **findfont** operation in line %36. Since the font has all the normal characters, you can use it for all the text on the page.

The text for the menu is printed in two columns, with the wine on the right and the matching food courses on the left. The two procedures, **ss** and **nextblock**, position the text as you want it on the page. The only further point for comment is the use of the special characters. As we discussed before, these characters do not appear on the keyboard; therefore, they must be placed into the display strings by means of the *ddd* convention. You see a typical example of this in line %42, where the characters *acircumflex* and *egrave* are printed by using their octal codes, *330* and *332*, in the output string.

There is one more point to make regarding these additional entries in the encoding vector. Remember that these characters exist in the PostScript font but are not encoded in the standard encoding array. If you look at the list of the standard encoding for a PostScript font, in addition to the alphabet and punctuation, you will see a series of individual accent marks. These marks, together with the appropriate letters, make up the additional accented letters that you called for when you reencoded the font. These accented characters are called *composite characters* because they are made up of two other characters. For example, the *acircumflex* that you used above in the exercise (*330*) is composed of the letter a (*141*) and the circumflex accent (*303*) in the font. Both characters that make up the composite character must be available in the new encoding array for the creation of the composite character to work properly.

This completes your exercise in reencoding a font. You can see how flexible and powerful the PostScript font machinery is and how you can work with it to take maximum advantage of its features.

You have been introduced to a number of new operators in this exercise. All of these operators are included in the "Operator Review" section at the end of the chapter, where they are presented in the standard format. I encourage you to look them up and review them to see their full range of capabilities.

OUTLINED LETTERS AND FONTS

There are other methods for manipulating the PostScript font characters. One of the most useful of these is to be able to use the fonts as either filled or outlined figures. In this part of the chapter, you will learn how to change specific PostScript fonts into outlined letters rather than filled letters.

This technique is only useful on those fonts that are generally filled, rather than stroked. You remember the **PaintType** indicator, from the font dictionary, which specifies whether a font is outlined or stroked. If the font is stroked, it is still possible to derive an outlined representation for it, but that representation is not what you might expect and is more complex to deal with. We will not cover this subject here. Of the standard PostScript fonts, only the Courier font family is stroked; both the Times-Roman and the Helvetica families and the Symbol font are outlined or filled.

This approach to the creation of outlined letters can be used on any string that will be displayed on the output page. For example, let's create a headline for the menu you just printed. This will be simple, just the words "DINNER MENU" in capitals across the top of the page. You will center the text 1 inch from the top of the page in 36-point Times-Italic and make the headline outlined type, rather than filled.

This program is easy enough (in contrast to the previous exercise) that it can just be listed here, without any additional preliminary setup work. The actual program is listed in Figure 5.9, which produces the simple line of output shown in Figure 5.10.

If you wanted, you could combine this program with the preceding one to produce the complete menu; however, this is similar to exercises you have done earlier in the book and not necessary to repeat here.

The program shown in Figure 5.9 has only one new feature: the display of the text string (DINNER MENU) in outlined rather than filled form.

```
%-----------------------Prologue -------------------------
/inch
      {        72 mul    } def

/centerText
      {        /Right exch def
               /Left exch def
               dup
               stringwidth pop
               2 div
               Right Left sub 2 div
               exch sub
               Left add
               Line moveto    }
      def
%-----------------------Script----------------------------
/Times-Italic findfont 36 scalefont setfont
/Line 10 inch def
(DINNER MENU)
1 inch 7.5 inch centerText
false charpath
stroke
showpage
```

Figure 5.9: Menu headline example

This changes two things in what you were previously doing. The first change is in the **centerText** procedure. In the version of this procedure that you were using before, the procedure finished with a **show** operator. This operator is now removed, so that you can change the string for outlined display.

The second change is the use of the new **charpath** operator. This operator changes the string to outlined form and adds the outlines to the current path. It requires two operands: the string to be changed and a boolean value that directs the operation. The boolean value, **false**, tells **charpath** that you want a path that is suitable for stroking; the value **true** would indicate that you want a path suitable for filling or clipping. (Clipping is an effect that we will discuss in detail in Chapter 7.) This distinction only becomes important in using stroked fonts such as Courier; that is, fonts with a **PaintType** of 1. For most of the fonts, which are outlined fonts and have a **PaintType** of 0 or 2, there is no difference in the resulting path, whether the boolean operand is **true** or **false**. However, you will always get the expected result if you use **false** when you are going to use **stroke** and use **true** otherwise. If you inadvertently use **charpath** with **true** and the Courier font, for example, you are likely to get unexpected and probably unsatisfactory results.

In this case, you have correctly chosen the Times-Italic font, which is an outlined font; and so the **charpath** operator returns an outlined image of each character that is added to the current path. When **charpath** is finished, you invoke the **stroke** operator to outline the letters. This **stroke** works the same way that it would for a box or any other figure you might

Figure 5.10: Menu headline output

create. In particular, the line width used is the current line width in the graphics state; in this case, it is the 1-point default line. Since the font is scaled to 36 points, this is fine; but if you were using a smaller point size, you might want to adjust the line width accordingly to avoid having the line overpower or even entirely fill some portions of a letter.

The program is now easy to follow. First you define the two procedures that you will require: **inch** and **centerText**. These are familiar; the

centerText procedure has the one change already discussed. Then you define the font you want to use, Times-Italic in this case, and you scale the font to 36 points and set it as the current font. Next you set the *Line* variable for the line you want the text to show on.

The actual text string is then pushed onto the stack, and the **centerText** procedure is invoked to center the string between the 1-inch and 7.5-inch margins. This procedure leaves the text string unaffected on the stack, where it becomes an operand for **charpath**. After the **charpath**, the resulting figures are stroked, and finally the entire page is printed.

It is also possible to change the **PaintType** code in the font dictionary to create an outlined font. To do so, you need to change the **PaintType** code from 0 to 2 and to create and set the **StrokeWidth** entry in the font dictionary. Doing this changes the font mechanism globally, rather than changing characters individually as you have been doing. The next section, "Font Metrics," covers the idea of global changes to the font dictionary, and it uses the same mechanisms and techniques that you would need to use in the process of changing from filled to outlined characters. After you have worked through that section, you will be able to do this as an exercise, if you want.

Before you leave this section, here is the new **charpath** operator in the standard format:

Syntax	Function
string bool **charpath** —	makes character-path outlines for the characters in *string* as if it were shown at the current point using **show**. These outlines are added to the current path and form shapes suitable for general filling, stroking, or clipping. If *bool* is *true,* the resulting path is suitable for filling or clipping; if *bool* is *false,* the result is suitable for stroking.

Remember that this distinction regarding *bool* only affects stroked fonts (**PaintType** 1); when the current font is an outlined font (**PaintType** 0 or 2), the results will be identical. Nevertheless, as discussed previously, I recommend that you use *false* for results that you want to **stroke** and *true* otherwise, since that will work regardless of the **PaintType**.

FONT METRICS

You have now worked through, in detail, the process of modifying individual characters. This section will discuss modification of the font dictionary in ways that change all the characters in the font at the same time, in the same way.

The most common global change made to a font is to change its size. Actually, you have performed this operation every time you have used a font, by using the **scalefont** operator. In this section, you will learn how to adjust the size of the font in a more general way. The measurement of size in a font and the coordinates used by the font are distinct from those in user space; these characteristics are called *font metrics*.

The changes to a font work in a way that is analogous to changes in the coordinate system in general. The main difference is that you can change the font coordinates without making any change to the page coordinates as a whole. This is what **scalefont** does; it works on the font coordinates in exactly the same way that the **scale** operator works on the entire page.

HOW FONTS ARE MEASURED

Before you can change the font measurements, you need to know how the characters within fonts are measured. Figure 5.11 shows two typical characters, the letter *g* and the letter *h*, positioned one after the other. The figure also shows some of the important measurements that affect characters and character placement.

Let's discuss these measurements in detail. First, all the measurements for characters are made in a separate *character-coordinate system*. This coordinate system is distinct from the coordinates in the user space and can use any scale that you want. For built-in fonts, the characters are usually scaled in a coordinate system of 1000 units. This works in the same way as the graphics procedures that you defined before: each character has its own *character origin* (0,0) that is separate from any page reference. You used this method to create, scale, and position the logo graphic in the last chapter.

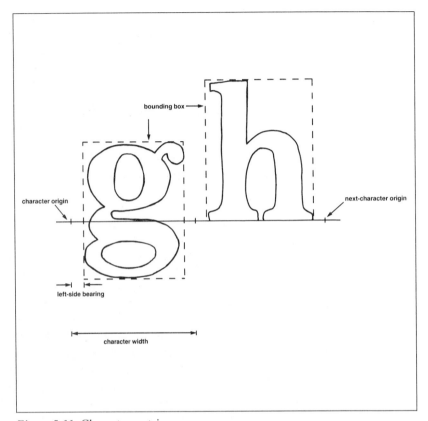

Figure 5.11: Character metrics

This character origin is also called the *reference point* and is the point that **show** (and other text-painting operators) will position on the current point of the user space when the character is painted onto the page. This point is the connection between character coordinates and user coordinates.

The *width* of the character is the distance between the origin of that character and the origin of the next character, when printing consecutively on the page. In other words, the *next-character origin* shown on the figure is the character origin plus the width; and this is the point that **show** will return to you as the current point if this is the last character in the string. As you noticed in the exercises where you used the **string-width** operator, character width is a vector in the character-coordinate system; it has both x- and y-coordinate values. For our purposes, the y-coordinate value will always be zero; but you should know that it exists.

The character is enclosed in a *bounding box*. This bounding box represents the smallest rectangle that will completely enclose all the marks that make up the character. You will remember the **FontBBox** entry in the font dictionary; that is the largest bounding box of all the characters in the font.

Finally, there is the *left-side bearing* of a character. This is the distance from the character origin to the left edge of the character's bounding box. This distance, like all the measurements for characters, is in character-coordinate units. Note also that it may be negative; that is, instead of starting on the right of the character's origin, the character may start on the left. This occurs, for example, in alphabets where the characters read from right to left.

MODIFICATION OF FONT METRICS

We have already discussed the most ordinary change that you might make to a font's size; namely, scaling it to the correct point size by using the **scalefont** operator. This is fast and convenient, but it doesn't have the flexibility that **scale** has, since you can only scale a font uniformly in both x- and y-coordinate units using **scalefont**.

The **scalefont** operator works by changing the **FontMatrix** array in the font dictionary. This array gives the transformation required to change the character coordinates into user coordinates. Since characters in the built-in fonts are typically sized in 1000 units, the typical **FontMatrix** before scaling divides all the character coordinates by 1000, by multiplying them by 0.001. The **FontMatrix** array contains six numeric entries that represent mathematical coefficients for the transformation, which sounds more formidable than it is. Let's examine the typical **FontMatrix** array before any scaling has taken place, which looks like this:

    [.001 0 0 .001 0 0]

The first element of the array is the multiplier for the x-coordinate. As expected, the multiplier is 0.001 to change from the 1000-unit character-coordinate system into 1 unit in the user-coordinate system. Similarly, the fourth element of the array is the multiplier for the y-coordinates. The rest of the six entries affect the font coordinates in other ways that we won't discuss here.

When you execute a **scalefont** operation, what you would see in the font dictionary is a revised matrix that would look like the following, if you scaled the font to 12 points:

[.012 0 0 .012 0 0]

As you see, you have simply multiplied the x- and y-coordinates by the scale factor of 12.

This example suggests how you can scale fonts in unequal proportions; you simply change the x- and y-coordinate multipliers in the **FontMatrix** by different amounts. This change can't be done by **scalefont**, but PostScript has thoughtfully provided another, more general, operator that will allow you to do it. This operator is called **makefont** and works like this:

Syntax	**Function**
font matrix **makefont** newfont	applies *matrix* to *font* and produces *newfont*, whose characters are transformed by the values in *matrix* when they are printed. The operator first creates a copy of *font* and then replaces the **FontMatrix** in the copy with the result of combining the original **FontMatrix** and *matrix*. The resulting *newfont* is returned to the stack.

This operator is used in the same place and in the same way as the **scalefont** operator, which isn't surprising, since **scalefont** is a special case of the more general **makefont**. In addition, the matrix that you use for the operation must have all six elements, not just two. However, the matrix looks just like the **FontMatrix** that we discussed earlier, so the first element is the x-scaling factor and the fourth element is the y-scaling factor.

You can make expanded and condensed fonts using the **makefont** operator. The short example that follows will show an arbitrary string in both expanded and condensed Helvetica down the page. The program for this is given in Figure 5.12, which produces the output shown in Figure 5.13.

```
%----------------------Prologue-------------------------
/inch
        {     72 mul    } def

/centerText
        {     /Right exch def
              /Left exch def
              dup
              stringwidth pop
              2 div
              Right Left sub 2 div
              exch sub
              Left add
              Line moveto
              show }
        def
%----------------------Script---------------------------
%first define the new condensed font
/Helvetica-Condensed
        /Helvetica findfont
        [ 10 0 0 12 0 0 ] makefont
def
%then define the new expanded font
/Helvetica-Expanded
        /Helvetica findfont
        [ 15 0 0 12 0 0 ] makefont
def
%finally define normal Helvetica for comparison
/Helvetica-Normal
        /Helvetica findfont
        12 scalefont
def
%now make test strings
/StrCond
(This is a test of Helvetica condensed font - units 10 on 12)
def
/StrExp
(This is a test of Helvetica expanded font - units 15 on 12)
def
/Str
(This is a test of Helvetica normal font - 12-point)
def
%now use each font
%first the normal 12-point
Helvetica-Normal setfont
1 inch 9 inch moveto
Str show
/Line 6 inch def
Str  0  8.5 inch centerText
%next condensed 10 on 12
Helvetica-Condensed setfont
1 inch 8 inch moveto
StrCond show
/Line 5 inch def
StrCond  0  8.5 inch centerText
%next expanded 15 on 12
Helvetica-Expanded setfont
1 inch 7 inch moveto
StrExp show
/Line 4 inch def
StrExp  0  8.5 inch centerText
showpage
```

Figure 5.12: Example of condensed and expanded fonts

The program itself is simple. You start by defining two of our old friends: **inch** and **centerText**. This is the original **centerText**, with a **show** at the end. Next you define three fonts: one condensed, one

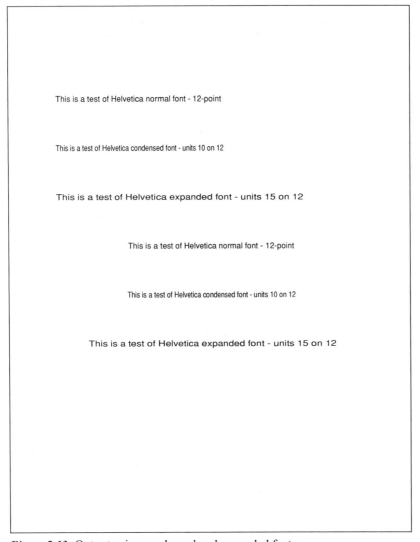

Figure 5.13: Output using condensed and expanded fonts

expanded, and one the normal Helvetica. These definitions all follow the same pattern. First you push the name for the scaled font onto the stack. Then you use **findfont** to get the basic font and put it onto the stack. Then you issue either **makefont** or **scalefont** with an appropriate operand.

In the case of the condensed font, the font is scaled by 10 units in the x-direction and 12 units in the y-direction. Because point size is a measurement of the font in the y-direction, this is a 12-point font. Since the x-scale is 10 points instead of 12, this will result in a condensed font; that is, the characters will take less room in the x-direction than in the y-direction. In the case of the expanded font, the reverse is true. Here the scaling is 15 units in the x-direction, but 12 units in the y-direction. You still have a 12-point font, but it is expanded by about 25%. Finally, you define a normal version of Helvetica, scaled to 12 points for comparison.

You will create three separate strings to test each of the fonts. The first portion of each string is the same in order to help you see the differences and similarities in the letters; the last portion of each string is unique to identify the different strings. Then comes the substance of the program. First you use the normal font, showing the normal string left-justified on a line 9 inches from the bottom of the page; then again, using **centerText**, you center it on a line 6 inches from the bottom. The centering is done between the edges of the paper, 0 and 8.5 inches respectively. Next you do the same thing for the condensed font, moving each line an inch below the previous normal text. Finally, you show the expanded text in the same way, 1 inch below the condensed font.

This is an interesting and instructive little program. It is the first time that you have defined fonts in this way and saved them for use in a multifont document. You will see more of this technique, and a discussion of the most efficient ways of handling fonts, in the next section.

There is one point to make about the "condensed" font that you have been using in this example. Adobe Systems, the creator of PostScript, distinguishes between "condensed" and "narrow" fonts. In this terminology, condensed fonts are fonts that have been designed to have tighter spacing than the normal font, whereas narrow fonts are mathematically reduced versions of the normal font. Therefore, a condensed font will have a **FontMatrix** that shows no scaling effect, that is,

[.001 0 0 .001 0 0]

while the narrow font will show different numbers as the x- and y-coordinate multipliers. By that definition, the font that you have created and used above is a narrow font, not a condensed font. This font closely approximates the Helvetica Narrow font that is part of LaserWriter Plus.

MULTIFONT DOCUMENTS

Text representation is one of the most time-consuming and resource-intensive activities normally performed in creating page descriptions, yet it is also one of the most common. PostScript has an efficient and well-designed mechanism for handling text, as you have read above. Nevertheless, you can do specific things to aid the interpreter in working on your pages, and you should avoid other things so that you don't slow the output down to a crawl. One area of special concern is pages that contain multiple fonts. A number of issues that are particularly important in dealing with multifont pages are discussed in the following sections.

EFFICIENT FONT CHANGES

The execution of the **findfont** and **scalefont** or **makefont** operators requires significant resources. You need to design your work to use these operators efficiently. The best way to do this is to avoid creating procedures that use these operations; instead, execute the operators once and save the resulting font dictionary for use later. You may have noticed that this was the technique you used in the last example; that was not accidental. In the last example, the overhead would have been the same whether you had made the font changes in-line, created procedures to do them, or used the saved font dictionaries as you did. Because there was only one use of each font on the page, each operation had to be executed once. But unlike the example, in many multifont pages it is not possible to predict where condensed text, for instance, will be positioned on the final page. In those cases, you would have to set the same font multiple times on the same page. As a result, the overhead of finding and scaling a font becomes significant. If you use the technique in the example, you will minimize that overhead.

STREAMLINING FONT HANDLING

There are some additional points to be sensitive to in handling PostScript fonts. Using many different fonts on a page is a potential problem. Setting aside the aesthetic considerations, the number of fonts that will fit into PostScript memory at one time is limited. Note that this is not a limitation of the PostScript language; this is a limitation of the realization of the language in a specific device. Each device has a specific amount of space for fonts to be stored and used internally. Some devices store the fonts externally in cartridges; and some fonts, like the built-in fonts that you have been using in the examples and exercises, are stored permanently in the device to increase speed of handling. All such efficiencies are device-dependent, however, and should not be relied on for most Post-Script pages.

To ensure that you have reasonably quick font handling, you want to use a minimum of font changes on a page. This is not intended to inhibit you from changing fonts; just be aware that every font change—and a change in point size is a font change for our purposes—has a cost in terms of performance and page output.

FONT-CACHE CONCERNS

Because font-character conversion is resource-intensive, PostScript uses the font cache as a means of speeding up text processing. Earlier in the chapter, you saw how the process works to insert characters that you are putting onto the page into the font cache for reuse. This is an important consideration in designing efficient PostScript code.

Here again, minimizing the number of font changes is important. Every character that differs from a preceding one in either size or style causes the interpreter to convert it from the font; whereas every character that is reused can be, and is, taken directly out of the font cache, rather than being reconverted. As we said earlier, the process of retrieving a character from the cache is almost 1000 times faster than the process of conversion. Whatever you can do to minimize changes that will call for additional conversion will improve your performance measurably.

You should also know that the PostScript interpreter stores particular fonts in the cache in its "spare time," so to speak. This activity takes place while the interpreter is between jobs. During that time, it converts selected fonts into images and stores them in the font cache. This is called *idle-time font scan conversion*. Obviously, it is device dependent; for the Apple LaserWriter, the fonts converted during this process are as follows:

- Courier, 10-point, full ASCII set
- Times-Roman, 10-, 12-, and 14-point, all letters and numbers and common punctuation
- Helvetica, 10-, 12-, and 14-point, all letters and numbers and common punctuation
- Times-Bold, 10-, 12-, and 14-point, lowercase letters only
- Helvetica-Bold, 10-, 12-, and 14-point, lowercase letters only

The 10-point Courier, 12-point Times-Roman, and 12-point Helvetica are permanently resident in ROM. Obviously, if you are running on an Apple LaserWriter, you may be able to accelerate the output substantially by using one of these fonts.

OVERLAY TECHNIQUES

The final point you might consider in looking at improvement of font handling is the method you use to generate multifont documents. Unlike most of the preceding techniques, this is not an issue that you will be able to control if you are using an application to generate most of your PostScript text. However, if you are generating your own text, as you have been in the exercises and examples above, then you can use this technique to improve performance for your documents.

This technique was used earlier to create the form with fill-in data. In that exercise, you created two separate, but matching, pages and overlaid one on top of the other. If you think about it, you will see how this technique can speed up the processing of the page. First, you can minimize the font changes required for page processing by putting all of one font on one overlay. In that way, the font cache can store the required characters efficiently even if you have a large page of text. In addition, you will be able to reduce the number of font accesses to limit the overhead lost to the font machinery.

This technique may not be practical, or even possible, in all cases. For pages of mixed text—for example, italic and regular text intermixed irregularly throughout many lines—it would be a horrendous task to compute or otherwise store the position of each different font. In this case, you should use the other techniques that we have discussed as the best answer for maximum performance. However, where you can delimit the different fonts, as you could on the form and fill-in, you can use this overlay technique to good effect.

FONT ADDITION

You have been well versed in the PostScript font machinery, and you have worked on various types of modifications that can be made to PostScript fonts. In all of this, you have been working with the built-in set of PostScript fonts. In this final section of the chapter, you will add more fonts to your PostScript device.

There are two ways to add more fonts to PostScript: to download additional fonts from your computer and to create your own new fonts. We will examine both of these methods in this section.

FONT DOWNLOADING

Probably the best way of adding fonts is to download fonts from your computer to your PostScript device. Downloading is the process of sending the font information, essentially the font dictionary and all its subsidiary information, to the PostScript printer and installing it so that the printer can use it.

This section of the chapter discusses downloading fonts in general terms and describes some of the things you need to keep in mind as you work with downloaded fonts. Specific directions on how to install, initialize, and download fonts for your system will be contained in the package when you purchase fonts for downloading.

DOWNLOADABLE FONTS (ADOBE-SUPPLIED)

There are several sources for PostScript-compatible fonts. The bibliography in Appendix E lists a book that contains an extensive compilation of available fonts. In this section of the book, however, we will only discuss those PostScript fonts that are available from Adobe Systems. These are probably the most common additional fonts that you may find, and the process of downloading is well defined for them, making these fonts the best choice as an example.

Fonts that are to be downloaded to the PostScript output device must have two things done to them before they are available for downloading. First, they must be initialized to the output device; and second, they must be installed on the host computer.

The initialization process essentially registers the font to a particular output device. This is a method of controlling the use of these fonts. Each font package that you purchase from Adobe will be set up to initialize either one or five printers, depending on whether you ordered the single-printer or multiple-printer option. In either case, first you must register the fonts into the printer. Once a font is registered to a printer, it can be used on that printer; if a printer is not registered, it cannot use the font. Any number of users or computers may use the font in their documents, as long as they are printing on the printer that was initialized for the font. The exact sequence of steps required to initialize a font is covered in the documentation that comes with the font.

Next you will have to install the fonts onto the host computer. Besides the installation of the font (or fonts) onto an accessible place (usually a hard disk), you must install the associated screen fonts and font-metric files. The screen fonts contain characters that accurately imitate the style and size of the printer fonts, so that your application programs can show you what your finished output will look like. The font-metric files have a file extension of .AFM (for *Adobe Font Metrics*) and provide the application program with information on the size and spacing for each character in the font. This information is important when the application is doing justification and kerning, for example.

There are one-time tasks that you must carry out to make the new fonts work on your system. They are not difficult, but they do take time. Of course, the instructions that are shipped with each additional font package are the final word on the correct procedures to follow for initialization and installation. This discussion is intended to give you a short overview of what has to be done to make these additional fonts work on your printer.

TYPES OF DOWNLOADING

Now that the new fonts are correctly installed, how can you make use of them in your documents? The basic concept should be clear. You must send the font information, essentially the font dictionary and all the supporting information that you learned about above, to the PostScript printer and have the interpreter enter the new font into the **FontDirectory**. Once that is done, you may use the font like any built-in font.

Adobe Systems provides a program called the *Font Downloader* for that task. It will process the font information from your disk, send it to the PostScript output device, and make the font available to the interpreter.

There are two methods of downloading fonts for a PostScript document. These methods do not differ in the process that is used; in both cases, the font-download process is as outlined above. Instead, the two methods differ in when the download is performed and in how much you, the user, have to be involved. The two methods are manual downloading and automatic downloading.

Some PostScript applications will automatically download the fonts that you request when you create a document using them. They check to see if the fonts are already on the printer; if not, they automatically look up the font information on the disk and download the required fonts.

If your application does not provide this service, or if you want to avoid using it, you may download the required fonts manually. There are important performance considerations in the automatic downloading process that we will examine in the next section of the chapter, which is why you might wish to avoid the process. Manual downloading means that the user controls the downloading process by sending the chosen fonts to the printer to be stored for subsequent use.

CONCERNS AND CAUTIONS

There is one main concern that you must have when you are downloading fonts. This has to do with the space available in PostScript memory to hold fonts. Earlier in the chapter, we briefly discussed the limitations on the number of fonts that could be held in any specific PostScript device. This limit specifically applies to downloaded fonts. Each font consumes memory resources, and inevitably, there is only a limited amount of memory in any device. Before you download a font, you must check the amount of memory available for the font before you issue the download. This operation is automatically performed by the *Font Downloader* supplied by Adobe Systems. The test is critical because, if you exceed memory, the printer will reset itself—just as if you turned it off and on again—and you will lose whatever is currently in the memory: procedures, fonts, and possibly your document.

You should also be cautious in your use of fonts, particularly when automatic download is part of your application. You may find that the application downloads the required fonts and then erases them after completing the individual document that used them. Most applications do this because of the memory limitations that we examined above; they are programmed to avoid leaving excess data in memory. However, if you're printing a series of documents that use a downloaded font, you will find that your documents print slowly because the application is downloading the fonts each time. Downloading is a lengthy process; there is a lot of information included in the font dictionaries. If you add this overhead to every document that you print, you will suffer severe degradation in performance. You can imagine the results if you have two or more fonts in your document that need to be downloaded.

You can avoid this problem by using manual downloading. In this case, you will control the downloading process, generally downloading once for your series of documents. Then, when the application is ready to do the automatic download, it "sees" that the fonts are already present in the printer and doesn't issue a download on its own.

FONT CREATION

In addition to adding fonts that are supplied by others, such as the Adobe fonts, you can also create your own fonts. The entire font-creation process requires much work and design and layout skills (not to mention PostScript procedures) that are beyond the scope of this book. However, we will look at the types of fonts that you might want to create and give you an overview of the process you would have to follow to create a new font.

TYPES OF FONTS

The fonts that you have been using, and all fonts that are supplied by Adobe Systems, are fonts in which the characters (the letters, numbers, and punctuation) are drawn using PostScript operations as we have discussed. We also mentioned bit-mapped fonts. These fonts are not drawn, but are a collection of dots that closely approximate a character in all aspects: point size, typeface, rotation, and so on. Generally, bit-mapped fonts are of significantly lower quality than drawn fonts.

You are most likely to encounter bit-mapped fonts when running applications that have fonts on the screen that are not (for one reason or another) available on the printer. Results in this case depend on the application and the hardware being used; but at least with the Apple Macintosh, you will be given bit-mapped versions of fonts if the correct fonts are not either already available on the printer or available to be downloaded to the printer. If this happens to you, consult your hardware documentation for corrective action; if you are using Adobe downloadable fonts, consult the *Adobe Type Library User's Manual* for further information.

You can also use a combination of reencoding and drawing to associate alternative shapes with various codes. You may use this technique to create bullets or small open circles to be used as part of an outline in your text. You could associate any arbitrary figure in place of a code; for example, you could take the logo graphic that we created earlier, in Chapter 4, and associate it with an arbitrary code or even replace a letter code, say L (for Logo) and have the graphic print out when you entered the code or the letter. Needless to say, I don't recommend replacing letters (or any keyboard character) in such a way; it would be confusing unless you had a specific purpose in mind. You can, if you wish, associate arbitrary graphic procedures with any character code, as well as the usual letter shapes. After all, the letters and other characters in a font are graphic shapes themselves.

HOW TO CREATE FONTS

Font creation in PostScript is similar to modifying the encoding vector, which you did earlier in the chapter as an exercise. It uses all the same techniques and adds a few others. Let's briefly look at the process of font creation.

To begin with, a user-defined font must follow all the rules laid down by PostScript for fonts. In particular, all the required entries for the font dictionary must be in place and be correct. This can be done using the same procedures that you used in the example of reencoding a font. The **FontType** must be set to 3, to indicate that this is a user-defined font. In addition, the font dictionary must contain a procedure named **BuildChar**, which is used to create characters in the new font.

The process works like this. When a PostScript program invokes an operator that displays a character, for example **show**, the interpreter first looks to see if the character is in the font cache. If it is, the image in the cache is used; but if it isn't (and no character of the new font will be at first), the interpreter pushes the current font dictionary onto the operand stack, followed by the character code (an integer number between 0 and 255), and then executes the font's **BuildChar** procedure.

This procedure must use the supplied information to construct the requested character, by determining what character has been requested. Normally, the procedure would determine this by using the character code as an index into the **Encoding** array, taking the key from the **Encoding** and looking up a procedure to create the character, supplying character-metric information, and finally, constructing the character and painting it by executing the procedure.

The **BuildChar** procedure must work within a **gsave**, **grestore** pair, so that changes to the graphics state do not affect other operations. It can assume that the coordinate system has been properly set to reflect both the font matrix defined in the current font and the current user coordinates. It should then use ordinary PostScript operators to construct the desired character and paint it.

Once the **BuildChar** is done, the interpreter takes the completed character and transfers it both onto the output device and into the font cache.

The character is included in the font cache only if that was requested within **BuildChar** by means of the appropriate operator.

This is all that we will present here regarding the creation of new fonts in PostScript. If you want more information, there is a discussion of the appropriate methods and procedures, including a much fuller discussion of the requirements for **BuildChar** and even a short example, in the *PostScript Language Reference Manual*.

OPERATOR REVIEW

This section presents in the standard format all the new operators that you have been introduced to in this chapter. Please look at each of these operators; in some cases, you will find that they are quite powerful and have additional capabilities that were not discussed in the text. Also, several of the operators are listed below in more than one section; most notably, **get**, **put**, and **copy**. Each of these performs somewhat different functions, depending on the nature of the operands that you give it; for that reason, the operators have been listed several times, under each of the types of operand that you might be using. Please note that it is the change in operand that determines how the operator's results change; there is no change in the operator itself.

DICTIONARY OPERATORS

Syntax	Function
int **dict** dict	creates an empty dictionary with a maximum capacity of *int* entries and places the created dictionary onto the operand stack. *int* must be a nonnegative integer.
dict **begin** —	pushes *dict* onto the dictionary stack and makes it the current dictionary.

Syntax	Function
— **end** —	pops the current dictionary off the dictionary stack and makes the dictionary that was immediately below it the current dictionary.
dict **length** int	returns *int* as the current number of *key,value* pairs in *dict* (see **maxlength**).
dict **maxlength** int	returns *int* as the maximum number of *key,value* pairs that *dict* can hold, as defined by the **dict** operator that created *dict*.
dict key **get** any	looks up the *key* in *dict* and returns the associated value. If *key* is not defined in *dict*, executes the error procedure **undefined**.
dict key value **put** —	uses *key* and *value* and stores them as a *key,value* pair into *dict*. If *key* is already present in *dict*, its associated value is replaced by the new *value*; if it is not present, **put** creates a new entry.
dict1 dict2 **copy** dict2	copies all elements of *dict1* into *dict2*. The **length** of *dict2* must be 0; that is, *dict2* must be empty when the **copy** takes place. **copy** returns the revised *dict2* onto the stack. *dict2*

must have a **maxlength**
that is at least as great
as the **length** of *dict1*.

ARRAY OPERATIONS

Syntax	Function
int **array** array	creates an *array* that initially contains *int* null objects as entries. *int* must be a nonnegative integer less than the device-dependent maximum array length.
array index **get** any string index	looks up the *index* in *array* or *string* and returns the element identified by *index* (counting from zero). The *index* must be between 0 and $n-1$, where n is the number of elements in *array* or *string*.
array index value **put** — string index value	stores *value* into *array* or *string* at the position identified by *index* (counting from zero). The *index* must be in the range 0 to $n-1$, where n is the number of elements in *array* or *string*.
array **length** int string	returns *int* as the number of elements that make up the value of *array* or *string*.
array1 array2 **copy** subarray2 string1 string2 substring2	copies all elements of *array1* or *string1* into *array2* or *string2*. The

Syntax	Function
	types of the two operands must be the same; that is, array or string. The length of the second operand must be at least the length of the first; **copy** returns the changed elements of the second operand onto the stack as *subarray2* or *substring2*. If the second operand is longer than the first, the remaining values are unaffected by the **copy**.
array **aload** a₀ ... a_{n−1} array	successively pushes all *n* elements of *array* onto the operand stack, where *n* is the number of elements in *array*, and finally pushes *array* itself.

FONT OPERATIONS

Syntax	Function
key font **definefont** font	registers *font* as a font dictionary associated with *key*, which is usually a name literal. **definefont** also creates an additional entry in the dictionary, whose key is **FID** and whose value is an object of type fontID; *font* must be large enough to add this entry.

Syntax				Function
font	matrix	**makefont**	newfont	applies *matrix* to *font* and produces *newfont*, whose characters are transformed by the values in *matrix* when they are printed. The operator first creates a copy of *font*, and then replaces the **FontMatrix** in the copy with the result of combining the original **FontMatrix** and *matrix*. The resulting *newfont* is returned to the stack.
string	bool	**charpath**	—	makes character-path outlines for the characters in *string* as if it were shown at the current point using **show**. These outlines are added to the current path, and they form shapes suitable for general filling, stroking, or clipping. If *bool* is *true*, the resulting path is suitable for filling or clipping; if *bool* is *false*, the result is suitable for stroking.

OTHER OPERATIONS

Syntax			Function
any$_1$ ... any$_n$ int	**copy**	any$_1$ ... any$_n$ any$_1$ ... any$_n$	when the top element on the operand stack is a

Syntax	**Function**
	nonnegative integer *int*, **copy** pops *int* and then duplicates the top *int* elements of the operand stack.
any$_{n-1}$ ... any$_0$ n int **roll** any$_{(j-1) \bmod n}$ ... any$_0$ any$_{n-1}$ ... any$_{j \bmod n}$	performs a circular shift of the contents of the operand stack. The top *n* objects on the stack are shifted by amount *int*. A positive value of *int* indicates movement up the stack, that is, toward the top of the stack; a negative value indicates movement down the stack. The operand *n* must be a nonnegative integer, and there must be at least *n* elements on the stack below the top two operands. The operand *int* must be an integer.
int1 int2 **idiv** result	divides *int1* by *int2* and returns the integer portion of the quotient as *result*; any remainder is discarded. Both operands must be integers, and the result is an integer.

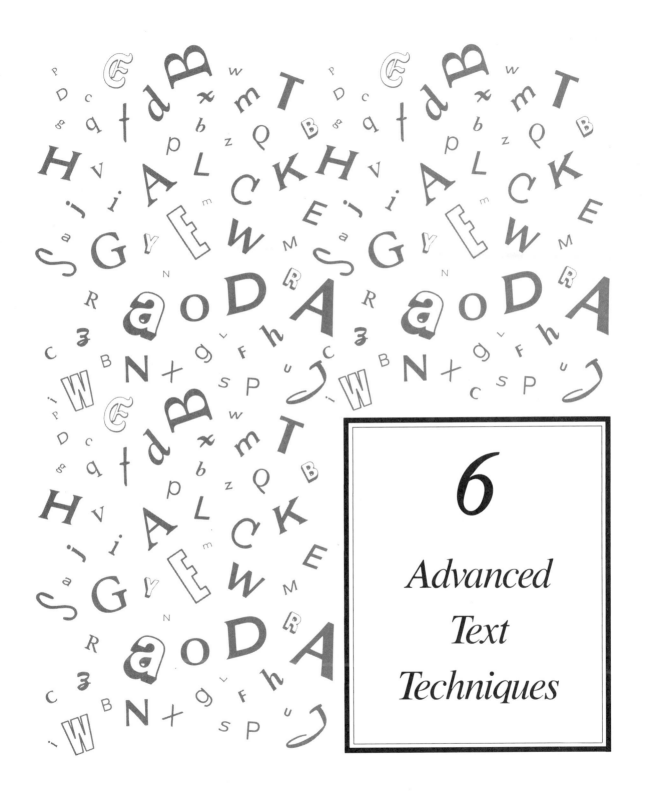

6

Advanced Text Techniques

THIS CHAPTER DEALS WITH ADVANCED TOPICS THAT RELATE TO HANDLING AND USING TEXT OUTPUT. THESE are important issues to understand if you are going to make the best use of your application software, and this chapter will clarify the techniques and procedures that might be used in typical applications to handle text processing. The primary objective is to help you understand and be able to read the PostScript code used by applications.

The first section of the chapter discusses advanced text-handling techniques. These techniques are concerned primarily with the adjustment of text strings during output for justification and for aesthetic reasons. The section begins with some new, advanced techniques for handling strings, which are the basic building blocks of all text output. Then the section continues with a discussion of several operators that can be used in place of the **show** operator to handle special spacing requirements during text output. Finally, you are introduced to an operator that allows you to control individual letter placement.

You will learn how to set text that is justified on both the left and right margins, using the string-handling operations identified earlier as part of a general text-justification procedure. This procedure is then included in a portion of a previous exercise to show you how easily you can revise most well-structured PostScript code.

The second section of this chapter covers handling text generated by application programs. There are two parts to this section. The first part discusses file transmission and file handling in PostScript; the second deals with understanding and changing output that has been generated by an application program.

The first part of this section examines two specific issues related to file handling. The first issue is very practical; you already may have been using it. This is a discussion of how to transmit files to your PostScript printer and how you might use this method to send PostScript programs to the printer for execution. The second issue is a brief overview of PostScript file-handling operations and an explanation of PostScript standard files.

The second part of this chapter deals with the use of applications to generate PostScript output and how you can modify that output to change the results, using the knowledge you have developed about the PostScript language. There are two basic methods for altering the PostScript output from an application. One is to add your own procedures to the output; the other is to modify the procedures provided by the application. Both methods are covered at a general level.

The chapter ends with the usual review of the operators that have been introduced in the chapter.

TEXT TECHNIQUES

This section of the chapter discusses techniques for handling text. Text is the most common object of PostScript processing and probably the most important topic for you to handle well. You have worked with basic text in a variety of situations and ways, all using the **show** operator. You have also worked with fonts, using simple font handling at first and then using more complex techniques in the last chapter. There you learned about the font machinery in detail, and you now have a working knowledge of PostScript font capabilities.

We are going to turn from concentration on the font mechanisms to text processing itself. We touched on these issues in the last chapter, when we discussed some of the concerns about the interaction of the font machinery and display operations for text via the font cache. The present section emphasizes the text-handling process that exists in addition to, and separate from, any of the font mechanisms or processes. Here you will learn how to use PostScript text-handling operations effectively.

STRING HANDLING

To learn more about PostScript text processing, first you must learn more about PostScript operations on strings. Strings are the fundamental objects that allow you to store and manipulate text, and PostScript has several operators that can carry out complex and useful actions on strings. Some of these operators are familiar to you, and some are new; but all of them are important in helping you work on strings, particularly text strings. This part of the chapter explores both the basic structure of strings and the operators that work on them.

TEXT AS STRINGS

Strings are the basic components of text in PostScript. Text strings were the first thing you worked with in the exercises and examples, and you have hardly had an exercise that has not included some text output. Like your font experiences before the last chapter, you have been working with text in a variety of formats but have not yet examined the operation of strings and text display in any depth. You have created strings and used the **show** operator to paint the strings onto the page, using the information provided by the current font.

There are additional points that have been made implicitly about strings that we shall review and make more explicit here. You will remember that a string essentially consists of a series of numbers, each number representing a single character in the current font. This was the basic concept that enabled the reencoding process you worked through earlier. You know that strings are enclosed in parentheses, ( ), and you have learned that there are a variety of ways of including characters within the string delimiters. The most usual way is to type the required characters within the bounding parentheses, but you can also use the \ddd notation and other special codes to include characters that are not otherwise readily encodable within the string.

From all of this, you can see that strings and text are inextricably connected within PostScript; and if you want to learn to handle text more accurately, you must first learn some of the more advanced operations that PostScript provides for handling strings.

OPERATORS ON STRINGS

Strings are composite objects, like arrays; and also like arrays, they can be accessed and worked on by using an index. Consequently, a variety of operators can be used with strings, in the same way that these operators are used with arrays. This concept is important to keep in mind as you are working with strings. Basically, any of the operations that you worked with in the last chapter on the encoding array, for example, can be adapted for use on strings. The following is a short list of the string operators that parallel the array operations that you used in the last chapter. Note that, in most cases, the operator is identical to the array operator; only the type of the operand (in this case, a string) determines the behavior of the operator. In the case of the **string** operator, the behavior is identical to the matching **array** operator.

Syntax	Function
int **string** string	creates a *string* that initially contains *int* characters of binary zero as entries. The *int* must be a nonnegative integer less than the device-dependent maximum string length.

Syntax					Function
string	index	**get**	any		looks up the *index* in *array* or *string* and returns the element identified by *index* (counting from zero). The *index* must be between 0 and $n-1$, where n is the number of elements in *array* or *string*. For *string*, the element returned will be the numeric value of the character and not a one-character string.
array	index				
string	index	value	**put**	—	stores *value* into *array* or *string* at the position identified by *index* (counting from zero). The *index* must be in the range 0 to $n-1$, where n is the number of elements in *array* or *string*. For *string*, the *value* should be an integer between 0 and 255, representing the numeric code of the desired character.
array	index	value			
string	**length**	int			returns *int* as the number of elements that make up the value of *array* or *string*. For a *string*, the value should be an integer from 0 to 255 representing the code of the character.
array					
string1	string2	**copy**	substring2		copies all elements of *array1* or *string1* into *array2* or *string2*. The types of the two
array1	array2		subarray2		

Syntax				Function

Syntax **Function**

operands must be the same, that is, array or string. The length of the second operand must be at least the length of the first; **copy** returns the changed elements of the second operand onto the stack as *subarray2* or *substring2*. If the second operand is longer than the first, the remaining values are unaffected by the **copy**.

string	proc	**forall**	—	
array	proc			

string   proc   **forall**   —

array   proc

executes the *proc* procedure for every element of *array* or *string*. The **forall** pushes each element from the array or string onto the stack and then executes the *proc* procedure, which may access the element on the stack. If the *proc* does not consume the element on the stack, it should remove it. Although **forall** itself does not leave any object on the stack, the elements of *array* or *string* will remain on the stack if *proc* does not clear the stack before exiting. In the case of *string*, the objects placed on the stack are the codes (numeric values) of the characters, not one-character strings.

Two additional operators are important in handling strings. These operators are quite different, but they each address an important issue in handling strings.

Syntax   **Function**

if found:
string   seek   **search**   post   match   pre   true
if not found:
string   seek   **search**   string   false

looks for the first time that the string *seek* occurs within *string* and returns the results of the search on the operand stack. The search is successful if any subset of *string* exactly matches the string *seek*. If there is such a match, **search** divides the *string* into three pieces and pushes them onto the operand stack: *pre*, the portion of *string* preceding the match; *match*, the portion of *string* that is identical to *seek*; and *post*, the remainder of *string*. Each of these is pushed onto the operand stack in the order indicated, followed by the boolean value *true* to indicate that a match was found. If no part of *string* is found to match *seek*, the operator returns the original *string* on the operand stack and pushes the boolean value *false*.

Syntax	Function
any string **cvs** substring	converts the object *any* to a string. The *any* is changed from its current form to an appropriate string representation and stored in the first section of *string*, which is overwritten. There must be enough room in *string* to hold the representation of *any*, or you will get an error.

This conversion process depends on a notion of what constitutes an appropriate string representation of each object type. The following table lists what that representation is and how **cvs** uses it.

Object	String Representation
string	copies the string object onto the first elements of the receiving string.
numeric	turns the numeric value into a string representation of the number; that is, the number 123 becomes the string (123).
boolean	returns the strings *true* or *false* as appropriate.
name	returns the text representation of the name.
operator	returns the text name for the operator.
any other	returns the string —*nostringval*—.

Each of these operators has a specific place in your PostScript repertoire. The **search** operator is used to analyze a string and break it up into appropriate units for processing. Later in the chapter, we will have some examples that make use of this operator.

The **cvs** operator is perhaps more difficult to understand, but its basic function is to turn other objects into strings for display or representation on an output page. For example, you cannot display a numeric object directly on a page; you must turn it into a string for the **show** operator to function correctly. This operator is one of several operators that begin with the character c (for convert) and that all perform conversions from one type or class of PostScript object to another. The complete set of these operators is presented in the *PostScript Language Reference Guide*. Remember these functions when you need to transform a result from one type of object to another.

JUSTIFICATION

This set of string operators is complemented by a set of operators that display strings on the output page. Until now, you have relied on the **show** operator to perform this function. The **show** will probably remain the most-used operator for your text display, but there are a variety of other operators, each of which has a specific focus and can facilitate operations that you will want to perform. The focus of these additional operators is to improve the process of justifying text strings.

WHAT JUSTIFICATION IS

Justification is the process of lining text up on both the left and right margins of a page or column. This process is generally used in high-quality publications for setting and displaying text; it is both laborious and resource-intensive. If a person is doing it, the primary resource consumed is time; if a computer is used, the time required is much less, but a high demand is placed on the computational resources within the computer.

Obviously, each line of text is a different length, because there are different numbers of characters in each line and because (if you are using proportional fonts) each character has a different width. Justification consists of adding space to a line of text to make that line the same length as all the other lines, usually a fixed width. The intention is to add space to the line in such a way that the additional space does not confuse the eye or detract from the legibility of the text.

This process can be accomplished in three ways. In the first method, additional spaces or fixed fractions of spaces are added at specific locations between sentences and words to align the lines. The second method is a refinement of the first, in which a smaller amount of space is added to all the spaces between words and sentences. This process inherently depends on the ability of the text to be adjusted by an arbitrary fractional amount, whereas the first method can be accomplished using whole and half-space increments, for example. The third way of adjusting the length of the text line is the most subtle, but it is also the most difficult. In this case, the necessary space is added between each letter, essentially incrementing the font width for each character on the line by the appropriate width adjustment. Notice that you can combine adjustments of the second and third type to make a line that is exactly justified and yet easy to read. PostScript provides the operators for each of these methods: space adjustment, character adjustment, and a combination of both.

SPACE ADJUSTMENT

The first method of justification mentioned above, adding full or fractional spaces at selected positions within the line, is the least desirable (and most obvious) method. The second method, character adjustment, is not so obvious and is a marked improvement on the first. PostScript has a specific operator, **widthshow**, that can help you perform this process as follows:

Syntax	**Function**
c_x c_y char string **widthshow** —	prints the characters of *string*, but adjusts the width of each occurrence of the character *char* in *string* by adding c_x to its x-dimension and c_y to its y-dimension, thereby adjusting the spacing between this character and the following character.

The **widthshow** operator works like the **show** operator for all characters except the selected character, called *char* above. Each time *char* occurs in *string*, the operator essentially modifies the width of the bounding box for the selected character by adding c_x and c_y to the box. The net result is to widen the line of text by the number of occurrences of the specified character multiplied by the width adjustment. This process is basically the same as the second method of justification given above; however, it is more general, since the **widthshow** operator can be used with any character, while the process outlined above will only add space between words and sentences. If that is what you want (and it usually will be), you would call the **widthshow** operator using the space character as the delimiter; in that way, you could add a specific amount to each of the spaces between words or sentences.

Clearly, an additional step must be performed before you can make effective use of **widthshow**. That is, you must know by how much you need to adjust each occurrence of *char* in order to get the line length you want. An exercise later in the chapter will show you how you might go about this process.

LETTER ADJUSTMENT

The other basic method of justifying text, as outlined above, is to add a smaller amount of space to each character within the text line. PostScript also has an operator for this process, as follows:

Syntax	**Function**
a_x a_y string **ashow** —	prints the characters of *string*, but adjusts the width of each occurrence of every character in *string* by adding a_x to its x-dimension and a_y to its y-dimension, thereby adjusting the spacing between all the characters.

The **ashow** operator behaves much like the preceding example. The only difference is that here each character in *string* is affected, where before only the specified character was modified. This operator conforms exactly to the third method of justification presented earlier, in which the additional space is evenly distributed across a line of type. The requirement to compute the necessary space adjustment has not gone away; the computation still must be done externally to this operation so that you know how much space to add to each character in order to justify the line.

COMBINED TECHNIQUES

Finally, PostScript provides an operator that combines both of the above processes. Not surprisingly, it is the **awidthshow** operator, which combines the two preceding operators and looks like this:

Syntax	Function
c_x c_y char a_x a_y string **awidthshow**	—

prints the characters of *string* and performs two adjustments. First, it adjusts the width of each occurrence of every character in *string* by adding a_x to its x-dimension and a_y to its y-dimension, thereby adjusting the spacing between all the characters. Second, it adjusts the width of each occurrence of the character *char* in *string* by adding c_x to its x-dimension and c_y to its y-dimension, thereby adjusting the spacing between this character and the following character.

The **awidthshow** operator provides the finest adjustment of the text line, but also requires the most computation for it to operate effectively. It combines the adjustment of a specific character, such as the space, with a uniform adjustment of all characters within the line. In this case, additional computation would be required to apportion the total space necessary for the justification of the line between the two methods of adding space.

KERNING

An additional topic related to justification should be discussed here. This is the process called *kerning,* which consists of adjusting the space between particular letters for aesthetic reasons. In fine typesetting, an adjustment is made to the width between specific letters, based on the fit of the two letters. Consider the letters in Figure 6.1.

As you can see, the letter W looks farther away from the letter A than from the letter H. This is an optical illusion, created by the fact that the side of the A slopes in the same direction as the side of the W, whereas the side of the H is straight. This effect can be compensated for by moving the A and the W slightly closer together. This process is kerning.

PostScript provides an operator, **kshow**, for such fine adjustment. The operator must look at each pair of characters in the string and perform an appropriate procedure for the ones that require adjustment. The exact format of the operator is as follows:

Syntax	**Function**
proc string **kshow** —	prints the characters of *string,* but allows the user to execute the *proc* procedure between each character of *string.* The operator shows each character of *string* in turn, adding the width of the character to the current point and then executing the *proc* procedure.

The name **kshow** is derived from "kern show," and the operator is intended to provide the facility for user-directed kerning operations. However, the operation is in no way constrained to performing kerning; any operation or procedure may be included. The procedure invoked may have any effects it wishes, including modification of the graphics state. If the procedure does modify the graphics state, those modifications will persist throughout the subsequent operation of **kshow** and afterward also. In other words, it is incumbent upon the procedure to control its effects and the results of its processing; the **kshow** operator will not perform any cleanup.

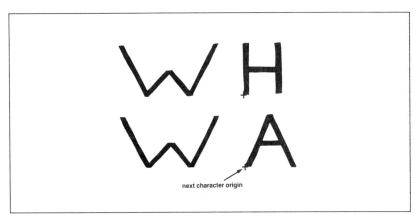

next character origin

Figure 6.1: Letters for kerning pairs

As an example, let us consider the operation of **kshow** on a short string, *(abcd)*. The operation would proceed in the following fashion:

1. The **kshow** operator displays the first character in the string, *a*, and updates the current point by the width of the character.

2. Next it pushes the character codes for *a* and *b* onto the stack, leaving *b* on the top of the stack, and then executes the procedure that has been defined. Typically, this procedure will alter the current point to affect the placement of the next character.

3. When the procedure is finished, **kshow** paints the character *b*, beginning at the current point as defined after the execution of *proc*, and updates the current point by the width of the character.

4. Then it pushes the character codes for *b* and *c* onto the operand stack, with *c* on the top of the stack this time and *b* underneath, and executes the procedure.

5. This process continues repeatedly until the string is exhausted. The final action is to show the character *d* and terminate the process.

Obviously, if you were going to kern, the procedure that you defined would compare the two characters on the stack with a list or table of character pairs. When you found a pair of characters that were in the table, the procedure would then adjust the current point by a fixed amount to adjust the positioning of the two characters relative to one another. Probably the easiest method for doing that task would be to have the desired adjustment for each pair of characters in the table, and simply take it from there.

The **kshow** operator, however, is not limited in any way. The procedure that you define can do anything that you want. For example, you might use the procedure to insert a particular character between each character in a string, or you might use it to perform tests on the current point to determine your position on the page and to take some action. You can use **kshow** in any way that you want; you are not limited by the implications of the name "kern show."

EXAMPLE

You have been reading about many operators; a practical example may help you see how you might use these operators. Obviously, not every one of these operators is used in a program; most of the time, only one of them is primarily used for justification in any program. For this example, you will use the **widthshow** operator to create several lines of justified text.

ANALYSIS

In this example, you will create a procedure, **justifyText**, that will take a string and justify it between preset margins. The example assumes that the string to be adjusted has already been fitted between these margins to the nearest word, or fraction of a word if hyphenation is being used. The task is a relatively simple one: to adjust the length of the string to match the line length. You will do this by using the simplest method of justification that we discussed above; namely, adding the required additional space to the existing spaces in the string. Note that there are some potential limitations on this process. If the string has only a few spaces, because it contains long words or is constrained by narrow margins (perhaps it's set in a narrow column), you may find that you have to add a lot of additional space to each space within the string to make the adjustment work. This would be obvious and disruptive; in such a case you would prefer to use another technique.

The justification process in this example will be less complex than that and will not perform any testing to determine whether to use alternative justification methods. The process at this basic level consists of three steps, as follows:

1. Count the number of spaces in the string.

2. Calculate the difference in length between the string and the line.

3. Adjust each space in the string by the difference in length divided by the number of spaces in the string.

This is the process that you will implement as **justifyText**. In the preceding steps, you can see where you could increase the sophistication of the process. For example, you could test the number of spaces that you count to determine whether it was greater than a desired amount and then choose the adjustment method based on that test. Or, with more sophistication, you could test whether the adjustment factor was greater than an acceptable maximum and take appropriate action to use alternative methods.

STRUCTURE OF THE ROUTINE

You already know how you are going to implement step 3, above. You can do this by using the **widthshow** operator on the output string. That leaves steps 1 and 2 for you to work out in the design of the procedure.

Step 2 is not difficult; you will subtract the length of the output string, which can be determined by the **stringwidth** operator, from the length of the line, which can be determined by subtracting the right margin from the left. This is similar to the process you used in some of the earliest examples to center text between two margins.

Step 3 is more complex. You need to examine the output string and count the number of spaces that you find there. You might use the **search** operator, which can do this fairly easily. As is always true in programming, there are alternative ways to achieve the same result. You also might design a loop, using **forall** and an **ifelse** test to tally the space characters. For the sake of instruction, we will use **search** here; but you should always keep in mind that there are often many approaches to a procedure and that you may need to choose one over another based on speed, efficiency, or another external consideration.

In either case, the processing loop for counting the blanks will be fairly complex. Let's analyze what you need to do. First, you want to create a procedure that you can call to count blanks in an arbitrary string. You can call this procedure **countBlanks**. The heart of such a procedure will be the **search** operator, which will take the string and break it up at each blank. That bit of code will have to look like this:

```
(string) ( )  search
```

This will return the following code onto the stack:

post match pre true	if found
string false	if not found

If a blank is found, you want to add 1 to a counter and continue to analyze the remainder of the string; if no blank is found, you're finished. At that point, the counter will contain the number of blanks in the string. This sequence naturally suggests the **ifelse** operator, since you would like to add 1 to the counter *if* there is a blank, or *else* you want to end the process.

The **ifelse** operator requires three operands: a boolean value and two procedures, one to be executed if the boolean value is true, the other to be executed if it is false. In this case, the boolean value will be supplied by the **search** operator, which leaves a boolean result on the stack; and the two procedures are as outlined above. They will look something like the following:

```
TRUE:    add 1 to counter
         clean up the stack for next search
FALSE:   clean up the stack
         end the process
```

You may wonder why you need to "clean up the stack." Remember that **search** leaves several results on the stack; the **ifelse** operator will remove the boolean result, but it is your responsibility to remove anything else. In the false case, you will need to **pop** the remainder of the string (presumably the final word on the line) before you exit the procedure; and in the true case, you will need to execute two **pop** operators to eliminate the *pre* and *match* results, and thus leave the remainder of the string on the stack for the next **search**.

The actual **ifelse** operation would then look like this:

```
(string) ( ) search                  % boolean
{ /BlankCtr BlankCtr 1 add def        % true procedure
  pop pop }
{ pop                                 % false procedure
  exit }
ifelse
```

You need to continue this process for the entire string, until the false result is returned by **search**. You can do this with the **loop** operator, which also has a matching **exit** operator to terminate processing. The **loop** operator requires one operand, which is the procedure to be executed repeatedly. The assumption is that an **exit** operator will be within the procedure to terminate the loop processing; otherwise, the processing would continue indefinitely in what programmers call "an endless loop." In this case, you have provided the **exit** operator as part of the false procedure within the **ifelse**. The loop process also requires one additional change from the **ifelse** outlined above: you need to remove the *(string)* reference, since the loop will be called with the string already on the stack.

This revised loop procedure will then form the major part of the **countBlanks** procedure. In addition to the loop, you will need to initialize the counter within the procedure, to ensure that it starts at zero. The entire procedure will look like Figure 6.2. With this process now in hand, you can proceed to constructing the full **justifyText** procedure.

CODE FOR JUSTIFICATION

The procedure shown in Figure 6.3 will require you to implement the steps outlined earlier for justification. The best way to approach the procedure is to look at it and then discuss it in detail.

The **justifyText** procedure starts out with two comment lines, designed to give you some helpful information about how to call and use it. Notice that these lines don't give you direct information about how the procedure itself is constructed; they merely remind you how to invoke and use the procedure when you need it. This is the kind of information that really should be kept in comments; otherwise, you would have to read the procedure to remind yourself how to use it every time you needed it.

The actual code begins on line %1 with a **dup** command. This command is necessary because you need to save the string on the stack for the **widthshow** on line %12, but you also need to use the string as an input to the **countBlanks** procedure on line %2. Because we have already analyzed this procedure, we don't need to say more here except to note that this takes care of the first step in the list of requirements.

Then you begin the computations to set up for step 2. This starts in line %3 by computing the *LineSize* as the difference between the left margin, *LM*, and the right margin, *RM*. The next step is to calculate the string length. In the same fashion as before, the **dup** on line %4 provides

```
/countBlanks
{     /BlankCtr 0 def                    % zero count
      {     ( ) search                   % boolean
            { /BlankCtr BlankCtr 1 add def    % true procedure
              pop pop }
            { pop                        % false procedure
              exit }
            ifelse    }
      loop }
def
```

Figure 6.2: The **countBlanks** procedure

```
/justifyText
% called as: (string) justifyText
% assumes variables LM (left margin) and RM (right margin)
{     dup                                            %1
      countBlanks                                    %2
      /LineSize RM LM sub def                        %3
      dup                                            %4
      /StringSize exch stringwidth pop def           %5
      /Space LineSize StringSize sub def             %6
      /BlankCtr 0 ne                                 %7
          {     /Space Space BlankCtr div def    }   %8
      if                                             %9
      Space 0 8#040                                  %10
          4 -1 roll                                  %11
      widthshow        }                             %12
  def                                                %13
```

Figure 6.3: The **justifyText** procedure

the operand for the **stringwidth** on line %5. Line %5 contains more than just the **stringwidth**, however. This line defines the variable *StringSize*, which is determined by the width of the string on the stack. Since the string is on the stack when the definition begins, you have to use the familiar **exch** to get the name and the value into the proper position for the definition. Once the name literal is beneath the string, the **stringwidth** operator is called, and it returns the x and y widths of the string. Remember that the y-width, which is on top of the stack, is always zero for English; therefore, you issue a **pop** command to throw away the y-width value, leaving the x-width on the stack. This width is now defined as *StringSize* by the **def** operator. Line %6 then subtracts the *StringSize* from the *LineSize* to determine the amount of *Space* that needs to be added to the string for it to fit perfectly within the two margins. This completes the second step.

Line %7 may surprise you until you think about it. It is possible that there were no blanks in the string—improbable, perhaps, but still possible. If there were no blanks, the **BlankCtr** will be zero, and division by zero is not defined mathematically and will result in a PostScript error. Therefore, you will only perform the division in line %8 if there are blanks in the string. This is determined by the test of **BlankCtr** for a zero value in line %7, which is matched by the **if** operator in line %9. The net result is that the division in line %8 is performed if the condition in line %7 is true, and not otherwise. Although the procedure will still execute if there are no blanks in the string, you should notice that the effect will be identical to **show**, since there will be no character for **widthshow** to add the extra space to.

Line %8 divides the total space required, which you have stored in the variable *Space*, by the number of blanks in the line, which was stored in the *BlankCtr* variable by the **countBlanks** procedure. The result is a real number that is the required adjustment for each space within the string and is stored back into the *Space* variable.

Line %10 begins the setup for the **widthshow** operator on line %12. This operator requires four operands: the additional x-distance, the additional y-distance, the character to be added to, and the string to be examined. On line %10, you push three of the four required operands in the correct order onto the stack. These three operands are the x-space adjustment, which has been stored in the *Space* variable; the y-space adjustment, which is 0; and the character that is to be adjusted, in this case the blank, which has character code octal 40, written *8#040* in PostScript. The string, which is the fourth operand, is already on the stack; but it is beneath the other operands and needs to be brought to the top of the stack. A **roll** operator does this in line %11. This use is similar to the one in the exercise regarding reencoding fonts; as in that exercise, you have all the required information on the stack, but not in the right order. This time, you have four elements to maneuver instead of three, and you need to move the bottom element of the stack to the top rather than the other way around. The four elements are represented by the 4 as an operand; and − 1 tells the **roll** that you are moving the contents of the stack down one by one, just as the 1 previously told it to move one element up at a time. The movement down pushes every item on the stack one level lower, except the string, which is the designated fourth element on the stack and therefore moves to the top. The top four elements on the stack are left in the desired order, and you now issue the **widthshow** command.

There are two other points to note about this procedure. First, the procedure assumes that the margins have already been set into the two variables, *LM* and *RM*, which is important. The second point is that **widthshow** is really a **show**, and just like **show**, it requires a current point and a current font to be set before you issue the procedure.

EXAMPLE OF JUSTIFICATION

The **widthshow** procedure is now in place, and you can use it in any of the text-handling examples that you have already completed. As a short example, here is a portion of the text-and-commentary example from Chapter 2. Notice how easily you can integrate this function into the previous work. I won't reproduce it all here, for space reasons, but you can easily complete the exercise if you want. The revised program is in Figure 6.4.

This example is only the first paragraph of the original exercise, and it produces a portion of the original output that looks like Figure 6.5.

```
%--------------------------Procedures--------------------
/inch                               %create a procedure
    {      72 mul }                 %to convert user units
    def                            %to use inch measurements

/advanceLine
    {      /NextLine
           NextLine LineSpace sub
           def   }
    def

/advancePara
    {      /NextLine
           NextLine ParaSpace sub
           def   }
    def

/countBlanks
    {      /BlankCtr 0 def
           { ( ) search
               { /BlankCtr BlankCtr 1 add def pop pop }
               { pop exit }
             ifelse       }
           loop    }
    def

/justifyText
    {      dup
           countBlanks
           /LineSize RM LM sub def
           dup
           /StringSize exch stringwidth pop def
           /Space LineSize StringSize sub def
           /BlankCtr 0 ne
               { /Space Space BlankCtr div def }
           if
           Space 0 8#040
           4 -1 roll
           widthshow     }
       def

/centerText
    {      dup
           stringwidth pop
           2 div
           RightMargin LeftMargin sub 2 div
           exch sub
```

Figure 6.4: Justified-text example

```
            LeftMargin add
            NextLine moveto
            show   }
      def
/bodyText
      {      SecondColumn NextLine moveto
             justifyText   }
      def

/rightJustifyText
      {      dup
             stringwidth pop
             RightColumn exch sub
             NextLine moveto
             show   }
      def

%-----------------------Named Constants----------------
/TopStart 9.5 inch def           %vertical start for head
/BodyStart 8.5 inch def          %vertical start for body

/LineSpace 14 def                %set line spacing (leading)
/ParaSpace 28 def                %set paragraph spacing

/LeftMargin .5 inch def          %set absolute left margin
/RightMargin 8 inch def          %set absolute right margin
/RightColumn 2.5 inch def        %set right edge of first column
/SecondColumn 3 inch def         %set left edge of second column

%-------------------Program (Title)----------------------
%Set up font for Title
/Times-Bold findfont 16 scalefont setfont

%Move to selected position
/NextLine TopStart def
(ACME WIDGETS INCORPORATED) centerText

/NextLine NextLine 20 sub def
(Fiscal Year 1986) centerText

%-------------------Program (Text Column)------------------
%Set up new font for Body Text
/Times-Roman findfont 12 scalefont setfont

/LM SecondColumn def
/RM 7.5 inch def

/NextLine BodyStart def
(Acme Widgets was founded in 1952 by Dippy and Daffy Acme) bodyText
advanceLine
(to produce high technology widgets for the growing aerospace) bodyText
advanceLine
(market. Acme was quickly recognized as being the best) bodyText
advanceLine
(widget works in the country. Continued investment in new) bodyText
advanceLine
(technology and manufacturing methods has kept Acme Widgets) bodyText
advanceLine
(in the forefront of this industry.)
dup /RM exch stringwidth pop def
bodyText

%---------------------Program (Titles)-------------------
%set font for Paragraph Titles
/Times-Bold findfont 12 scalefont setfont

/NextLine BodyStart def
(History: ) rightJustifyText
```

Figure 6.4 (cont.): Justified-text example

ACME WIDGETS INCORPORATED
Fiscal Year 1986

History: Acme Widgets was founded in 1952 by Dippy and Daffy Acme
to produce high technology widgets for the growing aerospace
market.   Acme was quickly recognized as being the best
widget works in the country.   Continued investment in new
technology and manufacturing methods has kept Acme Widgets
in the forefront of this industry.

Figure 6.5: Output from justified-text example

Insofar as this example is identical to the earlier exercise, it doesn't need
further explanation here. Let's briefly discuss the additional code that
was added to provide the justification mechanism.

First you had to add the two procedures **countBlanks** and **justifyText**
to the prologue. Then the **show** in **bodyText** was changed to **justifyText**.
Those were all the changes in the prologue. Notice how small these
changes are and how easily they can be inserted into the program as long

as the program is structured into a prologue and script.

In the body of the text, you had to add three statements. The first one sets the variable *LM* to the beginning position for the text column, SecondColumn. The second statement sets the variable *RM* to 7.5 inches. Because the body text was not justified in the original program, there was no reason to set the right margin precisely; now that you want to justify the right margin as well as the left, that margin needs to be precisely defined. In this case, you could have readjusted the *RightMargin* variable to the precise 7.5-inch value after centering the headline; or you could do as we've done here and simply set the *RM* variable to the precise value. The *RightMargin* variable had to be 8 inches initially to center the headline correctly between the edges of the paper.

The third additional line is the reset of *RM* just before the output of the last line of the paragraph. This is necessary because this line is deliberately short, and the right margin for it is not the same as that from the preceding lines. If you used the same value of *RM*, you would get too much space between the words because **justifyText** would space the words over the entire column. Since you don't want that, you set the value of *RM* to the precise length of the string that will be the last line, using essentially the same technique as you used earlier in the **justifyText** procedure.

REVIEW AND CONCERNS

The **justifyTest** example gives you an idea of how you can use the justification operators in actual text processing, and also shows you a use of the **search** operator. There are one or two points to review and discuss before we leave this topic, however.

The first issue is that of the proper, or appropriate, use of PostScript. PostScript is a page-description language; it is not designed or best used for calculation. In particular, justification of large amounts of text requires a fair amount of computation, as was mentioned earlier. Moreover, the presumption that we made, even for the justification above, was that the line of text was already fitted fairly close to the line length; that is, there was no room on the line for the next word in the text. Neither of these tasks really constitutes the appropriate use of PostScript.

The best approach to justification is for the word-processing program, or other application program that creates the text, to perform the necessary calculations before creating the PostScript output. This requires knowledge of the precise measurement of characters, so that the application can perform the equivalent of a **stringwidth**; this information is available in the font-metric files provided by Adobe Systems for each font. Using these font-metric files (which have an extension of .AFM), the application programmer can determine the length of a text string and calculate the adjustment factor required for justification in much the same manner as you did above.

This division of labor between the application and PostScript is more efficient than using PostScript for the entire process. Certainly you can perform all the calculations within PostScript; PostScript is a complete, general-purpose programming language and provides all the capabilities necessary for any processing that you need to do. The issue is not what you can do in PostScript (since you can do anything that you can in another language), but what is best done in each language, considering efficiency and the intrinsic facilities in each. PostScript is a language designed and best used to drive raster-output devices; it is not designed to compete with C, for example, in computational speed or facilities, just as C is not designed to draw arcs or to fill and shade letter shapes.

You should notice two things about inserting this additional code into the previous program. First, it is not difficult to add new features to properly structured PostScript. Although this has been noted before, it bears one more repetition. Besides the added procedures, you only had to change four lines of code to change from unjustified to justified text, and you wouldn't have had to change much more if you had wanted to adjust the entire page. That leads directly to the second point: with some redesigning, you could have eliminated the changes in the script entirely. To do that, you would need to modify the **bodyText** and **advanceLine** procedures so that the **moveto** was done in **advanceLine**; this would allow you to display the last line of each paragraph using a **show** operator rather than adjusting the *RM* variable. You would also need to provide the *RM* and *LM* variables in the prologue, in the same way the other variables are defined. Having done these two things, there would be no need for changes to the script. This type of consideration is of particular interest when you want to add or change PostScript code in applications, which we will discuss in the next section of this chapter.

TEXT APPLICATIONS

This section of the chapter covers two distinct PostScript topics. Both of these topics are related to text handling and processing, but each has a different emphasis. They are presented here in one section, since they both deal with the relation between PostScript and programs that generate PostScript code.

You have spent a lot of time and effort working on the various examples and exercises in PostScript. Almost all of this work has been undertaken one-on-one with the machine, using the interactive mode (if you have been following the examples). The single exception was the exercise in Chapter 4 that integrated the spreadsheet data with the PostScript form.

Obviously, this is not the typical method of dealing with PostScript. As explained when we discussed how to get started in Chapter 1, this is a good method for learning PostScript and an excellent way to analyze and debug PostScript routines, but it is not an efficient way to run in a production mode. Normally, you will be running PostScript files in a batch mode to the printer; and normally, those batch files will have been created, either entirely or partially, using an application program. You have now reached the point where you need to find out more about PostScript facilities in such a situation.

FILES AND FILE HANDLING

First we will examine two separate, but related, issues: the transmission of files to PostScript in your present circumstances, and PostScript files and file-handling operations. Each of these issues is important for you to be familiar with. The first issue is a practical one, however, while the second is primarily conceptual.

FILE TRANSMISSION

This subject was covered in detail in Chapter 4, when you were working with the spreadsheet output in preparation for integrating the data and the form that you produced. This section will review that information and expand on some of the points to help you make use of PostScript processing. Remember that all of this processing is still being done in the interactive mode; the transmitted file here represents the lines of code that you would otherwise have to type, and the PostScript interpreter is processing each line as though it came from your terminal.

The idea here is the same as it was before. You have prepared a file containing PostScript commands, using an editor or another method, and you want to transmit that file to the interpreter for execution. The easiest and most effective way of doing this is to use the same techniques that you have been using for the interactive mode. Start up PostScript to the PS> prompt, and then use your communications or terminal software to "upload" the file to the printer. The interpreter will read the lines of data as though they come from the terminal keyboard, and it will execute them in the identical fashion.

There are potential problems with this method. First, the transmission will tie up the link between the terminal and the printer, and you may not receive any error messages back over the link. Second, the transmission may be too long, and it may overrun the printer's buffer. The first problem can be solved in two ways. If you have the option of full duplex communication, that will allow the transmission of data in both directions simultaneously. It isn't likely that this option is available, but if it is, it can be an excellent solution. Another way to solve the problem is to wait until you produce an output page. If the output is not what you expected, you can often tell what the error is from looking at the output; at least, it provides a clue. You can also run each of the procedures individually, using **copypage** and **pstack** to help determine what exactly is happening within the procedure.

The second problem is essentially one of how the printer and the computer communicate. This subject was also discussed briefly in Chapter 1 and more extensively in Appendix C, with regard to specific hardware and software implementations. The secret here is to use a method that allows the printer to stop the data flow from the computer until the printer has room for more information. Generally, PostScript uses the XON/XOFF method of control; therefore, use that as your control. This method requires having some resident software that can perform XON/XOFF. If your computer doesn't have this feature, it is possible to change PostScript to use the other common method of controlling flow, called *DTR*. In either case, you should refer to your printer supplement for advice on handling the data-flow parameter.

POSTSCRIPT FILE OPERATIONS

The second issue is a discussion of PostScript files and file handling. PostScript has a small but useful set of file operators that you may want to know about. A complete discussion of the file operators is an advanced topic and beyond what we set out to do in this book; but you do want to know that the file operators exist, and you want to know something about PostScript standard files.

PostScript provides a complete set of file operations for use in programs. PostScript defines a file as a string of characters terminated by an end-of-file indication. Both input and output files can be used. The input files represent a source of data, or characters; the output files are a place for PostScript to write data. Each file is represented within PostScript by a file object. File objects are created by the interpreter upon execution of the **file** operator, which associates a specific file identifier with the new file object.

Once the file object is created, PostScript provides all the expected facilities for reading and writing the file. Note that most of the PostScript write operations may be buffered; that is, the write operation does not necessarily take place at the moment the command is issued, but instead may send characters to a buffer. However, PostScript does provide operators to deal with the situation when you require that the write operation take place immediately.

File operations follow a normal flow, and all the operations will return a standard end-of-file condition and execute standard error-handling procedures for exceptional conditions. An explicit operation closes a file when the program finishes the operation, disassociating the file object created earlier and the external file.

PostScript implements three standard files that have uniform names in all PostScript environments. Two of these are the *standard input file,* which is the source of the input to the interpreter, and the *standard output file,* which is the place where the interpreter writes error and status messages. There is also a *standard error file,* which receives certain types of low-level error messages and is typically the same as the standard output file. It is unlikely that you will have cause to use PostScript files other than the standard files.

Most of the PostScript file operations on the standard files are transparent to the user. The **executive** procedure that you have been using to start and run the interactive mode uses all the standard files. You simply need to know that there are standard files and that a set of operations and associated operators exists that you can take advantage of if you need them.

Application Interface

The second topic this chapter discusses is the relationship between PostScript, particularly the kind of PostScript that you have been utilizing in your programming exercises, and the "real world" of application output. After all, most PostScript code is generated by one or more applications that provide an interface for making the creation of text and graphics much simpler and more intuitive than writing PostScript code directly. As you worked through the examples and exercises, you must have realized how much effort is required to design and lay out even a relatively simple page. This should help you appreciate the magnitude of the task that your application program must handle.

Precisely because the transformation of pages of text and graphics into PostScript commands is such a large task, there is a place for and a purpose in understanding the underlying principles of PostScript. There will always be times when you want a result that the application either cannot handle or can handle only with difficulty. Because you have invested the energy in learning PostScript, you will be well-equipped to handle such situations by modifying the facilities provided by the application or by writing new code if necessary.

You might use several types of modifications for these purposes. In this portion of the chapter, we will discuss what, in my experience, are two of the most common modifications. These are embedding PostScript code in an existing application and modifying existing PostScript procedures provided by an application. Both of these modifications are highly dependent on the exact nature of the application program, and it isn't possible or reasonable to provide directions here on how to make them for specific applications. Instead, we will discuss the general approach that you should take to each of these kinds of changes, and you will learn some of the potential problems and opportunities—and how to avoid the former and take advantage of the latter. With this information, you should be able to use the application documentation to determine the precise methods for making whatever changes you want.

EMBEDDED POSTSCRIPT CODE

The first type of addition that you should think about is adding PostScript code directly into a file that is otherwise created by an application program. This is done by marking the PostSript code in such a way that the application program doesn't rearrange or process it. Successful embedding depends on the application; some applications that generate PostScript themselves make it easy to embed PostScript code, while other applications don't make it easy at all.

The most straightforward applications to work with are straight editor programs. These usually are designed for creating and modifying program text and will basically allow you to enter anything you want. For creating PostScript programs that you are going to send directly to the printer, these are the best tools. You can also create PostScript files with a word-processing program. Many word processors have a mode or method whereby you can enter text without having it edited; such a method is acceptable for creating and working with PostScript. In almost every case, you can direct the application output to a disk file, as you did in the exercise in Chapter 4, where it can be edited with either of the above techniques to include PostScript program text and to modify the application output, if necessary.

Some applications allow you to embed PostScript directly into the work that you are doing within the application. Two recent examples of applications that offer this facility are the Illustrator package by Adobe Systems and Cricket Draw. Each of these has explicit mechanisms for adding PostScript code into the application output file. Illustrator is particularly useful, because it also uses a version of a PostScript interpreter to paint the screen, so that you can see on the screen the changes you make to PostScript coding—a good feature for the budding PostScript programmer.

Sometimes it is possible to create a segment of PostScript within another text when you are using a word-processing program. When this can be done, you flag the PostScript code in the same fashion that you would flag printer-control codes. For example, in the Bank Street Writer (to take one fairly popular, simple word processor), you can bracket lines of PostScript with a FORMAT command that tells the word processor to ignore everything within the FORMATs and to transmit the text directly to the printer with no changes or formatting. Unfortunately, more sophisticated packages, such as WordStar, don't allow such simple techniques. For these applications, the best way to add PostScript is to print the file to disk and edit it there in nondocument or program mode, or to use a separate editor program on it.

MODIFICATION OF PROLOGUES AND PREP FILES

Another method of modification for application output is to modify the prologue for an application. You have been working with prologues and scripts for almost all of the book, so you are familiar with the concepts of prologues and scripts in your own programs. This structuring convention is also followed by most of the application programs that produce PostScript output. Typically, such prologues are called *prep files*, probably because the Macintosh version is called "Laserprep."

The typical application behaves in the following manner. There is a prep file that essentially consists of the procedure definitions that will be used by the application. This file is downloaded to the printer either at the start of a session or when you request printing for a specific file. The application output is then coded with procedure calls and data to generate the desired output. This process should certainly be familiar, since it replicates what you have been doing in all the exercises.

This replication is not an accident; nor is it just that the exercises follow the same structural guidelines as the applications (although we have). The basic reason for this compatibility in approach is the native structure of PostScript. You have seen, time and again throughout the book, how this approach is the only effective and sensible way to make use of PostScript's many facilities. So it is no surprise that the various application programs use the same technique.

This approach also allows you to change and modify the prep file for your application if you want to. This task is not trivial nor to be undertaken lightly. However, it can be done safely if you follow a few rules, and it is a useful technique. Again, we cannot give you a detailed look at any specific prep file; but we can discuss some of the practical rules that you should follow to protect yourself (and your output) from errors and provide some tips on how you might take advantage of this approach.

To begin with, the prep files are all readable. Like all PostScript code, they are essentially straight ASCII files and can be looked at using any simple text editor. I would strongly recommend that you take two important steps before you do anything further with your prep files. First, make a copy of the file and store it in a safe place with a new, but easily remembered, name. I assume that you already have a backup copy of whatever application software you're using; make sure that you include the new safety copy of the prep file on the backup as well. Second, use an editor to read and review the file; better yet, print the file out for reference. Then read and study the code used in the prep file. This will be straight PostScript code, and it will provide good exercise for you.

Although the code may be more complicated than what you have worked on so far in the book, you will see that it is similar to the exercises and examples that you have been working with. You may find that some routines are quite familiar, perhaps even identical to ones that you know; the reencoding routine that you worked with in the last chapter, or some variant of that, is one example of a fairly common routine.

The next thing I would recommend is to take a short, not too complex piece of output from the application and print it to the disk instead of to the PostScript printer. Then look at both the output and the prep file together, either printing both out or having one printed while you reference the other one on the screen with an editor. You will quickly see how the application uses the procedures in the prologue to produce its effects.

You should know one or two things about prep files at this point. First, when you look at the prep file or files that you may have available, you will notice that they use short names for procedures and variables, often only one or two letters. This is a matter of efficiency and space conservation within the interpreter. As stated previously, when you are creating procedures for your own use, it is recommended that you use names that have some relevance and mnemonic value; however, when you are using the application prep file, such names are not beneficial. Instead, the emphasis is on speed and efficient coding, which encourages the use of almost unintelligible names. If you are trying to follow the use of a specific procedure, you can use the global search-and-replace mechanism in your editor to change the name to something easily recognized; just remember to change the application output at the same time.

The second point to be aware of is that some techniques may be used in the application prologue that you have not been introduced to. Two of the most common are the use of special application dictionaries and the use of the **bind** operator to speed up the execution of PostScript code. Each of these techniques is clear once you understand the requirement that the technique is intended to address: this sort of thing is known generally in data processing as "clear if previously understood." To help you understand, we will examine each of these techniques in turn.

APPLICATION DICTIONARIES

Most application prologues begin with one or two lines of code that look something like this:

```
userdict /appldict known {stop} if
serverdict begin 0 exitserver
/appldict 100 dict def
begin
```

This sequence of code is intended to insert the application prologue into the PostScript memory in such a way that it won't be flushed out at the end of a job. The first line tests whether the name /appldict is already in **userdict**, by explicitly placing **userdict** onto the operand stack and testing to see if the name is present. If so, the **if** operator will execute the **stop** and end the current processing and wait for the next job. The name /appldict is the name of a private dictionary that will be created in line 3, which will hold all the procedure definitions for the application prologue. The intention here is to test, right at the start, whether the application has already loaded the dictionary. If it has, there is no point in reloading it; to do so would have some negative effects that we will discuss in a moment. However, if it hasn't been loaded, then the processing continues with line 2.

Line 2 performs a special PostScript function. It allows the application to bypass the normal processing mode of the interpreter and install the code that follows, up to the next end-of-file, into PostScript memory in such a way that the procedures and so on will not be removed until power-off. This process is device-dependent, and you don't need to know any more about it than the intention of the code in order to read and use the prologue file. However, do notice that once your printer is turned on and the prologue has been loaded, any changes you might make to the prologue will not be loaded until the next power-off. That will happen because the application dictionary, /appldict, is already defined in the system; therefore, the changed dictionary will not be loaded.

Lines 3 and 4 perform a function that you have worked with in the exercise on reencoding fonts. The new dictionary, /appldict, is defined to hold a specific number of items (in this case, 100) and then is pushed onto the dictionary stack as the current dictionary. After this action, all the code for the application prologue, usually consisting of procedures and perhaps some variables, will be stored in the application dictionary.

There is one issue regarding this type of mechanism that you should be aware of. This is the concern regarding the consumption of PostScript memory by the application prologue. Like every PostScript program, the application prologue takes up memory. However, unlike other programs, the application prologue will remain in memory even after the job is finished, until the power to the printer is turned off. It remains in memory because the procedures were loaded with the special commands that we discussed above, which store the prologue outside of the normal processing cycle. As a result, the prologue doesn't go away at the end of the job, a fact that has both good and bad implications. If you are running multiple jobs, all of which are output from the same application, this feature is good. It means that the prologue, which is relatively long and complex, doesn't have to be downloaded every time in order to print, which would be slow and inconvenient. However, it also means that the prologue remains in memory, in a place where you cannot remove it. For example, if you wanted to run another application, you would get the new application's prologue but not lose the old one. The net result is less memory for things like fonts and page descriptions of your own. This can be annoying in some circumstances.

If you are going to be running more than one application, or if you have any reason to suspect that you have multiple prep files in your printer, you can clear the memory and restore the maximum available space to the interpreter by shutting off the power to the printer and restarting it. This is the one sure and simple way to recover the memory used by such prep files. You can also see that you want to run all of one type of application in a group, as much as possible, to minimize the poor use of memory within the printer; and you may want to shut the printer off when you change to a new application to provide the maximum room for fonts and so on.

EARLY BINDING

Another common technique that you may see in a prep file is the use of the **bind** operator. This will catch you by surprise if you don't know what it is used for. A typical line of code that uses this operator might look like this:

```
/avg { add 2 div exch round } bind def
```

This is a simple averaging procedure, like those you have created before in the examples. The new feature is the insertion of the **bind** operator just before the **def**. This operator takes the executable procedure names in the preceding procedure and replaces them with their actual values, so that the interpreter doesn't have to do any additional lookup when it encounters **avg** in the script. This process is called *early binding,* because it happens before the normal binding process, called *late binding,* which occurs when the interpreter looks up the operator in **systemdict** at the time it executes the script. Early binding greatly improves the speed of execution of the procedures. You can ignore the **bind** operator whenever you find it, knowing that it is intended to accelerate the procedure immediately preceding it, but that it has no other effect.

This use of **bind** is one of a general class of techniques that are used to optimize PostScript performance. The complete range of such techniques falls into the category of advanced PostScript and, as such, is more complex than what we intended to discuss in this book. The use of **bind**, however, is important to mention so that, if you come across it in a prep file, you will understand that it does not change the operation of the procedure being defined.

OPERATOR REVIEW

This section presents in the standard format all the new operators that you have been introduced to in this chapter. As before, they are presented here as a combination reference and review.

Syntax	Function
int **string** string	creates a *string* that initially contains *int* characters of binary zero as entries. The *int* must be a nonnegative integer less than the device-dependent maximum string length.
string index **get** any array index	looks up the *index* in *array* or *string* and returns the element identified by *index* (counting from zero). The *index* must be between 0 and $n-1$, where *n* is the number of elements in *array* or *string*. For *string*, the element returned will be the numeric value of the character and not a one-character string.
string index value **put** — array index value	stores *value* into *array* or *string* at the position identified by *index* (counting from zero). The *index* must be in the range 0 to $n-1$, where *n* is the number of elements in *array* or *string*. For *string*, the *value* should be an integer between 0 and 255, representing the numeric code of the desired character.
string **length** int array	returns *int* as the number of elements that make up the value of *array* or *string*. For a *string*, the value should

Syntax				Function
				be an integer from 0 to 255 representing the code of the character.
string1 array1	string2 array2	**copy**	substring2 subarray2	copies all elements of *array1* or *string1* into *array2* or *string2*. The types of the two operands must be the same, that is, array or string. The length of the second operand must be at least the length of the first; **copy** returns the changed elements of the second operand onto the stack as *subarray2* or *substring2*. If the second operand is longer than the first, the remaining values are unaffected by the **copy**.
string array	proc proc	**forall**	—	executes the *proc* procedure for every element of *array* or *string*. The **forall** pushes each element from the array or string onto the stack and then executes the *proc* procedure, which may access the element on the stack. If the *proc* does not consume the element on the stack, it should remove it. Although **forall** itself does not leave any object on the stack, the elements of *array* or *string* will remain on the stack if *proc* does not clear the

Syntax	**Function**

stack before exiting. In the case of *string,* the objects placed on the stack are the codes (numeric values) of the characters, not one-character strings.

if found:
string   seek   **search**   post   match   pre   true
if not found:
string   seek   **search**   string   false

looks for the first time that the string *seek* occurs within *string* and returns the results of the search on the operand stack. The search is successful if any subset of *string* exactly matches the string *seek.* If there is such a match, **search** divides the *string* into three pieces and pushes them onto the operand stack: *pre*, the portion of *string* preceding the match; *match*, the portion of *string* that is identical to *seek*; and *post*, the remainder of *string.* Each of these is pushed onto the operand stack in the order indicated, followed by the boolean value *true* to indicate that a match was found. If no part of *string* is found to match *seek*, the operator returns the original *string*

Syntax	Function
	on the operand stack and pushes the boolean value *false*.
any string **cvs** substring	converts the object *any* to a string. The *any* is changed from its current form to an appropriate string representation and stored in the first section of *string*, which is overwritten. There must be enough room in *string* to hold the representation of *any*, or you will get an error.
c_x c_y char string **widthshow** —	prints the characters of *string*, but adjusts the width of each occurrence of the character *char* in *string* by adding c_x to its x-dimension and c_y to its y-dimension, thereby adjusting the spacing between this character and the following character.
a_x a_y string **ashow** —	prints the characters of *string*, but adjusts the width of each occurrence of every character in *string* by adding a_x to its x-dimension and a_y to its y-dimension, thereby adjusting the spacing between all the characters.
c_x c_y char a_x a_y **awidthshow** — string	prints the characters of *string* and performs two adjustments. First, it

Syntax	**Function**
	adjusts the width of each occurrence of every character in *string* by adding a_x to its x-dimension and a_y to its y-dimension, thereby adjusting the spacing between all the characters. Second, it adjusts the width of each occurrence of the character *char* in *string* by adding c_x to its x-dimension and c_y to its y-dimension, thereby adjusting the spacing between this character and the following character.
proc string **kshow** —	prints the characters of *string*, but allows the user to execute the *proc* procedure between each character of *string*. The operator shows each character of *string* in turn, adding the width of the character to the current point and then executing the *proc* procedure.

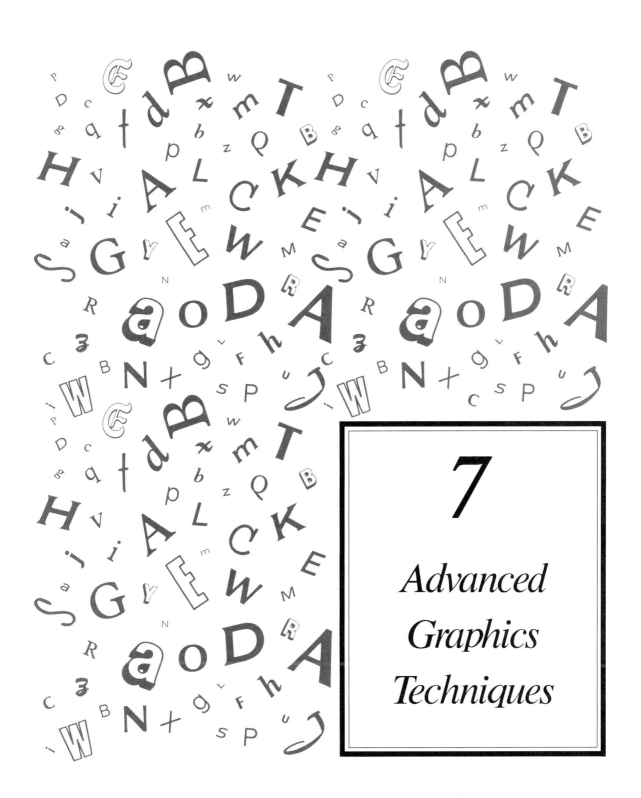

7

Advanced Graphics Techniques

THIS CHAPTER COVERS A VARIETY OF ADVANCED GRAPH-ICS OPERATIONS THAT ARE AVAILABLE IN POST-SCRIPT. You will see few examples in the chapter; to adequately explore the potential of most of the operations discussed here would require almost a separate chapter for each operator. However, you will learn what these operations are and how they work in general. In any case, you are now familiar enough with PostScript programs and programming to be able to work out examples and experiment with these new features on your own. If one of these operations seems interesting, try to create your own examples and work out the exact requirements and possibilities. This chapter will provide you with a basic framework for these operations, and you can then use the *PostScript Language Reference Manual* to guide you in the detailed requirements.

The first section of the chapter discusses several important graphics processes. The first of these is the clipping process, which is both easy and important. This PostScript operation functions in a manner similar to a common stencil, where you apply paint only where the cutout is. This is the one section in the chapter that contains examples for you to follow. The clipping operation is so straightforward and so useful that it is important to ensure that you feel fully comfortable with it.

The second subsection deals with the two processes of the creation and description of arbitrary curved-line segments and coordinate transformations. We covered both of these topics earlier in the book in a more restricted format. In both cases, the operators that you have learned and practiced represent the most common and accessible of each type of operation. This section introduces you to the general operators that lie behind the specifics that you have been using and discusses some of the mathematics that you need to understand in order to work with the general functions effectively.

The last process in this section discusses the manipulation of PostScript graphics. Specifically, it examines the methods that are available to determine the size and shape of a graphics object, such as might be described by the current path, within a PostScript program. Several operators provide this type of information, and this section both introduces you to these operators and discusses when you might want to use them.

The next section of the chapter covers processing general images in PostScript. These are the operations that deal with bit-mapped graphics and halftone images. An overview is provided for the concepts that are necessary to use these operations, including image-sampling techniques and control of such images on the output device. This type of work becomes intimately connected with the specific output device; and it is one of PostScript's many strengths that it provides remarkable control of these processes, including the ability to work at the device level if necessary, without sacrificing essential device independence. It is possible to create a PostScript program that will make maximum use of a specific device and yet still run correctly on any PostScript printer.

The last section of the chapter discusses various kinds of device-dependent PostScript operations and operators. Every time a PostScript interpreter is created in another output device, there are some operations and limitations that are specific to that device, and not necessarily to any other. PostScript handles this class of operations by providing both a special dictionary that contains all these parameters and a series of status operators that allow you to control such facilities. This section covers how to access and use this dictionary and the documentation associated with it.

ADVANCED GRAPHICS OPERATIONS

This section of the chapter will present several advanced techniques for handling graphics. In many ways, each of these techniques is different, but they all share a common point of reference: they all are extensions of graphics operations that you learned earlier. Each of them depends on one or more basic concepts and operations that thereby form the building blocks to develop progressively more powerful operations.

Other than this common genesis, however, each of these processes is distinct. Each one represents an important additional concept that you will want to understand and use in your PostScript programming; more important, perhaps, they also represent some of the most powerful graphics operators available. You will find these functions being used in some current applications, and I am sure that more and more graphics software will be taking advantage of these operations in the future.

CLIPPING

All of these advanced techniques include changing some feature of the current path. You are certainly familiar by now with the current path and the current graphics state. Now we are going to discuss several of the ways you can use or manipulate the current path by adjusting parameters in the graphics state.

CLIPPING PATH

The first of these ways is the clipping path. The *clipping path* is the path that defines the current boundary that crops, or limits, all output on the current page. This is similar to a current path in that it is a path in the user space that has been created by normal PostScript operations. It differs from the current path in that it is not stroked or filled, but instead defines a border that limits where marks can be made on the current page.

The clipping path starts out as the entire imageable portion of the current page, which is effectively the whole page. You may reduce it by means of the **clip** operator, which we will discuss in detail below. The new region defined by the clipping path must lie inside the current clipping region; you cannot expand it outside what is presently defined. The new region is reset to the entire page when you perform a **showpage**. You might think of this in the following way. You create an image on a temporary page, and then trim the page to the shape that you want with electronic scissors; you then paste the remaining material down on the current page to create your output. The clipping path defines the path that the electronic scissors will follow to cut, or clip, your temporary page to the shape that you want. This shape can be as arbitrary as you like; obviously, you should keep the path reasonable so that you know what is going to be inside and what outside. In particular, you may find that you want to use text characters as a clipping path. For example, you might create some outline text and want to fill it with a pattern of lines, other shapes, or even other text. All of these things can be done by means of the clipping mechanism. Further on in this section you will do an example that uses letters as a clipping path.

Notice one benefit to this model of what is happening. When you take a pair of scissors and cut something away, there's no way to put it completely back together. The same is generally true with the clipping function; once you have reduced the area on the page, using a new, larger clipping path will not restore the clipping area. However, by using **gsave**, **grestore** to bracket the clipping action, you can restore the clipping region to a larger, previous area. The clipping path is part of the current graphics state; and if you save the graphics state with a **gsave**, you also save the current clipping path, and it will be restored when you issue the matching

grestore. Any changes to the clipping path should be enclosed in the **gsave**, **grestore** pair even if you don't want to restore a larger path, for the same reason that we discussed earlier for all major changes to the graphics state: to insulate the rest of the page from the consequences of the changes.

CLIP OPERATIONS

Here is the complete description of the **clip** operator in the usual format.

Syntax	**Function**
— **clip** —	intersects the inside of the current path with the inside of the current clipping path to produce a new (smaller) current clipping path. Before creating the intersection, **clip** implicitly closes the current path.

When you are using the **clip** operator to generate a clipping region, you should remember that this operator, unlike **fill** and **stroke**, does not erase the current path when it has finished its operation. Therefore, if you want a new path, you will have to generate it by using the **newpath** operator. This is especially important in generating graphics; all procedures that construct graphics should begin with a **newpath** to be sure that no extraneous parts of the current path are left on the page.

SIMPLE GRAPHIC EXAMPLES

Let's illustrate these rather dry, abstract concepts by using them in some examples. A set of simple graphics will demonstrate the use of the **clip** operator in several ways. You will see what a clipping region is and how it appears on the page. In order to illustrate this, you will use several previous procedures and a new one. The new procedure is called **horizontalLines**, and true to its name, it generates a series of horizontal lines across a defined portion of the page. The other procedures are **screenBox** and **isoTriangle**, which you are familiar with. These can be combined into a general prologue file for use in all these exercises, which is shown in Figure 7.1.

The only new procedure here, as promised, is **horizontalLines**. Although this procedure is straightforward, let's look at a few points in it. First, you see from the comments that it is designed to produce rows of horizontal lines spaced 10 units apart with a specified height and width. The procedure starts with the necessary **newpath**, as we explained above. The height and width are on the stack when the procedure is called, and they are taken off in reverse order by the familiar method, using **exch**.

The heart of the procedure is a **for** loop, which produces the lines. Remember that **for** performs a procedure for a number of times, determined by incrementing a counter. The operator requires four operands: the initial value of the counter, the increment value, the end value, and

```
%Begin clipping prologue
%-----------------------Procedures----------------------
/inch
      {       72 mul }
      def

/screenBox
      %produces a square figure with rounded corners
      %called as: width screenBox
      {     newpath
          /Dim exch def
          .5 inch 0 moveto
          Dim 0   Dim Dim .25 inch  arcto
          4 {pop} repeat
          Dim Dim   0 Dim .25 inch  arcto
          4 {pop} repeat
          0 Dim    0 0    .25 inch  arcto
          4 {pop} repeat
          0 0      Dim 0  .25 inch  arcto
          4 {pop} repeat
          closepath }
      def

/isoTriangle
      %produces an isosceles triangle
      %called as: height base isoTriangle
      {     newpath
          /Base exch def
          /Hgt exch def
          /HalfBase Base 2 div def
          0 0 moveto
          HalfBase Hgt rlineto
          HalfBase Hgt neg rlineto
          closepath }
      def

/horizontalLines
      %produce a series of horizontal lines
      %  spaced 10 points apart
      %called as: height width horizontalLines
      {     newpath
          /Wdh exch def
          /Hgt exch def
          0 10 Hgt
          {     0 exch moveto
              Wdh 0 rlineto  }
          for
          stroke    }
      def
```

Figure 7.1: Prologue for clipping examples

finally the procedure to be executed. As **for** executes, the current value of the counter is placed on the operand stack while the procedure is executed, so it is available for the procedure's use. In this case, the counter will represent the y-coordinate for the lines; it begins at 0, increments by 10 units, and ends when the current value of the counter exceeds the height specified. The procedure being called first does a **moveto** to the point 0 and the current y-value, as stored on the operand stack by **for**. The **exch** is required to move the y-coordinate into the proper relationship for the **moveto**. Then the procedure makes a line from the current point horizontally for the designated width. This procedure is performed the required number of times by the **for**, the resulting lines are filled in by **stroke**, and the **horizontalLines** procedure is finished.

Let's see how the finished output from **horizontalLines** looks. Figure 7.2 is a short program that just uses the procedure alone. Remember that this program requires the prologue from Figure 7.1 before you can execute it. Once you have that, it produces a single page of output as shown in Figure 7.3.

Now let's add a clipping path to this exercise. This can be done as shown in Figure 7.4. Again, this assumes that the prologue from Figure 7.1 has been loaded into the interpreter. This program produces the page of output shown in Figure 7.5.

This program is simple; the only thing to explain is the use of the **clip** operator itself. The program begins with a translate to the same vertical position (5 inches) used in the preceding example, but moves in to the 3-inch position to center the figure more. Then it produces a current path in the familiar **screenBox** form, 3 inches on a side. This path is neither stroked nor filled; instead you issue the **clip** operator, which takes the current path and makes it into the clipping path. Now the only portion of the page that you can mark is the portion that lies inside the screen-box figure. To demonstrate this, the program sets 0.5 gray and, on the next line, again generates a 4-inch by 6-inch set of horizontal lines, as you did in the previous example. This time, however, the output only shows inside the screen box, as demonstrated in Figure 7.5. This shows you the most straightforward use of **clip**.

```
%------------------------Program----------------------
%first example - lines only
1 inch 5 inch translate
4 inch 6 inch horizontalLines
showpage
```

Figure 7.2: Program using **horizontalLines**

Figure 7.3: Output from **horizontalLines**

```
%------------------------Program-----------------------
%second example - clipped with screenBox
3 inch 5 inch translate
3 inch screenBox
clip
.5 setgray
4 inch 6 inch horizontalLines
showpage
```

Figure 7.4: Program using **clip**

Figure 7.5: Output using **clip**

The next example is more complex graphically, although not much more complex as a program. In this case, you are going to use two clipping paths and then paint the resulting area with the horizontal lines. This will demonstrate the discussion that you read above about the clipping path always getting smaller and never larger.

This example is done in two parts. The first part produces the figures that will be used for the clipping paths, strokes them, and prints them out to show you what they look like. Then the second part uses both of the figures, once to stroke them and a second time as clipping paths, and then prints a set of horizontal lines to show you what path remains after the two **clip** operators. Both parts of the program are in Figure 7.6. The first half of the program produces the page shown in Figure 7.7.

This output is what you might have expected, based on the first half of the program in Figure 7.6. This program creates an overlapping screen-box figure and an isosceles triangle. The two figures overlap so that a portion of each is outside the other. Before you go on, try to visualize what portion of this pair of figures will be retained by the **clip** operators. The result is shown in the output in Figure 7.8.

This program is easy to follow, so we won't spend any time in detailed analysis. The output, however, is more complex, and so the example both strokes the paths and uses them as clipping paths. This makes it easier to relate this figure to the preceding one and allows you to see exactly what the results of successive applications of the **clip** operator are.

Although the **screenBox** path was the last path used for **clip**, notice that the portions of the screen figure that lay outside of the previous clipping path, which was produced by **isoTriangle**, do not now become part of the new clipping region. This is also why you had to produce the screen box twice; in order to stroke the entire figure, you had to draw it and stroke it before the triangle was drawn, stroked, and used as a clipping region. Otherwise, you would only have been able to stroke the portion of the screen figure that lay within the triangle.

```
%--------------------------Program---------------------
%third example - screenBox and isoTriangle
%first half - page figures only
3 inch 5 inch translate
3 inch screenBox
stroke
5 inch 4 inch isoTriangle
stroke
showpage

%second half - as clipping paths also
3 inch 5 inch translate
3 inch screenBox
stroke
5 inch 4 inch isoTriangle
gsave
     stroke
grestore
clip
3 inch screenBox
clip
.5 setgray
4 inch 6 inch horizontalLines
showpage
```

Figure 7.6: Procedures for two figure-clipping regions

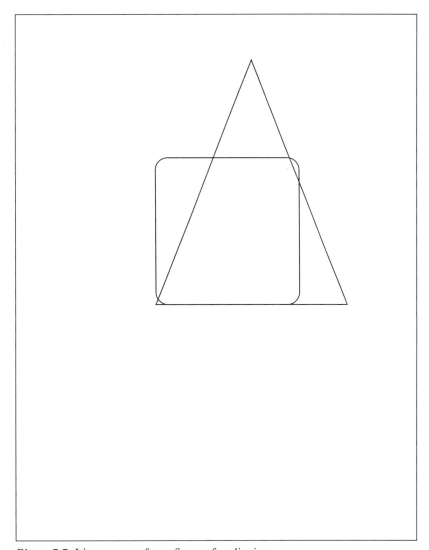

Figure 7.7: Line output of two figures for clipping

The use of **gsave** and **grestore** around the **stroke** for **isoTriangle** should be familiar; it is required so that the current path doesn't disappear when you stroke the triangle. An alternative would have been to issue the **clip** first and then issue the **stroke**. Because **clip** leaves the current path in place, that sequence would not have required a **gsave, grestore** bracket. The sequence as shown seems more natural and understandable to me, and that's why I used it here. It's just a matter of personal preference.

TEXT AS A CLIPPING PATH

Let's do one more clipping example to illustrate that you can use any arbitrary graphic as a clipping region. In particular, text in PostScript

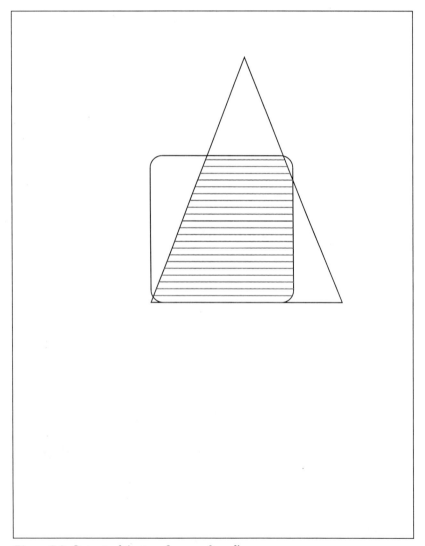

Figure 7.8: Output of the two figures after **clip**

(as you are well aware) is a graphic object. Therefore, one of the effects that you can generate with PostScript is to use the text as a clipping path and then show another graphic underneath it. The underlying graphic might be other text or any graphic image.

For this example, you will print the word "SUN" in 3-inch high, outlined letters in the Helvetica-BoldOblique font, and then use those letters as a clipping path for an image of the sun with rays radiating from it. This produces a fine graphic image, one that is beyond the reach of most applications except as a bit-mapped pattern.

There will be two procedures: **rays**, which draws only the rays, and **sunRays**, which draws the sun and the rays together. We won't spend much time explaining this; all of the techniques should be familiar to you. The program is shown in Figure 7.9. This program generates a complex graphic and uses large type; you can expect that it will take up to 2 minutes to generate the output shown in Figure 7.10.

Let's review what you did here. To begin with, let's examine the **sunRays** procedure. This procedure assumes that it will be called with an x- and a y-coordinate as operands. It then translates the origin to this location and uses the **rays** procedure to draw a set of 0.5-unit rays around a half circle, centered at the translated origin. Next it creates a half circle of 25 units, and both fills it with white (to erase the underlying rays) and strokes it with a 2-unit line. This will create the sun with rays as a graphic image that you want for the program.

The **rays** procedure also deserves some comment. This is a simple procedure that draws the rays by rotating the coordinates repeatedly and drawing a line directly along the x-axis from the center for 5 inches. The rotation and drawing are enclosed in a **gsave**, **grestore** pair to avoid affecting anything outside the procedure; in particular, to avoid the cumulative effect of the **rotate**. The entire procedure is repeated every 5° around a 180° arc, beginning with 0°; this repetition is performed by a **for** loop.

The body of the program begins by sizing and setting the font. Next the origin is translated to an appropriate point on the page, and a move to the origin is performed to set things up for displaying the string. Then you outline the string, using the techniques you learned in Chapter 5 when we discussed outlined fonts. Since you want to use the path in two ways, save it with a **gsave** before you stroke it, and then use **grestore** to bring it back for the **clip** operator. This generates the text outline on the page.

Now you need to generate the graphic to underlie the text. You start this with a **gsave**, remembering that these procedures will also modify the current graphics state. You decide to position the graphic in the center

```
%-----------------------------Prologue-------------------------
/inch
        { 72 mul  }
        def

/rays
        {       0  5  180
                {       gsave
                                rotate
                                0 0 moveto
                                5 inch 0 rlineto
                                stroke
                        grestore  }
                for  }
        def

/sunRays
        %called as: x y sunRays
        {       newpath
                translate
                .5 setlinewidth
                rays
                0 0 25 0 180 arc
                gsave
                        1 setgray
                        fill
                grestore
                2 setlinewidth
                stroke    }
        def

%-----------------------------Script--------------------------
%first set font and show letters
/Helvetica-BoldOblique findfont
3 inch scalefont setfont
1 inch 5 inch translate
0 0 moveto
(SUN) false charpath
gsave
        stroke
grestore
%now set clipping path from restored text path
clip
gsave
        (SUN) stringwidth pop 2 div
        -10 sunRays
grestore
showpage
```

Figure 7.9: Program for text-clipping example

of the string just below the baseline for maximum effect. To do this, you calculate the center of the string, using **stringwidth** divided by two, and then call the **sunRays** procedure with that result on the stack as the x-coordinate, adding a y-displacement of -10 units. This places the center of the "sun" exactly in the center of the text string and 10 points below the baseline of the text. The procedure does the rest, creating the graphic as you wanted it. Because the clipping path was set earlier, the graphic only shows up inside the outlines of each text letter, as you see in Figure 7.10.

Figure 7.10: Output using text clipping

ADVANCED LINE HANDLING

Another advanced tool that affects the current path is the variety of parameters that PostScript provides to control what happens when you issue a **stroke** command. Until now, you have used the default values for all the functions that we will discuss below, and you have not had any reason to be concerned. This is a good indication of how well the defaults have been chosen. However, now you want to learn how to change these defaults for the occasional special situation that requires it. Please don't worry about remembering all these variations; it will be enough to remember that such controls exist. When you need them, you can look up the exact use and syntax in the *PostScript Language Reference Manual*.

The first thing you need to know about the **stroke** operator is how it paints a line. Generally, since the lines that you use are relatively thin, you don't notice how the line is drawn. If you ever use a thick line, however, this will be important to know. The **stroke** operator draws the line evenly on either side of the current path; that is, if you are drawing a line that is 2 units wide, the line will extend 1 unit on either side of the current path. This can be especially important when drawing lines under or over text, where the baseline is the current path. Even though both current paths, the one for the text and the one for the line, may seem to be a sufficient distance apart, you may find that the line and the text run into one another. If so, usually this is because you have forgotten about the physical width of the line itself. It is possible to draw a very thin line by using a 0 line width; in this case, the line will be one *device* unit (one pixel or dot) wide. However, this is dangerous, since it is extremely device-dependent. For example, a one-dot line on a LaserWriter (at 300 dpi) is visible, but a one-dot line on a typesetter (at 1200 dpi or more) is virtually invisible.

LINE ENDING

One control that PostScript provides is control over how the ends of the lines are drawn. There are three possible methods of ending lines, as shown in Figure 7.11.

The interpreter uses a *line cap* code that is kept in the current graphics state to determine which of these endings is used when it draws a line segment. The line cap code can be changed by the **setlinecap** operator, which takes the new value from the operand stack and stores it in the current graphics state. The possible values of the line cap code are the following:

Value	Type of Cap
0	Butt caps. The line segment has square ends perpendicular to the path and ending at the

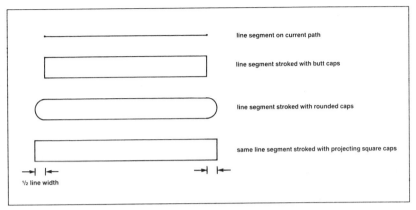

Figure 7.11: Line-ending appearance

	end of the path. This is the default PostScript line cap.
1	Rounded caps. The line segment ends with semicircular caps that have a diameter of the width of the line.
2	Projecting square caps. These are similar to butt caps in that they are square, perpendicular caps; but they extend out from the end of the line segment by one-half the width of the line.

LINE JOINING

As you might imagine, if you can control the ending of a line, you also can control the joining of a pair of lines. The *line join* parameter in the current graphics state controls this, and it is further affected by the *miter limit* parameter. The line join parameter works in a similar fashion to the line cap parameter. It controls the way PostScript paints the joints between line segments when they meet. If the segments merely cross, both continuing on the other side of one another, then there isn't any problem. The lines are merely drawn over one another, just as you might do with a pen. But if the lines end and join, then you have to decide how to paint the join. The three possible joins are shown in Figure 7.12.

Each of these joins again corresponds to a value of the line join parameter. The value of the line join parameter can be set by the **setlinejoin**

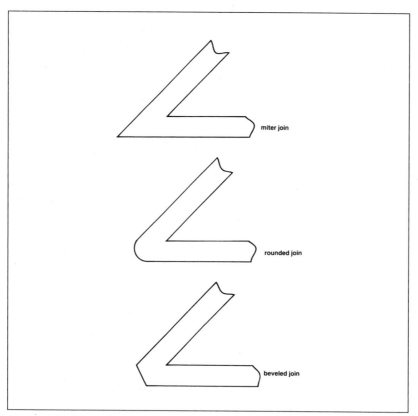

Figure 7.12: Line join appearance

operator. The three values for the line join are as follows:

Value	Type of Join
0	Mitered join. The edges of the lines are extended until they meet. This is the default line join, which is affected by the current *miter limit,* discussed below.
1	Rounded join. The line segments are connected by a rounded end, formed by a circular arc that has a diameter equal to the line width.
2	Beveled join. The segments are finished with butt end caps and filled in to form a bevel.

MITER LIMIT

When you are using a mitered join, which is the default join in PostScript, it is possible that the point on the join will extend some distance from the actual end of the line. This will happen when the lines meet at very small angles. This can be annoying under some circumstances; and to prevent such occurrences, PostScript changes from a mitered join (line join 0) to a beveled join (line join 3) at small angles. The precise angle at which this change occurs is controlled by the *miter limit* parameter in the current graphics state. This parameter defines the ratio of the line width to the length of the spike; when the ratio of these two for the actual join exceeds the miter limit, the join is turned from a mitered join into a beveled join. The default PostScript value makes this transition at about 11°. Because it is a ratio, the parameter works in a counterintuitive fashion, where smaller numbers for the miter limit make the transition at progressively larger angles. If you need to change it, you will probably have to experiment to discover the correct value for your application.

SOLID AND DASHED LINES

PostScript normally creates a solid line in the current color when you issue a **stroke** command. However, here again, this is controlled by the *dash pattern* in the current graphics state. This is not as simple as the previous controls; PostScript provides a flexible control for the line pattern.

Naturally, the default line is a solid one. The character of the line is set by the **setdash** operator, which takes two operands from the stack: an array and an offset. If the array is empty, the line is solid; if there are elements in the array, they determine the dash pattern for the line. The elements of the array specify alternately the length of the dash and the length of the gap along the line segment. Thus, an array with one element, such as [4], would produce a line composed of a 4-unit dash, followed by a 4-unit space, and so on until the length of the line was reached. Multiple elements in the array are each used in turn to determine the cycle of dashes and spaces along the line. You can generate some interesting patterns by using more complex arrays. It is not necessary for the line to be a multiple of the array factor; the array just stops wherever it may be in the cycle when it reaches the end of the line segment.

The offset operand determines when the array pattern starts on the line. The interpreter starts to process the array pattern, but doesn't actually paint anything until the total of the units used in the array equals the offset value. Then the pattern begins, starting at the beginning of the line. Notice that the offset affects the beginning of the pattern, not the beginning of the line. Let's use two examples to illustrate this process.

Suppose that you have an array and offset as follows:

[4]   2   **setdash**

You might think that the pattern should start 2 units into the line; in other words, that the line should start with a 2-unit space. That would be incorrect. When you stroke a line, the interpreter will begin processing the array, which specifies alternating 4-unit dashes with 4-unit spaces. But the actual stroking will not begin until 2 units of the array have been used; hence, the first dash will be only 2 units long, followed by a 4-unit space and then a 4-unit dash and so on throughout the remainder of the line. The first 2 units of the first dash were used by the offset parameter. The line, however, was stroked from the beginning; that is, the first 2-unit dash begins at the start of the line.

Another example is given by the following:

[4]   6   **setdash**

Here, the pattern defined by the array is the same as before, but the offset produces a slightly different pattern. This line will look the way we said the earlier line would not look; that is, the line begins with a 2-unit space. At the beginning of the **stroke**, the array is processed until 6 units are used. In the example, that uses up the first dash and 2 units of the first space; therefore, the line begins with the remaining space of 2 units, followed by a dash of 4 units, then a 4-unit space, and so on. In each case, you see how the interpreter used the offset against the array, not against the line.

All of these techniques are fairly exotic; the important point is for you to remember that they exist and that there are controls for you to work with if you ever need to. The default values work satisfactorily, and you should change them only for well-planned reasons.

ARBITRARY CURVES AND TRANSFORMATIONS

In previous chapters, you learned about various graphics operations that allowed you to draw circles and parts of circles and that allowed you to reshape the user coordinates in various ways. In both of these cases what you learned were special cases of a more general operation that PostScript implements. We covered these special cases because they are the most common, and most useful, variations of these general operations; and because of their utility, special operators perform those functions.

However, now we will discuss the two general operators that lie behind building curves and changing the coordinate system. These operators are mathematical because the underlying operations imply some complex calculations in order to generate the desired graphics functions. We are not going to go into much mathematical detail here; there are references in Appendix E, "Bibliography," that you can use if you want to know more about how these functions perform mathematically. Based on my own experience, it is almost impossible to use these functions effectively in ordinary PostScript without a good understanding of the mathematics involved. The intention here again is to provide you with a knowledge of the existence of these concepts and operators so that, if you need to use them, you will know that they exist and where to find them.

CURVED PATHS

PostScript describes all curved paths by using a mathematical function called a Bezier cubic section. The operators that you learned previously, such as **arc** and **arcto**, use this function to calculate the output paths that are drawn on the output page. This function can be used to produce any arbitrary curve on the output page, and it is invoked by the PostScript operator **curveto**. A detailed discussion of the **curveto** operator can be found in the *PostScript Language Reference Manual,* which you should read and understand if you are going to use this operator.

You should be aware of two points regarding these general arcs that PostScript produces. First, the other operators that produce curves use the **curveto** operator internally to generate the required shape. This means that, if you disassemble the path using the techniques we will discuss in the next section, you will get **curveto**s where the program issued operators like **arc**.

The second point is that the shape of the curve generated by **curveto** is a function of four points called *control points*. The first of these is the current point, where the curve starts. The last point is the end of the curve. The two points in the middle determine the motion and direction of the curve as it proceeds from one end point to the other. Although the first and last points lie on the curve, the two middle points do not; while they represent the motion and direction of the curve, they are not themselves part of it. If you drew a box connecting all four points, the curve generated by the **curveto** operator would always be inside the walls of the box and connected to only two of the corners. Of course, you understand that the "box" may have an arbitrary shape; there is no constraint on the position of the four control points.

This discussion is of most interest in utilizing some of the application software, such as Adobe's Illustrator package, which allows you to manipulate these control points directly to generate curves on the screen and then transfer them to the output page. Frankly, this is the only easy way to use **curveto**; it is extremely difficult to visualize the precise curve that will result from using a specific set of control points. If you have to use **curveto** in ordinary PostScript programming, you will want to experiment to find the exact points that generate the curve you need.

COORDINATE TRANSFORMATION

Just as general curves are an extension of circular arcs, so there is a general coordinate transformation that underlies the more specific operations of scaling, rotating, and translating coordinates that you worked with earlier in the book. This general coordinate transformation is done by the **concat** operator.

In order to understand what **concat** does, it is essential to review and expand the discussion of the PostScript coordinate system that we had earlier. Remember that PostScript transforms the user coordinates into device coordinates using a current transformation matrix, or CTM. This CTM is changed by operators such as **scale** and **rotate** to create the changed coordinates that are used in your programs. We discussed all this in Chapter 3, in the section "Measurement and Coordinates."

The mathematical operation of transforming one set of numbers, representing a two-dimensional space, into another set of numbers that represents a changed set of two-dimensional coordinates is performed by using a set of numbers called a *matrix*. In PostScript, the matrix for transforming one set of coordinates into another set is represented by six numbers in an array, like this:

$$[a\ b\ c\ d\ t_x\ t_y]$$

Before we explain the purpose of each number, let's define some terms to help us discuss them. These numbers are called *coefficients*, and they modify the current x- or y-coordinate values to determine the new x and y values. We will denote the current x- and y-coordinate values as x and y respectively, and the new x and y coordinates will be denoted by x′ and y′. The six coefficients have the following functions:

Coefficient	Function
a	multiplied by x (the original x-coordinate) as part of the determination of the new x′ (the new x-coordinate)
c	multiplied by y (the original y-coordinate) and added to the above as part of the determination of the new x′
t_x	added to both of the above as part of the determination of the new x′
b	multiplied by x (the original x-coordinate) as part of the determination of the new y′ (the new y-coordinate)
d	multiplied by y (the original y-coordinate) and added to the above as part of the determination of the new y′
t_y	added to both of the above as part of the determination of the new y′

This is a verbal description of what is represented, in mathematical terms, by the following equations:

$$x' = ax + cy + t_x$$
$$y' = bx + dy + t_y$$

The **concat** operator takes the 6-element array, described above, as an operand and *concatenates* it with the existing CTM to create a new CTM that is then placed into operation automatically by the interpreter. The operators that you studied and worked with previously are simply special types of **concat**. As one example, the **scale** operator is identical to a **concat** that changes only the a and d coefficients of the array. So when you issue the command

    72 108 scale

it is equivalent to the operation

    [72 0 0 108 0 0] concat

but the former is much easier to understand and remember.

As you may have noticed, this array looks similar to the array that you needed to use in the **makefont** operator; they are essentially identical. The **makefont** operator transforms the character-coordinate space in the same way, and using essentially the same mechanism as **concat,** transforms the user-coordinate space. You may want to review the "Font Metrics" section of Chapter 5 to see some of the transformations that were done there and that could be applied to the user space with **concat.**

GRAPHIC MANIPULATIONS

As the last part of this section on advanced graphics, we will discuss some of the operators that PostScript provides for determining the size and shape of graphic objects. Again, the intention is not to fully explore the use of these functions, but simply to let you know of their existence and to illustrate some of their possible uses.

GRAPHIC SIZE AND SHAPE

We will begin with the PostScript operator **pathbbox**. As you might guess from the name, this operator constructs a bounding box for the current path and returns two pairs of coordinates: the x- and y-coordinate values for the lower-left and upper-right corners of the box. The bounding box is the smallest rectangle that will completely enclose the points that make up the current path. The concept here is similar to the previous bounding boxes that we have discussed in regard to entire pages or groups of pages (in Chapter 2, the section on "Program Structure") and in regard to individual characters (in Chapter 5, the section on "Font Metrics").

You should note that the bounding box returned by **pathbbox** includes control points for any curved-line segments in the current path, as well as the actual lines themselves. If you think about it, this is reasonable. As we observed earlier, the control points of a curve form a rectangle that encloses the entire curve. These points, however, may not lie on the curve themselves, as we discussed above. Because the control points for a curved-line segment may be distant from the actual line that they define, PostScript provides another operator, **flattenpath**, that changes the curved-line segments into a short series of straight lines that closely approximates the curved segment. An example of this process is illustrated in Figure 7.13.

How close the approximation comes to the actual curve is a function of the *flatness* parameter in the current graphics state. This number

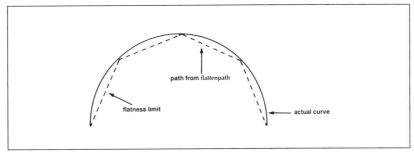

Figure 7.13: Illustration of curve approximation

varies for each PostScript device and is preset in the device setup routines to a value suitable for most applications using the device. We will discuss this, and other device-dependent information, in a later section of this chapter.

Because these are all straight lines, the bounding box that surrounds them will be closer to the actual paths than it will be with a curved segment. If you want a close fit on the bounding box, and the current path includes curved segments, you should use the **flattenpath** operator before you use the **pathbbox** operator.

COMMON APPLICATIONS

Not too surprisingly, the most common application of these operators is in determining bounding boxes for text characters. This is especially useful when you wish to scale another object to the current font. Typically, in such situations, the scaling will be done to a common letter, such as a lowercase m, that has no risers or descenders, or to a common capital letter. Once the bounding box is determined, the coordinates provided can be used to calculate the scaling factor. In such a case, it is essential that you use the **flattenpath** before you issue the **pathbbox**; otherwise, you will get different answers from those you anticipate and your scaling will be off.

IMAGE OPERATIONS

This section of the chapter presents the concepts behind PostScript's handling of images. PostScript provides sophisticated processing for transforming and rendering images. There is not room here for detailed examples and explanations of PostScript operations that process images; instead, we will try to develop and explain the concepts that lie behind these operations so that you can work with them comfortably.

In particular, we are going to explain the nature and representation of images from an internal standpoint and work from that basis to the PostScript operators that are provided to manipulate images. Some of this will repeat, but with more depth, information that was discussed in earlier portions of the book; and some of it may be information that you already know from other sources. In spite of this, the entire process will be presented here as a unit in order to allow the discussion to flow naturally, to be sure that all the information is covered, and to avoid the need to turn back and forth in the book.

IMAGE PROCESSING

An image is a representation of the outward appearance of something; in other words, an image is a form or shape that represents an object. Obviously, PostScript provides many facilities for creating and manipulating some common types of images, in that sense. Not all representations of forms or shapes can be easily described by the PostScript operators that you have used up to now, however. Complex images, such as photographs or even intricate, shaded line drawings, require alternate handling and processing. PostScript provides operators for such processing.

SAMPLED DATA AND IMAGES

To understand PostScript processing for complex images, we need to discuss how the computer stores and uses them. This kind of data is stored as an array of sampled data. The image is transformed, by the application of a grid, into a series of squares, and then a gray value is determined for each square. (If the image is processed in color, a set of color values is established for each square instead of a gray value. Black-and-white images will be used for our discussion, since they illustrate all the necessary points without the additional complexity of color; but all of the discussion applies to color as well.)

At the simplest level, each square can be either black or white, with no intermediate shades. In this case, the color of each square can be represented by a 0 or a 1; if we follow the PostScript conventions, we would use 0 for black and 1 for white (like **setgray**). Each square could also be given a range of gray values to provide additional shading of the image. We will discuss this process in more detail below; for now, let's look at the case where each square is black or white.

At this point, it may be helpful to look at Figure 7.14, which represents a simple image that is rendered into a grid format. The figure shows the image of the number 1 transformed into a grid. This is a simple image and could easily have been generated with ordinary PostScript operands, but it illustrates the processing mechanism. In actual practice, the images being used might represent the appearance of a natural scene or a complex, generated graphic. The simplicity of our example allows you to focus on the concepts involved.

The entire image is enclosed in a box that is 8 squares wide and 14 squares high. As stated previously, you can represent this image as a series of 0's and 1's (where 0 is black and 1 is white); it will look like Figure 7.15. This image is a *bit-mapped* representation of the number 1. Using this figure, we can discuss the PostScript mechanism for processing such images.

IMAGE REPRESENTATION

Each image is defined by three numbers: the number of columns in the image, the number of rows in the image, and the number of bits per sample. In our example, these are 8, 14, and 1, respectively. The number of rows and columns is easily understood; the number of bits per sample

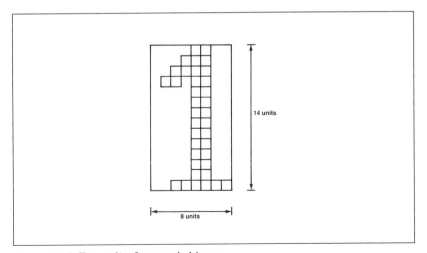

Figure 7.14: Example of a sampled image

may be less clear. This is a value for the gray level in the square represented by the sample. In the example, you have chosen to use either black or white; therefore, one bit is all that is required to represent the color value. PostScript allows you to use 1, 2, 4, or 8 bits per sample, giving you up to 256 gray levels for each sample square. This carries the obvious cost that you will have to process 2, 4, or 8 times as many bits to generate the image.

The sampled data that makes up the image is represented by a stream of characters. PostScript image processing obtains this data by executing a procedure that delivers the data, normally through reading a file that contains the data stream. The data is represented as a stream of characters, which is basically a stream of 8-bit integers in the range of 0 to 255. Each set of 8 bits represents from 1 to 8 sample squares, depending on the number of bits per sample. In this example, each character would represent 8 sample squares since each sample is only 1 bit. At the other extreme, if the samples were the maximum of 8 bits, each character would represent 1 sample square. Since the example in Figure 7.15 has 8 columns, each row can be represented by 1 character.

Image data must be presented in a defined order for processing. PostScript considers the image a rectangle, as we have illustrated above, and the coordinates for an image have the same structure as the coordinates on a page. The samples that make up the image are numbered (0, 0) from the bottom-left corner, proceed along the bottom row and then move up a row, and so on. In our example, that would make the bottom-left corner square (0, 0) and the bottom-right square (8, 0); the first square in the next row would be (0, 1), the top-left corner would be (0, 14), and the top-right corner, (8, 14). This is also the order that PostScript normally uses to assign values when it reads the data. That is, the first bits are applied to the bottom-left corner of the image, the

```
1    1    1    1    0    0    1    1
1    1    1    0    0    0    1    1
1    1    0    0    0    0    1    1
1    0    0    1    0    0    1    1
1    1    1    1    0    0    1    1
1    1    1    1    0    0    1    1
1    1    1    1    0    0    1    1
1    1    1    1    0    0    1    1
1    1    1    1    0    0    1    1
1    1    1    1    0    0    1    1
1    1    1    1    0    0    1    1
1    1    1    1    0    0    1    1
1    1    0    0    0    0    0    0
```

Figure 7.15: Bit representation of a sampled image

next bits are applied to the sample value on the left, and so on up the image until all the data is used.

The easiest way to encode bit-streams like this is to represent them as hexadecimal digits. PostScript provides a convenient notation for writing hexadecimal strings, by enclosing them in the characters < and >, instead of the usual parentheses. In that case, using hexadecimal notation, the rows of Figure 7.15 are equivalent to the hexadecimal values shown in Figure 7.16.

This set of numbers, or characters, would be sent to PostScript as the following hexadecimal string:

<c0f3f3f3f3f3f3f3f3f393c3e3f3>

As you see, it begins with the bottommost row and proceeds up the image to the top. The only point to watch out for here is that each row of the sample must start with a new character. For instance, if the example were 9 columns wide, you would have to put the ninth bit into a character by itself: the last 7 bits would be thrown out. To illustrate this, let's take the example above and add one column of white space on the right edge— another row of 1's. In that case, each row would have to add another character that would be the same for all the rows: an <80>, to set the last bit in the row. A single additional bit will not work. Then the string to represent the image would be changed as follows:

<c080f380f380f380f380f380f380f380f380f3809380c380e380f380>

IMAGE TRANSFORMATION

The coordinates actually used to generate an image may, of course, be different from those the PostScript interpreter uses to generate the

1	1	1	1	0	0	1	1	= <f3>
1	1	1	0	0	0	1	1	= <e3>
1	1	0	0	0	0	1	1	= <c3>
1	0	0	1	0	0	1	1	= <93>
1	1	1	1	0	0	1	1	= <f3>
1	1	1	1	0	0	1	1	= <f3>
1	1	1	1	0	0	1	1	= <f3>
1	1	1	1	0	0	1	1	= <f3>
1	1	1	1	0	0	1	1	= <f3>
1	1	1	1	0	0	1	1	= <f3>
1	1	1	1	0	0	1	1	= <f3>
1	1	1	1	0	0	1	1	= <f3>
1	1	1	1	0	0	1	1	= <f3>
1	1	0	0	0	0	0	0	= <c0>

Figure 7.16: Sampled image with hexadecimal equivalents

image. In particular, the PostScript operators that manage images allow transformations from the actual coordinates used by a device that produces the image into PostScript coordinates. This is accomplished by means of a transformation matrix, similar to the one discussed in the previous section of the chapter.

This transformation matrix maps the coordinates used in the source image into the user-coordinate space. The best and easiest method of handling this conversion is to do it in two steps. First, the image is converted into a unit square in user space by means of the transformation matrix mentioned above. Then that unit square is positioned and scaled on the page in the usual fashion. This process is familiar, since you used the same method to work with the logo graphic in the earlier exercises. In that case, the logo was defined in a procedure that was independent of the page itself; the entire object was positioned and scaled to fit the space reserved on the page for it. You should use this same technique for processing images.

This transformation matrix is identical in components and operation to the transformation matrix described earlier in the chapter as part of the **concat** operator. Thus, the process of scaling an image that is presented to the interpreter already in the expected sequence, like the string you developed above, would use the following matrix:

[8 0 0 14 0 0]

where the a and d coefficients represent the width and height of the sampled image, respectively. Remember that the a coefficient represents the x-coordinate, which is the width (or number of columns) of the image, and that the d coefficient represents the y-coordinate, which is the height (or number of rows). If you had an image that was scanned left to right, but top to bottom, instead of the bottom-to-top method expected by PostScript, the transformation matrix would look like this:

[8 0 0 −14 0 14]

This has the same width, but the y-coordinate is a negative height to indicate that the scan proceeds downward (in the negative direction) and the t_y coefficient is a positive 14 to move the starting point for the scan up to the top of the image. Using similar techniques, any form of scanned image can be converted into a PostScript unit square.

IMAGE-PROCESSING OPERATORS

Now that you have been introduced to the image-processing mechanism, we can discuss the actual PostScript operators that implement it. Two similar operators, **image** and **imagemask**, do this. These two are sufficiently alike that we will discuss **image** first and then explain the differences that distinguish **imagemask**.

The **image** operator takes five operands: sample width, sample height, number of bits per sample, the transformation matrix, and a procedure. You already understand the function of the first four items; only the procedure is new. This is the procedure that **image** executes, repeatedly if necessary, to get the data to generate the sample image. Typically, the procedure will read the image data from a file, often the current input file; that is, the same file that is supplying the PostScript commands. In that case, the data will be embedded into the command stream immediately after the **image** operator. In any case, the **image** operator obtains the data by executing the procedure. If the image area defined by the first three operands has not been filled by the time the procedure has completed execution, **image** will execute the procedure repeatedly until sufficient data has been obtained.

There are several advantages to this method of producing images on the device. To begin with, there is no need for the entire image to reside in PostScript memory in order for the image to be generated onto the output device. The sample data may also be processed as it is read, allowing various transformations to be performed on the file. For example, the data on the file might be compressed by an algorithm to conserve space and then decompressed by the input procedure to generate the final sample image. It is even possible to generate an image entirely internally, by using a procedure that calculates the necessary binary pattern instead of reading the data from some source.

The **image** operator produces images on the page by marking with an opaque paint, as always. Thus, each sample square is painted black, white, or a tone of gray, as selected by the bit/sample value. In this case, the usual PostScript rules apply, and the paint covers every part of the sampled image, overlaying anything that was on the page previously. This is the effective difference between the two operators **image** and **imagemask**.

The **imagemask** operator takes the data stream as a series of binary digits, 0 and 1, and uses these as a *mask* to control where the paint is applied. Let's look at Figure 7.15 again. We said earlier that this is a *bit-mapped* image of the number 1. When we were looking at this in relation to the **image** operator, the 0's represented black paint and the 1's were white paint. Now consider this same data as a mask. In that case, the 0's represent where the **imagemask** operator will apply paint—the current color, as set by **setgray**—and the 1's represent where no color is to be applied. Alternatively, the 0's could represent where no color was applied, and the 1's where the color was applied—the reverse of the preceding condition. This is the difference between the two operators: **image** paints the sampled data onto the page, whereas **imagemask** applies paint in the current color through the sampled data, using it as a mask.

The **imagemask** operator requires five operands, in the same fashion as **image**. The first and the last pair of operands are identical: the width and height, and the transformation matrix and the procedure. The difference is in the third operand. Here, **image** had the number of bits per sample, but since **imagemask** is a binary mask, there is always only one bit per position. Instead of bits/sample, **imagemask** has a boolean operand in this position: if the value is true, the 1's are painted and the 0's are blank; if it is false, the reverse occurs. Assuming that you wanted to paint the sample in Figure 7.15 in the current color, you would call the **imagemask** with the operands

    8 14 false [8 0 0 14 0 0] { procedure }

which would paint the 0's in the mask and leave everything else on the current page alone. This is an important point, particularly if you are developing bit-mapped characters. Any marks already on the page that lie under the nonpainted characters will not be affected by the operation. This ensures that, for example, if you had built your own font, the lines that you painted on the form in Chapter 4 would not be erased by the space character that prints on top of them. If you incorrectly used **image**, instead of **imagemask** with a bit-mapped space character, it would paint white over the line and would not be consistent with the behavior of the internal fonts.

DEVICE-DEPENDENT OPERATIONS

This last section of the chapter discusses a variety of PostScript operations that vary according to the device being used. This section does not discuss specific devices; insofar as there are specific device references in this section, they are here for illustration only. Specific information on the configurations used to produce the exercises and examples in this book is given in Appendix D.

DEVICE-SPECIFIC DOCUMENTATION

Along with the *PostScript Language Reference Manual*, Adobe Systems provides supplementary documentation covering device-specific features for each output device that supports PostScript. The device information for the Apple LaserWriter, which is contained in Appendix D of the *PostScript Language Reference Manual*, is typical of the information and layout of these supplements. Each follows essentially the same format, and generally contains at least the following sections:

1. Introduction
2. Basic operation
3. Communication
4. Details of server operation
5. System parameters

In all cases, the supplement for your output device contains useful and important information. Since all these supplements follow a similar format, we will discuss what information is typically contained in them and what some of the common information is used for.

BASIC OPERATION

This section covers the various modes of operation that are provided by the specific implementation of the PostScript interpreter in your device. This generally includes the *batch* mode, the *interactive* mode, and sometimes an *emulation* mode as well. The section discusses the standard flow of PostScript jobs into the device, status information displayed on the device (as it relates to PostScript), and overall server operations provided by the interpreter.

COMMUNICATIONS

The section on communications is important for setting up your particular output device and connecting it to the host computer. There is a variety of specific information on switch settings and other features that the device has for setting and changing communications parameters and modes of operation. Particular attention should be paid to this section, because a missetting of the communications parameters will often result in errors that are almost impossible to diagnose.

The communications section also includes device-specific information on cabling and the various communications options, which may be useful for you or your service technician in cabling devices together. There is also information on types of status queries supported by the device and on control of the communications channel. This is the section, for example, that describes the requirements for XON/XOFF protocol use.

SERVER OPERATION

Both general and specific considerations regarding server operation are covered in this part of the supplement. This section contains information on the size of paper supported during operation of the output device, manual-feed operation (when available), and a variety of specific parameters that are established for the device. There is also a list of fonts that are converted into character form and stored into the font cache during the time the device is not busy; this information is very device-specific, but it can be important in tuning page output (as described in Chapter 5).

OTHER DOCUMENTATION CONTENTS

The section of the supplementary information that deals with system parameters is so significant that it is treated separately in the next section of the chapter. However, a variety of other information may be included in any individual supplement.

Such information forms the subject of additional sections that are included in the supplement. Typical additional sections are the following:

- Other operating modes
- Known problems
- Disk- and file-system utilities

These sections are mostly self-explanatory and cover a wide range of information.

If your supplement contains a section on "Other Operating Modes," I strongly suggest that you read it. This section (if present) offers information regarding the interactive mode and the emulation mode of the device. You are familiar with the interactive mode; and in any case, it is not difficult to use or interpret. Most of the information in the supplement regarding this mode will already be familiar to you from the discussions earlier in this book, particularly in Chapter 1. The emulation mode, however, is often difficult to use and almost impossible to debug if the output goes wrong. The information in this section will be essential to you for setting up proper operation of the emulation function and controlling and correcting output, if you need or want to use the function.

SYSTEM PARAMETERS

Each PostScript device has a variety of features that are important to the users of that device and need to be controlled by PostScript to provide the output that users need. In addition, each device has a variety of internal settings that control its behavior and many facets of its operations. These controls are collectively known as *system parameters*. These parameters are stored inside the device, some in ordinary PostScript memory and some in nonvolatile memory where they will remain in effect even when the device is turned off.

All of these system parameters are stored in a special PostScript dictionary, called the **statusdict**, which is separate from other PostScript dictionaries, such as **systemdict** and **userdict**. This dictionary is where PostScript stores machine- and configuration-dependent operators and values; by definition, the information in **statusdict** varies from one PostScript implementation to another.

The parameters stored in **statusdict** can only be changed by an explicit access to **statusdict** itself. In this way, you don't need to worry about accidentally changing the parameters in an ordinary PostScript job. This access is done in typical PostScript fashion, by executing the command

statusdict begin

either from a PostScript program or in the interactive mode. This operation behaves like any other **begin** operation and pushes the requested dictionary, **statusdict**, onto the dictionary stack where it is available for access and change. From this point, the special operators that are defined in **statusdict** can be executed in the normal way by using their names, and the ordinary system parameters can be changed by using a **def** operator.

Some of the parameters stored in **statusdict** can only be changed by exiting the server loop. We discussed this process in Chapter 6, and it is fully discussed in the supplementary information for your device. If you need to access or modify this information, specifically if you need to modify the persistent system parameters, you should carefully study these references.

There is one point to make here regarding the use, and potential abuse, of the persistent system parameters. These are stored in special, non-volatile memory (called EEROM), which can be written to but not erased. There is a physical limit to how many writes you can perform to this memory before it is exhausted. Since the memory is intended for persistent system parameters that should never (or almost never) change once the system is installed in a particular configuration, this should not present a problem. However, some installations have apparently made a habit of issuing commands to change or set these parameters with each job that runs. If you allow that to happen, you will clearly run out of memory sooner or later, and you run the risk of massive printer failure. These parameters are collectively protected by a password and should not be modified in the course of ordinary processing. They should be reserved for their intended, exceptional purposes.

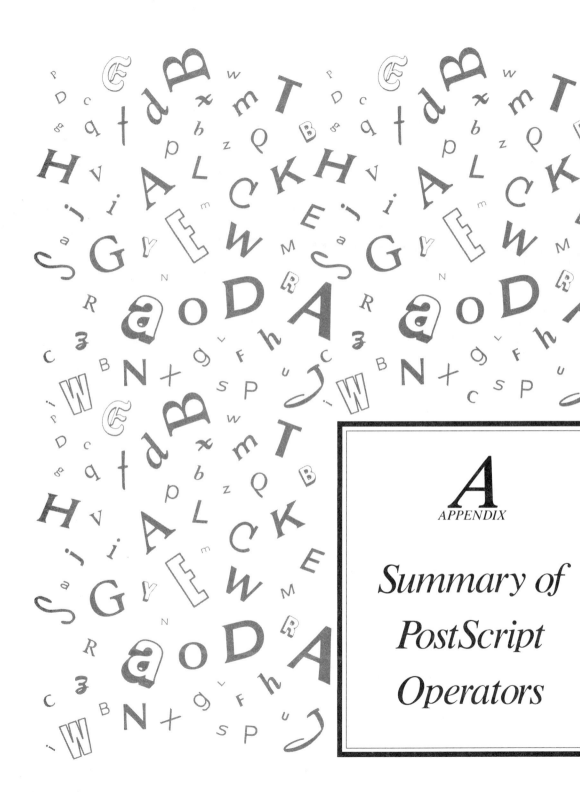

A

APPENDIX

Summary of PostScript Operators

We WILL NOW BEGIN OUR REVIEW OF THE OPERATORS THAT HAVE BEEN PRESENTED IN THIS BOOK. THIS SAME format has been used throughout all of the chapters to summarize the operators that have been used for the first time in that chapter. This appendix will help you to recall the operators in each chapter and also forms an informal index for review of the topics covered in the book.

Not every PostScript operator is presented in this appendix, but every operator that has been used in the book is included here. As was noted earlier, the best way to work with a language is to learn the primary functions in the language well and then to broaden your scope to include the more specialized operators. That is the rule that has been followed in this book; only the major functions are presented or used. Some related functions or operators have only been noted; others have been omitted altogether. If you want to use these other operators, be sure to consult the *PostScript Language Reference Manual* for full specification of their requirements and results.

This appendix is organized by operator type to enable you to find related operators quickly. A complete, alphabetical list of all PostScript operators is provided in the *PostScript Language Reference Manual* should you need it.

MATHEMATICAL OPERATORS

Syntax	Function
num1 num2 **add** sum	Adds *num1* to *num2*.
num1 num2 **sub** result	Subtracts *num2* from *num1*.
num1 num2 **mul** product	Multiplies *num1* by *num2*.
num1 num2 **div** quotient	Divides *num1* by *num2*.
num **neg** −num	Reverses the sign of *num*.
num1 **round** num2	Rounds *num1* to the nearest integer. If *num1* is equally close to its two nearest integers, the

Syntax	Function
	result is the greater of the two.
int1 int2 **idiv** result	Divides *int1* by *int2* and returns the integer portion of the quotient as *result*; any remainder is discarded. Both operands must be integers, and the result is an integer.

PATH OPERATORS

Syntax	Function
num1 num2 **moveto** —	Sets the current point to x-coordinate *num1* and y-coordinate *num2*.
num1 num2 **lineto** —	Adds a straight-line segment to the current path. The line segment extends from the current point to the *num1* x-coordinate and the *num2* y-coordinate. The new current point is (*num1, num2*).
num1 num2 **rmoveto** —	(Relative moveto.) Starts a new segment of the current path in the same manner as **moveto**. However, the new current point is defined from the current point (x, y) to x + *num1* as an x-coordinate and y + *num2* as a

Syntax	Function
	y-coordinate. The new current point is (x + *num1*, y + *num2*).
num1 num2 **rlineto** —	(Relative lineto.) Adds a straight-line segment to the current path in the same manner as **lineto**. However, the line segment extends from the current point (x, y) to x + *num1* as an x-coordinate and to y + *num2* as a y-coordinate. The new current point is (x + *num1*, y + *num2*).
x y r ang1 ang2 **arc** —	Adds a counter-clockwise arc of a circle to the current path, possibly preceded by a straight-line segment. The arc has radius *r* and the point *(x, y)* as a center. The *ang1* is the angle of a line from *(x, y)* with length *r* to the beginning of the arc; and *ang2* is the angle of a vector from *(x, y)* with length *r* to the end of the arc. If the current point is defined, the **arc** operator will construct a line from the current point to the beginning of the arc.
x y r ang1 ang2 **arcn** —	Performs the same function as **arc**, except in a clockwise direction.

Syntax	Function
x_1 y_1 x_2 y_2 **arcto** xt_1 yt_1 xt_2 yt_2	Creates a circular arc or radius r, tangent to the two lines defined from the current point to (x_1, y_1) and from (x_1, y_1) to (x_2, y_2). Returns the values of the coordinates of the two tangent points (xt_1, yt_1) and (xt_2, yt_2). The **arcto** operator also adds a straight-line segment to the current line, if the current point is not the same as the starting point of the arc.
— **newpath** —	Initializes the current path to be empty and causes the current point to be undefined.
— **closepath** —	Closes the segment of the current path by appending a straight line from the current point to the path's starting point (generally the point specified in the most recent **moveto**).

PAINTING OPERATORS

Syntax	Function
— **stroke** —	Paints a line following the current path and using the current color.

Syntax	Function
— **fill** —	Paints the area enclosed by the current path with the current color.
num **setlinewidth** —	Sets the current line width to *num*. This controls the thickness of lines painted by subsequent **stroke** operators.
num **setgray** —	Sets the current color to a shade of gray corresponding to *num*. The *num* must be between 0, corresponding to black, and 1, corresponding to white, with intermediate values corresponding to intermediate shades of gray.

STACK OPERATORS

Syntax	Function
any_1 any_2 **exch** any_2 any_1	Exchanges the top two elements on the stack.
any **pop** —	Discards the top element.
any **dup** any any	Duplicates the top element, and adds the copy to top of the stack.
$\vert$– any_n **clear** $\vert$–	Empties stack.
$any_{n-1}\ldots any_0$ n int **roll** $any_{(j-1)\bmod n}\ldots any_0$ $any_{n-1}\ldots any_{j\bmod n}$	Performs a circular shift of the contents of the operand stack. The top

Syntax	Function
	n objects on the stack are shifted by the amount *int*. A positive value of *int* indicates movement up the stack, that is, toward the top of the stack; a negative value indicates movement down the stack. The operand *n* must be a nonnegative integer, and at least *n* elements must be on the stack below the top two operands. The operand *int* must be an integer.
any$_1$...any$_n$ int **copy** any$_1$...any$_n$ any$_1$...any$_n$	When the top element on the operand stack is a nonnegative integer *int*, **copy** pops *int* and then duplicates the top *int* elements of the operand stack.

ARRAY AND STRING OPERATORS

Syntax	Function
int **array** array	Creates *array* that initially contains *int* null objects as entries. The *int* must be a nonnegative integer less than the device-dependent maximum array length.

Syntax	Function
array **aloa d** a$_0$...a$_{n-1}$ array	Successively pushes all *n* elements of *array* onto the operand stack, where *n* is the number of elements in *array*, and finally pushes *array* itself.
array index **get** any string index	Looks up the *index* in *array* or *string* and returns the element identified by *index* (counting from 0). The *index* must be between 0 and n − 1, where n is the number of elements in *array* or *string*. For *string*, the element returned will be the numeric value of the character and not a one-character string.
array index value **put** — string index value	Stores *value* into *array* or *string* at the position identified by *index* (counting from 0). The *index* must be in the range 0 to n − 1, where n is the number of elements in *array* or *string*. For *string*, the *value* should be an integer between 0 and 255, representing the numeric code of the desired character.
array **length** int string	Returns *int* as the number of elements that make up the value of *array* or *string*.

Syntax				Function
array1	array2	**copy**	subarray2	Copies all elements of *array1* or *string1* into
string1	string2		substring2	*array2* or *string2*. The types of the two operands must be the same, that is, array or string. The length of the second operand must be at least the length of the first; **copy** returns the changed elements of the second operand onto the stack as *subarray2* or *substring2*. If the second operand is longer than the first, the remaining values are unaffected by the **copy**.
int	**string**	string		Creates *string* that initially contains *int* characters of binary zero as entries. The *int* must be a nonnegative integer less than the device-dependent maximum string length.

Syntax			Function
string seek	**search**	*if found:* post match pre true *if not found:* string false	
			Looks for the first time that the string *seek* occurs within *string* and returns the results of the search on the operand stack.
any string	**cvs**	substring	Converts the object *any* to a string.

DICTIONARY OPERATORS

Syntax	Function
int **dict** dict	Creates a dictionary *dict* with the capacity for *int* value pairs. The *int* must be a non-negative integer.
dict **begin** —	Pushes *dict* onto the dictionary stack and makes it the current dictionary.
— **end** —	Pops the current dictionary from the dictionary stack.
key value **def** —	Associates *key* and *value* in the current dictionary.
dict **length** int	Returns *int* as the current number of key,value pairs in *dict* (see **maxlength**).
dict **maxlength** int	Returns *int* as the maximum number of key,value pairs that *dict* can hold, as defined by the **dict** operator that created *dict*.
dict key **get** any	Looks up the *key* in *dict* and returns the associated value. If *key* is not defined in *dict*, it executes the error procedure **undefined**.
dict key value **put** —	Uses *key* and *value* and stores them as a key,value pair into *dict*. If *key* is already present in *dict*, its associated

Syntax	Function
	value is replaced by the new *value*; if it is not present, **put** creates a new entry.
dict1 dict2 **copy** dict2	Copies all elements of *dict1* into *dict2*. The **length** of *dict2* must be 0; that is, *dict2* must be empty when the **copy** takes place; **copy** returns the revised *dict2* onto the stack. *dict2* must have a **maxlength** that is at least as great as the **length** of *dict1*.

RELATIONAL OPERATORS

Syntax	Function
any1 any2 **eq** bool	Tests whether *any1* is equal to *any2*.
any1 any2 **ne** bool	Tests whether *any1* is not equal to *any2*.
num1 num2 **ge** bool str1 str2	Tests whether *num1* or *str1* is greater than or equal to *num2* or *str2*.
num1 num2 **gt** bool str1 str2	Tests whether *num1* or *str1* is greater than *num2* or *str2*.
num1 num2 **le** bool str1 str2	Tests whether *num1* or *str1* is less than or equal to *num2* or *str2*.
num1 num2 **lt** bool str1 str2	Tests whether *num1* or *str1* is less than *num2* or *str2*.

LOGICAL OPERATORS

Syntax				Function
int1	int2	**and**	int	
bool1	bool2		bool	Logical or bitwise AND.
int1	int2	**or**	int	
	bool2		bool	Logical or bitwise inclusive OR.
int1	int2	**xor**	int	
bool1	bool2		bool	Logical or bitwise exclusive OR.
int	**not**	int		
bool		bool		Logical or bitwise NOT.
—	**true**	bool		Pushes the boolean value *true* onto the stack.
—	**false**	bool		Pushes the boolean value *false* onto the stack.

CONTROL OPERATORS

Syntax					Function
{proc}	**exec**	—			Executes *proc*.
int	{proc}	**repeat**	—		Executes *proc int* times.
init	incr	lim	{proc}	**for** —	Executes *proc* for values from *init* by steps of *incr* until reaching *lim*.
array	{proc}	**forall**	—		Enumerates the elements of the first operand, executing the *proc* procedure for each element. If the first operand is a *dict*, **forall** pushes a key and the associated value onto the operand stack and
string	{proc}				
dict	{proc}				

Syntax	Function
	executes *proc* for each key, value pair in *dict*. If the first operand is an *array* or a *string*, **forall** pushes an element onto the operand stack and executes *proc* for each element. If the first operand is empty, *proc* is not executed at all.
bool {proc} **if** —	Executes *proc* if *bool* is true.
bool {proc1} {proc2} **ifelse** —	Executes *proc1* if *bool* is true and executes *proc2* otherwise.
{proc} **loop** —	Executes *proc* an indefinite number of times.
exit —	Terminates the active loop.

TEXT OPERATORS

Syntax	Function
string **show** —	Paints the characters of *string* on the page at the current point in the current font.
c_x c_y char string **widthshow** —	Prints the characters of *string*, but adjusts the width of each occurrence of the character *char* in *string* by adding c_x to its x-dimension and c_y to its y-dimension, thereby adjusting the

Syntax	**Function**
	spacing between this character and the following character.
a_x a_y string **ashow** —	Prints the characters of *string*, but adjusts the width of each occurrence of every character in *string* by adding a_x to its x-dimension and a_y to its y-dimension, thereby adjusting the spacing between all the characters.
c_x c_y char a_x a_y string **awidthshow** —	Prints the characters of *string* and performs two adjustments. First, it adjusts the width of each occurrence of every character in *string* by adding a_x to its x-dimension and a_y to its y-dimension, thereby adjusting the spacing between all the characters. Second, it adjusts the width of each occurrence of the character *char* in *string* by adding c_x to its x-dimension and c_y to its y-dimension, thereby adjusting the spacing between this character and the following character.
{proc} string **kshow** —	Prints the characters of *string*, but allows the user to execute the *proc*

Syntax	Function
	procedure between each character of *string*. The operator shows each character of *string* in turn, adding the width of the character to the current point and then executing the *proc* procedure.

FONT OPERATORS

Syntax	Function
key font **definefont** font	Registers *font* as a font dictionary associated with *key*, which is usually a name literal. The **definefont** also creates an additional entry in the dictionary, whose key is **FID** and whose value is an object of type fontID; *font* must be large enough to add this entry.
font matrix **makefont** newfont	Applies *matrix* to *font* and produces *newfont*, whose characters are transformed by the values in *matrix* when they are printed. The resulting *newfont* is returned to the stack.
string bool **charpath** —	Makes character-path outlines for the characters in *string* as if it were shown at the current point using

Syntax	Function
	show. These outlines are added to the current path. If *bool* is *true,* the resulting path is suitable for filling or clipping; if *bool* is *false,* the result is suitable for stroking.

COORDINATE TRANSFORMATION OPERATORS

Syntax	Function
t_x t_y **translate** —	Moves the origin of the user space to (t_x, t_y) in the previous coordinate system.
angle **rotate** —	Rotates the user space around the origin by *angle* degrees.
s_x s_y **scale** —	Scales the user space by the factor s_x in the x-dimension and the factor s_y in the y-dimension.

STATE OPERATORS

Syntax	Function
— **gsave** —	Saves a copy of the current graphics state on the graphics-state stack.
— **grestore** —	Resets the graphics state by restoring the state on the top of the graphics-state stack and pops the stack.

Syntax	Function
— **save** savestate	Saves the current state of the PostScript virtual memory as *savestate*.
savestate **restore** —	Restores PostScript virtual memory to the state indicated by *savestate*.

OUTPUT OPERATORS

Syntax	Function
— **copypage** —	Prints out the current page onto the output device, and retains a copy of the current page and all current settings.
— **showpage** —	Prints a copy of the current page onto the output device and clears the page.

INTERACTIVE OPERATORS

Syntax	Function
= =	Shows the top element of the stack and removes it.
pstack	Shows the entire contents of the stack, but does not remove any element.
quit	Ends the operation of the PostScript interpreter.

B
APPENDIX

Structuring Conventions Version 2.0

This appendix explains the revised document structuring conventions released by adobe Systems in January, 1987. These conventions have been given version number 2.0; and they are a revision and extension of the original PostScript structuring conventions, which were version number 1.0 and which are discussed and explained in Chapter 2, in the section entitled "Program Structure and Style."

These new conventions primarily are an extension of the 1.0 conventions; in no case do they invalidate the previous ones or make them obsolete. If you follow the original conventions, you will automatically satisfy the requirements of the new 2.0 conventions. However, there are many new extensions to the original version, which allow new facilities and expand old ones substantially. If you require these extensions, you should add the new 2.0 conventions that implement them.

These 2.0 conventions are primarily designed to improve the handling of PostScript documents in multiuser, networked environments. They provide facilities that allow a class of programs, including print spoolers, device servers, and other postprocessors—known collectively as *document managers*—to manage printer resources efficiently and to process PostScript documents effectively in such environments.

The conventions generally allow complete cooperation between document managers at all levels, and they allow PostScript document descriptions to be created and printed to take maximum advantage of network facilities. These conventions are an external structure, neither imposed by the interpreter nor checked by it. They rely on the cooperation of the document-creation functions to implement as much, or as little, of specific conventions as are required and appropriate.

To aid in this process, Adobe Systems has created a series of Adobe Printer Description (APD) files, which provide printer-specific information in a standard format for use by document managers. The format of an APD file is available from Adobe Systems if you require it (see the address in Appendix D). The information contained in these files works in conjunction with the information provided by the structuring conventions to provide a mechanism for the specification and use of printer features and functions.

Because so many of these new conventions rely on site-specific information, we will not discuss many of the new comments extensively in this appendix. If you are working in an environment that implements these conventions, full documentation will be available from your network administrator regarding supported features and correct usage. If you are the network administrator and are trying to implement these conventions in a network, you can obtain a complete description of the 2.0 conventions from Adobe Systems. The address and ordering information are provided in Appendix D.

COMMENT CONVENTIONS

These conventions are still based on the comment structure described in Chapter 2. All of the structure comments begin with the character strings %% or %!. These strings indicate a comment to the PostScript interpreter and are sufficiently distinctive that they can be recognized by a document manager and parsed separately from the PostScript file itself. All comments start with a specific keyword that begins immediately after the %% or %! characters. Those comments that provide additional keyword values follow the format requirements set out in Chapter 2.

Three types of structural comments are defined in the 2.0 conventions. These are as follows:

- structure comments
- resource requirements
- query conventions

The *structure comments* are used to define various structural components of a PostScript document. These will generally include a prologue, script, and trailer; and they may include information regarding page breaks. Note that all the version 1.0 conventions fall under this category.

The *resource requirements* are comments that define exactly what resources are required within a PostScript document that have not been included within the text of the document itself; and they indicate, by their placement, where in the document these resources are required. These comments may include fonts, procedures (in the form of specific prologue information), and files. The requirements may also be device-specific or application- or environment-dependent, such as specific forms, paper colors, or collating order.

The *query conventions* are used to delimit PostScript programs that inquire about the availability of specific resources. These queries cannot be included within a conforming document, because they compromise the ability of document managers to process such programs. Therefore, they must be handled independently and can then provide valuable information for a PostScript programmer or application.

With this new set of conventions, PostScript has a new definition of a *conforming* page description. Previously, a concept of a minimally conforming PostScript document existed. This was a page description that did not implement the complete set of PostScript conventions, but nevertheless provided a specified minimum of structural information. Now a conforming program is one that implements any proper subset of the document conventions.

As mentioned in the body of the book, there are no longer any specific comments that must exist in a PostScript document in order for it to conform to the 2.0 standards. However, there is still a constraint on PostScript programs. Any PostScript document that uses the conventions must use them in a manner consistent with the standard usage as described in the following paragraphs. In particular, this implies that specific system-level PostScript operators must not be employed within a conforming program. Conversely, it also implies that a conforming document will provide the required structural information where appropriate.

Some general constraints apply to any conforming PostScript documents. The first limitation was discussed extensively in Chapter 2; the document must be divided into a prologue and a script, with no executable code allowed in the prologue and no definitions allowed in the script. The second constraint is that the **%%Page** comment, if used, shall apply only to pages that are independent of all other pages in the script; that is, pages that can be output using the information in the prologue and in the specific page description alone. Third, the lines within the document description shall not exceed 256 characters in length. This is not a PostScript limitation, but a limitation that is in many document processing and handling systems. If a comment must extend over more than one line, the 2.0 conventions provide a new facility for continuation comments. These comments shall continue on the next line after the keyword, on a line beginning with the string **%%+.** An example might be where there are a number of fonts to be used within a document. This could be recorded as in the following example:

```
%%Document Fonts: Helvetica Helvetica-Bold Helvetica-Narrow
%%+ Helvetica-BoldOblique  Symbol  Times-Roman
%%+ Times-Italic  Times-BoldItalic
```

Finally, there are specific constraints on PostScript operations that must be followed within a conforming document. First, the **showpage** operator shall be used outside of a **save**, **restore** pair that surrounds a page. This is required to ensure that the redefinition of **showpage**, which may be required in some complex environments, will work correctly.

Second, the PostScript program shall avoid using the operations listed in Figure B.1.

The only two of these operators that you have been introduced to are **quit** and **copypage**. The **quit** operator is an interactive operator and is used to terminate an interactive PostScript session that began with **executive**. That is how you have been using it, and it is correct to use it in that context. The **quit** operator should never be issued by a Post-Script page-description program that will be processed through a network spooler.

You have used the **copypage** operator in several exercises to show the present state of a page before adding more marks to that page. This is the correct use of **copypage**. It should not be used as a means of producing multiple copies of a finished page; you should use the **#copies** parameter for the **showpage** operator for that purpose.

This can be done by redefining **#copies** in the current dictionary. For example, suppose that you wanted to get three copies of the page you

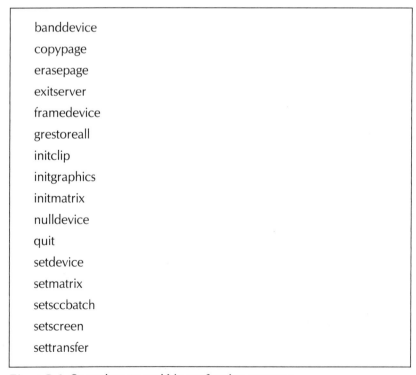

banddevice

copypage

erasepage

exitserver

framedevice

grestoreall

initclip

initgraphics

initmatrix

nulldevice

quit

setdevice

setmatrix

setsccbatch

setscreen

settransfer

Figure B.1: Operations to avoid in conforming programs

were about to output. Then you would issue the following commands:

```
/#copies 3 def
showpage
```

This is both the most correct and the fastest way to generate multiple copies of a page. Note that the redefinition of **#copies** remains in effect (like any other PostScript definition) until you end the job; it is not reset by the **showpage**.

STRUCTURING CONVENTIONS

The document structuring conventions are designed to allow document managers that are running in a networked environment to understand and, to some extent, manipulate document descriptions. This will inevitably be installation-specific in most cases. Ideally, applications that produce document descriptions in such an environment should be able to compose a document without any consideration of available resources and be able to rely on the document manager within the network to provide the necessary resources or provide the user with reasonable alternatives.

There are two ways to approach this ideal; neither excludes the other, but they represent somewhat different philosophies toward document preparation. In the first case, the document description relies on the document manager to generate or otherwise provide all necessary resources. In this case, the document description contains only structural and resource information that indicates a requirement for a particular resource. In the second case, the document description provides all the required resources itself, but delimits the resource-specific code with appropriate structural comments so that a document manager, if one exists, could remove these sections and substitute others as required.

Let us consider a simple example that may make this explanation clearer. Suppose you have generated a document that is intended to use a particular unusual font. If you are running on a dedicated printer, this represents no problem: either you have installed the font or you can download it before you print the document. If you are running in a networked environment, however, there is a problem. For several reasons, you do not know whether the font is available: you may not know which printer your document will print on, or you may not know when your document will print. In any case, you need to be sure that the required font is provided for your document.

In a dedicated environment, you would query the **FontDirectory** and determine whether the font was already loaded; if not, you would download the font and then print. In a network, such interaction with the printer is not feasible. Instead, you may use one of the two methods outlined above. First, you could simply indicate the need for this special font through the use of the established conventions as described below, relying on the document manager to perform the necessary query and download functions. Alternatively, your document could include the required font-downloading instructions within the document itself and thereby ensure that the font was on the correct printer at the required time. However, this makes the document longer to transmit and may possibly take it longer to execute. If you do use the second method, you want to delimit the font information using the appropriate conventions so that a document manager could remove or reprocess the document for more efficient execution. These two cases indicate the two alternative methods of handling resource-specific requirements.

Whichever method is chosen, there is a way to determine from the document structure in a consistent manner what functions need to be or can be performed on the document without altering the desired result. To implement both of these alternative approaches, the 2.0 structuring conventions contain a large number of new comments that represent *Begin* and *End* pairs of comments, which delimit printer-specific elements within a document. Similarly, the entire set of requirement conventions is newly developed to provide a mechanism for a document to request a resource (such as a font) or a device-specific feature (such as alternate paper) by means of *Include* comments.

There are three types of structure comments that make up the full set of Adobe 2.0 structuring conventions. These are

- Header comments, which occur only once in a document; as the name implies, they are placed before any executable PostScript code within the document.

- Body comments, which may appear anywhere inside a document and generally delimit the use of specific features or ingredients that are used in the document.

- Page comments, which are similar to header comments, in that they appear before each script page to define the page-level structure. They will occur before each page.

Header Comments

There are two requirements for header comments, as follows:

- The comments must all be contiguous. That is, when the document manager encounters the first instance of a noncomment line (one that does not begin with %%) within a document, it may stop checking for header comments.
- The first instance of any header supercedes and replaces any subsequent header with the same keyword.

The previous text discussion of header comments has not been changed; it has simply been repeated here to reinforce the points.

The following are the 2.0 header comments:

%!PS-Adobe-2.0

This version-identifier comment is identical in use to the similar 1.0 comment, except for the revision in version number. A new feature has been added to this comment; it may now contain one of three *keywords* following the 2.0. These keywords indicate to a document manager that the following document belongs to certain special classes of documents, so that it can change modes of processing, if required. These keywords are the following:

Syntax	Function
EPSF	Indicates that the following file is in a special format, known as "encapsulated PostScript." Such files primarily produce illustrations, and the format is designed to allow them to be included easily in other documents. The EPSF keyword can be followed by a version number (see Appendix C for more information about EPS files).
Query	Indicates that the entire job that follows consists of PostScript query commands. This is discussed below in the "Query Comments" section.
ExitServer	Indicates a job that will modify the persistent information within PostScript by issuing an **exitserver** operator.

The following comments are identical to the 1.0 comments of the same name and are fully described and discussed in Chapter 2. They are included here for reference only.

```
%%Title: text
%%Creator: text
%%CreationDate: text
%%For: text
%%BoundingBox: llx lly urx ury
%%Pages: integer [page order]
%%DocumentFonts: fontname fontname ...
%%EndComments
%%EndProlog
```

Some new header comments have been added, as follows:

%%Routing: text

This comment provides information about how to route a document in a networked environment. The contents and format are system- and site-dependent.

%%Requirements: keyword keyword ...

This comment contains keywords that define document requirements for specific physical features on a printer, such as duplex printing, collating, color printing, and so on. The nature and precise meaning of the keywords will be site-specific.

%%DocumentNeededFonts: fontname fontname ...

This comment, if used, lists the fonts that are required within the document and are not contained within it. These fonts would presumably be downloaded by the document manager prior to the execution of the document. It is assumed that corresponding **%%IncludeFont** directives will be provided for each font listed here.

%%DocumentSuppliedFonts: fontname fontname ...

This comment provides a list of all the fonts that are provided within the document description itself. It is assumed that at least one **%%BeginFont** and **%%EndFont** pair of comments will be provided within the document for each font listed here.

You should note two things about these conventions. First, the **%%DocumentNeeded** and the **%%DocumentSupplied** comments are complementary, since fonts that are included will not be provided by the document manager and vice versa. There are several more pairs of comments within the header that follow this same format and have essentially the same meaning. However, there is a difference between the two comments in that **%%DocumentNeeded** is essential if the corresponding **%%Include** is used, but the **%%DocumentSupplied** comment is optional. Second, not all fonts used in the document need to be listed in either of these comments, since it is possible that the document uses only fonts that are already loaded and available in the printer (as our own examples do).

There is a series of similar comments that we will list here without additional discussion.

> **%%DocumentNeededProcSets: name version revision ...**
> **%%DocumentSuppliedProcSets: name version revision ...**
> **%%DocumentNeededFiles: filename filename ...**
> **%%DocumentSuppliedFiles: filename filename ...**

These comments have the same format and perform the same function for procedure sets and files that the preceding ones had for fonts. They also have corresponding **%%Include**, **%%Begin**, and **%%End** comments.

With the release of Illustrator 88 in May 1988, Adobe has added some additional header comments that support color processing and color handling within a document. These comments are not required for most documents; however, if you are using color within your document, they may be essential to provide postprocessing by service programs such as Adobe's Separator (which can produce four-color separations from a color-encoded file). A full discussion of color printing and handling is beyond the scope of this appendix. The comments required for this type of color processing are presented here without much explanation; if you need further information, consult the documentation that is available from your device manufacturer or software supplier.

All of these comments are placed in the document header. The following are the color header comments.

> **%%ColorUsage: Black&White**
> or
> **%%ColorUsage: Color**

This comment allows you to specify whether the document uses only black ink (**Black&White**) or whether it uses all four process colors (**Color**). Note that these are specific names and must be used this way; also, **(atend)** is allowed for this comment.

> **%%DocumentProcessColors: name ...**
> **%%+ name ...**

where **name** can be Cyan, Magenta, Yellow, or Black. The document is expected to use just the process inks specified. If this comment does not appear, the document is expected to use all four process colors. The **(atend)** specification is allowed.

The following comments allow you to specify how custom colors are defined and used within a document. We will not discuss here the use and handling of custom colors, but you should have some knowledge of color printing requirements and color usage before you use these comments.

%%DocumentCustomColors: string

If this comment is absent, the document is presumed to use no custom colors. The **string** may be any name that describes the custom color; for example, it might be PMS 284 Yellow, or some other standard color nomenclature. The **(atend)** specification is allowed.

%%GreyCustomColor: gray string
%%RGBCustomColor: red green blue string
%%HSBCustomColor: hue saturation brightness string
%%CMYKCustomColor: cyan magenta yellow black string

All of these comments define a custom color's process color approximation. They all can be continued in the usual fashion, and the **(atend)** specification is allowed. The **string** value has the same function and contents as described above, and the other parameters are the numeric percentages of each of the referenced colors that are used to approximate the named custom color.

Finally, there is a series of document-level requirements that can be included in the header. These are mostly self-explanatory and are as follows:

%%DocumentPaperSizes: sizename sizename ...
%%DocumentPaperForms: formname formname ...
%%DocumentPaperColors: colorname colorname ...
%%DocumentPaperWeights: integer integer ...
%%DocumentPrinterRequired: networkname productname
[version] [revision] ...

BODY COMMENTS

Body comments may appear anywhere in a document and are designed to provide structural information about the organization of the document.

In particular, body comments should match related information provided in the header comments section.

%%BeginDocument: name [version] [type]
%%EndDocument

These comments delimit an entire document file when it is included within another document description.

%%BeginFont: fontname [printername]
%%EndFont

These comments delimit a downloaded font that is included within a document. The optional *printername* is intended for use in networked environments where fonts may be tied to particular printers, by license or other registration arrangements.

%%BeginProcSet: name version revision
%%EndProcSet
%%BeginFile: filename
%%EndFile

These comments delimit procedure sets and files contained within the document.

%%BeginBinary: bytecount
%%EndBinary

These comments delimit binary information included within a page description (such as data for the **image** operator). They are provided because binary data can cause severe difficulties for a document manager during processing.

%%BeginSetup
%%EndSetup

This pair of comments delimits information that performs device setup functions. This comment is unusual because it must come immediately after the prologue, that is, after the **%%EndProlog** comment. It forms the first part of the script, before any page output is generated.

%%BeginPaperSize: sizename
%%EndPaperSize

These comments delimit code that invokes procedures to set a particular paper size.

%%BeginFeature: featuretype [option]
%%EndFeature

These comments delimit code that invokes specific printer features as defined and described in the printer APD file (see the definition of APD files above). The *featuretype* must correspond exactly to one of the keywords in the APD file.

%%BeginExitServer: password
%%EndExitServer

These comments delimit code that exits the normal server loop and installs procedures or other code into the PostScript memory for retention beyond the end-of-job, as discussed in Chapter 7, "Advanced Graphics Techniques." If they are used, the job should begin with the *ExitServer* keyword in the version identifier comment. See the discussion of keywords for the version identifier, above.

%%Trailer

This comment remains the same as it was in the 1.0 conventions.

PAGE COMMENTS

These page-level comments are all self-explanatory; they mirror at the page level the information discussed above at a document level. They are as follows:

%%Page: label ordinal
%%PageFonts: fontname fontname fontname ...
%%PageFiles: filename filename filename ...
%%PageBoundingBox: llx lly urx ury
%%BeginPageSetup
%%EndPageSetup
%%BeginObject: [name] [code]
%%EndObject

This last pair of comments delimits individual graphic elements on a page, in circumstances where it is useful or necessary for the document manager to extract or recognize such portions of a page.

RESOURCE REQUIREMENTS

These comments may occur anywhere in a document and indicate that the named resource is required and should be included in the document at the point where the comment is encountered. It is essential that no resource request occur within the body of the document unless a corresponding comment indicating the requirement has been included in the header section.

These comments all form a matching set with previously discussed header comments, and so further discussion here is kept to a minimum. The resource requirement comments are as follows:

> **%%IncludeFont: fontname**
> **%%IncludeProcSet: name version revision**
> **%%IncludeFile: filename**
> **%%ExecuteFile: filename**

The last of these comments has the same function as the **%%IncludeFile** comment, but indicates that the requested file is an executable page description, rather than (for example) a prologue. Essentially, this means that the file probably contains at least one **showpage** operator.

> **%%ChangeFont: fontname**
> **%%PaperForm: formname**
> **%%PaperColor: colorname**
> **%%PaperWeight: integer**
> **%%PaperSize: sizename**
> **%%Feature: featuretype [option]**
> **%%EOF**

This last comment is used to request that the document manager transmit an end-of-file indication to the PostScript printer in any circumstance where the application itself cannot embed such a character into a file.

QUERY CONVENTIONS

A *query* is defined as any PostScript program that will generate a response back to the originator across the communications channel that links the host and the output device. Examples of operators that would qualify under this definition are = = and **pstack**. The query conventions defined in the 2.0 convention set are designed to allow applications to determine the status of particular resources before generating a page description.

All of the query comments consist of a *Begin, End* pair of comments with keywords indicating the type of query performed by the code contained within the comments. For all the comments, the *End* comment includes a *default value,* which the document manager will return to the application as a reponse if it cannot understand or does not support the given query. This default value is entirely dependent upon the application.

The possible queries are as follows:

%!PS-Adobe-2.0 Query

This form of the version identifier comment indicates that what follows is a query program rather than a page description. All queries, to be fully transparent in a network environment, should be sent as separate jobs.

```
%%?BeginQuery: identifier
%%?EndQuery: default
%%?BeginPrinterQuery
%%?EndPrinterQuery: default
%%?BeginVMStatus
%%?EndVMStatus: default
%%?BeginFeatureQuery: featuretype option
%%?EndFeatureQuery: default
%%?BeginFileQuery: filename
%%?EndFileQuery: default
%%?BeginFontQuery: fontname fontname ...
%%?EndFontQuery: default
%%?BeginFontListQuery
%%?EndFontListQuery
%%?BeginProcSetQuery: name version revision
%%?EndProcSetQuery: default
```

These sets all have specific applications, most of which should be obvious to you by now. The set **%%?BeginQuery** and **%%?EndQuery** is the only one that does not have a specific meaning; it is provided for installations that need to define installation-specific queries and can now do so using this method.

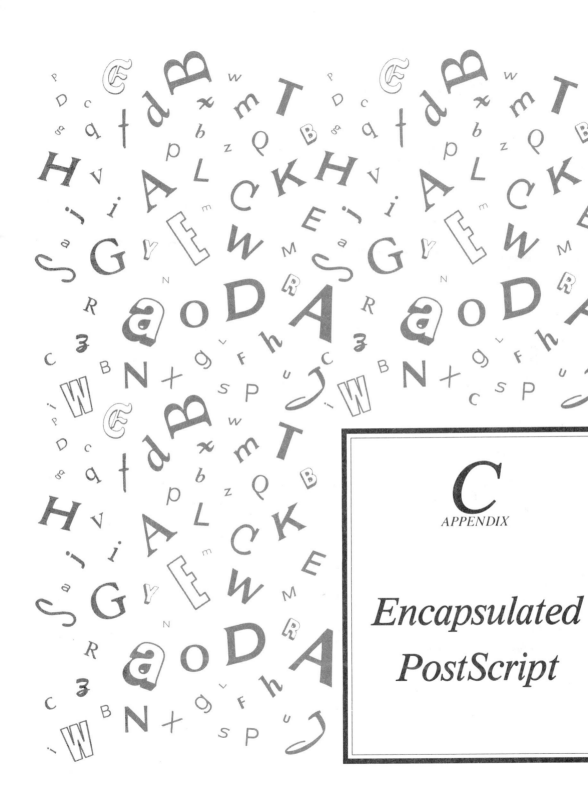

C
APPENDIX

Encapsulated
PostScript

ENCAPSULATED POSTSCRIPT IS A POSTSCRIPT FILE
THAT HAS A SPECIAL STRUCTURE. THIS STRUCTURE WAS
designed to allow other programs, particularly application programs that
produce PostScript output, to view a PostScript graphic and manipulate
it in certain limited ways. This structure is well-documented, and a full
description is available from Adobe Systems, the creator of PostScript.

USE OF EPS FILES

As the name implies, Encapsulated PostScript (EPS) files are intended
to be used as separate "capsules" of graphics. They are not designed to
interact in most ways with the rest of the *destination application's* (the
one that uses the file—Pagemaker, for example) output. The significant
deviations from this are the ability of the destination application to position the graphic on a page at any point and to crop, scale, or rotate the
graphic as required for correct placement on the output page. It is the destination application's responsibility to create the necessary changes in
the output environment to ensure that this occurs correctly, and to restore the original environment when it's done.

Generally, those file formats that contain preview graphics (EPS files)
cannot be edited with a simple text editor the way that simple PostScript
text files can be. This is because they have the graphic image embedded
within them. However, applications that understand the format (such as
Lasertalk, discussed in Appendix D) can edit the PostScript portion of
the EPS file with standard text-editing techniques; that portion of the file
is identical in all the output formats.

The destination program cannot redefine any details of the image. It
can simply transform the image, expanding or contracting each dimension
as requested; or it can crop the image as you might crop a photograph.
Destination applications can make these changes because they can interpret certain information about size and shape that is provided by the
EPS file format. They don't have to "understand" the PostScript code
itself; that is, the destination application does not use the PostScript
code to generate the screen image, nor does it interpret the PostScript
code that goes with the image. It takes the essential identity of the code
and image for granted.

The exchange of graphic information between the *source application* (the one that creates the EPS file, e.g., Adobe Illustrator) and the destination application, is quite simple from the user's point of view. You can easily insert EPS graphics into another application. Furthermore, the placement and transformation of such imported graphics within the destination application are always limited to a fairly basic set of options. Therefore, the role and work of each application is quite well-defined. To get the maximum productivity out of these graphic tools, you need to understand which application performs which functions.

EPS FILE FORMAT

The EPS file format consists of two distinct parts. The first contains the PostScript program created by the source that will generate the desired image on the output device. The second part, which is not required, contains a bit-mapped image of the resulting graphic. The bit-mapped image is used by the destination application for display purposes. The PostScript program follows a rigid structure, which also allows the destination application to translate, rotate, and scale the image as required for the new output that it is developing.

This section of the appendix discusses the format of each of these component parts of an EPS file. The PostScript structural requirements are described first, because they are the essential ingredients of an EPS file. The graphic attachment and its relationship to the display are discussed next.

SPECIAL POSTSCRIPT STRUCTURE

The EPS file format requires that the PostScript portion of the file follow the standard 2.0 structuring conventions. However, there are several comments that are part of the structure that take on new meaning and importance in EPS files. There is also some additional structural information that is very valuable in an EPS file. All of these are standard 2.0 comments, and their syntax and use are described in Appendix B.

REQUIRED HEADER COMMENTS

As is true for all conforming PostScript files, an EPS file must have a correctly formed version comment as the first comment in the header. This takes the following form:

%!PS-Adobe-2.0 EPSF-1.2

where the *1.2* may be replaced by any later version number of the EPS file format that is being followed.

This comment indicates to the destination application that the file conforms to both the structuring conventions generally and to the EPS format conventions in particular. The structure version number is given following the word *Adobe*, and the EPSF version number follows *EPSF*. This comment also indicates to a destination application that the file is intended for EPS use; without it, the destination application may reject the file or may not display the graphic information correctly.

Another required comment in the EPS file header specifies the area on the page that is included in the image produced by the PostScript program and represented by the graphic information. It takes the following form:

%%BoundingBox: *llx lly urx ury*

where the coordinates *llx, lly* are the position of the lower-left corner of the image in the default PostScript coordinates, and *urx, ury* are the position of the upper-right corner. These two corners are sufficient to define the entire box, which, as the name **%%BoundingBox** implies, completely encloses the graphic image being produced. As you will see later in the appendix, this information is the essential ingredient for placement and adjustment of the EPS graphic. If this comment is not present, the destination application may issue an error message and refuse to import the file.

OTHER HEADER INFORMATION

The following additional header comments are not required but are very useful. If an application cannot access the bit-mapped graphic in an EPS file or does not recognize the precise file format, it may be able to use the information provided in these comments to produce a text-identification block instead of the bit-mapped graphic.

```
%%Creator: name
%%Title: file name
%%CreationDate: date and time
```

These comments should contain the information suggested by their name, although there is no specific format required for the data.

The following comment explicitly terminates the header comments and is useful for destination applications that are examining the structure of the file.

```
%%EndComments
```

OTHER OPTIONAL COMMENTS

The EPS file format may also contain the following types of comments, which may help some destination applications provide the required resources for the EPS graphic. These comments are fully discussed in Appendix B, but we will briefly review each of them and their place in an EPS file.

If the EPS file has any text information, it will require one or more fonts. To enable the destination application to correctly integrate the EPS graphic and control the font handling for the entire output document, several font-management comments are useful.

The following comment lists all fonts used within the EPS file, whether they are included in the file itself or not:

```
%%DocumentFonts: font1 font2 ...
%%+ font3 font4 ...
```

This comment lists all the fonts that are required by the EPS file and are not provided within the file itself:

```
%%DocumentNeededFonts: font1 font2 ...
```

For each font listed in the above comment, there should be the following comment to indicate that the specified font must be made available for processing at this point in the file:

%%IncludeFont: *fontname*

The font may be downloaded at this point, or it may be a font that is globally available during the job (for example, because it is in ROM on the output device).

In addition to fonts, the EPS file may require procedure sets and/or files, which are provided for using the **%%DocumentNeeded...** and **%%Include...** comments, as described in Appendix B.

RESTRICTED OPERATORS

In addition to having the required structural comments, the PostScript code contained within the EPS file must follow certain rules and limitations regarding operator usage. The following operators are not to be used within EPS files, and most of them should not be used in any PostScript document that conforms to the 2.0 structuring conventions.

banddevice	initclip	renderbands
copypage	initgraphics	setdevice
erasepage	initmatrix	setmatrix
exitserver	note	setpageparms
framedevice	nulldevice	setscreen
grestoreall	quit	settransfer

The restriction on the use of most of these operators is easy to understand; they either modify the full-page image that is being created in raster memory (e.g., **erasepage** or **copypage**) or they become device dependent (e.g., by using **framedevice**, **nulldevice**, **banddevice**, or a related operator), or they modify the current graphics state in a way that prevents inclusion of the graphic within another PostScript page (e.g., **initgraphics**, **setmatrix**, or **note**). The **quit** and **exitserver** operators should especially be avoided. They perform functions that will significantly alter the processing environment and cannot ever be included within another page description; in fact, they are reserved for use only in certain specific and well-defined circumstances.

The **showpage** operator is also a problem for EPS files. Because it often exists within a file, it is not included in the list above; however, use of **showpage** within an EPS file will certainly cause all the problems that **copypage** or **erasepage** will. In this instance only, it is the destination application's responsibility to disable **showpage** to protect against any surprises, rather than the source application's responsibility to avoid using the operator.

GOOD POSTSCRIPT CODE PRACTICE

In addition to avoiding the operators listed above, and disabling the **showpage** operator, there are some good coding practices that should be maintained by an EPS file. First, all stacks must be returned to their original condition; no new information should be left on any stack after execution of the EPS file. This is essential so that the **save** and **restore** that bracket the EPS file will work correctly. Second, no global string should be changed. Doing so might affect the subsequent processing without warning. The recommended way to ensure against changing a global string is to have the EPS file create and use its own dictionaries, being sure to pop them off the dictionary stack when processing is finished by using the **end** operator. Finally, if any special dictionary is required for processing, or if any fonts require reencoding for the EPS file to execute properly, these resources should be provided for within the EPS file itself, and not presumed to be available.

BIT-MAPPED GRAPHIC FOR SCREEN DISPLAY

In addition to the PostScript code, EPS files may contain a bit-mapped image to be used by the destination application for screen display. The image is stored along with the PostScript file in a format that can be easily used by the destination application.

There are two forms of EPS files because of this potential to provide a bit-mapped image. The IBM and the Macintosh have quite different approaches to screen graphics, so source applications must provide two separate file types to generate the required screen graphic and link it correctly to the PostScript output. In addition, the IBM format of EPS files may use the Aldus/Microsoft TIFF graphic format or the MetaFile format for Windows to store the image, and any destination application that will display the image must be able to read one of these formats.

The Macintosh version of an EPS file contains a standard Macintosh QuickDraw PICT format graphic as the screen display portion of the file, which is stored in the resource fork. In both formats of EPS files, the bit-mapped images are produced at a resolution of 72 dots per inch. These bit-maps are not intended for final output; they are provided as an aid for page makeup and graphic placement within the destination application. The intention is that the final output will use the PostScript definitions of the graphic while the bit-mapped image is ignored.

The exact format, creation, and use of these bit-mapped images is beyond the scope of this appendix; however, more complete documentation is available from Adobe Systems and from Aldus Corporation in the following memos:

- *Encapsulated PostScript File Format*, EPSF Version 1.2, Adobe Systems, March 12, 1987

- *Encapsulated PostScript File Format for PageMaker Import*, Version 1.2, Aldus Corporation, January 5, 1987

Remember the inclusion of the bit-mapped image is not required for an EPS file. It is quite optional and, as long as you have structured your PostScript code correctly, you can create and import EPS graphics without worrying about the bit-mapped image. If you do want the bit-mapped image included in your EPS files, there is a utility that can accomplish this, which is discussed later in the appendix.

PRINTING AND DISPLAYING EPS FILES

When you display an EPS file by using the destination application facilities, you should have no problem including the EPS graphic, displaying it on the screen, or printing it. However, you may want to display an EPS file independently of any particular destination application, or, infrequently, the destination application may fail to handle the EPS file correctly. In these cases, you can print the EPS file yourself.

The basic requirements for printing an EPS file are quite straightforward. You must provide three things to display an EPS file: a **showpage** (if one is missing), positioning information for the graphic image, and a proper context for execution. In addition, you may wish to modify the image in some of the same ways that a destination application could: by transformation, rotation, or cropping.

An EPS file is designed to be included into a page generated by another PostScript program as a unit. That means that the source of the EPS file expects that you will take the entire PostScript output from the EPS file and include it with some other PostScript code. In order to do that successfully, or to print the file by itself, you need to define several things: where on the page you want to place the EPS graphic, what coordinates it uses, and what size you want it to be. The first two issues must always be addressed; the third only needs attention if you don't want to use your graphic at the same size as you created it.

PAGE SETUP

All these issues can be taken care of by two PostScript operators. The first is **translate**, which can be used to both position the graphic on the new output page and adjust the coordinates. The second is the **scale** operator, which will set the size of the graphic on the new page. In all cases, you also need to do some housekeeping to ensure that the EPS file does not interfere with your work in the process of generating the output to be included on the page. This is done by using paired **save** and **restore** operators.

The first change that you have to make is to correct for the default coordinates used in the EPS file. Without any adjustment, there is a good chance that the EPS graphic will be drawn off the bottom of the normal output, and you won't be able to see it. Furthermore, you cannot rely on the fact that the EPS file uses the default page origin. Because the origin of a PostScript page can be moved anywhere, you need to have an adjustment mechanism that allows you to readjust the coordinates independently of the default settings.

The necessary adjustment can be made by using the information provided by the **%%BoundingBox:** comment. You will remember that this comment is followed by four numbers. These represent the lower-left and upper-right corners, respectively, of the graphic that will actually be created by the EPS file, and in the coordinates that the file was created in. In particular, the x and y coordinates of each of these corners provide the necessary information for positioning and adjusting the coordinate system on the output page.

The first requirement is to move the lower-left corner of the EPS graphic to the new origin. This can be done most easily, conceptually, by doing a **translate** that first moves the origin to (0, 0) in the normal PostScript coordinates and then **translate** again to the new position that you want.

The first move is done by the following PostScript command:

    llx neg lly neg translate

This readjusts the coordinates for the output to a position that is −llx and −lly, because the **neg** operator just reverses the sign of the given number. That will mean that the EPS graphic will begin at the point (llx − llx) and (lly − lly), or (0, 0), since subtracting something from itself will always result in zero. After the origin of the graphic is translated to (0, 0), the coordinates on the EPS page will map correctly into those of the output page.

After you have positioned the EPS output at (0, 0) on the new output page, it is quite straightforward to move it to any desired location on the new output page by using another **translate**. As is always the case in PostScript, you will reposition the lower-left corner of the image by repositioning the origin. If you want to move the output graphic so that its lower-left corner is at the new position (nx, ny), you would follow the command above with the command

    nx ny translate

which moves the graphic to the point you want. Although the order in which you issue the commands is irrelevant to the PostScript interpreter, I would strongly recommend that you do them in some consistent and logical order; for me, that means doing the **translate** to (0, 0) first, and then moving to (nx, ny).

SCALING THE IMAGE

Another change that you may want to make to your EPS file output is to scale it to fit on a defined space in the new page output. This also can be done with the help of the **%%BoundingBox:** information. In this case, you want to adjust the height and width of the existing output to fit into some new space.

Suppose that the new space to be filled has a width of w and a height of h. Scaling the EPS graphic to this window means simply that the width of the graphic must be scaled to w and the height, scaled to h. For example, if the window that you wanted to fit were 1 unit by 1 unit, and the graphic was 2 by 4, you would have to scale the graphic by 1 divided by 2 in width and 1 divided by 4 in height.

This is the general approach for scaling a graphic: the new dimension divided by the old dimension is the scale factor for that coordinate. The width of the graphic is determined by subtracting the two x coordinates from one another, and the height by subtracting the two y coordinates. Therefore, the scale factor for width will be $w / (urx - llx)$, and for height it will be $h / (ury - lly)$. You can use the same method to compute the width and height of the new window as you use to compute the width and height of the EPS graphic: by subtracting the x and y coordinates of the lower-left and upper-right corners. Using this technique with a new window whose coordinates for those points are given by (nlx, nly) and (nux, nuy), the PostScript commands for the scaling operation are as follows:

```
nux nlx sub        %calculate the width of new window
urx llx sub        %calculate width of graphic
div                %use two results on stack for ratio
                   %and leave result on stack
nuy nly sub        %calculate the height of the new
                   window
ury lly sub        %calculate height of graphic
div                %use two results on stack for ratio
                   %now both x and y scale are on stack
scale              %so issue scale command
```

This can be compressed down into one or two lines of PostScript code, but I expanded it here to help you see all the operations and the stack results more clearly.

The following code demonstrates the techniques described in this section. It takes a generic EPS file titled (EPSF test art) and rescales, translates, and displays it within a new file titled EPSF enclosure example.

```
%!PS-Adobe-2.0
%%Creator: David Holzgang
%%Title: EPSF enclosure example
```

```
%%CreationDate: 6/10/88 6:42 AM
/Save_state save def      % save the current state
/workdict 5 dict def      % define a working dictionary
workdict begin            % and start using it
/showpage {} def          % redefine showpage to avoid accidents
neg 103 neg 352           % move to (0, 0)
translate
100 200 translate         % and reposition on page
% now scale graphic to fit new box on page
%       with coordinates 100 200 300 500
%       as discussed in the text
300 100 sub               % calculate ratio of new x width
277 103 sub               % to old x width
div
500 200 sub               % and ratio of new y width
608 352 sub               % to old y width
div
scale                     % and scale to those dimensions
%insert actual EPS file (in its entirety) here
%The following is a sample EPS file header generated using
%       Adobe Illustrator 88 (TM)
%!PS-Adobe-2.0 EPSF-1.2
%%Creator: Adobe Illustrator 88(TM)
%%For: (David Holzgang) (SYBEX)
%%Title: (EPSF test art)
%%CreationDate: (6/8/88) (6:20 AM)
%%BoundingBox: 103 352 277 608
... and the rest of the EPS file follows here
%%Trailer
... a variety of comments finish this EPS file
```

The following three lines of code are added to the end of the file, after the **%%Trailer** comment.

```
end                       % terminate use of workdict
Save_state restore        % restore saved state
showpage
```

The state of the printer is restored by the **restore** command on the next to the last line, while the page output is produced on the last line by a **showpage** command. The **showpage** is only inserted to generate the page output; if you included this file within some other PostScript program, you would omit this operator until you completed the page description.

OTHER TRANSFORMATIONS

You can use the same technique described above for a **scale** operation to perform more advanced transformations on EPS graphics. You can rotate the graphic image by using the **rotate** and **translate** operators in sequence, as you did earlier in the book to generate output in landscape mode. You can also use the **clip** operator to crop the image to a particular size, if you don't want the entire image to display. Do remember, however, that clipping is an expensive and time-consuming operation; if you use it, expect to wait for the output.

CREATING EPS FILES

Basically, any correctly structured PostScript program can be used as an EPS file. The essential ingredients are, as you have seen, the bounding box information and the structural comments. It is not essential, although it is useful, to have the bit-mapped image attached to the file.

There is no simple way to include your own bit-mapped image in an EPS file for transfer. If your bounding box information and other header comments are in place, most destination applications will at least show you the bounding box rectangle and include within it or next to it the text information from the header comments. This actually works fairly well for many purposes.

This section will briefly review the requirements for an EPS file and provide some general comments and guidance that you can adapt for your programs.

HEADER INFORMATION EXAMPLE

A good example of the required header information for an EPS file is shown below. It is the header from the Adobe Illustrator file shown earlier.

```
%!PS-Adobe-2.0 EPSF-1.2
%%Creator: Adobe Illustrator 88(TM)
%%For: (David Holzgang) (SYBEX)
%%Title: (EPSF test art)
%%CreationDate: (6/8/88) (6:20 AM)
%%BoundingBox: 103 352 277 608
```

The easiest way to access and use this information, in my experience, is to create it as a separate file and then just include it, using a program editor, at the beginning of your PostScript program.

BOUNDING BOX INFORMATION

The most difficult part of this is determining the bounding box information. Unfortunately, there is no easy answer here. You probably know the lower-left corner of your image on the page, but establishing the upper-right one can be tricky. It is easiest if you have some help, like the Lasertalk programming environment, where you can see the image on the printer along with coordinates. Before I had that facility, I used a physical ruler (typesetter's rulers are great, because they have point measures that more or less correspond to the PostScript coordinates) or printed special index marks on a sample page. Both work but are time-consuming.

However, you want to make your best effort at calculating the bounding box correctly. If your box is too small, you may lose some of the image. If it is too large, your placement of the image on the output page may be faulty. However, if you have to guess, make it too big rather than too small.

USING UTILITY PROGRAMS

There is one utility that I know of that can provide you with a bit-map of any PostScript file, provided that you have a PostScript printer attached to your system. This is the SmartArt program, produced by Emerald City Software, whose address is listed in Appendix D.

SmartArt provides the bit-map by downloading the PostScript file to the printer, retrieving the bit-map from the printer's frame buffer, and constructing and combining the bit-map with the script to form an EPS file. This utility is particularly useful for showing the precise placement of text. No other application program (including Adobe Illustrator 88) displays the actual printer font bit-maps in an EPS file. SmartArt is designed as a desk accessory so that it can be used in conjunction with graphics and test application programs.

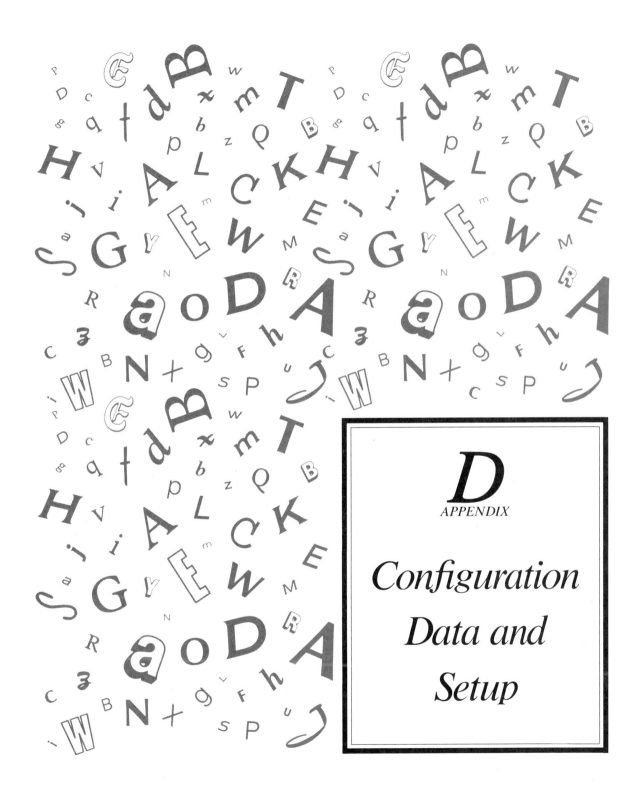

D
APPENDIX

Configuration Data and Setup

THIS APPENDIX CONTAINS TWO SAMPLE CONFIGURA-
TIONS THAT HAVE BEEN USED TO CREATE AND EXECUTE
the examples in this book. The purpose of these examples is to provide
you with two working models of actual configurations that can communicate with a PostScript printer and will run in the interactive mode.
These models should function both as examples and as a mechanism for
review in case you have problems getting your own configuration to run
correctly.

There are two example configurations described in this appendix: one
for an IBM PC, the other for an Apple Macintosh. Between them, they
represent probably 95 percent of the basic configurations that are likely to be used by the readers of this book. However, any computer
that supports communication through an RS-232 port can be used to
communicate with most PostScript devices, certainly with an Apple
LaserWriter.

The selection of hardware and software listed here should not be taken
as a recommendation. The various elements were simply what I had
available to do the tasks that needed to be done to communicate between
the computer and the printer and to create and run the exercises.

The configurations that are presented here are by no means unique.
Multiple configurations could be used to achieve the same results. I have
tried to describe the configurations in detail, so that they may provide
some guidance for you if you have a problem making your configuration
work. Many specifics of these two configurations—memory size, features available, and so on—should not be taken as limitations; they are
presented only as examples of working configurations. So if your configuration differs from one of these, don't try to match what is listed here;
first try out what you have, and only modify it if it won't work.

IBM PERSONAL COMPUTER

Most of the initial development of exercises and examples for this book
was done on an IBM PC clone, with the configuration described here. I
found it to be convenient and responsive. It is not hard to set up, either
for interactive or batch processing. The only real problem is that the
Apple LaserWriter manual provides almost no information on how to
connect and run the printer from anything but an Apple Macintosh, so

you need to read between the lines. There is also much valuable information in Appendix D, "Apple LaserWriter," of the *PostScript Language Reference Manual,* particularly section D.3, "Communication."

CONFIGURATION: HARDWARE

The hardware in this configuration is as follows:

IBM PC XT (clone)
    10-megabyte hard disk
    640K memory
    1 serial port (COM1:)

Apple LaserWriter
    base model

The two devices are connected by a standard 25-pin, RS-232 cable with a "null modem" pin assignment—pin 2 at the printer is connected to pin 3 at the computer, and pin 3 at the printer is connected to pin 2 at the computer. This arrangement reverses the data signals and is required because both devices would otherwise be trying to send and receive data over the same wire.

The baud-rate switch at the rear of the Apple LaserWriter is set to 9600. Consult the LaserWriter manual or Appendix D in the *Language Reference* for more information on the function of this switch.

CONFIGURATION: SOFTWARE

There are two important pieces of software that you must have to create and run exercises on the LaserWriter: a communications program and an editor. The communications program makes your PC behave like a terminal, sending data down the communications line to the printer. The editor provides a means to create batch jobs to send to the printer and is necessary for some of the exercises to modify disk output from applications into a valid format for the PostScript interpreter.

The communications program that I used was PC-TALK III. This is an excellent, inexpensive communications program that can be obtained from several bulletin boards and other sources. Since you need only the most rudimentary communications support for this work, you don't need anything more than a program like this.

I used several different editors at various times; all worked well. The three that I used were

- **WordStar**. This must be run in "nondocument" mode to create the PostScript files for processing; otherwise, it modifies characters to mark words and (I think) some special status information. The "nondocument" mode ran successfully, however.

- **Bank Street Writer**. This is an excellent, simple word-processing program that includes a surprising range of features. It provides facilities that can be used to embed PostScript commands within a print file, or it can be used to create PostScript programs.

- **Norton Editor**. A great editor for doing any kind of programming.

The communications with the LaserWriter are set up as follows:

1. Execute a batch file similar to the following, which sets the mode on the communications port and starts up the communications program:

```
ECHO OFF
MODE COM1:9600,N,8,1,P,X
PC-TALK
CD C:\
CLS
```

2. Enter the communications program dialing menu, and (the first time) create a new entry with the correct communications parameters: 9600 baud, 8 data bits, no parity, 1 stop bit, no echo. DO NOT ENTER ANY TELEPHONE NUMBER. All other settings were allowed to default.

3. Remove all modem commands from the menu item that you have created to access the LaserWriter. These are usually commands that begin with "ATDT". Replace them with the "executive" (all lowercase letters) command.

4. "Dial" the entry. I put quotes around that because the communications package doesn't actually issue any dialing commands; it simply opens the COM1: port and sends the "executive" string down the line. This will start the interactive mode on the LaserWriter.

There is one additional comment to make. I use a Leading Edge, with a version of MS-DOS that includes support for the XON/XOFF protocol as part of the operating system. It is invoked as part of the DOS MODE command. The complete batch file that I use to access the LaserWriter is shown in step 1 above.

Then you would proceed with the steps outlined in Chapter 1 to complete the connection to the LaserWriter, and you would begin interactive operations.

APPLE MACINTOSH

There are two ways to send and receive data from a LaserWriter on a Macintosh. One way—the one most talked about in the LaserWriter documentation—is through an AppleTalk network. This is fairly straightforward from a user's viewpoint; you just purchase an AppleTalk kit from your Apple dealer, connect the LaserWriter and the Macintosh as instructed, and begin running jobs. That would be all that needed to be said, except that AppleTalk won't allow you to run in the interactive mode without some help.

The AppleTalk connection by itself, only allows you to prepare PostScript jobs and send them, as batch files, to a LaserWriter. You can do the exercises in this book using this method. If you are on an AppleTalk network with other users, you will probably have to do this. If you are going to do the exercises that way, software is available that provides semi-interactive access to the LaserWriter. There is a software package listed below that will send your batch job to a LaserWriter over the AppleTalk network and return any errors or output information that belongs to your job back to your terminal. If you are running alone on the network, this is almost the same as interactive use; if more than one person is running, you will have to be careful about mixing up your jobs with other people's.

Since the first edition of this book, one software package has come onto the market that allows full interactive access to your LaserWriter (or any other PostScript printer) over the AppleTalk network. This is the Lasertalk product from Emerald City Software (address and ordering information below).

CONFIGURATION: HARDWARE

The hardware in this configuration is as follows:

Apple Macintosh
>internal and external disk drives (I only used one)
>512K memory
>cable M0150 (ImageWriter cable)

Apple LaserWriter
>base model

The cable connects the modem port on the back of the Macintosh to the LaserWriter. The LaserWriter mode switch was set to 1200; presumably, you could use the 9600-baud setting by choosing the higher speed at the computer end. The advantage of the 1200-baud setting is that it forces the LaserWriter to a specific state; see Appendix D of the *PostScript Language Reference Manual* or your LaserWriter manual for details.

Alternatively, as discussed above, you can use an AppleTalk connection and Lasertalk to provide interactive access.

CONFIGURATION: SOFTWARE

As in the case of the IBM PC, you will need two kinds of software to run your PostScript jobs interactively: a communications package and an editor. Any reasonable editor will do; I believe that you could use MacWrite if you wanted to, but I didn't have it available for testing. The software used to test the programs in this book consisted of the Mac-Terminal communications program and the Microsoft Word editor.

Communications are set up with the following sequence of steps:

1. Start up MacTerminal by double clicking on the MacTerminal icon. This opens a session window.

2. Set the communications parameters in Terminal, Compatibility, and File Transfer as follows:

Terminal: Terminal = VT100, Mode = ANSI, Cursor Shape = underline, Character Set = US, LineWidth = 80 column. Select the following parameters: On-Line, Auto Repeat, Auto Wraparound.

Compatibility: Baud Rate = 1200, Bits per Character = 8 bits, Parity = none, Handshake = none, Connection = another computer, Connection Port = modem.

File Transfer: Transfer Method = text.

Now you are in communication with the LaserWriter and can begin your interactive PostScript session as described in Chapter 1.

If you have AppleTalk, you can save yourself a substantial amount of work and worry by purchasing the following software, which will provide immediate interactive access (as described in Chapter 1).

Lasertalk
Emerald City Software
P.O. Box 2103
Menlo Park, CA 94026
(415) 324-8080

Lasertalk provides all the communications and editing facilities that you need to create and maintain PostScript programs. In fact, Lasertalk provides a complete PostScript programming environment, not just interactive access. This includes an editor with a number of features, a dictionary browser, on-line access to the operator definitions, and a unique preview mode that allows you to see what is on the page before printing (thus eliminating the need for frequent use of the **copypage** operator).

Lasertalk provides the best environment for learning PostScript and for using it, and it is completely compatible with all the exercises and examples in this book. In fact, it comes with the exercises and examples already keyed into an Examples folder.

LASERWRITER COMMANDS

There are a few commands that you can use to control the LaserWriter while you are in the interactive mode. These commands fall into two groups: communications functions that are available from the keyboard, and some limited editing functions that can be used while you are in the interactive mode. Most of these functions are invoked by means of the Control key (on the IBM) or the Command key (on the Macintosh) along with one of the characters shown in the following table. For convenience, these are all designated "Ctrl-"; you should understand that this means to hold down the Control (or the Command) key and press the designated letter.

COMMUNICATION FUNCTIONS

Key	Function
Ctrl-C	interrupt; stops the execution of a PostScript program
Ctrl-D	end-of-file
Ctrl-S	stop output (XOFF)
Ctrl-Q	start output (XON)
Ctrl-T	status query; causes the interpreter to respond with a one-line status message
Return	end-of-line; equivalent to the PostScript newline character
Line-Feed	end-of-line; equivalent to the PostScript newline character. When both a *Return* and a *Line-Feed* are received in succession, only one newline is executed.

EDITING FUNCTIONS

Key	Function
Ctrl-H	backs up and erases one character
Ctrl-U	erases the current line
Ctrl-R	redisplays the current line
Ctrl-C	aborts the statement and starts over
Backspace	backs up and erases one character
Delete	(same as *Backspace* above)

E

APPENDIX

Bibliography

This APPENDIX LISTS BOOKS ON A VARIETY OF TOPICS RELATED, MORE OR LESS DIRECTLY, TO THE SUBJECTS of PostScript and PostScript programming. The list is neither complete nor authoritative. It represents my own personal prejudices and some intensive looking in technical bookstores and reference libraries for current, and currently available, materials. There may be other, better, books on any of these topics; I just haven't found them.

PostScript References

Adobe Systems. *PostScript Language Reference Manual.* Reading, Mass.: Addison-Wesley, 1986.

Adobe Systems, *PostScript Language Tutorial and Cookbook.* Reading, Mass.: Addison-Wesley, 1986.

Adobe Systems. Glenn C. Reid. *PostScript Language Program Design.* Reading, Mass.: Addison-Wesley, 1988.

Apple Computer. *LaserWriter Reference Manual.* San Jose, Calif: Apple Computer, 1987.

The last book can be ordered from Apple at the following address:

Apple Computer Incorporated
467 Saratoga Avenue, Suite 62
San Jose, CA 95129

Additional reference materials, in the form of a *Language Supplement,* are available from Adobe Systems regarding almost every kind of PostScript-equipped output device, including revised and updated information about the Apple LaserWriter and LaserWriter Plus. You can also get the complete description of the 2.0 structuring conventions, if you need them. You can write to

Adobe Systems Incorporated
1870 Embarcadero Road
Palo Alto, CA 94303

COMPUTER GRAPHICS AND PROGRAMMING

Cox, B. J. *Object-Oriented Programming: An Evolutionary Approach*. Reading, Mass.: Addison-Wesley, 1986.

Foley, J. D., and Van Dam, A. *Fundamentals of Interactive Computer Graphics*. Reading, Mass.: Addison-Wesley, 1983.

Hughes, Michton, and Michton. *A Structured Approach to Programming*. Englewood Cliffs, N.J.: Prentice Hall, 1987.

Kruse, R. *Data Structure and Program Design*. Englewood Cliffs, N.J.: Prentice Hall, 1987.

Newman, W. M., and Sproull, R. F. *Principles of Interactive Computer Graphics*. 2nd Edition. New York: McGraw-Hill, 1979.

Stern, N., and Stern, R. *Structured COBOL Programming*. 4th Edition. New York: J. Wiley & Sons, 1985.

COMPUTER OPERATIONS

Books on MS-DOS and PC-DOS and the operation of the IBM PC (and clones), mostly at a beginner's level, are the following:

King, R. *The IBM PC-DOS Handbook*. 2nd Edition. Alameda, Calif.: SYBEX, 1986.

King, R. *The MS-DOS Handbook*. 2nd Edition. Alameda, Calif.: SYBEX, 1986.

Miller, A. *The ABC's of MS-DOS*. Alameda, Calif.: SYBEX, 1987.

Norton, P. *MS-DOS and PC-DOS User Guide*. New York: Brady, 1984.

Books on the Macintosh seem to be fewer, and they generally focus on more advanced topics—I suspect because the Macintosh is much easier for a beginner to understand. The LaserWriter references above contain useful information about connecting and using the LaserWriter and the Macintosh. The two books below give some good introductory material along with more advanced topics.

Lu, C. *The Apple Macintosh Book*. 2nd Edition. Redmond, Wash.: Microsoft Press, 1985.

Apple Computer. *Inside Macintosh, Volume I*. Reading, Mass.: Addison-Wesley, 1985.

PAGE DESIGN AND LAYOUT

Bove, T., Rhodes, C., and Thomas, W. *The Art of Desktop Publishing*. New York: Bantam Computer Books, 1986.

Bowman, W. *Graphic Communication*. New York: J. Wiley & Sons, 1980.

Rardin, K. *Desktop Publishing on the MAC*. New York: The Waite Group, New American Library, 1986.

Ryan, T. and Miles, D., eds. *The Macintosh Book of Fonts*. Santa Barbara, Calif.: SourceNet, 1987.

Tufte, E. R. *The Visual Display of Quantitative Information*. Cheshire, Conn.: Graphics Press, 1983.

White, J. *Mastering Graphics*. Chicago: R. R. Bowker, 1983.

PRINTING AND TYPOGRAPHY

Burke, C. *Printing It*. Berkeley, Calif.: Wingbow Press, 1972.

This remarkable little book, subtitled "A Guide to Graphic Techniques for the Impecunious," is now a little out of date with regard to some of the techniques, but it is an invaluable guide to the arcane world of the printer. It also teaches (and practices) some timeless lessons about making beautiful and effective printed output.

Gill, E. *Essay on Typography*. London: J. M. Dent & Sons, 1960.

Johnston, E. *Writing, Illuminating and Lettering*. New York and Chicago: Pitman, 1939.

In my opinion, these two books are classics and teach much more than their titles may suggest.

INDEX

Selections from The SYBEX Library

DESKTOP PUBLISHING

Mastering Ventura
(Second Edition)
Matthew Holtz

600pp. Ref. 581-6

A complete, step-by-step guide to IBM PC desktop publishing with Xerox Ventura Publisher. Practical examples show how to use style sheets, format pages, cut and paste, enhance layouts, import material from other programs, and more.

Ventura Tips and Techniques
Carl Townsend/Sandy Townsend

424pp. Ref. 559-X

Packed with an experienced Ventura user's tips and tricks, this volume is a time saver and design booster. From crop marks to file management to using special fonts, this book is for serious Ventura users. Covers Ventura 2.

Ventura Instant Reference
Matthew Holtz

320pp. Ref. 544-1

This compact volume offers easy access to the complex details of Ventura modes and options, commands, side-bars, file management, output device configuration, and control. Written for versions through Ventura 2, it also includes standard procedures for project and job control.

Mastering PageMaker
on the IBM PC
(Second Edition)
Antonia Stacy Jolles

400pp. Ref. 521-2

A guide to every aspect of desktop publishing with PageMaker: the vocabulary and basics of page design, layout, graphics and typography, plus instructions for creating finished typeset publications of all kinds.

Mastering Ready, Set, Go!
David A. Kater

482pp. Ref. 536-0

This hands-on introduction to the popular desktop publishing package for the Macintosh allows readers to produce professional-looking reports, brochures, and flyers. Written for Version 4, this title has been endorsed by Letraset, the Ready, Set, Go! software publisher.

COMPUTER-AIDED DESIGN AND DRAFTING

The ABC's of AutoCAD
(Second Edition)
Alan R. Miller

375pp. Ref. 584-0

This brief but effective introduction to AutoCAD quickly gets users drafting and designing with this complex CADD package. The essential operations and capabilities of AutoCAD are neatly detailed, using a proven, step-by-step method that is tailored to the results-oriented beginner.

Mastering AutoCAD
(Third Edition)
George Omura

825pp. Ref. 574-3

Now in its third edition, this tutorial guide to computer-aided design and drafting with AutoCAD is perfect for newcomers to CADD, as well as AutoCAD users seeking greater proficiency. An architectural project serves as an example throughout.

Advanced Techniques in AutoCAD (Second Edition)
Robert M. Thomas
425pp. Ref. 593-X

Develop custom applications using screen menus, command macros, and AutoLISP programming—no prior programming experience required. Topics include customizing the AutoCAD environment, advanced data extraction techniques, and much more.

WORD PROCESSING

The ABC's of WordPerfect 5
Alan R. Neibauer
283pp. Ref. 504-2

This introduction explains the basics of desktop publishing with WordPerfect 5: editing, layout, formatting, printing, sorting, merging, and more. Readers are shown how to use WordPerfect 5's new features to produce great-looking reports.

The ABC's of WordPerfect
Alan R. Neibauer
239pp. Ref. 425-9

This basic introduction to WordPefect consists of short, step-by-step lessons—for new users who want to get going fast. Topics range from simple editing and formatting, to merging, sorting, macros, and more. Includes version 4.2

Mastering WordPerfect 5
Susan Baake Kelly
709pp. Ref. 500-X

The revised and expanded version of this definitive guide is now on WordPerfect 5 and covers wordprocessing and basic desktop publishing. As more than 200,000 readers of the original edition can attest, no tutorial approaches it for clarity and depth of treatment. Sorting, line drawing, and laser printing included.

Mastering WordPerfect
Susan Baake Kelly
435pp. Ref. 332-5

Step-by-step training from startup to mastery, featuring practical uses (form letters, newsletters and more), plus advanced topics such as document security and macro creation, sorting and columnar math. Includes Version 4.2.

Advanced Techniques in WordPerfect 5
Kay Yarborough Nelson
586pp. Ref. 511-5

Now updated for Version 5, this invaluable guide to the advanced features of Word-Perfect provides step-by-step instructions and practical examples covering those specialized techniques which have most perplexed users—indexing, outlining, foreign-language typing, mathematical functions, and more.

WordPerfect 5 Desktop Companion
SYBEX Ready Reference Series
Greg Harvey/Kay Yarborough Nelson
1000pp. Ref. 522-0

Desktop publishing features have been added to this compact encyclopedia. This title offers more detailed, cross-referenced entries on every software features including page formatting and layout, laser printing and word processing macros. New users of WordPerfect, and those new to Version 5 and desktop publishing will find this easy to use for on-the-job help. For Version 5.

WordPerfect Tips and Tricks (Third Edition)
Alan R. Neibauer
650pp. Ref. 520-4

This new edition is a real timesaver. For on-the-job guidance and creative new uses, this title covers all versions of Word-Perfect up to and including 5.0—covers streamlining documents, automating with macros, new print enhancements, and more.

WordPerfect 5 Instant Reference
Greg Harvey/Kay Yarborough Nelson
316pp. Ref. 535-2

This pocket-sized reference has all the program commands for the powerful WordPerfect 5 organized alphabetically for quick access. Each command entry has the exact key sequence, any reveal codes, a list of available options, and option-by-option discussions.

WordPerfect Instant Reference SYBEX Prompter Series
Greg Harvey/Kay Yarborough Nelson
254pp. Ref. 476-3

When you don't have time to go digging through the manuals, this fingertip guide offers clear, concise answers: command summaries, correct usage, and exact keystroke sequences for on-the-job tasks. Convenient organization reflects the structure of WordPerfect.

The ABC's of Microsoft WORD
Alan R. Neibauer
321pp. Ref. 497-6

Users who want to wordprocess straightforward documents and print elegant reports without wading through reams of documentation will find all they need to know about MicroSoft WORD in this basic guide. Simple editing, formatting, merging, sorting, macros and style sheets are detailed.

Mastering Microsoft WORD (Third Edition)
Matthew Holtz
638pp. Ref. 524-7

This comprehensive, step-by-step guide includes Version 4.0. Hands-on tutorials treat everything from word processing basics to the fundamentals of desktop publishing, stressing business applications throughout.

Advanced Techinques in Microsoft WORD
Alan R. Neibauer
537pp. Ref. 416-X

The book starts with a brief overview, but the main focus is on practical applications using advanced features. Topics include customization, forms, style sheets, columns, tables, financial documents, graphics and data management.

Mastering DisplayWrite 4
Michael E. McCarthy
447pp. Ref. 510-7

Total training, reference and support for

users at all levels—in plain, non-technical language. Novices will be up and running in an hour's time; everyone will gain complete word-processing and document-management skills.

Mastering MultiMate Advantage II
Charles Ackerman
407pp. Ref. 482-8

This comprehensive tutorial covers all the capabilities of MultiMate, and highlights the differences between MultiMate Advantage II and previous versions—in pathway support, sorting, math, DOS access, using dBASE III, and more. With many practical examples, and a chapter on the On-File database.

The Complete Guide to MultiMate
Carol Holcomb Dreger
208pp. Ref. 229-9

This step-by-step tutorial is also an excellent reference guide to MultiMate features and uses. Topics include search/replace, library and merge functions, repagination, document defaults and more.

Advanced Techniques in MultiMate
Chris Gilbert
275pp. Ref. 412-7

A textbook on efficient use of MultiMate for business applications, in a series of self-contained lessons on such topics as multiple columns, high-speed merging, mailing-list printing and Key Procedures.

Introduction to WordStar
Arthur Naiman
208pp. Ref. 134-9

This all time bestseller is an engaging first-time introduction to word processing as well as a complete guide to using WordStar—from basic editing to blocks, global searches, formatting, dot commands, SpellStar and MailMerge.

Practical WordStar Uses
Julie Anne Arca
303pp. Ref. 107-1

A hands-on guide to WordStar and MailMerge applications, with solutions to comon problems and "recipes" for day-to-day tasks. Formatting, merge-printing and much more; plus a quick-reference command chart and notes on CP/M and PC-DOS.

Mastering WordStar Release 4
Greg Harvey
413pp. Ref. 399-6
Practical training and reference for the latest WordStar release—from startup to advanced featues. Experienced users will find new features highlighted and illustrated with hands-on examples. Covers math, macros, laser printers and more.

WordStar Instant Reference
David J. Clark
314pp. Ref. 543-3

This quick reference provides reminders on the use of the editing, formatting, mailmerge, and document processing commands available through WordStar 4 and 5. Operations are organized alphabetically for easy access. The text includes a survey of the menu system and instructions for installing and customizing WordStar.

Understanding WordStar 2000
David Kolodney/Thomas Blackadar
275pp. Ref. 554-9
This engaging, fast-paced series of tutorials covers everything from moving the cursor to print enhancements, format files, key glossaries, windows and MailMerge. With practical examples, and notes for former WordStar users.